From Savannah to Yorktown

From Savannah to Yorktown

The American Revolution in the South

by Henry Lumpkin

Paragon House Publishers
New York

First U.S. Paperback Edition 1987

Published by
Paragon House Publishers
2 Hammarskjöld Plaza
New York, New York 10017

Copyright 1981 by Henry Lumpkin

First published by
University of South Carolina Press
Columbia, South Carolina

Library of Congress Cataloging-in-Publication Data

Lumpkin, Henry, 1913–
  From Savannah to Yorktown.

  Originally published: Columbia, S.C.:
  University of South Carolina Press, 1981.
  Bibliography:
  Includes index.
    1. Southern States—History—Revolution, 1775–1783—
Campaigns. I. Title.
E230. 5. S7L85 1986   973.3'3   86-22583
ISBN 0-913729-48-5

This book is dedicated to my wife, ROSA STONEY LUMPKIN, and to my three brothers, WILLIAM, JOHN and ROBERT.

Contents

Acknowledgments

The author acknowledges with profound gratitude the courtesy, interest, guidance, and active contributions of the following persons and institutions.

He thanks particularly Robert Wilson of Woodruff, South Carolina, whose distinguished paintings of the battles of Kings Mountain, Cowpens, and Ninety Six and many of the leaders in the South during the Revolution have added immeasurably to the historical accuracy and interest of this book. The author also thanks Hubert Hendrix, the editor and publisher of the Spartanburg, South Carolina, *Herald*, who graciously provided copies of Wilson's paintings of the battles and personalities of Kings Mountain and Cowpens. He appreciates greatly the generosity of W. Bruce Ezell who, with the city of Ninety Six, gave permission to use Wilson's paintings of the battle of Ninety Six and the leaders in that engagement.

The author wishes to express his deep appreciaton to the United States National Park Service, the Yorktown Colonial National Historical Park, and the Guilford Court House National Military Park. The Yorktown Park through the courtesy of James N. Haskett, park historian, permitted the use in this book of the Sidney King painting of British officers on the ramparts at Yorktown and photographs of the several eighteenth-century artillery pieces preserved at the Yorktown Colonial National Park. (The photography of Thomas Williams of Williamsburg, Virginia, who made the copy of the painting and the pictures of the artillery pieces is excellent.) The Guilford Court House Military Park through the efforts of Willard W. Danielson, park superintendant, and Scott Culclosure, park technician, allowed use of the painting by Frank E. Buffmire (copying a lost work by F. C. Yohn) of the First Maryland Regiment charging the British Guards at the battle of Guilford Court House.

The author expresses his sincere gratitude to the South Caroliniana Library of the University of South Carolina, its director, E. L. Inabinett, the reference librarian, Eleanor Richardson, and Charles Gay, technical assistant. The research facilities of that library and the continued assistance of its director and staff have been an invaluable help in the successful completion of the book.

The author wishes to acknowledge and thank Warren Moore of Ramsey, New Jersey, a distinguished authority on eighteenth-century arms. Moore very generously has permitted the use in this book of photographs from his own weapons collection and copies of paintings of American, British, French, and German soldiers in the correct uniforms of the period. His contribution has added greatly to the book's historical validity.

The Maritime Museum of Newport News, Virginia, has given useful guidance, and the author appreciates profoundly the permission granted by the National Maritime Museum of London, England, to use copies of the two contemporary drawings of the "Battle of the Virginia Capes, September 5, 1781."

The author's thanks are due to the Georgia Department of Archives and History, which provided the picture of Elijah Clarke, and the South Carolina Historical Society in Charleston, which permitted use of the copy of its etching of Sir Henry Clinton by H. B. Hall.

A most sincere expression of appreciation also goes to the Library of Congress, which has allowed the use of a copy of Pierre Ozanne's Map of the Siege of Savannah, Georgia, from the Ozanne Collections, No. 22, in the Geography and Map Division of the Library of Congress.

Thanks also are due to the Smithsonian Institution, which, through the efforts of Craddock Goins, curator of the Division of Military History, provided a photograph of the Ferguson rifle preserved in the James Watts De Peyster collection.

The author wishes further to express his gratitude for their outstanding help in research and research materials to Dr. Robert L. Stephenson and Dr. Stanley South of the Institute of Archaeology and Anthropology at the University of South Carolina and Charles Lee, director of the South Carolina Department of Archives and History, and his excellent staff, particularly Terry Lipscomb, whose knowledgeable guidance in the question of correct dating for many pertinent events was essential to the historical accuracy of the book. In this matter of dates, the standard reference works frequently disagree, and the author makes no claim that his dates are beyond dispute; whenever possible, the dates for the American Revolution given in the oldest documents have been used. Profound thanks also are owed to Kenneth Toombs, director of libraries at the University of South Carolina, and the staff of the Thomas Cooper Memorial Library for their help in many facets of the research.

The author is greatly indebted to his good friends and former colleagues Dr. Robert Bass and Dr. Francis Lord, both distinguished scholars of eighteenth-century military history, for their wise and courteous guidance. He also wishes to thank Dr. John Sproat, head of the Department of History at the University of South Carolina, for his continued and friendly support. Henry Cauthen, president and general manager of South Carolina Education Television, and David Smalley are owed particular appreciation since it is the ETV program "And Then There Were Thirteen," which Mr. Cauthen authorized and David Smalley directed with distinction, which established the concept of this book.

The author appreciates, more than he can say, the efforts of the secretaries of the Department of History of the University of South Carolina who typed this manuscript with patience, good humor, and always creditable skill. He also thanks Rose Wilkinson of the Sandlapper Store, Inc., who gave permission to reprint the maps of the siege of

Ninety Six and the battles of Blackstocks and Quinby Bridge from the books *Ninety Six* and *Gamecock* by Robert Bass.

General John W. Richardson of Longboat Key, Florida, has graciously contributed a copy of the portrait of his ancestor, Richard Richardson, and this too is very much appreciated. The author appreciates deeply the courtesy of the Carolina Art Associaton/ Gibbes Art Gallery which provided the copy of the miniature of Colonel William "Danger" Thomson attributed to Edward Savage.

Since her contribution has meant so much, the author thanks his wife, Rosa Stoney Lumpkin, who loyally, patiently, and skillfully completed the book's index and to whom this book is dedicated with his brothers, William, John, and Robert.

Illustrations Credits

Figure 1, courtesy of Brigadier General John W. Richardson, USAF Ret. Figure 2, courtesy of the Carolina Art Association/Gibbes Art Gallery. Figures 3, 4, 7, 9, 10, 11, 14, 15, 18, 23, 77, 81, 83, 93, and 98, courtesy of the South Caroliniana Library, University of South Carolina. Figure 5, courtesy of the Ozanne Collection, Geography and Map Division, Library of Congress. Figure 8, courtesy of the South Carolina Historical Society. Figures 12, 80, and 90, courtesy of Mr. Robert Wilson. Figure 13, courtesy of the Georgia Department of Archives and History. Figures 16, 17, 19, 21, 22, 25, and 89 Copyright© Artco, Ltd., courtesy of Mr. Hubert Hendrix, editor and publisher of the Spartanburg, South Carolina, *Herald*. Figures 20, 88, and 91, reprinted with permission of the Sandlapper Store, Inc. Figures 26, 28, 29, 30, 31, 32, 33, 42, 43, 44, 45, 46, 47, 48, 49, 50, 51, 52, 53, 54, 55, 56, 57, 58, 59, 61, 62, 63, 64, 65, 66, 67, 68, 69, 70, 71, 72, 73, 74, 75, and 76, courtesy of Mr. Warren Moore. Figures 35, 36, 37, 38, 39, 40, 41, and 97, courtesy of the U.S. Park Service Colonial National Historical Park, Yorktown, Virginia. Figure 34, courtesy of the James Watts De Peyster Collection, Smithsonian Institution. Figures 27 and 60, courtesy of Dr. Francis Lord. Figures 82 and 78, courtesy of the U.S. Park Service Guilford Court House National Park, Guilford County, North Carolina. Figures 79, 85, 86, and 89, courtesy of Mr. W. Bruce Ezell and the city of Ninety Six, South Carolina. Figures 95 and 96, courtesy of the National Maritime Museum, London, England.

The War Begins

The first shots of the American Revolution had been fired at Lexington and Concord, Massachusetts, on 19 April 1775, and the British had taken Bunker Hill and Breeds Hill by direct bayonet assault and with heavy losses on 17 June before any military operations took place in the South.

Fighting started in South Carolina during October 1775 when Loyalist Patrick Cuningham and 60 armed men seized wagons loaded with 1,000 pounds of gunpowder and 2,000 pounds of lead being sent by the Council of Safety in Charleston as a peace gesture to the Cherokee Indians. Major Andrew Williamson of the Ninety Six district marched against these Loyalists with 562 Patriot militia. On 19 November 1775 Patrick Cuningham and a superior force of pro-British backcountrymen launched a two-day attack on Williamson and his men defending a hastily built fort near Ninety Six. Archaeologists from the University of South Carolina have discovered the fort to have been of stronger construction than the literary sources indicate, with a vertical palisade anchored on two log barns used as redoubts that enclosed an area 85 by 150 feet and a defense ditch covering the north and northwest approaches. One man was killed outright and several were wounded on each side before the skirmish ended ingloriously with a truce. Blood had been shed in South Carolina for the first time in the Revolution. Andrew Williamson served later with Colonel Richard Richardson against the Loyalists in the Snow Campaign, led South Carolina militia in the punitive expedition to break the power of the Cherokees in 1776, and commanded South Carolinians at the siege of British-held Savannah in 1779. After the capture of Charleston by Sir Henry Clinton in 1780, Williamson signed his parole and joined the British. His changing stance is a grim commentary on the complex and agonizing nature of loyalties in the South during these years.

In Virginia, military action began when prominent citizens of Norfolk, feeling their interests threatened by the activities of the Whig assembly meeting at Williamsburg, called on the royal governor, John Murray, the Earl of Dunmore, to occupy the town. When the American Patriots mustered 300 militia from Princess Anne and Norfolk counties to counter this move, Lord Dunmore assembled his few regulars, a handful of Scottish clerks, and a contingent of armed slaves. With this makeshift force Dunmore attacked the Whig militia at Kempville and drove them from the field. This successful action

[1]

prompted several thousand men to come to Norfolk and swear allegiance to the king. Dunmore raised two Loyalist regiments, the Queen's Own Loyal Virginia Regiment and the Royal Ethiopian Regiment, a black unit, and raided the coastal counties of Virginia, freeing slaves who deserted their masters and joined his growing army.

Lord Dunmore was defeated and his forces scattered on 11 December 1775 when Colonel William Woodford with 700 Virginia and 200 North Carolina militia attacked the royal governor and his 500 British regulars and Loyalists as they attempted to hold a position at Great Bridge, commanding the road to Norfolk. Lord Dunmore's troops were driven in rout, and Norfolk was burned by the vengeful Virginia militia as a center of pro-British sympathies.

In the late fall of 1775 the seventy-year-old Colonel Richard Richardson and that dour frontier fighter Colonel William "Danger" Thomson, with 2,500 men pushed into the backcountry of South Carolina to dissipate the strong concentrations of Loyalists gathering under Patrick Cuningham and Colonel Thomas Fletchall. As Richardson and Thomson advanced, the Loyalists, after brief fighting stands, retreated deeper into the wilderness. No decisive engagement occurred, but several important Tory prisoners were taken, among them Fletchall, whom Thomson's Rangers discovered hiding in a hollow sycamore tree after a skirmish.

With the arrival of 1,100 reinforcements from North Carolina and 800 South Carolinians led by Major Andrew Williamson, Colonel Richardson could muster about 4,000 Patriot militia. This force penetrated four miles beyond the Cherokee tribal boundary to the Great Canebrake on Reedy River. Scouts brought back word that Patrick Cuningham and his force were camping at the Canebrake. Richardson sent "Danger" Thomson with his 3d Ranger Regiment and support forces, about 1,300 men, to attack the Loyalists. Toward daylight on 22 December 1775 William Thomson had almost surrounded the area when sentries belatedly gave the alarm. A sharp fire fight followed with 6 Loyalists killed and 130 taken prisoner. Thomson only had one man wounded, but his main quarry—Patrick Cuningham—escaped, riding a horse bareback and shouting to his followers to shift for themselves.

His mission accomplished, Colonel Richard Richardson dismissed the North Carolinians and marched homeward. Heavy snow fell during the last days of the operation, thus it was known as the "Snow Campaign." This was Richardson's first and last active duty in the Revolution. He was promoted to brigadier general and captured by the British after the fall of Charleston in 1780, probably at his home near Summerton, South Carolina. He died that same year at the age of seventy-five after several months of harsh imprisonment imposed because the old gentlemen refused to accept the terms offered by his captors.

Significant military operations first occurred in North Carolina during January of

Figure 1.
Brigadier General Richard Richardson

Figure 2.
Colonel William "Danger" Thomson,
attributed to Edward Savage

1776 when Josiah Martin, the royal governor, ordered the Highland Scot settlers in the colony, most of them Loyalists, to rally about the king's standard raised by Brigadier General Donald McDonald. The Scots were to assemble at Cross Creek as secretly as possible, supported by other Loyalists, mostly members of the old backcountry Regulator movement. Prior to the Revolution the Regulators had rebelled against the tidewater political domination of the colony. Because the planters and merchants of the coastal area generally supported American independence, with varying and changing degrees of enthusiasm, many of the former Regulators in both Carolinas were loyal to King George. This force of Scots and other Loyalists was ordered to march toward the coast, where Governor Martin expected units of the royal fleet to arrive escorting transports with reinforcements from Ireland. With these regular troops and the pro-British elements he was organizing, Martin planned to launch a campaign to suppress the rebellion in North Carolina and secure the colony for the king.

It seems strange that the Highland Scots, who had suffered so terribly at the hands of the House of Hanover after the lost battle of Culloden in 1746, should fight for a Hanoverian king. There is an interesting horticultural comment on Highland Scottish sentiment in this matter: the flower "Sweet William" was given that name in England to honor William, Duke of Cumberland, who smashed Bonnie Prince Charles's army and drove him into permanent exile; in Scotland the same plant is still called "Stinking Billy." The generous royal land grants in North Carolina and the pledge of loyalty to George II given by the Scottish survivors of Culloden probably are the reasons for the Highlanders' support of Josiah Martin. They also may have fought for the king because most of their political enemies, the Presbyterian Lowland Scots and the Scots-Irish settlers, favored the Revolution.

Donald McDonald and Captain Donald McLeod originally had been sent to North Carolina by General Thomas Gage, the British commander in chief in America, to recruit for the Royal Highland Emigrant Regiment then being raised in Boston. McDonald and McLeod both had served at Bunker Hill and Breeds Hill. Donald McDonald was a veteran of Culloden and a cousin of Allan McDonald, the husband of the famous Flora McDonald, who had helped Bonnie Prince Charlie make a successful escape after his last battle. Allan and Flora were leaders in the Scottish settlements in North Carolina, so Brigadier General Donald McDonald found relatives and influential sympathizers in the area when he arrived.

The Highlanders, having surrendered all of their firearms after Culloden, were armed mainly with the traditional basket hilted broad- or backsword and dirk. The column that marched from the assembly point at Cross Creek to the coast numbered about 1,600, of whom 1,300 were Scots. Eighty picked Highland swordsmen under Captains John Campbell and Alexander McLeod led the advance, followed by the main body, variously equipped, and a contingent of approximately 300 musket and riflemen, probably the regulators, at the rear. Meanwhile, the American Patriot forces were gathering to oppose the Scots and the regulars from Ireland when the latter were put ashore. Colonel James Moore marched from Wilmington toward Cross Creek with 650 men of the 1st North Carolina Continental Regiment supported by five guns. He was met on 18 February 1776 by Colonel Alexander Lillington leading 150 North Carolina militia, followed by Colonel James Kenan with 200 additional militia and Colonel John Ashe at the head of 100 rangers. On 25 February, Lillington and Ashe reached Moore's Creek Bridge some seventeen miles from Wilmington on the route the Loyalists would follow to reach their coastal rendezvous with Josiah Martin and the hoped-for British reinforcements. Colonel Richard Caswell joined Lillington and Ashe on 26 February with additional militia. The combined forces crossed Moore's Creek and built earthworks on the west bank. Fearing that he could not hold these against the expected attack, Caswell abandoned his fieldworks and fell back to the east bank, where the three commanders fortified their position and waited.

The Americans, expecting the Scots to charge, removed the planks from the middle of the bridge and greased the stringers with soft soap and animal fat. Two cannon, known as "Mother Covington and her Daughter," commanded the bridge, and the North Carolina Patriot militia lay behind earthworks along the stream bank. The Loyalists apparently were unaware of the missing planks and approached the bridge on 27 February, bagpipes skirling a wild clan march and the eighty chosen swordsmen leading the attack. When the Scots reached the bridge, they drew blade and charged with the war cry, "Broadswords and King George." Reaching the unexpected gap the eighty hesitated and then came forward with reckless gallantry balancing on the greased stringers and using their sword points to steady the uncertain footing. The charge was met by point-blank canister and musket fire. Thirty of the Highlanders were killed as they advanced, including their two commanders, John Campbell and Alexander McLeod, and forty were wounded. Some fell from the greased stringers into the creek and were drowned. The North Carolina militia on the east bank suffered only two casualties—one man dead, John Grady of Anson, and one wounded.

The Loyalists, disheartened by the heavy losses, broke and scattered, but the Patriot militia did not press the victory. Instead, they stopped and looted the baggage wagons abandoned by the fleeing Highlanders and their supporters. Colonel Moore and his Continentals, who had not appeared in time to take part in the battle, arrived, and Moore promptly organized a pursuit. Although most of the Regulators safely escaped, 850 Highlanders were captured at Black Mingo Creek. Brigadier General Donald Mcdonald, an old man, was taken later still in camp, as he slept in his tent unaware that his little army had been routed.

After the battle, Donald McDonald and Allan McDonald were jailed by the Americans, but most of the Highlanders accepted parole and returned to their homes, pledging never again to bear arms against the colonists. Some ten thousand Highland Scot settlers lived in North Carolina, and most remained strongly pro-British; many served in Loyalist regiments during the southern campaigns of 1780 and 1781. Lord Charles Cornwallis on his march to Wilmington after the battle of Guilford Court House on 15 March 1781 was able to halt and rest his battered army with the Scots at Cross Creek, still a center of Loyalist sympathy.

Moore's Creek Bridge was unquestionably an important victory in the war for American independence, even though casualties were comparatively light and the encounter was of short duration. The engagement prevented early British domination of North Carolina. That state was never occupied by British forces. John Rutledge, then governor of South Carolina, took refuge in North Carolina following the fall of Charleston in 1780, and Nathanael Greene, after assuming command of the Southern Department on 2 December 1780, used North Carolina as a staging base for his campaign in the Carolinas, Georgia, and Virginia. Fighting between Patriot and Loyalist continued throughout the South. It was to be waged with increasing hatred and intensity—an unceasing, merciless internecine conflict the civilized British found difficult to comprehend and impossible to counter.

These early southern actions, however, while important to the overall picture of the war, were military sidelights to the main theater of operations. From 1775 until late in 1778 almost all of the major actions took place in the northern states and Canada.

George Washington of Virginia, selected by the Continental Congress as commander in chief of the newly established Continental Army of America, forced the British to evacuate Boston, Massachusetts, after a siege of almost a year. This victory on 17 March 1776 was balanced by a tragic American failure. Two American columns marched into Canada: one, under Richard Montgomery, pushed north via Lake Champlain and captured Montreal; the second led by Benedict Arnold and Daniel Morgan moved up the Kennebec River in Maine and into Canada over the wild watershed called the Height of Land. The forces converged on Quebec, ably defended by Sir Guy Carleton. The attack launched on 1 January 1776 failed. Montgomery died in the assault, and most of the Kennebec column, including Daniel Morgan, were captured. Carleton, having received reinforcements, marched south and on 8 June 1776 defeated an American army at Three Rivers, Canada. After this, British control in Canada was never threatened again.

The war in the North through the summer and fall of 1776 was marked by a series of disasters for the Americans. On 27 August 1776 Sir William Howe and Sir Henry Clinton, supported by the royal fleet, badly defeated George Washington at Long Island. After the battle Washington managed to extricate most of his army under the cover of darkness and a providential fog. The British occupied New York, and, after two hard-fought actions at Harlem Heights on 16 September and White Plains on 28 October, George Washington was forced to cross the Hudson River and retreat through New Jersey with Lord Cornwallis in pursuit. Two American strong points, Fort Washington overlooking the northern end of Manhattan Island and Fort Lee guarding the Jersey side of the Hudson, fell to British attack on 16 and 20 November respectively. The British army and navy thus held New York, its harbor, and immediate environs, a position they were to maintain until the peace treaty was signed in 1783.

During the night hours of 25 December 1776 George Washington crossed the ice-laden Delaware River with 2,400 men and eight guns and at eight in the morning of 26 December struck Colonel Rahl's Hessian brigade quartered in Trenton, New Jersey. The Germans were caught by surprise and lost 32 killed and 886 taken prisoner. Rahl was mortally wounded in the attack. After this brilliant little action the Americans marched on Princeton, where they smashed Charles Mawhood's brigade holding the town as Cornwallis's rear guard. Lord Cornwallis moved against Washington with his full army; the American commander in chief, having shaken the British badly, broke off operations and went into winter quarters in the forested country near Morristown.

During the winter of 1777, the British evolved a strategic concept designed to win the war: a push from Canada down Lake Champlain and the Hudson Valley coordinated with a supporting drive from Oswego through the Mohawk Valley, both to be met at Albany by a large force moving from New York City up the Hudson River. This would separate New England from the middle states, and whatever resistance remained could be destroyed sector by sector. Sir William Howe, the commander in chief, had different ideas and proceeded with most of his army against Philadelphia. General John Burgoyne, marching south from Canada presumably to meet supporting forces coming up the Hudson, fought major engagements at Freeman's Farm on 19 September and Bemis Heights on 7 October. The second battle was a severe British defeat, and Burgoyne, surrounded by greatly superior American forces, surrendered his entire army of some 5,000 effectives to General Horatio Gates at Saratoga, New York, on 17 October 1777. A column detached from Burgoyne's army had already been badly beaten at Bennington, Vermont, and Barry St. Leger attacking from Oswego down the Mohawk Valley had been forced to raise the siege of Fort Stanwix and retreat. The entire British invasion from Canada collapsed in disaster. This splendid American victory saved New England and the war in the North, but it was one of the few bright spots in an otherwise terrible year for the cause of independence.

While the long-range importance of Saratoga to eventual American victory cannot be overestimated, it was offset in 1777 by three serious American defeats, all in Pennsylvania: Brandywine on 11 September, Paoli on 21 September, and Germantown on 4 October. At Brandywine, Sir William Howe drove Washington's 11,000 men from the field with losses estimated at 300 killed and about 600 wounded. The fighting was sustained and heavy, the British casualties numbering 576. At Paoli, the British General Charles "No Flint" Grey, in a night attack with the bayonet, caught Anthony Wayne's rear guard by surprise and killed, wounded, or captured some 400 Americans.

Sir William Howe occupied Philadelphia on 26 September 1777 and deployed his army in and around the city. George Washington moved against the British lines, and on 4 October at Germantown the two armies fought a savage and confused two-and-one-half-hour engagement in a dense fog. Washington once more suffered defeat, although he came very close to victory. In General Anthony Wayne's harsh judgment, the Americans ran away from victory. It probably was a case of British discipline winning over the still raw and half-trained American Army.

George Washington retreated to quarters at Valley Forge about twenty-five miles up the Schuylkill River from Philadelphia; there the miserable winter of 1777–1778 dragged by. It was through this ordeal of starvation and deprivation and the strenuous efforts of Washington and such foreign military advisers as the Prussian drillmaster, Baron Frederick von Steuben, that the regular American army was born. In February, 1778, through the patient and wise diplomacy of Benjamin Franklin and other American envoys, the Franco-American alliance was announced, and the British now faced a European war with the ever-present probability of active French intervention by sea or land in the American theater of operations. This turn of events would strongly influence British strategic thinking henceforth.

Sir William Howe was relieved as commander in chief at his own request and replaced by Sir Henry Clinton. Clinton realized that a French fleet and expeditionary force cooperating with the American army could seriously threaten British strength, divided as it was between Philadelphia and New York. He therefore decided to abandon Philadelphia and establish the main British operating base in and around New York City, where an excellent harbor and easily defended island positions permitted effective support by the Royal Navy.

Philadelphia was evacuated between 7 and 18 June 1778, 3,000 Loyalist residents of the city going by sea in fleet-supported transports and the army marching overland. George Washington left Valley Forge and followed the retirement. On Sunday, 28 June, at Monmouth Court House, New Jersey, Sir Henry Clinton halted his march to New York and fought a hotly contested battle with Washington and his trained and reconstituted army. Action halted at nightfall, and Clinton, having achieved his objective of saving an essential baggage train, marched off during the night leaving the field to the Americans. George Washington reported Monmouth Court House as a victory to the Continental Congress, but losses on both sides were equally heavy. The engagement was in no way decisive, and Sir Henry Clinton reached New York safely and with no further serious military interference. Possibly the main American gain from the operation was that some 600 German mercenaries and British soldiers deserted Clinton during his march north. Monmouth Court House was also the last major field action in the northern theater betweem the regular British and American armies.

Sir Henry Clinton held New York in strength, and the Royal Navy dominated American waters launching successful amphibious attacks along the coast without interference. These included the action at Castine, Maine, in 1779 when a British squadron forced Commodore Dudley Saltonstall to run his ships up the Penobscot River where he beached and destroyed them and the burning of New London, Connecticut, by a British landing force on 6 September 1781. George Washington encamped his army around New York; plagued by treason, mutiny, and lack of supplies, he was without sufficient strength to drive Clinton from his main positions. The entry of France into the conflict, however, demanded a new strategy, and the British accordingly devised one.

With the war stalemated in the North and Canada strongly held and safe from American attack, the British high command in New York decided to move major operations to the South with the hope that the Loyalists might rise in full support of a British invasion. This decision was based on reasonably sound intelligence—pro-British feeling did remain strong in the South throughout the war. Loyalty to an abstract ideal, however, and willingness to fight and possibly die for that ideal are two different matters. Former royal governors in their reports consistently overestimated the number of men actively ready to take up arms for the British and against their own people. This fact would be decisive in the entire southern campaign.

The British reasoned quite correctly that the northern states could be contained by naval blockade and by the constant offensive threat of powerful forces in New York and Canada. This obvious strength would permit transfer of the necessary troops to attack and systematically reduce Georgia, the Carolinas, and Virginia. Once accomplished, New England and the middle states, outflanked north and south, harassed by Indian attack in the west, and blocked from outside help by sea, could not maintain a successful, long-term resistance.

Strategically, this was an excellent plan.

It almost worked.

CHAPTER I

The British Attack on Charleston, 28 June 1776

During the first two years of the American Revolution, Virginia, the Carolinas, and Georgia were torn by bitter fratricidal civil war between pro-British Loyalists and Americans supporting the cause of independence. Skirmishes, raids, and counterraids occurred, including a brutally successful frontier campaign against the Cherokee Indians and their royalist agents. No major action involving British regular forces in strength took place in the South until Lieutenant General Sir Henry Clinton and Admiral Sir Peter Parker attacked the outer defenses of Charleston, South Carolina, in June of 1776. At that time Charleston and Savannah, Georgia, were the two principal seaports in the southeast.

Clinton, field commander of the army forces assigned by the British high command in North America to the southern theater, had originally planned joint operations with Admiral Parker and his fleet units in the Chesapeake Bay area. The admiral, however, received intelligence information that the works on Sullivan's Island protecting the entrance into Charleston harbor were unfinished. These might be taken by a *coup de main* and Sullivan's Island held thereafter by a small British force of infantry and artillery, supported by a frigate or two. This would effectively seal Charleston harbor to all important shipping, although smugglers could get into the city via the network of tidal rivers and creeks cutting through the salt marshes around Charleston that are navigable to smaller craft at high tide.

Apparently Sir Henry Clinton, lacking sufficient troops for a prolonged siege operation, had no plan or expectation at that time of capturing Charleston itself. Sullivan's Island was another matter; seized quickly, it could prove a very important acquisition for the British and greatly facilitate any subsequent move against the port itself. Undisputed control of coastal waters by the Royal Navy would permit a steady supply of provisions for the garrison from the sea island farms to the south of Charleston. These islands could not be defended successfully against naval landing parties, striking at random and will, without seriously depleting the militia units guarding Charleston, and that was impossible with the town threatened by British pressure at the harbor entrance. The British overall strategic concept thus showed wisdom and imagination.

On 1 June 1776 Admiral Parker dropped anchor a few miles north of Charleston with fifty vessels, including troop transports. John Rutledge, at that time president of South Carolina, ordered the alarm guns fired and that the militia be put in the best posture to withstand an expected attack. Six days later, on 7 June, most of the British transports and lighter frigates were brought over the Charleston bar into five fathom hole beyond the harbor's entrance, leaving the heavy units outside. Admiral Parker wished to put the troops ashore on the northern end of Sullivan's Island. The assault force, covered by the guns of the fleet, would take the fort from the rear where the defenses were still incomplete. Clinton refused to accept this plan because he feared the heavy surf would damage the ships' longboats and barges used as landing craft. Clinton also believed the shallow shelving beach areas would prevent the larger warships from standing in close enough to provide the necessary support fire for the amphibious attempt.

To understand properly the action at Sullivan's Island it must be remembered that a 32- or 24-pound smoothbore ship's long gun, firing a solid cast iron round shot, had a maximum flat range of two miles. It was reasonably accurate at about 500 to 600 yards. Ammunition designed to cut standing rigging or for antipersonnel purposes—chain shot, grapeshot, canister, or bag shot used in the same guns—carried effectively a little over 500 yards. No long gun of the period could be employed with the spherical explosive shells equipped with powder-train fuses; these shells were fired on land from short, specially constructed field howitzers or from high-trajectory siege mortars. The latter also could be placed on fleet units, not part of the regular battle line, for use against harbor or coastal defenses. These were usually smaller vessels, bomb sloops, schooners, or brigs with heavy reinforced spar deck mountings to absorb the terrible down recoil of the squat, massive, wide-mouth ordnance.

Admiral Parker apparently did not try to overcome General Clinton's objections to a landing on Sullivan's Island, and Clinton decided to put his ground forces ashore on Long Island (now the Isle of Palms) just across Breach Inlet and to the north of Sullivan's Island. Clinton had been informed that Breach Inlet was only eighteen inches deep at ebb tide and thus assault troops could wade across easily, supported by field artillery emplaced on Long Island. To his dismay he found instead that the inlet even at dead low was a dangerous stretch of water scoured by the running tide and with numerous seven foot holes. Boats would be needed, and only fifteen flat-bottom barges were available for a cross-inlet attack.

It seems strange that Clinton, who later made a personal two-night reconnaissance by small boat of the marshes and salt creeks behind Long and Sullivan's Islands, accepted a hearsay report and did not have Breach Inlet checked by a scouting party before he put his people on the beach. Unfortunately for the British joint command, this decision to use Long Island as the base for army operations prevented 2,200 well-trained regular infantry and artillery from participating effectively in the coming engagement.

Some knowledge of South Carolina coastal geography is just as necessary as an understanding of eighteenth-century gunnery to realize the problem of war in that area. Charleston is built on the lower end of a peninsula between the Ashley and Cooper Rivers. It could be cut off from relief from land and sea (a fact Clinton would exploit in 1780). But the peninsula above the town, the harbor, and both banks of the two rivers contiguous to Charleston would have to be seized and held for this to be accomplished. In front of the city and all down the coast of South Carolina and Georgia lie the sea islands, large and small, separated from the mainland by miles of salt marshes intersected by mud-buttomed creeks running full and deep at high tide and almost empty at low. In either condition they presented a nearly impassable barrier to a fully equipped army with horse-drawn vehicles and field guns. Two of the sea islands form natural defenses for Charleston harbor: Sullivan's Island, which stretches for about four miles from the northern entrance of the harbor, and the smaller Morris Island to the south. The mud and oyster bank where the famous Fort Sumter was later built supported no fortifications in 1776, although there were batteries and installations across the harbor at Fort Johnson on James Island to command the southern approaches.

The appearance of the British fleet and seaborne army off Charleston rallied in defense of the town many of those who had previously opposed the cause of independence. Batteries were established along East Bay, and shops and warehouses were leveled to give free field of fire on the waterfront. The harbor defenses consisted of these batteries and fleches and bastions that began on the peninsula just south of Comings Point on the Ashley River and extended along South Bay and East Bay to Gadsden's Wharf on the Cooper River (at the foot of the present Calhoun Street). Forces manning these various works and the outer forts on Sullivan's Island and James Island numbered 6,522 men. These included 1,950 South Carolina regulars, 700 Charleston militia, and 1,972 country militia, supported by 1,400 North Carolina militia and 500 Virginia Continentals.

While the town prepared for the impending attack, Major General Charles Lee arrived from the north sent by the Continental Congress to command the defense of Charleston. His record in Europe as a soldier of fortune was most impressive: he had fought the Turks, commanded Russian Cossacks, talked with King Frederick the Great of Prussia, and been aide-de-camp to the King of Poland. He also served with the British army in North America during the Seven Years' War and been adopted by the Mohawk Indians and given the name "Boiling Water." Charles Lee's later dubious and bizarre career demonstrates the Indians' perceptiveness in judging his character. The people of Charleston were greatly pleased at his arrival. Charles Cotesworth Pinckney, commanding the batteries at Fort Johnson, however, observed caustically that he found General Lee clever but, socially speaking, a strange creature.

Fort Sullivan on Sullivan's Island, as the main defense of the northern approaches to the harbor, was the objective of the primary British attack. It had been built as a square with a bastion at each angle, sufficiently large to contain approximately 1,000 men. Instead of masonry, it was constructed of palmetto logs laid one upon the other in two parallel rows some sixteen feet apart. The rows were connected at intervals with bolted and dovetailed heavy timbers; the space between the logs filled with sand. A dark blue flag with a silver crescent in the upper left field (and possibly the word "Liberty" embroidered on the center field) was fixed on the southeast bastion. Three 18-pounders and two 9-pounders had been mounted on the southeast bastion, while two English 18-pounders and two 9-pounders were placed on the southeast curtain. The southwest curtain and bastion had three 12-pounders and three 9-pounders. Two flanking fieldworks, epaulements or cavaliers, were hastily built to guard the sea face of the fort, with three 12-pounders mounted on each. There also were loopholes in the top logs of the fort for musket or riflemen if the British ships came in close enough for small arms fire or if a direct assault by landing parties was attempted. The northeast curtain and northwest curtain and bastions were unfinished at the time of the attack; the logs were still being cut and laid in position. After a first inspection, Charles Lee had ordered William Moultrie to build a defensive work or traverse behind the fort. This was not completed in time, which meant that British infantry attacking in force could have taken the exposed position from the rear. A British frigate, worked up the mouth of the creek running between Sullivan's Island and the mainland, would have been able not only to block reinforcements from Charleston but, by long-range gunfire, to make the unfinished fort difficult to hold or even untenable. Major General Lee on his inspection visit called Fort Sullivan indefensible and a potential slaughter pen. William Moultrie said that he could and would defend it and proceeded to prove his statement.

The fort was garrisoned by the 2d South Carolina regiment of 413 men and a detachment of the 4th Regiment's artillery with 22 men. These 435 soldiers of the state's regular line were encamped inside the uncompleted defenses. Across the harbor on James Island, Fort Johnson mounted a mixed battery of twenty guns, 26- and 18-pounders, now under the command of Christopher Gadsden. The two forts thus guarded the northern and southern approaches to the inner harbor. There were some 1,200 defenders on Sullivan's Island but only 10,000 pounds of powder for the guns, an insufficent supply if the engagement involved an extended cannonade. In addition to the 435 men in Fort Sullivan, Colonel William "Danger" Thomson held the northern end of the island across Breach Inlet from Long Island with 780 troops. These included 300 men of his own 3d South Carolina Regiment of rangers with one company of about 30 Catawba Indian riflemen led by Captain Samuel Boyakin (an ancestor of the present Boykin family of Camden, South Carolina), 200 North Carolina Continentals commanded by a Lieutenant Colonel Clark, and Colonel Daniel Horry's 200 South Carolina state troops with Captain John Allston's Raccoon or Foot Rover Company of 50 Peedee, Waccamaw, Cheraw, and Catawba Indian riflemen.

Figure 3.
Major General William Moultrie

Captain Ferdinand de Brahm, a military engineer attached to the Charleston garrison, had supervised the erection of a sand and palmetto log breastwork facing Breach Inlet. This mounted one 18-pounder long gun and a brass 6-pounder fieldpiece. With 2,200 British regulars assembled on Long Island, the problem of guaranteeing reinforcements from Charleston to Sullivan's Island remained an imperative. Charles Lee, who had assumed overall command of the defense on 8 June without consulting President John Rutledge (a fact which did not increase his local popularity), ordered the construction of a pontoon bridge from the battery at Haddrell's Point to Sullivan's Island. This primitive makeshift of hogsheads and boats with planks laid over them promptly sank under Clark's North Carolinians, and small craft had to be used for future crossings.

On the morning of 28 June, William Moultrie and "Danger" Thomson riding together to inspect the troops and defenses on the northern end of Sullivan's Island saw the British warships at anchor off Long Island loose their topsails. Moultrie galloped back to Fort Sullivan and ordered the drums to beat to quarters, calling all men to battle stations. A captain of a Charleston-based privateer named Clement Lempriere, present at the time, told Moultrie that when the British fleet came alongside it would knock his fort down in thirty minutes. In that case, the doughty Moultrie informed him, he and his garrison would lie behind the ruins and prevent the enemy from landing.

Two 50-gun ships, five frigates, and four smaller armed vessels mounting altogether 270 guns moved down the coast of the island to engage Fort Sullivan. Between ten and eleven o'clock, *Thunder*, a bombship with heavy spar deck mounted mortars, anchored about a mile and a half from the fort, and with cover, from *Friendship*, an armed vessel, began to throw shells. Most of these landed and buried in the sand outside the works or within the fort perimeter and exploded without doing any material damage. Ordered to fire at too long a range, the mortar crews overcharged their guns, and, after a few relatively ineffective salvos, the recoil ruptured the heavy beams of the mortar beds and *Thunder* was out of action.

With the wind from the southwest on the starboard bow quarter and a strong flood tide, *Active*, 28 guns, *Bristol*, 50 guns, *Experiment*, 50 guns, and *Solebay*, 28 guns, soon came within range. The fort opened fire first from the southwest bastion. The first ship in line, the frigate *Active*, approached the fort and, dropping bow and stern anchors, delivered broadsides. According to Admiral Parker, *Active* took position at approximately 400 yards with spring lines on her cables for winding the ship into better firing positions. *Bristol*, *Experiment*, and *Solebay* anchored astern of *Active* and also opened broadside fire on Fort Sullivan. The fort replied with a slow, steady aimed fire from the southeast and southwest bastions and curtains, supported by the six 12-pounders on the flanking cavaliers.

Figure 4.   Battle of Fort Sullivan, South Carolina, 28 June 1776, by N. Pocock

All military actions produce legends destined to become part of the folklore of a people, and this was a very unusual action—anchored, wooden warships fighting a close-range gunnery duel with a land-based fort. The first South Carolinian killed in the engagement was a corporal of grenadiers. According to the story, the men of his gun crew immediately threw the body from the firing platform and vengefully returned to their posts. Even though this was their first battle, they behaved like veterans. A sergeant named MacDonald in Captain Frank Huger's company was almost torn in half by a round shot. As they carried the dying man away, he is reported to have implored his comrades loudly not to let liberty expire with him. Soldiers so badly wounded usually go into shock and say little or nothing at all, and the story may be apocryphal. This, however was the eighteenth century, and possibly men in that era were made of sterner stuff.

The greatest story of heroism in the battle is known to be true. Bernard Elliot reported that a round shot carried away the flagstaff at the height of the fighting. Seeing this, his old grenadier sergeant William Jasper shouted to Colonel William Moultrie not to let them fight without a flag. Jasper then on his own volition mounted the parapet swept by British broadsides and, fixing the blue flag to a gun sponger, placed it on the merlon of the bastion next to the enemy. The sergeant's courage was publicly recognized when South Carolina President John Rutledge presented Jasper with his own sword. In 1779 during the French and American attack on British-held Savannah, Sergeant Jasper fell mortally wounded bearing the colors of the 2d South Carolina Regiment at the head of the column frontally assaulting the fiercely and successfully defended Spring Hill redoubt. Very properly, there are monuments to Sergeant Jasper in both Charleston and Savannah.

In the course of the action at Fort Sullivan the defenders ran out of powder, and John Rutledge sent 500 pounds to the island by small boat along with predictions of both honor and victory. With the ammunition shortage in mind, he instructed William Moultrie not to make free with his cannon but to stay cool and do mischief. Major General Charles Lee came over to the fort from Charleston, ascended the firing platform, and discharged a gun. He then went back to the town stating that the garrison had no occasion for him. This was his only command visit during the entire battle.

The British ships fired fifty shots to each one fired by Fort Sullivan, but only twelve men of the fort's garrison were killed. With *Thunder*, whose mortar bombs delivered from a proper range might have changed the day, out of action early in the fight, the round shot broadsides of the four units engaged either buried in the spongy palmetto logs or dug harmlessly into the sand. A ship anchored in shallow water is never a steady artillery platform, and the royal fleet traditionally fired at the beginning of the down roll to take effect on an enemy's hull and gun decks. The British losses compared to those of the defenders were very heavy indeed. *Bristol*, whose captain lost an arm and later died, had forty-four killed and thirty wounded. *Experiment*'s captain also lost an arm, and the ship suffered fifty-seven killed and thirty wounded. *Active* had one officer killed and one man wounded, while *Solebay* lost two of its crew with three or four wounded. Quite obviously the fort directed its heaviest fire on the two 50-gun ships, the frigates being lesser targets. As part of the operation Admiral Parker had ordered the three other frigates to enter the harbor and move up the creek behind the island as far as water permitted to cut communications between the fort and the mainland. All three vessels ran aground on the shoal where Fort Sumter later was to be built. Two were worked free, but *Acteon* remained stuck fast and was burned by its crew with the loss of one man.

During the action the guns in the fort were silenced temporarily for lack of powder. The British thought the position had been abandoned, which they expected because there was general confidence that colonists would not stand for long against the broadsides of the Royal Navy. The heat was intense in a South Carolina June, and the defending gunners discarded uniform jackets and shirts. Some of these articles of clothing were tossed into trees inside the fort's perimeter by plunging shot. British lookouts at the mastheads called down that members of the garrison were being hanged, presumably for desertion in the face of the enemy.

The fort and its fighting garrison survived, although on one occasion three broadsides struck at the same time, and the entire log-sand structure jumped and quivered at the impact. To alleviate the fierce early summer heat, grog (rum and water) was served around the guns in fire buckets. William Moultrie, who fought and on this occasion drank with his men, said afterward that he never had a more agreeable draught than the one he took in the middle of a battle from a fire bucket.

The British also mounted an assault from their base on Long Island across Breach Inlet, covered by the armed schooner *Lady William*, a shallow-draft gunship, and a flotilla of troop-laden longboats from the fleet with light guns placed in the bows. This was part of the overall plan launched by Sir Henry Clinton and Lord Cornwallis in coordination with the naval attack on the fort. The little fleet advanced bravely, but Colonel William Thomson opened at point-blank range with his one 18-pounder and the 6-pounder field gun supported by rifles and muskets of the defending infantry. The advancing British landing craft and gunships were swept by canister and small arms fire. After suffering heavy casualties, Clinton sent orders for the boats to pull back, and the amphibious attempt failed. Late that afternoon Thomson was reinforced by 700 Virginians and South Carolinians commanded by Colonel Peter Muhlenberg, and the British did not try a second attack.

This action ended the battle of Sullivan's Island. Sir Peter Parker picked up the troops on Long Island and sailed north, badly battered and nursing his wounds. He had suffered the personal indignity of having his trousers split in the rear by a passing round shot which undoubtedly did not improve his temper or ameliorate the humiliation of the occasion. Mere colonials had met and beaten back a joint assault by units of the proud Royal Navy and the British regular army.

After the engagement William Logan of Charleston sent his compliments to Colonel

William Moultrie, the officers, and soldiers on Sullivan's Island and begged their accep-
tance of a hogshead of old Antigua rum. The victorious Moultrie laconically reported
that Logan's gift was gratefully received and forthwith enjoyed.

Admiral Sir Peter Parker stated later that the ships fired on the fort at 450 yards or
less. He also admitted that this had been too great a range, an interesting comment on
effective eighteenth-century gunnery. Clinton maintained that the fleet anchored between 800 and 400 yards from Fort Sullivan and that many of the shots from the upper
gun decks went over the low-lying log fortifications. The fact that Admiral Parker very
clearly did not employ short-range, antipersonnel ammunition against the defenders
would seem to support General Clinton's contention. Canister and grape would have
been deadly effective against exposed personnel fighting from open gun platforms. Parker's guns were not loaded with canister and grape because the ships lay too far out
from the fort. In 1780 when the British captured Charleston, Clinton had soundings
made in the water approaches to Fort Moultrie and concluded from his findings that the
fleet could have anchored almost within musket range, in other words, at less than 400
yards. He always blamed the defeat on the position taken by the larger vessels and the
failure to bring the three frigates that ran aground into the mouth of the creek behind
the island to cut communications with Haddrell's Point and thus the mainland. General
Clinton apparently forgot he had persuaded Admiral Parker that an amphibious landing
on Sullivan's Island was not feasible because of shoal waters off the beach. The aborted
attempt to force a crossing of Breach Inlet from Long Island was an important contrib-
uting factor to the British failure.

Charleston, however, was saved and rested secure behind its fortifications and guns,
at least in the minds of its citizens, until 1780. In that year Clinton, supported by fleet
units under Admiral Mariot Arbuthnot, took the town. The fleet ran the forts at the
harbor entrance, and Arbuthnot brought his guns to Charleston's waterfront. The British army under Clinton and Charles Lord Cornwallis carried out a classic European-style
siege operation down the peninsula. The British high command had learned from their
failure in 1776 how Charleston could be attacked and taken. The city's defenders had
not profited from the same experience and failed to realize in time that a fleet commanded
by a clearly excellent sailor like Arbuthnot may run land forts. Also, any amphibious
assault across the Ashley River to cut off the Charleston peninsula would have to be met
and thrown back at the beach head—precisely what Colonel William Thomson had accomplished at Breach Inlet. Quite obviously, these facts were not appreciated by the
American commander, Major General Benjamin Lincoln, or the town fathers in 1780
when they lost Charleston.

CHAPTER II

The Cherokee War

On 1 July 1776, only two days after the unsuccessful British attack on the outer forts guarding Charleston, the entire southern frontier erupted in savage warfare. Fortunately for the backcountry settlements, only the powerful Cherokee Nation took the hatchet. The equally strong Creeks and Choctaws and the numerically weaker but exceedingly warlike Chicasaws, all lying further west, generally maintained an uneasy neutrality.

The Cherokee at that time probably numbered 12–14,000 with a fighting potential of as many as 3,000 musket-armed warriors. The white settlers of the frontier, trained by often tragic experience against these formidable and totally merciless antagonists, were to introduce in the coming war against each other and the British a concept of battle to the death—a total departure from the formalized, limited warfare of eighteenth-century western Europe.

The royal superintendent of Indian affairs for the whole southern district was a Scot, Captain John Stuart. He was responsible for the tribal territories along the frontiers of Virginia, North and South Carolina, Georgia, and Florida and all the Indian peoples dwelling therein. He was trusted completely by the tribes, exerted great influence among them, and was a most loyal subject to King George III. Under his guidance the Indians, increasingly resentful at illegal white pressure on tribal lands, also were loyal to the British king, whom they considered to be their protector.

Realizing that events in the South were moving toward a crisis, John Stuart in June of 1775 left Charleston (where his mansion still stands) and went to Florida. His wife and daughter, Mary Fenwick, remained in the port town. The Provincial Congress sitting in Charleston promptly issued an order confining the two women to their home, thus in effect making them hostages for John Stuart's behavior. The Stuart house was placed under military guard; no person was permitted to visit without Colonel William Moultrie's permission. Mrs. Fenwick eventually was released, but Mrs. Stuart escaped by night, apparently with the help of her son-in-law, Edward Fenwick. She joined her husband in Florida, but Edward Fenwick was arrested by the Charleston authorities and held for some time in the town jail.

John Stuart in Florida established communications with the Cherokee chiefs in upper South Carolina, western North Carolina, northern Georgia, and present-day eastern Tennessee. He also wrote on 3 October to the British commander in chief for the thirteen colonies, Lieutenant General Thomas Gage, stationed at Boston, Massachusetts, asking that he coordinate any possible military or naval operations in the South with his Indian allies. Stuart's letter reported to the general that a large majority of the backcountry white settlers were loyal to their king. He strongly opposed indiscriminate attack by the Indians along the frontier, but would try to use them in a concerted plan against the rebels in conjunction with their Loyalist neighbors. Stuart sent his brother, Henry Stuart, and another Scot, Alexander Cameron, as his personal emissaries and agents to the Cherokees. Moses Kirkland, a dedicated South Carolina Loyalist, was employed as John Stuart's messenger to General Gage.

The intelligent and benevolent policies of the royal government in dealing with the Indians assured that the great fighting tribes, North and South, were either neutral or on the British side during the American Revolution. Among the southern Indians, only the Siouan Catawbas in upper South Carolina actively aided the revolutionary cause, and the Catawbas were hereditary enemies of the Cherokees. The major tribal groups' antagonism to the element of the white population supporting the revolution is both a commentary on British policy on the Indians and on American frontier attitudes toward most of their red neighbors.

The letter sent by John Stuart to General Gage fell into the hands of the Continental Congress when the vessel in which his agent, Moses Kirkland, sailed was captured by an American privateer. Its subsequent publication by the Congress profoundly influenced public opinion by its implication of British willingness to unleash the known horrors of Indian warfare on the southern frontier.

The Cherokees struck on 1 July 1776 from Virginia to Georgia, killing and burning. Apparently the attack was meant to be coordinated with British operations at Charleston, but news of the arrival of Admiral Parker and Sir Henry Clinton off that port did not reach the Cherokees until two days after the British repulse. Charleston was about two hundred miles from tribal territory, much of the way through wilderness or semiwilderness over incredibly bad roads, and information traveled slowly. Difficult terrain, great distances, harsh climate, disease, and poor communications were to present almost insuperable difficulties to all forces engaged in the southern fighting throughout the war.

The first information concerning the Indian attack was brought to Francis Salvador at his plantation on Corn Acre Creek in the Ninety Six district. Aaron Smith, son of a nearby settler, rode up desperately, two fingers shot away, to bring word that his father, mother, five smaller brothers and sisters, and five black slaves had been butchered by the Cherokees. Francis Salvador, a twenty-nine-year-old English Sephardic Jew who had taken up seven thousand acres near Ninety Six, was a person of considerable prominence in the backcountry. He was an active member of the Provincial Congress and a leader in the defense affairs of his district. Salvador promptly ordered his best horse saddled and rode to Major Andrew Williamson's house, twenty-eight miles away, to raise the Ninety

Six district against the attack. Casualty reports now began to come in from outlying settlements. Among others, the Hampton family who farmed near the Tyger River in what is now Spartanburg County, had suffered heavily. The original settler, Anthony Hampton, his wife, a son named Preston, and an infant grandson all died in the attack. Fortunately for the family but not for the British, Loyalists, and Cherokees, five sons survived—Edward, Henry, John, Richard, and Wade Hampton—each one destined to distinguish himself as a leader in the coming war.

The Indian rising terrified the backcountry from Virginia to Georgia. Everyone knew from dreadful experience what it could and probably would mean. Eighteenth-century Indian warfare was totally brutal—in surprise attacks on unsuspecting and isolated homesteads white and black inhabitants were tortured, mutilated, and murdered without regard for age or sex. The frontier settlers in the South reacted in kind against the tribes, whom they considered less than human. But this warfare provided a grim battle training for the Americans.

A letter written by William Drayton in Charleston to Francis Salvador dated 24 July 1776 illustrates fear of and hostility to the Cherokees very clearly. Drayton advises Salvador to make smooth work as he and the South Carolina militia carry out the planned campaign. Drayton recommends that every Indian town be burned, all the cornfields destroyed, and Indian prisoners made slaves of the takers. The nation must be extirpated, and its lands should become the property of the public. Drayton believed there could be no peace with the Cherokees until the whole people were removed beyond the mountains. His advice was carried out with bitter thoroughness.

To complicate the military situation on the frontier, most of the best rifles and muskets in the backcountry had been sold to the militia regiments called up to meet the British threat against the coastal area. Panic-stricken families fled before the Indian attack, and Major Andrew Williamson, to whom Francis Salvador had brought the first information of the massacre, could raise only 40 men in the first few days of the crisis. Militia and volunteers slowly began to gather, and when Williamson's little force reached 220 he marched to DeWitt's Corner (now Due West, South Carolina) and established a camp about four miles from the Cherokee line. By mid-July, Andrew Pickens had arrived with reinforcements, and Williamson advanced with 450 men to Baker's Creek in what today is Abbeville County. The settlers along the Saluda River had gathered with their families in an old stockade called Lyndley's Fort, on Rayborn Creek. Here on 15 July they were attacked by 88 Cherokee warriors and over 100 Loyalists, dressed and painted as Indians. The few defenders holding Lyndley's Fort had been reinforced the evening before by 150 men. Thus strenghtened, the impromptu garrison repelled the attack and pursued their enemy. Nine of the war-painted white men were captured and sent under escort to Ninety Six where they were jailed.

This small victory gave heart to the embattled frontier. When news of the British defeat at Charleston finally reached the backcountry many doubters were persuaded and began to arrive in numbers to join Andrew Williamson and Andrew Pickens in a punitive expedition against the Cherokees. Further strengthened by a Georgia militia regiment led by Colonel Jack, the force of Georgians and South Carolinians mustered about 1,150 muskets and rifles. Ranger scouts meanwhile brought word that John Stuart's agent Alexander Cameron, had come to South Carolina from the Over-Hill Cherokee towns (those lying west of the mountains) with only thirteen white Loyalists and was camped about thirty miles away on Oconore Creek. Andrew Williamson decided to move out at once and capture Cameron.

Williamson's force was operating deep in Indian territory, but he apparently was ill-prepared to conduct a wilderness campaign against savage and well-armed opponents on their home ground. Although the experienced Indian fighter Andrew Pickens warned him sternly not to do so, Williamson stubbornly sounded morning and evening formations in true militia fashion, thus loudly advertising his presence to any possible enemy.

About six o'clock on the evening of 31 July 1776 Williamson with 330 mounted militia marched against Alexander Cameron. He was guided by two Loyalist prisoners whom his scouts had captured, and these unhappy men were warned that instant death would follow any attempt to give warning of the column's approach.

Alexander Cameron's camp lay on the other side of the Keowee River. Williamson therefore used the Esseneca Ford, the only crossing on that stretch of the Keowee and obviously watched by Cameron's spies. Williamson advanced against a supremely woodscrafty enemy with a mounted column whose shod horses could be heard at a considerable distance through the still night forest. He did not throw out a proper screen of dismounted scouts, nor did he possess adequate knowledge of the possible numbers facing him.

At approximately two o'clock in the morning of 1 August, Andrew Williamson and his 330 men were ambushed by Alexander Cameron and 1,200 Cherokee warriors who had joined him at his camp as planned—undetected by Williamson. Williamson's force, completely surprised, broke and retreated in confusion. Francis Salvador was shot from his horse and scalped while still alive by the pursuing Cherokees. Captain Smith, son of Aaron Smith murdered by the Indians in the first attack, viewed the scalping, but in the wild confusion of ambush and retreat, Smith thought the dark figures bending over the helpless Salvador were his servants trying to aid their master. He therefore did not ride to the rescue but continued to fall back with his men. Francis Salvador died later of his wounds and horrible mutilation, an early casualty in the War for Independence.

Fortunately, Lieutenant Colonel Leroy Hammond of the South Carolina militia rallied some twenty soldiers and led a mounted charge in the darkness against the advancing warriors. They successfully checked the undisciplined Cherokees so that the rest of Williamson's army could escape. Andrew Pickens at the head of a support force came up just before daylight, occupied a low ridge commanding the area, and in turn surprised the Indians with a hot and well-directed fire. The Cherokees withdrew at sunrise leaving one dead and three badly wounded warriors on the field. Andrew Williamson lost three men killed and fourteen seriously hurt in the brief but chaotic engagement. Under the circumstances—an ambush in the early morning darkness by an enemy greatly superior in numbers—he was fortunate and owed his escape to the basic military disorganization of the Cherokees, Leroy Hammond's cool courage, and the timely arrival of Andrew Pickens.

When full daylight came, Williamson and Pickens reassembled the demoralized column and pressed forward. They found the two Esseneca towns on both sides of the Keowee River deserted by their Indian inhabitants and burned these to the ground, also destroying some 6,000 bushels of stored corn. Fearful of advancing because of their partial defeat in ambush, they decided to leave the burned towns as a warning and fall back to Twenty-Three Mile Creek on the edge of Indian territory. Here a base camp could be established, militia reinforcements brought in, and a major expedition planned against the Cherokees.

Before his appointment as commander in chief of the field army Andrew Williamson had been only a major of militia, outranked by several of his officers. To quell the considerable jealousy aroused by his promotion, President John Rutledge made Williamson a colonel of the Ninety Six militia regiment, and shortly thereafter new operations were initiated against the Indians.

On 2 August 1776 a ruthless campaign was launched from the base on Twenty-Three Mile Creek to break permanently the effective fighting power of the Cherokees. A strong column sent out on 4 August destroyed the lower Cherokee settlements of Sugar Town, Soconee, and Keowee. Six days later 640 men of the South Carolina militia razed the towns of Estatoe and Tugaloo. The Indians fell back into the mountains with their women and children and waited for the warriors to gather.

The South Carolinians pushed into what is now Pickens County in the northwest corner of the state and pitched camp by the Little River. From here Andrew Pickens, with 25 chosen men guided by a half-breed scout named Cornell went on a reconnaissance mission that ended with his famous ring fight. The scouting party had proceeded about two miles from Williamson's camp when they were surprised and surrounded by almost 200 Cherokees as they were crossing an abandoned cornfield grown up in brush and tall grass.

Pickens ordered his men to form a counter circle and to fire in relays, two men discharging their weapons and crouching in the grass to reload, the next two firing and crouching in turn. The Indians tried to rush the ring, and the few who broke the line were killed by bayonet, hatchet, and knife in vicious hand-to-hand combat. The remainder finally broke off the action and retreated when Joseph Pickens, Andrew's brother, heard the shots and came up from his camp with a volunteer rescue party.

Williamson now advanced with his full force and on 12 August met and defeated a large Cherokee war party. The South Carolinians suffered only six killed and seventeen wounded in this engagement. The Cherokees left sixteen dead on the field and retreated, carrying their wounded. Williamson and Pickens then burned the abandoned towns of Tomassy, Chehohee, and Eustash, destroying all the dried corn and peas the Indians had stored for winter food and forcing the Cherokees of the lower settlements to survive through the cold months on a diet of roots, winter-killed wild fruit, and whatever game or fish they might take.

Following this operation the South Carolinians returned to the advance base on Twenty-Three Mile Creek where Williamson and Pickens found to their consternation that many of the troops detailed to hold the outpost had gone home. These were militia, to whom discipline was foreign or distasteful, and they behaved accordingly. Most of the men who remained lacked the necessary clothing for a winter campaign in the mountains and were given furloughs. Orders were issued, however, that all should report for duty on 28 August at the agreed rendezvous of Esseneca. After these plans were established, Andrew Williamson marched back to that ruined town with his 600 remaining men and built Fort Rutledge, named in honor of the state's president. There he and Pickens collected supplies and waited for the army to reassemble in late summer.

After the first Cherokee attack, the government of South Carolina had sent hasty dispatches to North Carolina, Virginia, and Georgia suggesting a coordinated offensive against the Indians. The three states had agreed and begun to raise the necessary forces for a joint campaign. The North Carolinians under General Griffith Rutherford were to act with the South Carolinians against the lower and middle Cherokee settlements lying east of and in the mountains. The Virginians, commanded by Colonel Christie, would march west of the ranges and carry the war to the Over-Hill Cherokees. The Georgians were to strike north against the Indian towns in the upper sections of the state. Williamson and Pickens already had destroyed a large number of the lower Cherokee towns before Rutherford took the field.

On 13 September, Andrew Williamson, assigning 300 men to guard Fort Rutledge at Esseneca (now Seneca, South Carolina), advanced with 2,000 militia to join his force with General Rutherford and the North Carolinians. Guided by Catawba Indian scouts, the South Carolinians passed through Rabun Gap and marched down the ancient path by the headwaters of the Tennessee River. There are two excellent eyewitness accounts of Williamson's campaign, one a diary of a soldier named Arthur Fairies and the other by a Captain Ross. Both describe in harrowing detail the narrow trails up the mountains, flanked by impassable laurel thickets where scouts could not be thrown out to guard against surprise and ambushes might be expected at every dark turn. They also tell of the wounding of an Indian woman as she ran out on the path before the advance troops. The soldiers promptly shot the injured squaw like a dog. Ross states that the militiamen scalped Indians after a fight. He relates how, during the skirmish at Tomassy, one young South Carolinian engaged a Cherokee warrior in single combat. The soldier gouged the Indian's eyes, then threw the man down and scalped him while still alive. He finished off his opponent by beating out his brains with a gun butt. These narratives are mordant commentaries on the southern frontier fighting.

Andrew Williamson's column reached the town of Coweechee on 17 September where they hoped to join General Rutherford and his North Carolinians. Finding that Rutherford had not arrived, the South Carolinians pressed forward, following the Coweecho River through the wild hill-country, and on 19 September walked into a major ambush at a steep-sided, heavily wooded river gorge known as the "Black Hole," about nine miles south of present Franklin, North Carolina. Fairies and Ross describe the bloody battle of the Black Hole, which lasted two hours and cost the South Carolinians thirteen killed and eighteen wounded. There was no way to counterattack except forward, which the army did, clearing the enemy positions by direct frontal assault. Again, discipline defeated an undisciplined enemy.

The militia from North and South Carolina finally met at Hiwassee on 26 September, forming a combined force of almost 4,000. They listened to the Reverend James Hall, chaplain of the North Carolinians, offer public prayers for the safety and success of the expedition. Hall's words reflected the strain of grim, self-righteous, combative Calvinism prevalent in the early southern backcountry. The Indians were referred to as murderous heathen, and the troops accordingly considered themselves engaged in a holy war in which all actions against such an enemy were justified.

General Rutherford had passed through the Blue Ridge at Suwannanoa Gap with about 2,000 men and marched down the French Broad River fording at a shallow run later called the War Ford. He then moved up the valley of Hominy Creek and pushed over Cowee Mountain to the Tennessee River for his rendezvous with Williamson. On the march the North Carolinians, under constant, harassing sniper fire, destroyed towns, cut up the Cherokees' standing corn, and drove off their cattle.

The junction of the forces at Hiwassee gave them sufficient strength to complete the task, and the militia of the two Carolinas went through the valleys literally with fire and sword, burning out the remaining tribal settlements in the mountain area. The Virginians and Georgians, coming in from the north and south, carried out the same ruthless policy west of the Appalachians. The defeated and starving Cherokees sued for peace.

The South Carolinians had experienced the heaviest fighting, but the entire campaign cost the state only 99 men killed and wounded. The casualties for Virginia, North Carolina, and Georgia were even lighter. The Cherokee dead, however, were estimated at over 2,000, probably including all ages and both sexes. A large proportion of Cherokee fighting manpower thus was eliminated, and the tribal lands were totally devastated. This campaign is undoubtedly the reason why the Cherokees did not join the British and Loyalists in force after the capture of Charleston and the American rout at Camden in

1780. The tribe no longer possessed the military power or will to intervene successfully when their intervention might have been of signal aid to the then triumphant British cause.

On 20 May 1777 representatives from Georgia, South Carolina, North Carolina, and Virginia met with the paramount chiefs of the Cherokees. At this conference a treaty of pacification was signed in which the tribe ceded a large portion of its lands in upper South Carolina, including the present counties of Anderson, Pickens, Oconee, and Greenville, the Indians retaining only a small strip along the Chattooga River. The Cherokee war chief Atta-Kulla-Kulla tried to appease his American conquerors by offering 500 warriors to fight against the British. This offer was never accepted and feelings remained bitter on both sides. Some of the Cherokee clans, led by the war chief Dragging Canoe, refused to honor the treaty and went down the Tennessee River to Chickamauga Creek where they established a new settlement. Here this undefeated remnant was joined later by disaffected Creeks, Shawnees from north of the Ohio, and even a few white Loyalists. Swearing to support the British and remain at war with the four states, Dragging Canoe and his warriors conducted hit-and-run forays along the southern frontier throughout the war, including attacks on the Watauga and Nolichucky settlements successfully countered by John Sevier and Isaac Shelby and a dreadful massacre in November 1781 at Thomson's Fort in upper South Carolina. On the latter occasion a band of Loyalists dressed and painted like Indians, supported by some Cherokee warriors, all led by a sadistic white renegade known as Bloody Bates, captured Fort Thomson. They killed and horribly mutilated almost every man, woman, or child who had taken refuge within the stockade. A few mangled survivors managed to escape and brought word of the tragedy.

A strong force of South Carolinians and Georgians led by Andrew Pickens and the famous Georgia partisan leader Elijah Clarke finally put an effective end to Cherokee raids in 1782. Pickens' brother had been captured and roasted slowly to death by the Cherokees; it was therefore fitting that the stern Presbyterian fighting elder should wreak ultimate defeat on the Cherokees. Permanent peace with the tribe, however, was not established until ten years after the war.

The people settled along the Indian border believed, with considerable reason, that by encouraging the Indian raids the British authorities had launched a savage war against the backcountry. This feeling undoubtedly exerted strong influence on many people of the region to support the revolutionary cause. In full justice, the royal agent, Captain John Stuart, had opposed indiscriminate use of Indians, knowing exactly what the result would be. The Indians had indeed attacked, inflicting all the horrors for which they were noted, and this was the fact the settlers remembered.

CHAPTER III

Savannah, 1778–1779

After the first British failure at Charleston in June 1776 and the Cherokee War during the late summer and early fall of the same year, no major fighting occurred in the southern theater of operations until 1778. Charles Lee in his brief tenure as commander in South Carolina and Georgia launched an abortive invasion of British-held Florida that withered on the vine as Major General Augustine Prevost, the British commander in the area, fell back before the American advance, allowing the summer climate and disease to do his fighting for him. Lee undertook his ill-advised expedition in the worst possible season for yellow fever and malaria. The troops did not meet or even see an enemy but sickened and died in the swamps and marshes of the Ogeechee River.

Many Loyalists had fled from South Carolina and Georgia to East Florida. From Florida, rangers led by Thomas Browne and Daniel McGirth raided deep into Georgia. Both Browne and McGirth had suffered outrageous treatment from their former friends and neighbors for their unswerving loyalty to King George. Thomas Browne had been tarred and feathered and his bare feet held to a fire and severely burned; Daniel McGirth had been publicly whipped. Both clearly felt totally justified in organizing and leading fellow Loyalist refugees in a bitter, vindictive guerrilla war against supporters of the Revolution.

In 1776, after Major General Charles Lee's Florida fiasco, Augustine Prevost built and garrisoned a fort on the St. Mary's River which served as a pivot of maneuver for the British and Loyalist forays into Georgia. To counter these raids Major General Robert Howe, who had succeeded Charles Lee as American commander in the South, led a second and equally ill-fated expedition in 1778 against the British in Florida. Howe's little army marched south through an increasingly desolate terrain where neither bud nor berry was to be seen. The horses died for lack of fodder, the men from malaria, yellow fever, dysentery, and the intense heat of a south Georgia coastal summer. Torn by command disagreements and factional conflict, the Americans finally retreated without fighting a single battle, but 500 soldiers had died in the disastrous operation.

Robert Howe had left Colonel Lachlan McIntosh with a small force to hold Sunbury, Georgia. Prevost followed Howe's army with orders to take Sunbury and move from there to take Savannah. A second and seaborne column was instructed to sail from Florida and cooperate with Prevost at Sunbury and later at Savannah. The two forces never made a junction, and General Prevost invested Sunbury with his own unsupported troops. Lachlan McIntosh was summoned to surrender, and the doughty Scot sent word to the British to come and take the town if they could. Prevost declined this grim invitation and marched back to Florida, receiving a serious check on the way when he had to fight his way across Ogeechee Ferry against Lieutenant Colonel Samuel Elbert with some 200 Georgia Continentals whose mission was to harry the British retreat. With an enthusiasm exceeded only by the stupidity of the act, Augustine Prevost on his return march laid waste an already devastated country, thus permanently antagonizing the few inhabitants still trying to scratch a miserable living from a barren land.

According to the new British strategy to win the war, Georgia, the newest and weakest of the southern colonies, was considered the most vulnerable point to attack. A captured and pacified Georgia and South Carolina could supply the important West Indian sugar islands with food. With this objective, Sir Henry Clinton, now commander in chief for American operations stationed in New York, dispatched Lieutenant Colonel Archibald Campbell in November of 1778 to attack Savannah with 3,000 soldiers, all crack troops. These included the 71st Regiment of Foot (Highland Scots), four battalions of German mercenary infantry, two battalions of North and South Carolina Provincials (Loyalists trained and equipped as British regulars), a very fine northern Loyalist Provincial regiment, the New York Volunteers, and a strong detachment of Royal Artillery. The North Carolinians were commanded by Colonel John Hamilton, a veteran of Culloden Moor and now a wealthy southern planter. The South Carolinians were led by Colonel Alexander Innes, former secretary to Lord William Campbell, royal governor of South Carolina.

On 27 December 1778 the fleet from New York, commanded by Commodore Hyde Parker, arrived off the Savannah River, successfully crossed the bar on a rising tide, and dropped anchor in the river mouth. During the morning of the 29th the first troops came ashore below Savannah at Girardeau's plantation where a narrow causeway with a quarter drain (a deep, water-filled ditch) on either side led from the plantation landing across a rice field to higher ground.

The light infantry of the 71st Regiment under Captain Cameron formed, fixed bayonets, and advanced in column across the causeway, officers in front. A small American force assigned to watch the plantation landing fired one volley which killed Cameron, but the Highlanders promptly charged and cleared the high ground, its defenders retreating on the main American position just downriver from Savannah.

The British forces, 3,000 strong, completed the landing operation and moved toward the town. General Robert Howe, the American commander, had only some 700 men, many of them raw, untried militia, but General Benjamin Lincoln was expected to bring reinforcements from South Carolina. Realizing that any delay in battle action could only profit Savannah's defenders, Campbell wisely decided to attack before nightfall.

Robert Howe, badly outnumbered and outgunned, should have retreated northward to join his forces with those gathering in South Carolina. Instead, he called a council of war, which voted to stay and fight. General Howe had selected a defensive position that appeared to be a wise disposition of his available forces. In front and parallel to his line of battle lay a lagoon, and the bridge crossing it had been destroyed to impede the British advance. Howe's right was protected by a wooded swamp with a few houses on higher ground, and these were held by American riflemen. The river marshes covered his left, while the American army's rear rested on the town and some old fieldworks along the Savannah River. The army was divided into two wings with General Isaac Huger of South Carolina commanding the right and Lieutenant Colonel Samuel Elbert of Georgia the left.

Archibald Campbell, a truly professional soldier, already had conducted a thorough reconnaissance and discovered a path through the swamp on Howe's right. He detached his regular light infantry under Sir James Baird and the New York Volunteers, and these units, led by a black slave, passed unnoticed through the swamp and reached the rear of Savannah's defenders. Meanwhile, the British made a strong demonstration on Howe's front to hold his attention. As soon as Baird sent back word that he was in position, Campbell's feint was converted into a direct assault across the lagoon. The Americans fell back, Baird attacked from their rear, and after a few minutes of desperate fighting, the battle became a rout. General Howe managed to escape with a few men and officers into South Carolina, but his army suffered about 550 killed or captured out of 700 effectives and lost all of its artillery and support vehicles. There were 26 British casualties, 7 killed and 19 wounded.

Savannah now was secured, giving the British an excellent base for their next move. Most of the people in the lower part of the state came in and took the oath of allegiance to King George III. From among the Georgia Loyalist elements, new and old, Lieutenant Colonel Campbell began to form rifle and musket companies or dragoon squadrons. South Carolina had become an American march province with active enemies along its southern and western frontiers.

In establishing the British position strongly in Georgia, Archibald Campbell proved to be an equitable and just conqueror. If he had remained in command, the war in the South might have had different and far more serious results for the American cause. Fortunately for the Americans, he was relieved and was succeeded by less honorable, exemplary, and intelligent men.

Except for a few high moments, the next few months proved disastrous for American arms. Major General Augustine Prevost came up from Florida and joined forces with Lieutenant Colonel Campbell at Savannah. On Prevost's march north he took Sunbury, the disheartened American garrison losing 212 prisoners and 40 pieces of artillery. The able Loyalist Colonel John Hamilton, with 200 mounted infantry, was sent upriver toward Augusta to show the flag and encourage pro-British or wavering elements among the inhabitants. It was during this operation that the British suffered their only serious reverse in the Georgia campaign. Colonel Andrew Pickens, the fighting Presbyterian elder, marched against the Loyalists with 500 American militia from Georgia and the Ninety Six district of South Carolina. At the same time a strong force of Loyalists from North Carolina led by Colonel James Boyd were pushing through South Carolina to join Hamilton on the Savannah River. Pickens and his militia first attacked Hamilton and were beaten off, then turned against Boyd. They followed the North Carolinians to Kettle Creek where, in an action lasting less than an hour, Boyd was mortally wounded and his followers killed, captured, or scattered. According to legend, Andrew Pickens, who had known Boyd before the war, found his dying opponent and told him he was sorry to find him suffering for such a cause. Boyd replied that he gloried in his cause and proudly gave his life for his king. He asked Pickens to take a brooch he wore to his wife and requested that two men be assigned to stay with him until he died. A person of stern integrity in all matters, Andrew Pickens honored both requests. Kettle Creek, fought near the present city of Washington, Georgia, on 14 February 1779, was one of few American successes. By the middle of February 1779 the entire state of Georgia seemed firmly in British hands.

Congress, at last aware of the gravity of the military situation in the South, had sent Benjamin Lincoln to replace Robert Howe as commander in the Southern Department. He arrived in Charleston on 19 December 1778, just ten days before the fall of Savannah, and found only 1,500 men available to march as a relief force. Desperately calling up militia, General Lincoln finally increased his forces to 3,500 and marched on British-held Savannah, taking position at Purysburg, South Carolina, just across the river from Ebenezer, Georgia. Major General Augustine Prevost, now in overall command of British and Loyalist forces in Georgia and Florida, countermoved on 3 February 1779 by making an amphibious landing on Port Royal Island with 200 men under Major Gardiner, supported by the naval squadron that had escorted Archibald Campbell's transports from New York. General William Moultrie and Brigadier General Stephen Bull with 300 South Carolina militia crossed the waterways surrounding the island and drove the British from their beachhead. It is interesting to note that the best unit in William Moultrie's attack force was the Charleston Battalion of Artillery, organized and trained by Christopher Gadsden and recruited from the town's best families. Major Thomas Grimball commanded the battalion, and the two companies were led by Captains Thomas Heyward and Edward Rutledge, both signers of the Declaration of Independence.

This action at Port Royal and the victory of Kettle Creek were the only real successes the Americans could claim in the early southern campaign. On 3 March 1779, General John Ashe of North Carolina was routed at Briar Creek by Lieutenant Colonel Mark Prevost, the general's younger brother. Ashe lost his artillery, all the ammunition and baggage, and about 400 men killed, wounded, or captured. The British suffered 16 casualties. After this defeat, Benjamin Lincoln marched up the Savannah River toward Augusta with most of his army, leaving William Moultrie behind with an inadequate force to guard the key port of Charleston. The reason's for Lincoln's departure remain obscure, but Prevost promptly took advantage of his absence, crossed the river, and drove on Charleston, brushing aside Moultrie and his covering force. He arrived on the peninsula above the town, and the Charlestonians, who had been so courageous and steadfast in 1776, seriously considered becoming neutral for the rest of the war. Although accounts of the terms differ, the town apparently made an offer of neutrality to Prevost, which he naturally rejected because all military advantages lay with the British. Benjamin Lincoln, however, informed by dispatch rider of the situation, was marching back at his best speed from the Savannah River with a force larger than Prevost's 3,000 men. Prevost found the town defenses stronger than he had expected. Lacking time for a siege or the numbers to warrant a direct assault, Prevost withdrew and retired to Savannah via the coastal sea islands. The offer by Charleston's leaders to become neutral remains unexplained, but it probably reflected the strong sense of weary defeatism that permeated the American cause at this time, both North and South. After four years of fighting the Americans had achieved only one outstanding success—the defeat and capture of General Burgoyne's army at Saratoga in 1777. The mood throughout the thirteen states generally was one of apathy or active despair. Charleston's desire for neutrality could be seen as a precursor of the later unsuccessful defense of the town against General Sir Henry Clinton's all-out attack in 1780.

General Prevost retreated southward from Charleston with Benjamin Lincoln following closely. The main British force withdrew safely to Savannah, but Lieutenant Colonel John Maitland, commanding Prevost's rear guard, fought a savage delaying action against Lincoln's pursuing army on 20 June 1779 at Stono Ferry near the present town of Rantowles.

Maitland's rear guard consisted of the first battalion of the 71st Regiment of Foot (Highland Scots), part of a Hessian regiment, the North and South Carolina Provincial infantry regiments, and a small unit of artillery mustering altogether about 500 effectives. According to Charles Stedman, whose information is based on General Prevost's field report, Lincoln led some 5,000 men supported by light guns. These included Continental infantry, a North and South Carolina militia brigade, a Virginia militia brigade, Casimir Pulaski's cavalry, and a small contingent of North Carolina horsemen under William Richardson Davie, who was destined to become one of the great partisan leaders of the war in the South. The 5,000 American effectives and eight guns reported by Prevost undoubtedly are an exaggeration. Though they outnumbered Maitland seven or eight to one, Lincoln's army later at the siege of Savannah probably did not exceed 3,000 men with five guns.

Maitland had built temporary earthworks and an abatis at the ferry and sent out two companies of Highland Scots to make contact with the approaching Americans. Moving about a quarter of a mile from the British position, these troops encountered the Continentals, and a hot fire fight promptly ensued. The Scots resisted so stubbornly that all of their officers were killed or wounded, and only eleven survivors of the two companies fell back, still fighting, on the fieldworks. A general engagement followed, and the Hessians on Maitland's left were pushed back in confusion by the North and South Carolina militia stationed on the American right. John Maitland, a cool and wise commander, promptly threw the remainder of the 71st's battalion from his right to the left wing and restored the British line. The Hessians rallied, and the battle continued with even greater intensity.

After an hour of close fighting Lincoln's battle line became disorganized and he ordered a tactical retreat covered by a cavalry charge against the advancing British. Maitland halted his small force, formed a bristling bayonet front, and drove back American horsemen with disciplined volley fire. The Virginia brigade, which Lincoln had held in reserve, came up and delivered a crashing volley, but Maitland, his mission of delaying the Americans effectively accomplished, broke off the action and crossed the Stono River unmolested. British casualties in the engagement numbered 129, including 26 killed. The Americans suffered about 150 killed and wounded. Lincoln retired to Charleston with his still somewhat disorganized army, having failed with greatly superior forces to destroy a rear guard with its back to a river.

The battle of the Stono thus could be called a draw, without real advantage to either side. The heroes of the day were the gallant Highlanders whose staunch fighting abilities undoubtedly saved Maitland from disaster.

The French alliance had been consummated by Congress on 6 February 1778 and seemed at last to be bringing results. Admiral d'Estaing had provided naval support for the capture of Grenada and St. Vincent in the West Indies and defeated the British Vice Admiral, the Honorable John "Foul Weather Jack" Byron, in a hard-fought naval engagement in the summer of 1779. Governor John Rutledge of South Carolina, General Benjamin Lincoln, and the French consul in Charleston, Monsieur Plombard, wrote several letters to d'Estaing requesting his aid in a combined attack on British-controlled Savannah. In response, the French admiral sailed up from the islands, arriving off Charleston bar in the first week of September 1779 with a powerful fleet and 4,000 French troops. An officer came ashore by ship's pinnace and informed Benjamin Lincoln that the Count d'Estaing was ready to support an attack on Savannah but urged haste because it was dangerous for the big French naval units to remain in southern coastal waters during the hurricane season.

The British did not know of d'Estaing's arrival until 4 September, when scout frigates sighted the French fleet of thirty-seven sail south of Tybee Island, Georgia. General Prevost was informed immediately and desperate efforts were begun to put Savannah in a proper state of defense against an expected French-American assault.

Colonel John Harris Cruger, a brilliant New York Loyalist officer, was ordered to bring his garrison up from Sunbury. Guns were landed from the small British naval squadron stationed at Savannah and emplaced on the town fortifications, and several of the ships were sunk in the channel below the town to prevent the French fleet from working frigates upriver to attack the defenses with direct broadside fire. A log boom was constructed and anchored across the river above Savannah to prevent fire ships from being sent down on the current. One armed British vessel remained in the river above the sunken hulls to offer resistance if crossings were attempted at that point.

On 5 September General Benjamin Lincoln published orders for all officers and soldiers of Continental and militia regiments to rejoin their respective units. As his forces gathered, he took command at Sheldon on the road to Savannah; William Moultrie was designated the commander in Charleston. The French fleet anchored off Savannah bar as planned on 9 September, but the big line-of-battle ships could not approach the shore where the shallows began. Small boats had to be obtained from Charleston, and it was not until 12 September that 3,000 of d'Estaing's 4,000 soldiers finally were put on the beach, of necessity at Beaulieu on Ossabaw Sound, a few miles south of Savannah.

Admiral the Count d'Estaing moved on his objective without waiting for Benjamin Lincoln and the American army marching south to join him. On 16 September d'Estaing invested Savannah and demanded that Prevost surrender the town in the name of his most Christian majesty, King Louis XVI of France. This summons contained no reference, verbal or written, to d'Estaing's American allies pushing down from Sheldon. The French admiral also vaunted with considerable arrogance his successful capture of Grenada and threatened to hold Prevost personally responsible for a useless prolongaton of the fighting. When they learned of d'Estaing's messages, the American commanders became resentful of his apparently uncalled-for discourtesy, and they feared that d'Estaing might capture Savannah and then hold the town in the name of King Louis XVI. After his arrival, Benjamin Lincoln protested, and though the French admiral apparently made some explanation of his conduct, distrust of him persisted.

General Augustine Prevost answered d'Estaing's summons to surrender most correctly, according to formal European military usage, and asked for twenty-four hours to consider the terms under which a submission might be made. Admiral d'Estaing somewhat foolishly granted the request—he could have taken Savannah by direct assault without American assistance because the town's defenses were incomplete and undermanned. The delay permitted Prevost, with details of soldiers, citizens, and black slaves laboring night and day, to finish his fortifications and summon Lieutenant Colonel John Maitland with much needed reinforcements from the advanced British outpost at Beaufort, South Carolina. Maitland, the excellent soldier who had checked Benjamin Lincoln in the hot retreating action on the Stono River, promptly evacuated Beaufort and marched south. Although seriously ill with the fever that eventually killed him, Maitland pushed his command at double time to the north bank of the Savannah. The French held the lower river, so Maitland and his men, guided by black Gullah fisherpeople, followed Walls's Cut, a little-known passage behind Daufuskie Island, dragging and poling their heavy boats through miles of deep mud and shallow, winding salt creeks. Maitland arrived with 800 veterans, but the rest of the Beaufort garrison could not be transported for lack of boats and remained with the armed galleys under Captain Christian of the Royal Navy. With retreat prevented by Benjamin Lincoln's advance, Christian dug in at Callibogue Sound where the French and Americans did not try to dislodge him. The town of Savannah now was properly held, and General Prevost immediately sent a defiant message to Admiral d'Estaing rejecting out of hand the proposed terms of surrender. By his procrastination even after the time limit of twenty-four hours expired, the French commander had lost the crucial moment for attack. An equally advantageous second chance would never occur.

On 23 September Benjamin Lincoln finally joined Admiral d'Estaing before Savannah. With the Georgia and South Carolina Continentals plus militia units, Lincoln's army counted 3,000 effectives. The combined French and American troops available for the operation thus numbered about 7,000. Prevost with Maitland's reinforcements commanded some 2,500 to defend Savannah.

Even after General Lincoln arrived, a scarcity of horses and artillery carriages prevented an expeditious landing from the ships and emplacement of the heavy French artillery. Thus delayed again, the allied armies did not break ground for the first siege parallel until 24 September, and the big guns were not in position until 4 October. These lost days would prove disastrous to French and American plans.

While the allies were establishing the first siege approaches, two sorties by the British garrison effectively interrupted the work on the parallel. The first led by Major Graham of the 16th Regiment reached the French-American lines and threw them into total confusion. When the raiding party retired in good order to Savannah, the Americans followed so closely that they lost heavily to musketry directed from the works. The second sortie, under Major Archibald MacArthur of the 71st (Highland) Regiment, was carried out so adroitly that it accomplished its mission of disruption and also produced an exchange of fire between the French and American troops manning the lines.

In the meantime the entire British and Loyalist garrison, assisted by a large number of black slaves, worked incessantly under the very able direction of Captain Moncrieff, the military engineer officer on Prevost's staff. When the French first landed, the fortifications around Savannah mounted about a dozen pieces of artillery. Before the siege ended more than 100 guns were in position.

On the morning of 4 October, the batteries of the besiegers opened on the town with the fire of 53 heavy cannon and 14 mortars. General Prevost, fearing for the lives of the noncombatants, sent out a flag requesting that the women and children be permitted to leave Savannah and go on board vessels anchored in the river. These would be placed

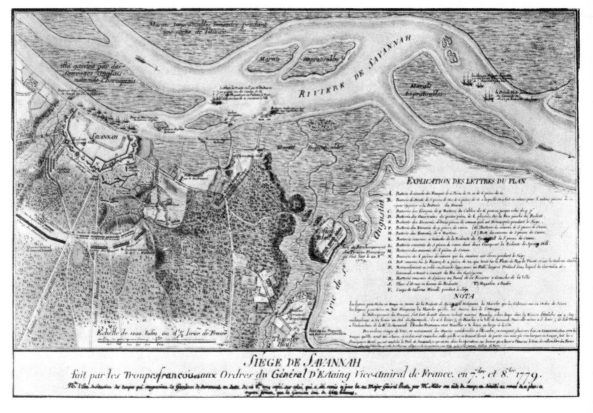

Figure 5.   Siege of Savannah, Georgia, 16 September–19 October 1779, by Pierre Ozanne

under the protecton of Admiral d'Estaing to await the outcome of the siege. This humane proposal was rejected by the French and American high commands who apparently feared that Prevost would use the temporary cessation of hostilities to strengthen his works further—a specious and somewhat tardy consideration. Fortunately, the cannonade and bombardment, which lasted from 4 to 9 October, cost few civilian or military lives and did little material damage to the defenses.

Savannah is situated on the southern bank of the river. In the eighteenth century the town was secured on two sides, the Savannah River protecting its northern front and a heavily wooded swamp draining into the river above the town covering the western side. The southern and eastern sides were open to the country which for several miles had been cleared of forest and thus offered a level area for attack. By the time the battle took place, Augustine Prevost had established a line of works, the right and left of his area defended by redoubts and the center by seamen's batteries. These works around the town were strengthened by abatis, while impalements and traverses had been put up in the rear to protect troops from high-trajectory enemy fire.

There were three redoubts on the right toward the swamp. The center redoubt under the command of Lieutenant Colonel John Hamilton was garrisoned by two companies of Loyalist Georgia militia with the North Carolina Loyalist Regiment in support. On the right were Captains Raworth and Wyley with the South Carolina corps of King's Rangers. Captain Tawse with his South Carolina Provincial Dragoons held the left, called the Spring Hill redoubt. He was supported by a regiment of South Carolina Loyalist infantry led by the same Lieutenant Colonel Thomas Browne who in 1775 had been tarred, feathered, and had his bare feet held to a fire for expressing loyalty to his king. To the right of the redoubts, covering the river approaches, Prevost had set up a naval battery of 9-pounders supported by a company of the British Legion, an elite Loyalist unit commanded by Captain Stewart. Between the center and the Spring Hill redoubt was a second naval battery under Captain Manby, and posted behind were the grenadiers of the 16th Regiment of Foot plus the marines from the British ships of war, all led by Lieutenant Colonel Glazier. This entire force on the right of the lines was commanded by the gallant but mortally ill Maitland, who had brought his troops through the coastal forests and marshes from Beaufort.

On the left of the lines facing the open country were two strong redoubts constructed like Fort Moultrie at Charleston of spongy palmetto logs filled with sand and mounting heavy guns. One of these was commanded by Lieutenant Colonel John Harris Cruger with a unit of de Lancey's New York Brigade and the other by Major James Wright, the son of the royal governor of Georgia and grandson of a chief justice of South Carolina. His redoubt was garrisoned by a strong contingent of Georgia Loyalists. In the center of the works protected by impalements and traverses were two battalions of the 71st Regiment, two regiments of Hessian mercenaries, the New York Volunteers, a battalion of de Lancey's Loyalist foot, and the light infantry of the British regiments. This reserve was placed under Major Graham with orders to come rapidly to the support of any part of the lines heavily attacked. As was often the case in the southern fighting, more than half the defenders were Americans loyal to their king, opposed to Americans supporting the Revolution and their new French allies, the latter soldiers and sailors of a nation that had been the bitter enemy of the British and colonists alike throughout the colonial period.

A five-day cannonade and bombardment did not dislodge the defenders or destroy their works. Admiral d'Estaing already had spent a month in front of Savannah in an operaton the French originally had expected to last ten or twelve days. The continued delays, however, proved fatal to allied plans. General Augustine Prevost now was ready to repel any attack. The hurricane season was well advanced, causing Admiral d'Estaing and his senior officers increasing concern about the safety of the ships. In addition, the French feared the possible arrival off Savannah of a strong British fleet capable of cutting them off from their base in the West Indies. D'Estaing therefore informed Benjamin Lincoln that the siege must be raised or the town stormed forthwith. Lincoln agreed.

During the early morning of 8 October, Major L'Enfant of the French army with five volunteers tried to burn the abatis. A heavy fire by the alert defenders, the greenness of the wood, and the damp morning frustrated the attempt. The wooded swamp on the British right, however, presented an approach to the defenses via a sink that ran along its margin. Thus protected, troops could move along the edge of the swamp under cover and launch an assault, exposed only briefly to enemy fire before reaching the works. This seemed to the French and American commanders the best approach for an all-out attack. Prevost, however, was aware of the danger presented by the sink and had guarded that portion of the defenses with his best troops.

On the evening of 8 October, General Benjamin Lincoln and Admiral d'Estaing established their order of battle. The troops assigned to carry out the assault were divided into two groups, the first composed of a strong French column supported by light infantry drawn from the American Continental regiments, the second under the command of Lieutenant Colonel John Laurens. The second group included the regular line infantry of the Continental regiments and the first battalion of the Charleston militia. This entire force was ordered to parade at one o'clock in the morning of 9 October. The invalids were assigned to guard the camps and keep the camp fires burning as usual.

The American cavalry were to parade at the same hour, and all mounted troops were instructed to follow the column of French assault troops and precede the attached American light infantry. Their orders were to try to penetrate the enemy lines toward the river. The American field artillery would follow the French artillery in the rear of the formations.

Elements of South Carolina militia from the 1st and 2d Brigades under Brigadier General Andrew Williamson who had led the expedition against the Cherokees in 1776 and the second battalion of Charleston militia commanded by Brigadier General Isaac Huger formed a secondary assault force. Huger's 500 men were to move as quietly as possible toward the left of the British lines and remain there in readiness. The other 500 under Williamson would be stationed in the advanced parallel at four o'clock in the morning. The full 1,000 were to advance and attack the enemy left. Huger was to hit the defense as near to the river as possible. This would be a feint in force, but if the opportunity presented itself Huger was to convert the feint into full attack and rush the works.

The Spring Hill redoubt held by Captain Tawse with his South Carolina Provincial Dragoons and Thomas Browne's South Carolina Loyalist infantry would be the main point of attack on the British right. The assault forces designated to carry this redoubt were the South Carolina Continentals and the 1st Battalion of Charleston militia. Thus, as so often tragically happened, South Carolinian was to fight South Carolinian.

The general attack on the British right would be in two columns, the first column of French and American troops led personally by Admiral d'Estaing and General Benjamin Lincoln. A second allied column under the Irish-French Count Dillon was to move along the edge of the swamp around the redoubts and attack the town toward the river.

Delays of the sort that had plagued the entire operation prevailed, and the assault planned for the predawn hours did not take place until broad daylight, thus losing the advantage of surprise. No adequate reconnaissance had been conducted, and Isaac Huger advancing with 500 men on the British left found himself in a flooded rice field, his equipment-burdened soldiers struggling through semiliquid mud. When he finally reached dry ground before the defenses, his force was met with a blast of artillery and musket fire that sent the untried militia retreating far faster than they had advanced.

Count Dillon's column lost its way in the swamp, an easy thing to do in the darkness, as anyone knows who has shot or fished in South Carolina and Georgia swamps. Dillon's column did not emerge until full daylight and promptly came under a hot and well-directed artillery and musket fire. They were unable to form and fell back into the woods for protection.

General Lincoln and Admiral d'Estaing, covered by darkness and the swamp-edge sink and with the advantage that the British were occupied by Huger and Dillon, approached closely to the Spring Hill redoubt before they were discovered, and here the main battle was fought. The remainder of the 4,000 French troops on the ships had been brought ashore. D'Estaing at the head of some 3,500 soldiers and Lincoln leading 600 South Carolina Continentals supported by 350 Charleston militia tried to storm the redoubts by frontal attack. The French and Americans were met by a withering cross fire of canister and musketry, but the South Carolina Continentals commanded by Lachlan McIntosh pressed forward and forced the abatis. The South Carolina Loyalist Captain Tawse died defending the gate of the redoubt, his sword through the body of the third fellow South Carolinian he killed that day. French and South Caolina assault troops actually reached the parapet and planted their standards on the redoubt. The 2d South Carolina Continental Regiment led by Lieutenant Colonel Francis Marion carried a beautiful pair of silk colors, one flag red and the other blue, presented by Mrs. Barnard Elliott of Charleston as a reward from the ladies of the town for the regiment's outstanding conduct under fire at Fort Sullivan. Both flags were placed on the ramparts and both color bearers were killed in the process. One was Sergeant William Jasper who had raised Colonel Moultrie's flag on the sponger staff at Fort Sullivan. The dying Jasper handed the red colors to the already seriously wounded Lieutenant John Bush, who fell shortly afterward with the flag under his body. It was captured there by the defenders during the counterattack. Lieutenant James Gray, who carried the blue colors, also was mortally wounded, but a Sergeant McDonald picked up the flag, charged forward, and placed it on the rampart. When the retreat was ordered, McDonald brought these colors back to safety.

This was the climax of the attack—French and American flags planted on the parapet and the assault columns pressing forward over their own dead and wounded through a vicious point-blank cross fire. If the allies were not halted, the British and Loyalist garrison might lose Savannah. It was at this crucial moment that Lieutenant Colonel Maitland sent in his reserves, placed there for this very purpose. The grenadiers of the 16th Regiment and the Royal Marines charged with the bayonet and thrust the French and Americans from the ramparts into the ditch below the fraise, where, huddled and helpless, unable to advance or retreat, they were slaughtered unmercifully by artillery and musket fire.

At the same time that Maitland forced the assault troops from the parapet, Casimir Pulaski leading a badly timed but desperate charge of 200 horse tried to force his way between the redoubts and get behind the defenders. Such a direct mounted attack on emplaced infantry and artillery is not a proper use of cavalry, but the horsemen were pressing forward with pistol and saber when an apparently chance round shot from the British armed vessel, firing high-elevation harassing broadsides from the river, mortally wounded Pulaski. Demoralized by the loss of their leader, his troops retired in disorder from the fruitless attempt.

After standing to the defenders' concentrated fire for forty-five minutes, d'Estaing and Lincoln pulled back their shattered troops. The French suffered 828 casualties and Admiral d'Estaing, personally leading his troops, was wounded twice. The South Carolina Continentals lost 250 out of the 600 men engaged, and the Charleston militia had one man killed and six wounded. While reasonably heavy, these were not prohibitive losses considering the numbers of allied troops engaged in an assault against a strongly held and fortified position.

An attempt to take the town by siege was begun again, but Admiral d'Estaing's senior officers impressed on him the dangers of hurricane and British naval attack. They urged that the French fleet be gotten out to sea as quickly as possible. Much disaffection was felt between the defeated allies. The French behaved with unwarrranted arrogance to the Americans, referring to them contemptuously as "insurgents." French officers even informed General Augustine Prevost, with apologies, that the Americans were wholly to blame for not permitting the women and children to leave the town and remain in safety on the ships as Prevost had requested. Since this had been an allied command decision, the Americans deeply resented the slur.

After a few days' delay Admiral d'Estaing reembarked his army and sailed away, returning with part of the fleet to France and sending the remainder to the West Indies. On 19 October Benjamin Lincoln, deserted by his allies, raised the siege and retreated to Ebenezer Heights, proceeding from there with the army to Charleston. After his arrival, smallpox broke out in the town, and the disheartened, defeated militia, fearful of catching the disease, dispersed to their homes.

The allied siege of Savannah thus ended in defeat, comparatively heavy losses, and disillusionment and altercation with the French ally whose hoped-for military assistance had proven strangely ineffective. The British now held Georgia, and the scene was set for the fall of Charleston in 1780 and the British occupation of key towns and areas in South Carolina. The British campaign in the South had begun with victory for them and their Loyalist supporters. In its first real test the French alliance had failed the Americans, and civil war in Georgia, the Carolinas, and Virginia was about to increase with savage and vindictive fury.

CHAPTER IV

Sir Henry Clinton's Capture of Charleston, 1780

The first British attack on Charleston, South Carolina, in 1776 had failed for two reasons. Admiral Peter Parker underestimated South Carolina's resolution to defend the city and tried to shoot it out at close range from anchored wooded ships with a land-based fort mounting heavy guns. The British army forces under Sir Henry Clinton were landed on Long Island instead of Sullivan's Island where the works were placed, and Breach Inlet running between the two islands proved too deep, even at low tide, for the soldiers to wade. The ground troops therefore could not be used, as planned, to support the naval attack.

General Clinton succeeded in his second attempt to take Charleston, and the capture of the town in 1780 is a superb example of a beautifully coordinated eighteenth-century joint operation. Although Clinton's investment of Charleston was extended over several months, this may have been part of a deliberate plan. The results attained by delay were far greater than could have been achieved by a quick victory.

In the first attack Parker and Clinton made all the mistakes. During the second operation of 1780 the American commander, General Benjamin Lincoln, and the State Council of South Carolina committed almost every error possible. Lincoln's decision to stay and hold Charleston doomed him to lose the key port with all of his defending army and the naval squadron sent by Congress to aid him. This defeat inevitably led to the British occupation of South Carolina and two years of a bitter, relentless war of subjugation that merged into an equally bloody civil war.

British strategic plans to defeat the American revolutionaries in 1779 were concentrated on the South. Aside from the belief, held with some justice, that royalist sympathies remained strong in those colonies, the broad southern waterways, such as Chesapeake Bay, and the great river systems navigable far into the interior made fleet-supported amphibious operations possible and practicable. Completion of the Continental Congress's working alliance with France in 1778 made a quick British victory in North America imperative. The southern strategy therefore was established by the British government, and General Clinton, supported by Admiral Mariot Arbuthnot, was given direction of the overall attack plan. Three thousand fresh reinforcements had ar-

rived at New York from England, bringing to about 39,000 the number of British, Loyalist, and German soldiers stationed in the thirteen rebellious colonies. These forces were
sufficient to guard the northern theater and carry out offensive operations in the South
at the same time.

After establishing the necessary arrangements for the defense of New York with General Wilhelm von Knyphausen of the German mercenaries, Clinton sailed from Sandy
Hook to Tybee, Georgia, on 26 December 1779 with a field force of 8,500 men. This
included four flank battalions, twelve regiments and corps, British, Hessian, and Loyalist
Provincials with a powerful artillery detachment, and 250 cavalry. Pushed eastward by
the Gulf Stream, the fleet was dispersed by the usual seasonal storms. One ordnance
vessel foundered and all the artillery horses' legs were broken in the holds of the rolling,
pitching ships, necessitating destruction of most of the horses en route. A vessel with
Hessian infantry was forced by bad weather to sail across the Atlantic to England. Small
supply craft loaded with cavalry equipment became separated from the main convoy and
were captured by American privateers. The main fleet finally made rendezvous at Tybee
on the coast of Georgia, disembarked part of the army, completed temporary repairs on
the extensive storm damage, and sailed north for Charleston with 5,000 men. A primitive
coastal waterway behind the sea islands existed even then, and Clinton wanted to send
part of his army via this inland route. His naval advisers protested, but the 250 cavalry,
locally remounted on sorry marsh tackeys, was detached toward Augusta as a diversion
with orders to proceed from there to Charleston.

Admiral Arbuthnot planned originally to effect a landing on Johns Island by Stono
Inlet, but Captain George Keith Elphinstone of his flagship persuaded him to try the
North Edisto River, and the fleet came in by Deveaux Bank. This is still a tricky piece of
water, and Arbuthnot must have been a superb sailor, for the transports anchored without mishap off Simmons Island (now Seabrook Island) behind Deveaux Bank the day
after the ships sailed from Tybee.

The four battalions of light infantry and the grenadiers of the flank corps, who were
assigned specialized tasks, landed on Seabrook Island and marched inland on 11 February 1780, meeting no opposition as Elphinstone had surmised. The rest of the army
came ashore without incident during the next day. Seabrook Island lies about thirty miles
south of Charleston, and the light troops advanced rapidly on the town across Johns
Island and James Island. A scout force in shallow-draft boats maneuvered through the
marsh creeks and seized Fort Johnson on James Island, Perroneau's Landing, and Wappoo Cut, thus securing the defenses on the southern side of the harbor and the Ashley
River bank across from Charleston. The fleet meanwhile proceeded up the coast and
blockaded Charleston harbor while a battery of heavy guns was brought from the base at
Seabrook Island and established on the south side of the Ashley, covering the bridgehead
for the impending attack on the town.

Sir Henry Clinton now moved with all the majestic deliberation of formal eighteenth-century siege warfare. He carefully established and garrisoned fortified posts on his line of communications with the Stono and North Edisto rivers to preserve contact with his supply bases and the fleet. This took time, and it was not until 20 March 1780 that his advance elements passed the Ashley River at Drayton Hall, again uncontested, and successfully established defense positions on Charleston Neck above the town.

The Assembly was sitting in Charleston when the news came of the British landing in force on Seabrook Island. The members promptly delegated Governor John Rutledge power to do everything necessary for the public good except to execute a citizen without trial. In effect Rutledge was made a dictator, and he held the reins of government in South Carolina after his escape from Charleston for two long and terrible years of war, moving from place to place ahead of the British columns fanning out over the state.

John Rutledge promptly called the militia and all the inhabitants and owners of property to join the American garrison and defend the city under pain of confiscation. The country militia were afraid of smallpox, then prevalent in the town, and few reported for duty. Clinton had the perspicacity to offer a free and general pardon to all who came in and swore allegiance to the crown, while threatening severest penalties to those who failed to accept the offer. If nothing else, the proclamation thoroughly clouded the issue of resistance or nonresistance to the British.

In 1779 Spain had joined France in the alliance against Great Britain. Governor Rutledge accordingly sent a French volunteer officer, a Colonel Ternant, to Havana, Cuba, with a request for immediate Spanish military help and an offer in return of 2,000 men for a later combined attack on British-held St. Augustine, Florida. The Spanish governor of Cuba apparently doubted his authority or ability to mount a major expedition against Clinton and made no move. The Spaniards, striking from New Orleans, were later able to mount a diversionary attack on British West Florida that reduced the town and fort of Mobile but did not affect the war in any material way.

Commodore Abraham Whipple had been sent by Congress to Charleston with a small naval squadron of frigates and armed vessels to aid in the defense of the port. He soon discovered that the American ships could not lie at anchor close to the bar or keep station under sail in the face of a rising tide and a strong east wind. Since the British needed these conditions to bring their heavy units across the bar, the American naval command faced an insoluable tactical dilemma. If the bar could not be held, what was the best use of available American naval strength? Whipple decided to pull his ships back and anchor in a position to rake the channel, aided by the guns of Fort Moultrie.

This anchorage was abandoned, however, when the commodore decided that the obstructions placed in the channel after his withdrawal from the bar were neither numerous nor large enough to stop Admiral Arbuthnot. In the meantime, the British ships *Renown* of 50 guns, *Roebuck*, 44 guns, and *Romulus*, also 44 guns, were lightened and passed the bar with no opposition except from some American galleys that came up under oars and fired on the British longboats sounding the channel.

Commodore Whipple's squadron then retreated to the inner harbor where it was decided to sink seven of the vessels across the Cooper River from the Exchange building in the town to the marsh opposite. This tactic successfully prevented Admiral Arbuthnot from working frigates up the Cooper River and placing them in positions to fire on Charleston's defenses from behind. The crews and guns of the sunken units were added to the town's defenses, but the American naval squadron as such ceased to exist.

Charleston lies on a peninsula between the Ashley and Cooper rivers. In the eighteenth century, a defender had to hold the bar across the mouth of the harbor to prevent a fleet from running the outer forts and placing its guns on the town itself. Once big warships passed Fort Moultrie and Fort Johnson and land forces seized Charleston Neck above the town and the two river banks across from the peninsula, there was no escape and Charleston inevitably would fall. General Benjamin Lincoln apparently never fully

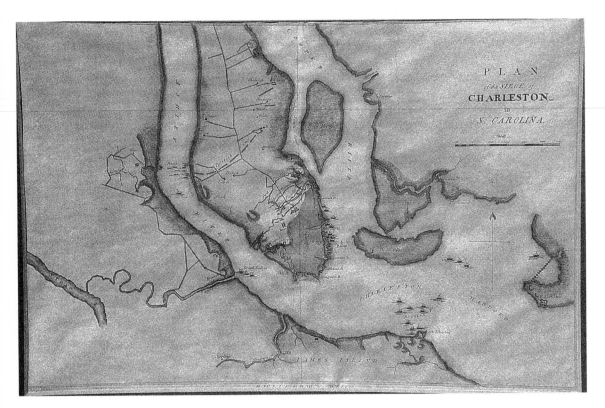

Figure 6.   Map of Sir Henry Clinton's siege of Charleston, South Carolina, 29 March–12 May 1780

Figure 7.
Major General Benjamin Lincoln

Figure 8.
Sir Henry Clinton, etching by H. B. Hall

perceived these facts until too late. The town council, naively secure behind the all too inadequate fortifications and serenely confident that the victory of 1776 would be repeated, furiously and adamantly rejected any suggestion that the army strategically depart. Clearly unsure as to the best course of action, General Lincoln yielded to civilian pressure, and each American reinforcement that arrived only increased Sir Henry Clinton's eventual "bag."

The British army crossed the Ashley River at Bee's Ferry and landed on Charleston Neck several miles above the town. The flat-bottomed boats used in the operation had been brought through the creeks and inlets that interlace the marshes all the way from the North Edisto where the transports still lay at anchor. Captain Elphinstone of the Royal Navy conducted the river crossing and landing of the troops on the peninsula, covered by armed galleys.

On 30 March, the day after the passage of the river, Sir Henry Clinton sent strong patrols of light infantry, grenadiers, and jäger riflemen to probe the American outworks. They encountered no resistance until they approached Gibbes's farm about two miles from the town, where Colonel John Laurens came out with a battalion of infantry and was later reinforced by Major Philip Love with 90 men and 2 fieldpieces. This force skirmished with the British advance guard until nightfall and then fell back on the lines.

Brigadier General James Patterson with 1,500 men of the Savannah garrison and

Lieutenant Colonel Banastre Tarleton commanding 250 dragoons had joined Clinton's army on 25 March. With Charleston Neck secured, these troops were brought directly across the river from Wappoo Cut to Gibbes's Landing, and the British army above Charleston established direct communications with the navy and could receive reinforcements, ammunition, and supplies as needed. With all necessary support moving smoothly and steadily, Major Moncrieff, the chief army engineer who had distinguished himself in the defense of Savannah, supervised on 1 April the breaking of ground for the first British siege parallel, about 800 yards from the American lines.

Since Charleston's waterfront geography has changed markedly with landfills extending the city over what once were tidal areas, the original land defenses are difficult to trace. They apparently began near the Cooper River some distance below the present Cooper River Bridge, where Chapel Street crosses East Bay. The lines ran from there close by the modern locations of the New Tabernacle Fourth Baptist Church on Elizabeth Street and the Second Presbyterian Church on Meeting Street. They then crossed Meeting Street where a strong masonry hornwork was built, a remnant of which still is preserved on Marion Square. The works continued through what is now Vander Horst Street, then crossed the site of the present St. Paul's and St. Luke's Episcopal Cathedral (consecrated in 1816), extending thence to the Ashley River marshes. They ended and were anchored on the complex of marsh and creek which at that time bordered and flowed into the river where the old Charleston Museum now stands.

In front of the lines a canal or wet ditch was dug, deep enough to fill with seepage water, and from the dams at each end of this ditch, placed to prevent drainage, the marshes on both rivers constituted effective barriers to flanking attacks. There were two rows of abatis behind the canal and a second, more shallow ditch directly under the works protected further by a double fraise. The masonry hornwork secured the center, and the works on the right and left were pushed forward to provide enfilade fire covering most of the wet ditch.

To guard the river and harbor fronts a battery had been established on Coming's Point between Bull and Beaufain streets and a line of works constructed along South Bay, extending from the Ashley to the Cooper rivers including a strong point at Granville's Bastion. St. Michael's tall white steeple, painted black to prevent the enemy artillery from spotting it at night, was used as an observation post. Ironically, the British reported after the siege that the black steeple stood out better than a white one would have.

On 9 April, the day British artillerists erected heavy batteries in a completed first parallel, Admiral Arbuthnot, aided by a strong southeast wind and a rising tide, ran Fort Moultrie and entered the inner harbor. His fleet included eight ships of the line and six frigates with additional support vessels. Peter Timothy, a militiaman on watch in St. Michael's steeple, saw the fleet come in. He reported later that they made a most noble appearance in the disciplined, intrepid way each ship approached, received, and returned the fire of Fort Moultrie, then came to and dropped anchor off Fort Johnson, just out of range of the town's batteries. One frigate lost a topmast to a round shot; 14 seamen were killed and 15 wounded, a small price to pay for the results gained. There were no casualties in the fort, but a British store ship following Arbuthnot's attack squadron into the harbor grounded near Haddrell's Point. This vessel was abandoned and burned by the crew after Colonel Charles Cotesworth Pinckney sent Captain Thomas Gadsden with two fieldpieces to bring her under close-range fire. Charleston now was almost completely invested except for landings at Haddrell's Point, Lempriere's Point, or Hobcaw, four miles across the Cooper River.

The garrison still could have been evacuated using small boats. Instead, three days before, on 6 April, Brigadier General William Woodford had brought in 750 North Carolina and Virginia Continentals after a 500-mile march in twenty-eight days—and the trap already was closing.

Once the fleet was in the harbor, on 10 April Sir Henry Clinton summoned the town under a flag of truce, according to proper eighteenth-century usage, and offered terms, threatening the resentment of an angry soldiery if surrender were delayed. Benjamin Lincoln firmly refused this first offer on the basis that sixty days had passed since the defenders knew the British intentions were hostile. During that period Charleston could have been abandoned, but Lincoln considered it his duty to support the defense until the last extremity.

After refusing the first summons, General Lincoln called in Governor John Rutledge and urged him to leave town with part of his council while this still was possible. Rutledge agreed and on 13 April was ferried across the Cooper River to safety with Colonel Pinckney, Daniel Huger, and John Lewis Gervais. It was decided that Thomas Ferguson, David Ramsay (who later wrote a history of the Revolution in South Carolina), Richard Hutson, and Benjamin Cattell, all of the council, would stay. Christopher Gadsden was appointed lieutenant governor and remained in Charleston to replace Thomas Bee, who was in Philadelphia at the Continental Congress. It is interesting that Rutledge took with him the council's conservatives, leaving the younger, more radical members behind.

The British on 14 April began to move against the last escape routes. They knew that General Isaac Huger with Daniel Horry's horse, a remnant of the dead Casimir Pulaski's dragoons, and a force of cavalry recently arrived from Virginia under William Washington had been stationed by Benjamin Lincoln at Monck's Corner thirty-two miles from Charleston. These mounted troops supported by a force of militia infantry were assigned to patrol the passes and forks of the Cooper River and maintain communications with the town via Hobcaw and Haddrell's Point. To counter them Clinton detached Lieutenant Colonel James Webster with 1,400 men including the 33d and 64th infantry regiments, reinforced by Major Patrick Ferguson's Loyalist infantry with the dragoons and infantry of Banastre Tarleton's Legion. On the march up the peninsula Tarleton's scouts intercepted a black slave carrying a message from Isaac Huger to Benjamin Lincoln whom they bribed to guide the British to the American position. Huger's cavalry were camped by the river on the town side, and the militia were posted at and around the Meeting House that commanded Biggin's Bridge. Tarleton and his legion, marching as advance guard of the British and Loyalist troops, were led by the slave through back paths in the forest. They suddenly emerged from the woods, overran Huger's sentries, and killed, captured, or routed the astonished American horsemen. Major Cochrane, following with the legion infantry with fixed bayonets, drove the militia across Biggin's Bridge and completely scattered them. Isaac Huger and William Washington with a few of their men escaped on foot through the nearby river swamps, but a Major Vernier of the late Casimir Pulaski's Legion was mortally wounded and captured. He died shortly after the engagement, cursing in fury the conduct of the Americans and the barbarity of Tarleton's Loyalist troops for refusing him quarter. The British captured in this engagement 42 wagons, 102 wagon horses, and 83 dragoon horses plus ammunition, supplies, and numerous prisoners. Most of Tarleton's men could now be properly mounted, an advantage that became very important in the days immediately ahead.

The victory at Monck's Corner gave Clinton a passage to the country across the Cooper River from Charleston. Additional reinforcements under Lord Cornwallis and Francis Lord Rawdon had arrived from New York, and Clinton now commanded 13,572 troops supported by a strong fleet. He detached a powerful force under Cornwallis with orders to march down the Cooper River and close off all remaining avenues of escape. A battery of two guns on James Island, for some reason called by the citizens of Charleston the "Watermelon battery," opened harassing fire, and one round shot ironically carried off the arm of the statue of the great British statesman William Pitt, erected at the intersection of Broad and Meeting streets in 1770. (It still stands armless in City Hall Park.) The second parallel about 250 yards from the American lines was opened on 20 April. From there the short-range mortars and howitzers rained explosive shells, red hot shot, and incendiary carcasses (combustibles confined in iron hoops) on the town. By 28 April Cornwallis's force had seized Lempriere's Point, Hobcaw, and Haddrell's Point and the fleet swung at anchor in the roadstead with its guns on the town. A third parallel between 80 and 150 yards from the American lines was finished on 6 May and the jäger riflemen moved in, killing any man who showed his head above the ramparts, while British engineers working at night sapped and drained the canal thus opening the way for a direct assault on the main defenses. Fort Moultrie, held so gallantly in 1776, surrendered without firing a shot on 7 May when a landing party of 200 Royal Marines and sailors led by a Captain Hudson of the navy came in from behind. On the preceding day the broken remains of the American cavalry under Colonel Anthony White were surprised again by Banastre Tarleton at Lenud's Ferry on the Santee River and defeated by the hard-riding British horsemen.

Surrounded and besieged on all sides, Benjamin Lincoln continued to vacillate. He was in sole charge of the military forces and the defense of the city but consistently made the grave error of deferring to the civilian government. General Lincoln even took the strong-willed Christopher Gadsden into his confidence and shared command responsibilities with him. Thomas Ferguson of the council said openly that if the Continental troops tried to evacuate the town, he personally would open its gates to the enemy and aid them in attacking the departing American regulars. This of course was sheer idiocy, but it was effective. Benjamin Lincoln succumbed to civilian pressure and stayed in Charleston with his doomed army as each possible avenue of escape was closed. Brigadier General Louis Du Portail, a French military engineer sent by Congress, made his way through the British lines and, after an inspection, declared the American defenses to be totally untenable. After hearing this grim pronouncement, Benjamin Lincoln refused to let Du Portail leave on the somewhat specious basis that his departure might injure troop and city morale. The unhappy brigadier thus shared the fate of the town garrison when Charleston surrendered.

The people of Charleston finally recognized the inevitable and on 10 May requested Benjamin Lincoln to surrender. On the next day, British attack groups covered by the jäger riflemen crossed the drained canal and dug in for the final assault. General Lincoln, realizing that the entire defense position was impossible, agreed to capitulate on British terms. He requested that the American garrison might proceed to the surrender area with the bands playing a British march, according to the honorable custom of the period. This courtesy was refused to "rebels" and on 12 May, 2,650 American Continentals paraded and piled arms on the left of the hornwork. Among the captured were one major general, six brigadier generals, nine colonels, and fourteen lieutenant colonels—a good bag for the British. Also taken were 3,034 militia, 1,000 sailors, including French seamen caught in the siege, and 154 guns in battery. The militia were paroled to their homes and the Continentals imprisoned, a far greater disaster to American arms than Saratoga had been for the British. A bitter commentary on the siege was the remark of a British officer to the captured William Moultrie that Charleston had made a gallant defense but the town contained a great many rascals (he mentioned their names) who came out every night and gave Clinton information concerning the garrison and its dispositions.

The casualties for a long siege were comparatively light: 89 American soldiers killed, 138 wounded, and 20 civilians killed by chance shell fire. The attacking British lost only 78 killed and 189 wounded.

After four years of war, with Saratoga the one great victory, American hopes seemed dim. Savannah and Charleston were in British hands, and many honest Loyalists and many honest American patriots, including Governor John Rutledge of South Carolina, had come to believe that final separation from Great Britain was a mistake.

Major Banastre Tarleton emerged as a ruthless, fighting cavalry commander in a tragic anticlimax to the capture of Charleston. Colonel Abraham Buford, who had arrived too late to reinforce the town, was retreating northward with 350 Virginia Continentals and the remainder of William Washington's shattered cavalry. Tarleton was ordered to destroy Buford's command and, with 270 dragoons, rode 154 miles in 54 hours to catch him at the Waxhaws on the North Carolina border. Buford was informed of the British approach and sent his wagons and artillery ahead and took up a position across a road. Apparently Buford made the grave error of holding fire until the charging cavalry were only ten yards away. The volley emptied a few saddles but there was no time to reload, and the saber-armed horsemen were over and through Buford's formation with the steel, literally tearing it apart. Tarleton's men all were northern Loyalists whose hatred for "rebels" was great and abiding. No quarter was given—113 were killed outright and 150 badly wounded. Only 53 Americans were taken prisoner, and the British losses were negligible: 5 killed and 14 wounded. Abraham Buford, who escaped the disaster, claimed the white flag had been raised before the butchery started. Tarleton said later that he was temporarily dismounted, his horse having been shot in the charge, or he would have stopped the sabers. But "Tarleton's quarter" set the tone for the war in Georgia and the Carolinas which, strangely and terribly, even after the fall of Savannah and Charleston, had just begun.

At least one Patriot remained honorable to his cause despite inducement to the contrary following the fall of Charleston. Charles Greville Montagu, a former royal governor of South Carolina, wrote to his friend William Moultrie, a prisoner in British hands, offering him the command of his own Loyalist regiment recruited from captured Americans and the return of Moultrie's family estates after the war if he would come over to the British. Moultrie replied indignantly that he would not listen to such dishonorable proposals—that if he were guilty of such baseness he would hate himself and shun mankind. Benedict Arnold in the North, not a prisoner of war and with far less inducement and provocation, chose the opposite course. It is an interesting comparison: Moultrie, the great gentleman, and Arnold, the traitor.

CHAPTER V

The Loyalists in the South

It has been said, somewhat facetiously, that of about three million inhabitants settled in the thirteen British colonies at the time of the Revolution, one million supported the Revolution, one million supported the British, and one million didn't give a damn. Although that statement is an oversimplification of a very complex period in American history, it still has considerable validity. This chapter, therefore, is devoted to an often forgotten or neglected element in eighteenth-century America—the many Loyalists who supported their king and fought with dedication, courage, and at the end, great sacrifice for the British cause.

There were 73 known Loyalist units of various strengths and designations serving with the British army during the Revolution, and some 25,000 Americans wore the king's uniform as trained Provincial regulars between 1775 and 1783. Other Loyalist regular units undoubtedly existed whose military records have not been preserved. William Dobein James, who served with Francis Marion, cites, for example, black dragoons recruited by the British command in Charleston from among the escaped slaves in the town.

The best of these Provincial formations, such as Banastre Tarleton's Legion, Francis Lord Rawdon's Volunteers of Ireland, John Simcoe's Queen's Rangers, Patrick Ferguson's Rangers and his independent command of North and South Carolina backcountrymen, Oliver de Lancey's New York Loyalist Brigade of Foot, the New Jersey Volunteers, or Thomas Browne's King's Carolina Rangers were as well equipped and effective as British regulars or German mercenaries. American Loyalist soldiers knew the terrain, were inured to the climate, and understood their enemy and thus probably were more effective than British or German troops against fast-moving American partisans.

A commentary on the numbers of Loyalists in the royal forces is the fact that the American Continental regulars after 1776 never totaled 36,000 soldiers at any single time. During some periods in the war, such as the terrible winters of 1779 and 1780, George Washington would have had difficulty fielding 5,000 Continentals. By the Reorganization Act of 1780, which created a permanent American army, the total Continental army, on paper, came to 36,000 men. No more than half this number ever were in the field simultaneously, and the full force never was recruited.

Thus the number of Americans serving with the British Provincials often equaled and on occasion exceeded those serving in the Continental line. These figures, of course, do not include Patriot state militia—or Loyalist militia—called up for service in specific regional campaigns or battles.

As was stated earlier, the revolutionary war in the South developed into an increasingly brutal civil war. The eighteenth-century South was a wild, harsh, and violent land, inhabited by a hard and violent people. The southern Loyalists fought their former friends, cousins, and neighbors who supported the cause of American independence with a cruel and sanguinary ferocity exceeded only by the cruel and sanguinary ferocity with which the American Patriots fought them.

William Dobein James, Francis Marion's young follower, says that the people of the old Cheraw district waged an unrecorded war of extermination with the Loyalists on their borders. The murderous Colonel William Cuningham, a Loyalist partisan leader in South Carolina, was known to his American opponents as "Bloody Bill," and the name was fully justified. According to legend, Cuningham developed an implacable hatred for all supporters of the Revolution after the brutal murder in 1778 of his crippled and epileptic brother John by Patriot partisans. True or not, "Bloody Bill" Cuningham's wild and sanguinary exploits directed against his Whig neighbors became legend still remembered in his native South Carolina. One such tale says that because he did not have a horse he walked from Savannah to Ninety Six where he personally shot dead Captain William Richie, reputedly the murderer of his brother. The irony in this story is that Cuningham and Richie had served together in the Cherokee War of 1776 under Andrew Williamson.

Later, Cuningham, mounted on his famous horse Ringtail (given to him, according to family tradition, by his cousin Patrick Cuningham), raised a Loyalist raiding force of 300 men and on 17 November 1781 hit by surprise a party of 30 American Patriots under Captain James Butler camped near Clouds Creek in Edgefield County, South Carolina. Having barricaded themselves in a nearby unfinished log house, Butler and his small detachment fought for some time against hopeless odds but finally surrendered unconditionally. All of the prisoners were butchered on the spot except two who managed to escape and carry the story.

William Cuningham then forded the Saluda River and rode on to Hayes's Station in Laurens County, an American post held by Colonel Joseph Hayes and fifteen men. After a stout resistance of several hours, Cuningham managed to set fire to Hayes's fortified house and the little garrison, driven out by the flames, surrendered. Cuningham hanged Hayes. When the improvised gallows broke, "Bloody Bill" murdered with his sword the half-strangled man and sabered another whom he also had hanged on the same pole. The rest of the survivors (two had fallen in the action) were butchered by Cuningham's men.

Cuningham's raiders finally were defeated by Captain William Butler, a son of the murdered James Butler, and his Rangers, but Cuningham escaped and survived the war with other Loyalist exiles.

The Loyalist leadership in the South, as in the Northern states, included men and families of substance and social standing. Thomas Browne, a leading citizen of Augusta, Georgia, was physically tortured by his own neighbors for expressing too forcibly his support of the king's cause. After this grim experience, he fled to British Florida where he organized his Rangers from among other Loyalist refugees and harried the Georgia border country. On his return to that state with Clinton's invading army, he was made a lieutenant colonel and commanded the King's Carolina Rangers. Later in 1781 with these troops and other Loyalist units, Browne defended Augusta with stubborn gallantry against overwhelming odds. When the town finally surrendered, Henry Lee and Andrew Pickens granted him safe-conduct to British-held Savannah and provided an escort to ensure his protection as a tribute to his obstinate courage.

Lieutenant Colonel John Hamilton of the Royal North Carolina Regiment was a prominent merchant and planter and an outstanding Loyalist officer. His somewhat uncommon mercy to those American soldiers who fell into his hands won for him the lasting respect of his opponents. The Loyalist Charles Stedman, who served under Sir William Howe, Sir Henry Clinton, and Lord Cornwallis, says that the British nation owed more to John Hamilton than to any other individual Loyalist in the British service. Hamilton fought in nearly every major action in Georgia, the Carolinas, and Virginia. After the war he moved to England, where he died in 1817.

Major James Wright, the son of a royal governor of Georgia, commanded Georgia Loyalists at the siege of Savannah in 1779. Another prominent Loyalist, Alexander McDonald, was a major in the regiment of North Carolina Highlanders. A distinguished North Carolina Scottish Loyalist, Brigadier General Donald McDonald, raised the royal standard in January 1776 and rallied his clansmen and other Scottish settlers around it. A South Carolina Loyalist, Robert Cuningham, had been a judge in the Ninety Six district before the war. Lord Cornwallis made him a brigadier in 1780, and he took the field with Loyalist militia. His brothers Patrick, David, and John all were substantial citizens of South Carolina and served the British cause during the war with steadfast loyalty.

Tough old Micajah Ganey, a hard-fighting Loyalist partisan commander, was one of Francis Marion's greatest opponents in the South Carolina lowcountry, as was Colonel John Coming Ball, of a notable Charleston family. The latter lost his favorite horse to Francis Marion in one engagement; Marion renamed the animal "Ball" and rode him throughout the war.

Edmund Fanning of North Carolina became a general in the British army. Another North Carolinian, David Fanning, whose narrative is a fascinating source for the southern war, was a scourge to his Whig neighbors. Colonel Hector MacNeil and Colonel David Fanning on the morning of 12 September 1781 with 640 Loyalist partisans surprised Hillsboro and captured there some 200 prisoners, including Governor Thomas Burke of North Carolina, his state council, several Continental officers, and over 70 American regular soldiers. This victory was accomplished with only one Loyalist casualty, although MacNeil died in a skirmish at Rain Creek on the partisans' return march to the coast. Most of the Loyalists, however, arrived safely at Wilmington and turned over their prisoners to Major Craig, the British commander at that base. This feat was accomplished after the battle of Guilford Court House when British fortunes in the South already were declining.

These few men are only some of the more outstanding Loyalist commanders in the South. Many people declared for the king and formed the backbone of great fighting units that served with distinguished courage on many battlefields.

Thousands of Highland Scots had migrated to the Carolinas after the disaster to Stuart arms at Culloden. In a strange *volte face*, the same men who had fought against the Hanoverian kings of England, or their sons born in America, now supported a Hanoverian king against the American cause of independence. Elements among the old backcountry "Regulators" also rallied to the royal standard. Prior to the Revolution the Regulators in the two Carolinas had opposed, sometimes with armed violence, lowcountry domination of the economic and political life of those colonies. Since leadership and support for the Revolution in its early stages came chiefly from the tidewater area, some of the Regulators took a stand for the king and thus against their old enemies. Support for the British could be found among the German Lutheran settlers in the Carolinas who had been granted a religious and political haven by the royal government. Naturally grateful and fearing the loss of their grants, they gave logistic support to the British and Loyalist columns operating in German-settled territory.

About half the men serving in the British armies during the Southern campaigns of 1778 to 1782 were Loyalists, soldiers in regular Provincial units. When Benjamin Lincoln and Admiral d'Estaing attempted to take Savannah, Georgia, in September and October of 1779, Loyalists comprised more than 50 percent of Major General Augustine Prevost's defending garrison. These included Lieutenant Colonel John Hamilton's Royal North Carolina Regiment, the South Carolina King's Rangers, the South Carolina Dragoons, a company of the British Legion, one battalion of de Lancey's New York Brigade led by Lieutenant Colonel John Harris Cruger, and a battalion of Georgia Loyalists under Major James Wright.

During Clinton's siege of Charleston, South Carolina, in the spring of 1780, Lieutenant Colonel Tarleton's Legion of horse and foot, who were with the exception of a few British officers Northern Loyalists, surprised and scattered Isaac Huger's and William Washington's cavalry at Monck's Corner on 14 April 1780. This was the same Loyalist legion that later struck and cut to pieces without mercy Buford's 3d Virginia Regiment retreating northward after the fall of Charleston.

The entire left wing of Lord Cornwallis's victorious army at the battle of Camden,

South Carolina, fought on 16 August 1780, was composed of Loyalists from the North and South. These were Francis Lord Rawdon's Volunteers of Ireland, recruited in Philadelphia mainly from Irish deserters who had fled the American army, Banastre Tarleton's Legion infantry, and part of Lieutenant Colonel John Hamilton's Royal North Carolina Regiment. Lieutenant Colonel Samuel Bryan's North Carolina Volunteers and Tarleton's Loyalist cavalry were in support behind the main battle line.

At the battle of Camden, Lord Rawdon's Loyalist left wing engaged the American right wing composed of the 2d Maryland brigade of Continental infantry and the Delaware Line regiment, some of the finest regulars in American service. The two wings, Tory and Whig, attacked and counterattacked each other in fierce successive bayonet charges until the American commander Major General Johann de Kalb fell mortally wounded. The Marylanders and Delawares supported by Dixon's North Carolina battalion made a brief stand, but broke when attacked on all sides by overwhelming force.

At Kings Mountain, South Carolina, about 800 North and South Carolina Loyalists reinforced by 100 Loyalist rangers from the North were surrounded and almost annihilated on 7 October 1780 by American riflemen from Georgia, Virginia, and the two Carolinas. American fought American; the only British soldier present at the engagement was Major Patrick Ferguson, the commander of the Loyalist force. He died, sword in hand, attempting by a desperate mounted charge to break the encircling ring. A South Carolina Loyalist officer, Major Daniel Plummer, and a North Carolina Loyalist, Colonel Vesey Husbands, fell with him. The best eyewitness account of the engagement was written by Lieutenant Anthony Allaire, a New York Huguenot Loyalist serving with Ferguson's 100 Rangers.

At the battles of Blackstocks, 20 November 1780, Cowpens, 17 January 1781, and Guilford Court House, 15 March 1781, Banastre Tarleton's Loyalist dragoons formed the main part of the British cavalry present.

The battle of Hobkirk Hill was fought outside of Camden, South Carolina, on 25 April 1781 by approximately equal numbers on both sides. On this occasion the British commander Francis Lord Rawdon successfully forced the Americans under Major General Nathanael Greene from the field. Rawdon's small army of 900 men included only one regular British regiment, the 63d Foot; all the rest were Loyalists. Again, Americans fought Americans and the Loyalists won.

The town of Ninety Six, which Nathanael Greene and Henry Lee tried to capture by siege and assault from 22 May until 19 June 1781, was defended successfully by that most gallant of New York Loyalists, Lieutenant Colonel John Harris Cruger. His garrison of 550 men was composed entirely of Loyalists: Cruger's own battalion of de Lancey's brigade, the 2d Battalion of New Jersey Volunteers and 200 South Carolina Loyalist militia. When the latter were given a choice of retreating with their families to British-held Charleston or remaining to defend Ninety Six, they released their excellent horses in the woods and decided unanimously to stay and fight with Cruger and his northern troops. In the final stages of the siege, while Rawdon's relief force marched up from Charleston and Greene was desperately trying to take the fort by direct assault, the 60 bayonet men who came around the ditch defending the star fort and drove out the American attackers in hand-to-hand fighting were chosen from the New Jersey Volunteers and de Lancey's New York battalion.

At Eutaw Springs, where Nathanael Greene was forced to retire from the field on 8 September 1781 after almost winning the battle, about half of Lieutenant Colonel Alexander Stuart's opposing army of 2,000 men were Loyalists. When the British center and left were driven back by the American advance early in the battle, Major Henry Sheridan of the New York Volunteers with a detachment of his battalion held a sturdy brick house in the middle of the battlefield against all attacks until Stuart could reform his lines and continue the engagement.

During the last phases of the war in the South, an outstanding Loyalist cavalry leader emerged: Colonel Benjamin Thompson of Massachusetts, later elevated to the British peerage as Lord Rumford. Thompson came to Charleston late in 1782 and formed a striking force of 200 cavalry, 500 infantry, and an artillery contingent with two field guns from resident Loyalist militia, the Volunteers of Ireland, German mercenary riflemen (jägers), and a few British regulars. With this mixed legion he attacked and defeated Francis Marion's brigade at Wambaw Bridge on 14 February 1782. In Marion's absence, the brigade was led by Peter Horry. Several days later, at Tydiman's plantation, with Francis Marion present on the field, Thompson beat the famous brigade for a second time. This brief flare-up of Loyalist military leadership proved to be ephemeral. Thwarted in an attempt to surprise Nathanael Greene at Ashley Hall above Charleston, Colonel Benjamin Thompson left the South, his short if brilliant military career finished.

By this time the war had lasted seven long years with inconclusive results and the loyalties of many in this basically civil conflict were thoroughly confused. In the last phases of the fighting a large proportion of each Loyalist Provincial regiment was recruited from American deserters, while American Continental units were filled with discharged soldiers and deserters from British or Hessian formations. General Nathanael Greene said that at the close of the war he fought the enemy with British soldiers and they fought him with those of America. Many Loyalists, however, remained true to their convictions throughout the Revolution. At the end of the war, their lands and possessions confiscated, they were forced to leave and start a new life in the Bahamas, Nova Scotia, New Brunswick, or across the sea in Great Britain. These were our own people and some were our forebears. They included both villains and heroes, and they held true to their convictions despite the hardships often caused by their loyalty. The Loyalists' suffering is part of the total suffering that in agony and war was the price of the nation's birth.

CHAPTER VI

The Battle of Camden, 16 August 1780

In April 1780 General George Washington ordered two Maryland Line regiments and the Delaware Line regiment supported by the 1st Continental Artillery Regiment with eighteen guns to the threatened southern theater of war. Major General the Baron Johann de Kalb was given command.

Of the many European volunteers and soldiers of fortune who offered their swords to the American cause, Johann de Kalb is one of the most interesting. A Bavarian by birth, he apparently was not actually a baron but served as an officer in the French army and assumed both the prefix "de" and the title, because it was most difficult to achieve high rank in European armies of the period if one lacked distinguished lineage. Whether born to the purple or not, this man was an aristocrat in the best sense of that word, a particularly fine soldier and the only towering figure, both literally and figuratively, on the American side at the battle of Camden. His aide-de-camp, Nicholas Rogers of Baltimore, describes him as more than six feet tall, with a high forehead, aquiline nose, hazel eyes, and a strong chin. De Kalb preferred marching on foot with his men to riding and could hike twenty to thirty miles a day. He drank only water and was a completely sober, frugal, and controlled person. Wrapped in his horseman's cloak, Johann de Kalb would sleep by a camp fire with his soldiers, the perfect field commander in the classic tradition. His conduct and personality are strongly reminiscent of the officer cited by that great soldier and brilliant military scholar, the victor at Fontenoy in 1745, Maurice, Count de Saxe, a marshal of the armies of King Louis XV of France. Saxe said the the best field commander he ever had known was the French count who led in battle by stepping out in front of his regiment, drawing his sword, and simply saying, "follow me." Johann de Kalb was to fall, mortally wounded, at Camden, after leading his Maryland and Delaware troops in repeated desperate and hopeless bayonet charges, continuing even after the last unbeaten fragment of the American army was completely surrounded.

The reinforcements sent by Washington in April arrived in the South too late to save Charleston, so General de Kalb remained with his troops at General Parson's plantation in Granville County, North Carolina. It was hoped that the presence in the area of these well-trained and reasonably well-equipped Continentals would act as a spur to American morale and entice recruitment after the disasters at Charleston and the Waxhaws. Unfortunately, few recruits appeared. As the British had estimated correctly, Loyalist sympathy was strong in the South, and the capture of its two main ports, Savannah and Charleston, seriously deterred honest neutrals or waverers. Johann de Kalb and his soldiers also experienced the dubious joys of campaigning in the South in late spring and early summer. Redbugs, also known as chiggers, and ticks infested their camping area, and de Kalb wrote to his wife in France that his entire body was covered by the stings of these insects. Chiggers burrow under the skin, causing severe inflammation, swelling, and an almost intolerable itching. They must have subjected him and his troops to sheer torture.

Probably suffering from an apathy or loss of morale because of a succession of almost catastrophic defeats, the North Carolina and Virginia militia refused to join de Kalb when requested to do so. Major General Richard Caswell, commanding a strong force of North Carolina militia, offered excuses, as did General Edward Stevens and Lieutenant Colonel Charles Porterfield of Virginia. Short of proper food, many of his men sickening from the unaccustomed heat and poor diet, Major General de Kalb moved the troops to Buffalo Ford, a crossing at Deep River, where he first learned about his new commander. De Kalb was a splendid professional soldier, but he also was a foreigner and possessed very little influence with the Continental Congress, where decisions of command were made. He was passed over for General Horatio Gates, the victor and hero (whether justifiably or not) at the battle of Saratoga. George Washington had preferred the steady, dependable Nathanael Greene, who, ironically, was to replace Horatio Gates in the South after the latter's rout at Camden. Congress, however, admired Gates and assigned him the responsibility of retrieving, if possible, the American military position in the southern theater of operations. Strangely, Congress did not ask George Washington's advice, although his opinion of Gates was well known.

With this appointment begins the tragic story of mistake added to mistake, bad judgment compounded by worse judgment, and finally, inevitable disaster.

Horatio Gates was at home on his Virginia farm when the news of his selection arrived by courier. A man of total self-assurance (Gates believed himself a far better general than Washington), he accepted the responsibility with complacent pride. The only sour note in the affair was his neighbor Charles Lee's cynical and unhappily prophetic comment that Gates take care lest his northern laurels turn to southern willows.

Horatio Gates and Johann de Kalb met at the Deep River in North Carolina with all proper ceremony, including a 13-gun salute. Gates took over command of the entire Southern Department and Major General de Kalb was confirmed in his leadership of the Maryland and Delaware Line regiments, a division of the "Grand Army" as Horatio Gates pretentiously called it, although no real army as yet existed. For want of horses, de Kalb had been forced to leave behind at General Parson's plantation 10 of his 18 guns, a grim deficiency in the battle ahead. The "Grand Army" therefore consisted of de Kalb's Continental infantry, three companies of artillery with 8 guns, and Colonel Charles Armand's Legion of 60 dragoons and 60 foot soldiers.

De Kalb had planned a march to Camden, southwest through Salisbury, North Carolina, knowing that the people of this area were, for the most part, strongly anti-British and that the rich farming countryside would provide subsistence. Such a roundabout route did not suit the hero of Saratoga, who decided instead to push from Deep River directly on to Camden. Although this was fifty miles shorter than de Kalb's route, it traversed the sand hills, a poor, barren country of sparse pine and jack oak forests, numerous unbridged, shallow streams, and the usual tangled southern river swamps. Gates's route also ran through the Cross Creek country, one of the most pro-British areas in the Carolinas, and the few inhabitants ran away as the Americans approached. No food could be found except small herds of bony, stunted, half-wild cattle, a little green corn, and ragged peach or apple orchards. The officers even used their hair powder to thicken what little soup could be made from available rations. This adversity meant that it was a hungry, sick army that struggled along the sand roads and through the creeks and swamps.

When the troops finally reached the Pee Dee River, they found good crops of corn on its wide bottomlands. Though still green, this was harvested and eaten, with inevitable consequences. Colonel William Washington and Colonel Anthony White, who had been badly beaten by Banastre Tarleton at Monck's Corner and Lenud's Ferry, had taken refuge with the remnants of their cavalry in North Carolina. They rode to Horatio Gates's camp expecting to join forces. General Gates informed them that he did not want their help because he did not feel cavalry was useful for the southern field—a nonsensical view. The Southeast was especially well adapted to use of cavalry because of its wide reaches of open pine barrens, broad savannahs, great distances, wild forests and swamps for concealment, and year-round natural forage for the horses. Francis Marion, William Davie, Thomas Sumter, and Elijah Clarke—all the great partisans on both sides—were to prove time and again the value of fast-moving, heavily armed, well-mounted men in southern warfare. What is more, the people of the countryside were bred to the saddle, natural horse soldiers. Horatio Gates's uninformed and foolish decision was to deprive his army of an essential scouting and shock arm in the battle to come. He had only a very small force of cavalry to scout his advance or cover his retreat.

On 3 August, Lieutenant Colonel Charles Porterfield, a fine officer with an excellent record as captain of Continentals, arrived at Gates's camp with 100 Virginia state troops. The army then crossed the Pee Dee and continued its march through a semiwilderness country inhabited chiefly by enemy sympathizers. Major William Seymour of the Delaware Line wrote in his journal that on a fourteen-day march the men drew only half a pound of flour for rations. Sometimes the soldiers received half a pound of beef, "so miserable and poor" it almost was inedible. Weak, sickly, and surrounded by a hostile population, the troops lived mainly on green apples and peaches.

Richard Caswell at last arrived on 6 August, and Horatio Gates added 2,100 North Carolina militia to his slowly growing army. Francis Lord Rawdon, watching the approaching Americans with a strong reconnaissance force, retired before Gates's advance without offering battle and took a defensive position on the other side of Little Lynches Creek. Despite Johann de Kalb's advice to outflank Lord Rawdon by a forced night march, Gates pushed forward in broad daylight. Rawdon called in his garrison from Colonel Henry Rugely's mill and fell back on Log Town, a mile above Camden. Gates arrived at Rugeley's, halted, and was joined by General Edward Stevens with 700 Virginia militia.

Brigadier General Thomas Sumter, the very aggressive but not always fortunate South Carolina partisan leader, had been operating on the British supply line to Charleston. He sent a dispatch rider to Horatio Gates requesting reinforcements to attack a British wagon train bringing supplies and ammunition to the main upcountry base at Camden. General Gates sent 100 Maryland Continentals, some of his best troops, and 300 North Carolina militia with two fieldpieces, thus reducing his artillery to seven guns, an additional one having come in with the militia.

Lord Cornwallis, meanwhile, informed by courier of Gates's advance, had ridden from Charleston to Camden in four days. He also detached four companies of light infantry on a forced march from Ninety Six to Camden. When these troops arrived, Cornwallis and Rawdon led 2,239 men, mostly British regulars or highly trained Provincials. The combat elements included three companies of the 23d Regiment, the 33d Regiment, five companies of the 71st Regiment (Highlanders), Banastre Tarleton's Legion of horse and foot, the Royal North Carolina Loyalist Regiment, Francis Lord Rawdon's Volunteers of Ireland, made up almost entirely of Irish deserters from the American army, 26 pioneers, 170 men of the royal artillery with four 6-pounders and two 3-pounders, and 300 South Carolina Loyalist militia.

Horatio Gates's Maryland and Delaware Continentals had been reduced to 900 infantry by sickness, desertion, and the 100 soldiers detached on Thomas Sumter's request. There were 60 horsemen and 60 foot soldiers of Charles Armand's Legion. Lieutenant Colonel Charles Porterfield commanded 100 Virginia light infantry (state troops and better trained than militia), while Edward Stevens and Richard Caswell led 2,800 Virginia and North Carolina militia. The South Carolina militia had sent 70 mounted volunteers, and the artillery mustered 100 men with seven guns. The American army thus numbered about 4,100 regulars and militia including officers, but only 3,052 were fit for duty.

For reasons that remain unknown, Gates thought that he had over 7,000 effectives. When Otho Williams of Maryland, his deputy adjutant general, informed his commander that only 3,052 were in fighting condition, Gates with his usual blind self-confidence stated that these were enough troops for the purpose. With an army composed chiefly of militia, General Gates decided on a night march in column on a prepared enemy position, a difficult and complicated maneuver even for well-trained regulars to perform.

Beef, corn meal, and molasses had been procured locally in adequate quantities to issue rations. The men gathered wood, lit their fires, and prepared a meal before the march began. There is a theory that corn meal mush mixed with molasses and wolfed down with campfire-baked bread and fresh-killed beef will act like a charge of explosives in the stomachs of a famished army. The soldiers no doubt already were half sick from the diet of green fruit, green corn, and bad water, as well as the exertion of a long, difficult march in hot August weather. The hastily cooked supper probably merely capped the digestive climax. In any case, Otho Williams grimly tells of men breaking ranks through necessity all night long. The army that went into action the next day was thoroughly debilitated.

The American forces began their march after full dark with Charles Porterfield's 100 Virginians and Major John Armstrong's battalion of North Carolina militia serving as light infantry, deployed in single file about 200 yards on the right and left of the head of the column. Charles Armand's 60 dragoons had been assigned the task of leading the van. Horatio Gates ignored Armand's protests that cavalry had no place in the lead because the horses' hooves could be heard for a great distance. In line on the road behind the cavalry and the flanking light infantry came the 1st and 2d Maryland brigades with the Delaware regiment. After the Continentals marched the North Carolina and Virginia militia in that order, then the seven guns of the artillery, and last the mounted South Carolina militia, patrolling the road and watching the baggage train. According to tradition, as Horatio Gates watched the column file by, he is said to have stated that he would breakfast the next morning with Earl Cornwallis a prisoner and guest at his table. Gates would have been the guest instead, if his horse had been a little slower.

The first encounter took place very early in the morning of 16 August 1780. By pure coincidence, and battles are often decided by such chance happenings, Earl Cornwallis and Lord Rawdon had decided to march that night from Camden and surprise Horatio Gates, just as Gates had determined to advance from Rugeley's Mill to surprise Cornwallis. To the astonishment of all, Banastre Tarleton's dragoons, riding ahead of the British forces, suddenly ran head-on into Charles Armand's horsemen. After some wild pistol fighting in the dark, the always aggressive Tarleton ordered a saber charge and smashed Armand's cavalry (an undisciplined lot at best, mostly British deserters) back on the leading elements of the American infantry. Charles Porterfield and John Armstrong, commanding coolly and well, swung their flanking light infantry out of the woods and caught Tarleton's dragoons in an enfilading fire, forcing them to withdraw. It was here that Charles Porterfield fell, mortally wounded by a stray bullet in the confused night skirmish. The British infantry steadily moving up into the line checked the flank attacks and after fifteen or twenty minutes of generally disorganized fighting both sides fell back to regroup. It was then, for the first time, that Gates discovered he had literally stumbled into Cornwallis and over 2,000 experienced soldiers.

With an army composed chiefly of inexperienced militia, most of them sick, it was

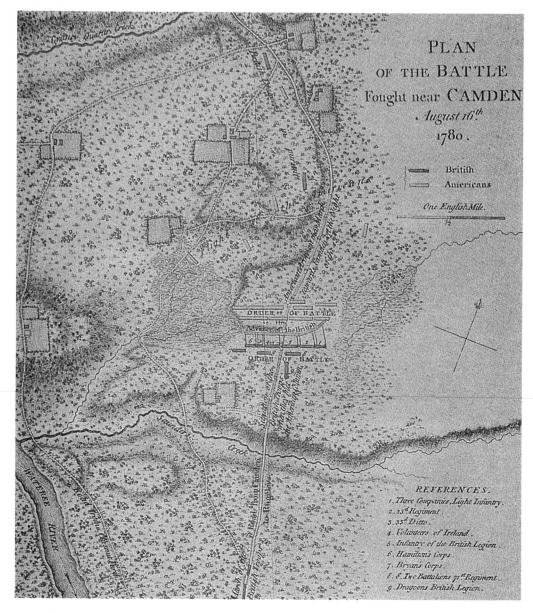

Figure 9. Plan of the battle fought near Camden, South Carolina, 16 August 1780, from *A History of the Campaigns of 1780 and 1781 in the Southern Provinces of North America*, by Lieutenant Colonel Banastre Tarleton (London, 1787)

clear that the only wise move for Horatio Gates was to retreat in good order, take up a strong defensive position, and await the British attack. This was the advice of the brilliant Otho Williams of Maryland, who expected the general to do so. Gates, vacillating and unsure of himself in a time of crisis, instead called a battle council of his field commanders. He told them they understood the situation and asked their opinion. Apparently no one spoke until Edward Stevens of the Virginia militia finally broke the strained silence suggesting it was too late to retreat and the army must fight. Lacking either agreement or disagreement among the officers present, Gates finally concurred and ordered his officers to their posts.

The battle was fought astride the Charlotte road with a narrow, open forest of pines, almost free of undergrowth, on both sides. Flanking the pine woods were wide swamps impassable to an army moving with wheeled equipment. The Americans held a better position on slightly rising ground with a clear escape route behind them. A wide creek ran across the British rear, a potential trap in case of defeat, but Cornwallis's line rested on the swamps so he could not be easily outflanked. The pine forest was wider where the American army was stationed, leaving its flanks open if the British should win.

Horatio Gates's line was drawn up as follows: Mordecai Gist's 2d Brigade of three Maryland and one Delaware regiments were stationed to the right of the road. On the left from the road, Richard Caswell's North Carolina militia and Edward Stevens's Virginia militia stood in that order with Charles Armand's small legion in support. William Smallwood's 1st Maryland Brigade was held in reserve behind the 2d Maryland, and the few pieces of artillery, some seven guns, were placed on the road in front of the center and between Caswell and Stevens. Johann de Kalb was given the place of honor, command of the right wing, while Horatio Gates with his staff took post some 600 yards to the rear.

Cornwallis formed his line with the Royal North Carolina Regiment, the infantry of Tarleton's Legion, and Lord Rawdon's Volunteers of Ireland from left to right on the road. Samuel Bryan's North Carolina Volunteers were stationed a short distance behind on their left flank. Francis Lord Rawdon commanded this wing facing de Kalb. The right wing from the swamp to the road was composed of a detachment of light infantry, three companies of the 23d Regiment, and the 33d Regiment. Lieutenant Colonel James Webster, a very good soldier, commanded the right wing. The five companies of Highlanders from the 71st Regiment were placed in reserve behind the center with two 6-pounder field guns. Two 6-pounders and two 3-pounders were placed in front of the British center, and Banastre Tarleton's dragoons rode in column on the road to the rear of the battle line, ready to exploit any retreat by the enemy.

In the very early morning, Colonel Otho Williams, riding along the waiting American line, saw the British advancing up the road. He summoned Captain Singleton of the artillery who said the enemy column could not be more than 200 yards away because he could distinguish the grounds of their uniforms. Williams ordered him to open fire, and Singleton did. The British promptly unlimbered their advance field guns and replied. The battle was joined. Williams rode back and reported to Gates that the enemy were deploying from column into battle lines and that he could attack them before they were fully formed. Gates replied that Williams was correct and the attack should be made. This, it would seem, was the last recorded command Horatio Gates gave in the battle.

Edward Stevens on the left was ordered to move his Virginians forward into action, and the inexperienced militia responded with hesitation. Otho Williams dismounted and called for volunteers, leading some 80 or 90 men to within 40 yards of the deploying British where, taking cover behind trees, they delivered harassing fire at close range. The alert Cornwallis, however, had observed the Virginia militia's clumsy attempts to form for an advance and ordered James Webster to countercharge. Webster, leading the 23d and 33d regiments, closed ranks, fixed bayonets, and the men drove forward on the double, shoulder to shoulder. The Virginia militia heard the deep British cheer and saw the steel-tipped, scarlet line sweep toward them in perfect order. They hesitated, wavered, and fell back in dismay. A few Virginians fired their muskets and a few redcoats went down, but this was the first time most of the militia had been in battle or seen an enemy, and war suddenly became to them personal and very dangerous. In spite of the desperate shouted exhortations of Edward Stevens to use the bayonet, the Virginians simply broke and ran. Seeing the Virginians' precipitate retreat and the British advance, the North Carolinians on their right also ran without firing a shot, throwing away muskets and equipment as they fled. Over 2,500 running militia broke through the 1st Maryland Brigade stationed in reserve behind the line, throwing that steady unit into confusion. Horatio Gates, the hero of Saratoga, mounted on a famous racer and believing the day lost, left the field at full gallop and did not spare spur until he reached Charlotte and safety sixty miles away. His later excuse for deserting his men and the battle was that he recognized defeat and went to Charlotte where he might rally the survivors. Although exonerated officially for his conduct by Congress and the army, he never held command again.

Johann de Kalb and Mordecai Gist with the American right wing and the 1st Maryland Brigade in reserve still held the field. One regiment of North Carolina militia under the command of Colonel Henry Dixon did not join in the general flight of the left but fell back fighting and linked up with the Delawares. De Kalb called for the reserve, and Otho Williams, finding that its commander, William Smallwood, also had fled the battle, tried to bring these regulars to the left of the 2d Brigade and Dixon's militia to form an "L" of defensive fire. The British already had advanced strong elements between the two brigades, and the gap could not be closed. Charles Cornwallis sent in James Webster and his regulars against the 1st Marylanders. They fought, retreated, rallied around their colors, and finally broke completely, some of them escaping safely through the swamp.

Figure 10.   Battle of Camden, South Carolina, 16 August 1780 and the death of de Kalb.
From a painting by Chappel; engraver unknown

Only the 2d Maryland Brigade, the Delaware regiment, and Henry Dixon's North Carolinians continued unbeaten resistance, 600 men against 2,000. They already had driven Lord Rawdon's left wing back with repeated bayonet charges and even had taken prisoners. For another hour they charged, reformed, and charged again, with de Kalb leading them personally, on foot and sword in hand, his horse having been killed early in the battle. Urged by his officers to retire while they still could, de Kalb refused to consider retreat. His head laid open by a saber cut, de Kalb led one more charge, killed a British soldier opposing him, and finally went down, mortally wounded, after sustaining eleven sword, bayonet, and bullet wounds. His men closed ranks and repelled with magnificent courage still another bayonet attack. Banastre Tarleton had returned with the dragoons from an immediate pursuit of the fleeing militia and Cornwallis threw in his horsemen with the saber on the American rear. The last remnant of the 2d Maryland Brigade, the Delawares, and Dixon's North Carolinians stood and fought for a few moments, then broke and ran. The battle of Camden was over.

John Eager Howard, John Gunby, and Robert Kirkwood, all fine soldiers, rallied

about 60 Marylanders and Delawares and retreated from the battle through the surrounding woods in a compact fighting group. The rest of Horatio Gates's "Grand
Army" were killed, captured, or scattered through the forests and swamps. Johann de
Kalb was left on the field. When British soldiers ran up to finish off the "rebel" general
with their bayonets, his aide, the Chevalier de Buysson, interposed his own body, shouting out de Kalb's name and rank. The wounded general was propped against a wagon
wheel by his enemies and sat there, dying, until Lord Cornwallis rode by and, recogniz-
ing the famous European soldier, had him carried into Camden on a litter and given the
best possible medical treatment.

According to the legend, and there is no reason to doubt it, Lord Cornwallis discovered that Johann de Kalb was a Mason, as he was himself. When de Kalb died with great
courage and dignity three days later, Cornwallis had him buried with full military and
Masonic honors. Cornwallis, Lord Rawdon, and all the British and Loyalist officers attended the funeral, a poignant note in an otherwise tragic and bloody affair.

With the battle over, Banastre Tarleton returned to his pursuit of the American fugitives and followed the broken army for twenty miles, killing as he rode. Charles Stedman, who served with the British army, left an eyewitness description of the road from
the battlefield to Charlotte, North Carolina: broken wagons, dead horses, abandoned
weapons or equipment, dead, dying, or badly wounded Americans lining the road and
roadside for miles, the dreadful debris of defeat and rout. At Rugeley's Mill, Colonel
Charles Armand with his 60 dragoons tried to save the American baggage left behind
when the march on Camden began, a hurried task doubly complicated because the North
Carolina and Virginia militia had stopped to loot the baggage. Tarleton came up with his
cavalry, ruthlessly broke what little resistance was offered, captured the baggage, and
continued the pursuit.

The British casualties at Camden were 331 of all ranks out of the 2,239 engaged.
This included 2 officers and 66 men killed, 18 officers and 227 enlisted personnel
wounded, and 18 men missing. The American losses never were fully reckoned, but 3
officers died in action and 30 were captured. From 650 to 700 of Horatio Gates's soldiers were either killed or taken out of a total of 3,052 effectives engaged in the battle.
This disaster to American arms approached that of Charleston. Saratoga had been thoroughly avenged.

Further American defeat was to come. Thomas Sumter asleep under a wagon, barely
escaped, without hat, boots, or coat and astride a saddleless horse. His surviving partisans with a few of their reinforcements were scattered over the countryside.

Major William Davie of North Carolina, a splendid cavalry soldier who raised and
equipped his own legion of dragoons and infantry and was probably the best swordsman
in the American army, had not taken part in the engagement. Instead, he had been on
detached duty, escorting wounded from the attack on the British post at Hanging Rock

to the field hospital at Charlotte. Riding down to join Horatio Gates, he first received information of the battle from one of the fugitives, whom he promptly arrested as a deserter. The tragic news of the American defeat and rout was confirmed by the sudden appearance of Horatio Gates himself, shouting to Davie as he rode that Tarleton and his dragoons were hard behind. Davie replied that his men were accustomed to Tarleton and not in the least afraid of him. Gates did not stay to discuss the matter but proceeded at all speed to Charlotte. General Isaac Huger then rode up, and Davie inquired how far the orders of General Gates should be followed. Huger told Davie to follow them as far as he pleased, because they never would see Horatio Gates again. Davie then sent an officer after Gates, who overtook him, halted him, and asked if the general wished Davie and his dragoons to ride toward Camden and bury the American dead. Gates replied that retreat was now the only possible course of action—the dead could bury the dead.

Thus the battle of Camden ended in panic, defeat, and disgrace. A numerically inferior force of British regulars and Loyalist Provincials, led with masterly skill, had thoroughly beaten a larger but less experienced American army. The American rout was redeemed only by the magnificent courage of Johann de Kalb and his brave Maryland and Delaware Continentals with Henry Dixon's North Carolinians.

CHAPTER VII

Brigadier General Francis Marion

War never is a particularly romantic business, but occasionally it produces a truly romantic figure. Francis Marion of South Carolina, one of the great partisan leaders of all times, must be considered high among these.

Francis Marion belonged to that steadfast, valiant group of French Protestants, the Huguenots, whose immediate forbears came to South Carolina in the late seventeenth and early eighteenth centuries after the revocation of the Edict of Nantes by King Louis XIV. Marion's grandfather settled with other Huguenot families near the lower Santee River in what was then and remains today in some areas a brooding, lost wilderness. Young Francis grew up amid the great swamp forests. He hunted, fished, and rode with his brothers and cousins, a wild, natural life that provided superb training for the guerrilla fighting in which he later was to excel.

Francis Marion served with distinction as a junior officer of South Carolina colonial militia in two Cherokee wars (1759 and 1761) when that powerful Indian tribe of the upper foothills and southern Appalachian ranges attacked the colony. These were real wars, since the Cherokees could field from 3,000 to 4,000 well-armed warriors and fought with courage and savage cruelty. Marion gained early experience as a lieutenant under the command of Captain William Moultrie, with whom he would stand again at Fort Sullivan in 1776. Moultrie reported after the Cherokee campaigns that Marion was a brave, hardy, and active soldier and an excellent partisan officer.

Francis Marion served with equal distinction as captain and then major in the 2d South Carolina Line Regiment of infantry raised in 1775 by the Provincial Congress. He was promoted to the rank of lieutenant colonel after Admiral Peter Parker and his fleet were driven from Charleston in 1776 by the guns of Fort Sullivan, later to be called Fort Moultrie in honor of its gallant commander. The 2d Regiment helped to man the sand-filled palmetto log defenses and Marion's cool courage in that engagement was noted by his colonel.

Lieutenant Colonel Francis Marion was second in command of the 2d Regiment at Savannah, Georgia, in 1779 when the unit participated in the desperate but unsuccessful assault on the town's fortifications. The 2d South Carolina Regiment, officers and colors in front, attacked the Spring Hill redoubt, one of the strongest points of the Savannah defenses, but finally was driven back with heavy loss after planting the regimental flags and fighting hand to hand on the berme below the main parapet.

When General Sir Henry Clinton took Charleston in 1780, capturing in the process General Benjamin Lincoln and most of the American army of the Southern Department, Marion was not among the prisoners. Prior to Clinton's attack, Marion, an officer in the town garrison, attended a regimental drinking party. The host locked the doors of his Charleston home to prevent the guests from escaping, thus ensuring the continuation and success of the affair. Francis Marion, a confirmed teetotaler, refusing to be constrained by this social device, leaped from a second story window and either broke or badly sprained an ankle. He was recuperating with friends at an outlying plantation when the town fell.

Governor John Rutledge, directing the state from an enforced exile in North Carolina, subsequently dispatched one of the few regular officers left uncaptured—Lieutenant Colonel Francis Marion—to take command and organize resistance in the Santee-Pee Dee districts. This move brought Marion home to his own swamps and forests, the area that would be his battleground and the site of his most famous exploits.

An excellent eyewitness description portrays Marion as lean, swarthy, and short, with an aquiline nose, a projecting chin, a large, high forehead, and black, piercing, steady eyes. He was already forty-eight years old when the war began, but hard, wiry, a superb horseman, and a born partisan leader. Marion became a model field commander, riding into battle at the head of his men but seldom participating in the actual fighting. Instead, he directed and controlled the action with calm brilliance, attacking savagely or pulling back from an engagement as the situation demanded. A famous story concerns Marion's sword. He never adopted the long cavalry saber favored by most of his men, wearing instead a short infantry officer's sword of his old 2d Regiment. On one battle occasion he tried to draw the short sword and found, to his dismay, that it had rusted into the scabbard.

Marion's style and original concept of warfare would bring him fame as well as the name "Swamp Fox," according to legend an angry epithet bestowed by a frustrated British pursuer, Lieutenant Colonel Banastre Tarleton. Marion operated successfully for almost a year without any logistical support. His men were unpaid volunteers, mostly untrained in formal warfare, using whatever weapons they already possessed or could capture from the enemy: sabers hammered by local blacksmiths from plantation wood saws, shotguns, hunting rifles, smooth-bore British army muskets, cavalry carbines, or pistols. Their favorite close-range load was number 2 goose shot; at 20 or 30 yards the pattern would tear a man apart.

Francis Marion's favorite tactic when pursued was to retire at his own pace until he came to a stream running through heavy swamp timber. After crossing, Marion would conceal his partisans on the other side in plentiful cover and wait for the enemy. When they arrived and tried to use the ford or primitive bridge, the British and Loyalist soldiers would be caught in a deadly enfilade fire from hidden rifles and muskets. If a crossing were forced, the enemy would find the ambush abandoned. Francis Marion already had fallen back to a different prepared position, deeper in the swamp, on the further side of still another stream. The unpleasant and bloody process would have to be repeated and then repeated again until Marion's opponents grew weary of the costly game and called off the operation. Francis Marion with his men was known to ride fifty miles in a night, attack by surprise a post or camp in the early morning, then fade back into his familiar fastnesses whenever faced by superior forces.

When Major General Horatio Gates marched into South Carolina in the summer of 1780 to reestablish American military power in the South after the fall of Charleston, Francis Marion rode up from the Santee-Pee Dee country with twenty followers to offer his services. Colonel Otho Williams wrote in his journal that Colonel Marion, a gentleman of South Carolina, had joined General Gates with twenty mounted men, black and white, wearing small leather caps, all badly equipped and wretchedly attired. The American army found this ragged nucleus for later glory a source of vast amusement, and the pompous Horatio Gates, who never understood the importance of cavalry in country to which it was best suited, was delighted to detach Marion and his little command back to their own territory with orders to watch enemy movements and furnish intelligence.

In mid-August 1780 word came to Francis Marion of the defeat and total rout of Horatio Gates and his entire army at the battle of Camden. A few days later news arrived of the near destruction of Thomas Sumter's command by Banastre Tarleton at Fishing Creek. During the last four months of 1780, Marion and his raiders, cut off from all support, were the only Americans still active against the British in the South Carolina lowcountry.

This period was the nadir of American military hopes in the South. With no regular organized forces opposing them, the British established chains of forts and outposts in Georgia and South Carolina from the coast to the foothills, an interlocking, mutually supporting network of garrisoned strong points to control and pacify the vast territory. At this time, with Savannah and Charleston in British hands, the two main American armies in the area captured or routed, and Loyalists rallying to the royal standard, the great southern partisans took the field: Francis Marion, Thomas Sumter, Elijah Clarke, William Davie, and others, desperate, ragged men striking savagely from swamp, savannah, mountain, or forest. The British and their Loyalist allies held the fortified towns and outposts, but the wild hinterland belonged to the American partisans.

During this period Francis Marion with his able lieutenants and followers—Peter Horry, Hugh Horry, John Van de Horst, Keating Simons, John Gavin and William James, Hezekiah Maham, Daniel Conyers, Thomas Waties, Henry Mouzon, John and James Postell, William McCottry, Gavin Witherspoon, Thomas Elliott, Lewis Ogier, and many others—were able to hold the country between the Santee and Pee Dee rivers up to the High Hills of the Santee and to make forays down to Charleston and beyond. In recognition of his services, Marion finally was commissioned a brigadier general of state militia by Governor John Rutledge on 30 December 1780, but his "brigade" ranged from 30 to 1 ,400 men. He made his lair on Snow's Island, guarded by Lynches River, Clark's Creek, and the wide Pee Dee with its great river swamps.

The Pee Dee is an area still rich in animal, bird, and fish life. Marion's men lived and fought on a diet of corn meal, molasses, sweet potatoes, hominy and hominy grits, game, fish, tough stringy beef from the half-wild scrub cattle wandering the woods, or pork from feral hogs, an animal that roams the same swamps today. The main difficulty was a serious lack of salt, rum, or other spirits unless these could be captured or were brought in by friendly farmers. Legend, immortalized in a painting, depicts the British officer who came under a flag to Marion's headquarters on Snow's Island and was entertained at a dinner that consisted wholly of sweet potatoes baked in the ashes of a campfire. According to the story, the envoy was astounded that men were willing to fight and die for any cause while living on such meager fare and on his return to Charleston refused to serve any longer against such a dedicated enemy. Whether true or not, the tale is part of the Marion mystique and reflects the hold he achieved on the imagination of his followers and the people in the surrounding country.

Figure 11.   Francis Marion entertains a British officer with a meal of sweet potatoes.
Engraving for Currier and Ives from the painting by John Blake White

Marion did not drink wine or spirits of any sort; his canteen usually held water with an infusion of vinegar. Since the eighteenth-century French army, following the old Roman custom, was issued this same mixture for its water bottles on the known basis that vinegar had certain purifying properties, it may be conjectured that Marion was a more knowledgeable and sophisticated soldier than he usually is given credit for being. At any rate, his favorite drink probably kept him much healthier than his comrades.

Francis Marion's first military operation of any consequence occurred just after the rout at Camden when he surprised a British escort conducting 150 American prisoners to the main base at Charleston. In a brief early morning attack, Marion and Peter Horry with a few followers captured or killed 22 British soldiers and 2 Loyalist guides. The freed prisoners were soldiers of the Maryland line brigades, but to Marion's vast and angry astonishment, 85 of the released Marylanders refused to join him and insisted on proceeding to Charleston as prisoners of war. Marion sent word of the raid to the defeated and discredited Horatio Gates, who was licking his wounded vanity in North Carolina. Gates informed Congress of this one piece of cheerful news in an otherwise grim picture, and the item appeared in some northern newspapers. For the first time a dispirited and apathetic country heard of Francis Marion.

Marion now was to move from hard fought victory to hard fought victory, none individually vitally important but cumulatively a steady drain on British resources and a constant threat to the supply lines from Charleston to the outposts. Near the Little Pee Dee River, Marion defeated a strong force of Loyalists under Major Micajah Ganey and Captain Jesse Barefield. During this engagement Major John James of Marion's command, charging alone on his horse Thunder, routed a Loyalist unit by shouting to imaginary followers, "Come on, boys, here they are. Here they are" When enemy reinforcements arrived, Marion according to his custom fell back, hotly pursued by superior forces. Halting at Blue Savannah he set an ambush in a thick wood of young pines. Carried away by the excitement of close pursuit, the Loyalists rode into the trap, and Marion cut them to pieces.

In a following skirmish, Marion surrounded Colonel John Coming Ball and 46 Loyalist partisans camped on the edge of Black Mingo Swamp. Attacked suddenly from three sides in the darkness, the Loyalists were completely broken by the onset and scattered wildly through the woods by way of the one side of their bivouac that remained open. Probably through a natural tactical instinct, Marion thus provided his opponents with Scipio Africanus's "Golden bridge of retreat." A surrounded enemy with all avenues of escape closed may fight to the death, but if a way is left open to run, the enemy will usually take it.

During the late evening of 25 October 1780, Francis Marion attacked Lieutenant Colonel Samuel Tynes and his Loyalist raiders at their camp by Tearcoat Swamp on the upper Black River. Again, as at Black Mingo, Marion ordered his men to charge in from three directions. Tynes escaped but 3 of his followers were killed, 14 wounded, and 23

Figure 12.   Brigadier General Francis Marion, by Robert Wilson

captured. The pro-British elements in the Santee-Pee Dee district were becoming thoroughly intimidated.

The merciless ambush at Blue Savannah and the defeats of Ball and Tynes brought Marion to the attention of Earl Cornwallis, the British commander in South Carolina and Georgia following the return of Sir Henry Clinton to New York. After Camden and Fishing Creek, South Carolina was presumed to be conquered with only the process of pacification and organization remaining. The ubiquitous American "gadfly," Francis Marion, must be sought out and destroyed. The ruthless Lieutenant Colonel Banastre Tarleton was given the task of hunting down and finishing off Marion. Tarleton, with his green-jacketed legion, a picked force of dragoons, and mounted infantry, advanced into the Santee-Pee Dee country, and Marion with 400 men rode to meet him. His scouts, fanning out in advance of the column, discovered Tarleton's Legion camped at the late Brigadier General Richard Richardson's plantation. When the report came back of the enemy's numbers, the cool and cautious Marion, realizing the odds were against him, swung his command around and galloped away through swampy forests and across slow, shallow, black water streams to the wild pine lands south of the Black River. Tarleton, alarmed by an escaped prisoner, mounted and followed hard on Marion's track for seven hours. At Ox Swamp, which lies some twenty miles from Kingstree, Tarleton finally halted his weary men and horses. It may be true that Tarleton, in tired and frustrated desperation, called off the operation, saying that he and his legion should return to the upcountry and find the "Gamecock," referring to the always aggressive Thomas Sumter, but as for the "damned old fox"—Francis Marion—"the devil himself could not catch him." There seems little reason to doubt that this was the time Marion received the name by which he is known to history: the "Swamp Fox."

During this time also Marion suffered a cruel personal tragedy. Young Gabriel Marion, his nephew, was unhorsed and captured in a skirmish by Loyalist partisans. Because he was a close kinsman of the hated Swamp Fox, his captors held a buckshot-loaded musket against his chest and blew it apart. When the suspected murderer, a Loyalist mulatto named Sweat, was caught in a later operation by Marion's men, they shot him. It is a measure of Marion's moral stature that, though personally bereaved, he was furious at his own men's treatment of a disarmed prisoner and publicly reprimanded the vengeful partisan who pulled the trigger.

A Scottish major, Robert McLeroth, was the next British officer to meet and, in this case, outwit Marion. McLeroth was leading recruits for the Royal Fusiliers from Charleston to join Cornwallis's army at Winnsboro, South Carolina. Marion, riding up the Santee road beyond Nelson's Ferry with 700 men, overtook the unhappy major who promptly ordered his raw troops to take positions behind a rail fence in an open field and wait for the attack. A parley was called and flags exchanged between the two forces. It was agreed that 20 marksmen should be selected from each side who would meet in the field and carry out a mass duel to determine by mortal combat the fighting qualities of the antagonists.

Francis Marion named Major John Van der Horst to command his team with Captain Samuel Price of All Saints Parish as second in command. Van der Horst carefully chose the best marksmen, including a crack shot named Gavin Witherspoon. He asked Witherspoon what would be the surest distance to strike with buckshot, and Witherspoon informed him that 50 yards was best for the first fire. John Van der Horst told his 20 marksmen that he was not a good judge of distance, but at 50 yards Witherspoon would tap him on the shoulder. At that moment on the order, they should form on his left facing the British Fusiliers. Each partisan was immediately to fire his load of buckshot at the man opposite. Van der Horst assured them that few of the enemy would survive for a second volley.

As the two forces closed to 50 yards without firing, a British officer swung out and passed along the red-coated line, which shouldered its muskets, performed an about-face, and marched away. John Van der Horst and his men returned in glory to the American position without firing a shot.

This was one occasion when the Swamp Fox was outfoxed by a wily Scot. Major McLeroth had seized the opportunity and time consumed in arranging the formal duel to send for help and get the rest of his column on the road. The British had a head start of several hours, but Marion promptly sent a well-mounted detachment to cut them off and hold them until he could come up with the rest of his command.

Marion's men passed the British on the march, swung around them, and occupied a house covering the road. As McLeroth came up, to his amazement, the prepared ambush suddenly dissolved. The Americans had discovered to their horror that the entire Singleton family, owners of the house, were seriously ill with smallpox. They ran out as the astonished British watched, mounted, and rode away in frightened haste. Robert McLeroth got safely away with his recruits, although, ironically, he later was cashiered for not being sufficiently aggressive in his activities against the "rebels."

Major General Nathanael Greene, George Washington's original choice for the post, assumed command of the Southern Department on 2 December 1780 at Charlotte, North Carolina, replacing the unfortunate Horatio Gates. Greene promptly began to assemble a new army for a campaign in South Carolina. He also immediately realized the potential of Francis Marion as a genius of partisan warfare and sent Lieutenant Colonel Henry Lee of Virginia and his legion of horse and foot to cooperate with the Swamp Fox. Lee's crack legion uniformed in green jackets, black boots, white trousers, and brass helmets with horsehair plumes would fight beside Marion's tattered guerrillas.

To Nathanael Greene's surprise, Lee and Marion got along famously and made a magnificent fighting team. Lee profoundly respected Marion's brilliance as a partisan commander and his moral and steadfast character. Marion admired Lee's dash, gallantry, and educated good breeding.

Working together Francis Marion and Henry Lee almost captured strongly held Georgetown, South Carolina, by a combined amphibious surprise attack in boats from the river and a fast land assault with mounted troops. The town commandant was taken, but some of the garrison, retreating into a strongly fortified area, held out and Georgetown remained in British hands.

Just before Lee joined Marion one of the more dramatic incidents of the fighting around Georgetown occurred. Peter Horry, following Nathanael Greene's orders to secure information, encountered and forced back a detachment of Queen's Rangers patrolling near Georgetown. The stout old Tory Micajah Ganey rode out with reinforcements from the town to support his retreating comrades, and Peter Horry drove in with the saber to meet him. Ganey's Loyalist horsemen fled before the attack, and Ganey was pursued as he galloped for Georgetown by Sergeant McDonald, a big redheaded Scot, one of Marion's best soldiers. Just before Ganey reached the outskirts of town and safety, McDonald, close behind him, rose in his stirrups and lunged with a bayoneted musket, literally driving the blade through Ganey's body. The bayonet pulled loose, and Ganey rode into town, fainting, bleeding, his body pierced from back through chest. The man must indeed have possessed a sturdy constitution, for he recovered from his dreadful wound.

After Banastre Tarleton was thoroughly defeated by Brigadier General Daniel Morgan in a stand-up soldier's battle at Cowpens on 17 January 1781, Cornwallis made the fatal decision to pursue Nathanael Greene across North Carolina. Henry Lee was detached from Marion's area, his legion covering Greene's long retreat, and these months were Marion's greatest ordeal. The "Gamecock," Thomas Sumter, was operating in the backcountry almost 200 miles away. A very able British commander, Francis Lord Rawdon, lay between the two partisan leaders with a strong force of regulars and Loyalist Provincials.

Lieutenant Colonel John Watson, leading 500 Loyalists and a fine British regiment, the Buffs, was ordered by Rawdon in March 1781 to move on Marion's headquarters at Snow's Island. Lieutenant Colonel Welbore Doyle with a second British and Loyalist column marched at the same time in a pincher movement down Lynches River. Marion's scouts, working all the way to Camden, brought him word of the double approach, and Marion, never a man to avoid a fight if he thought victory possible, chose his opponent and waited for John Watson at Wiboo Swamp on the Santee River.

Watson came up, and Peter Horry defended the swamp approaches until dislodged by cannon fire. Marion, meanwhile, had pulled the rest of his 400 partisans into the swamp and across a narrow causeway. Horry retired in good order to join him, and Gavin James, the last man in the retreat, held the causeway alone, mounted and using his empty bayoneted musket as a lance. He killed two of Watson's men as they charged him, stabbed a third man, and then fell back, dragging his enemy out of the saddle and along the causeway some 40 yards before the blade came free. Marion, still falling back and still pursued, crossed the Black River and halted, ordering Major John James with William McCottry's riflemen to defend the bridge near Kingstree . John Watson arrived and tried to force the bridge, but after five of his men were killed and several wounded by long-range rifle fire, Watson broke off the engagement, stating that he had never seen such shooting in all of his life—the American riflemen were killing his men at well over 200 yards.

After this series of bloody little skirmishes, Marion chivalrously granted a written pass to Lieutenant Colonel Watson authorizing him to send his wounded back to the coast through partisan country, a humane act in an otherwise ruthless war. Watson finally reached Georgetown with two wagon loads of wounded, but in Marion's absence Welbore Doyle captured the base at Snow's Island. Its defenders had destroyed all of the carefully gathered and hoarded supplies before leaving.

This could have been the low moment for Marion and his brigade, but Nathanael Greene had decided after Cornwallis's pyrrhic victory at Guilford Court House in North Carolina to march south again, and Henry Lee with his legion was detached to find and cooperate with Marion.

After some difficulty, Marion and his partisans were discovered and the two commanders again joined forces. They decided that their first operation should be to attack and capture Fort Watson on Scott's Lake, a key British outpost guarding the line of communications from Charleston to the backcountry. Fort Watson had been constructed on an ancient Indian mound rising over 30 feet above the surrounding Santee swamp. It was heavily stockaded with three rows of abatis and a garrison of 80 British and 40 Loyalist soldiers under Lieutenant James McKay.

The besiegers took post on 15 April 1781 between the fort and Scott's Lake, an arm of the Santee, to cut off the water supply; but McKay, a thoroughly efficient officer, sank a well under cover of night just outside the stockade that could be defended by a covered trench or rude caponier extending out from his fort. The forest also had been cleared around the defenses to give a free field of fire, and the Americans were completely exposed to enemy musketry. Lee and Marion were forced to sit down and carry out a time-consuming investment of the outpost. Speed was necessary lest Fort Watson might be relieved. Without artillery, the stockade could not be breached, so Marion sent a courier to General Greene who had advanced to Hobkirk Hill, about a mile and a half from Camden, and asked for a fieldpiece. Greene complied, but the fort fell before the gun arrived.

Lieutenant Colonel Hezekiah Maham, one of Marion's officers, suggested that a log tower be built high enough to overlook the fort with a protected platform for riflemen on its top. A very thorough exploration of Fort Watson's site was conducted in 1972 and 1973 by the Institute of Archaeology and Anthropology of the University of South Carolina. The quantity of flattened lead rifle balls found in the eastern and southern halves of the area clearly within the eighteenth-century stockade proves that the tower was located northwest of the mound. Since the balls obviously struck with sufficient force to distort their shape, it is evident that the tower had to be well within effective rifle-killing range—under 300 yards. The mound itself is still 33 feet high, and, to provide adequate protection, the stockade must have been 6 or 7 feet tall. Sound speculation, based on the available archaeological evidence, would locate the tower about 40 or 50 yards from the northwest parapet. To cover the interior of the fort and place the rifle balls where they were found, the tower would have to be something over 40 feet in height. (When used later, such towers always were called Maham Towers.)

The tower was constructed at night from logs notched and laid crosswise, using the timber available in the swamp. From its top, rifles in the hands of a selected group of Marion's best marksmen brought the interior of the fort under direct aimed fire. No one could move inside the stockade, and a volunteer detachment of Henry Lee's men rushed the defenses protected by the tower's riflemen and began to pull away the abatis. Lieutenant James McKay, seeing the legion infantry lining up for a final bayonet assault, realized his position was hopeless and surrendered. This capture of Fort Watson eliminated a strong point in the British defense system and severed the essential suppply line from Charleston.

After acquiring the 6-pounder field gun from Nathanael Greene, Marion and Lee marched up the Santee and a major tributary, the Congaree River, on 8 May 1781 to invest Fort Motte, the most important depot for convoys moving from Charleston to Camden, Fort Granby, and Ninety Six. Lieutenant Donald McPherson with about 140 British and Hessian infantry supported by a small contingent of dragoons had taken over and fortified a handsome house, Mount Joseph Plantation, the property of Mrs. Rebecca Motte, and had evicted her; she was living nearby in her overseer's cottage. McPherson's defenses consisted of a deep, wide trench around the house with a high, wide earthwork parapet on the inner side of the ditch. The strongly constructed plantation home itself constituted the main fortress. The British garrison defended the post with stubborn gallantry and surrendered only after the besiegers succeeded in setting fire to the roof of the big house itself, preventing the defenders' attempts to extinguish the blaze with discharges of well-aimed canister from the 6-pounder. After the British raised the white flag, Marion's partisans, Lee's Legion, and the defending garrison all cooperated in putting out the fire.

Mrs. Motte is said to have given permission as a patriotic duty for Marion and Lee to fire the house and then offered a bow and fire arrows presented to her husband by the captain of an East Indiaman. The roof shingles were ignited by these arrows. William Dobein James, however, who served with Marion and was present at the action, says that a private in Marion's brigade fired the house with a ball of ignited brimstone hurled with a sling. The latter seems the more likely account.

After the battle, Mrs. Motte entertained both the victorious and the conquered officers at a dinner party set up outside the overseer's cottage. A much grimmer tale states that on that same evening Marion angrily saved the lives of certain British prisoners whom Lee's men were in the process of hanging—another comment on Marion's moral standards and the savage nature of the war in South Carolina.

This last action signaled the end of Marion's partisan days. With the British falling back on Charleston, Marion was to serve and command with gallantry and distinction at Quinby Bridge and Eutaw Springs. He no longer was the elusive guerrilla but a field officer again, proudly leading his brigade into full battle.

Ironically, in three final engagements of the war, Francis Marion was beaten by his British opponents. Colonel Benjamin Thompson, a brilliant Loyalist cavalry leader from Massachusetts, defeated the brigade at Wambaw Bridge on 14 February 1782 and again at Tydiman's Plantation eleven days later. Marion's last battle fought at Fairlawn Plantation on 29 August 1782 also ended in a British victory, although as usual Marion extricated his command and fell back in good order. On this occasion a desperate, forlorn-hope charge by Major Thomas Fraser's Royal Dragoons broke through the American position, causing the horses of Marion's ammunition wagons to bolt with the wagons. Though deprived of his reserve powder and shot, Marion beat back the charge and broke off the action. It was his last fight in the revolutionary war.

Another event provides further insight into Francis Marion's personal ethical standards. During the autumn of 1782 when General Alexander Leslie, commanding the British troops in Charleston, prepared to evacuate the town, Marion refused to shed further blood. The British were filling their water casks for the long voyage home across the Cooper River at Lempriere's Point. Nathanael Greene suggested but did not order that Marion ambush the watering parties. Marion flatly replied, "No," stating that if he were ordered to attack he would obey, but that not another life should be lost with his consent, even if the event brought him the highest personal honor as a soldier. Marion added that he would prefer to send his troops to protect the British rather than attack them. It is a tribute to Marion's reputation that Nathanael Greene did not press the point.

Francis Marion was unquestionably the most distinguished of the partisan leaders on either side in the revolutionary war. Personally courageous, humane when possible, cunning, cautious, if need be totally ruthless, Francis Marion possessed what the ancient Romans called *virtus*—"all that goes to make a true man."

He died on 27 February 1795 and lies among his kinspeople under the great oak, pine, and tupelo trees of a private burial ground on his brother's plantation, Belle Isle. The inscription on the monument reads as follows:

> This tribute of veneration and gratitude is in commemoration of the noble and disinterested virtues of the citizen and the gallant exploits of the soldier who lived without fear and died without reproach.

CHAPTER VIII

The Fighting Partisans of the Backcountry

After the British capture of Charleston, South Carolina, in May of 1780, Francis Marion, the Swamp Fox, kept the war alive for over a year in the swamps and forests of lower South Carolina. The backcountry, that wide and wild land lying between the Cherokee tribal frontier, the mountains, and the coastal plain of Georgia, the Carolinas, and Virginia was the fighting territory of many other partisan leaders. Three of the greatest were Thomas Sumter of South Carolina, William Richardson Davie of North Carolina, and Elijah Clarke of Georgia.

Like Francis Marion, the backcountry partisans continued a fierce resistance to the British occupation without pay or logistical support except what they could levy by ruthless force from Loyalist farmers or capture from their British enemies. The guerrillas ranged throughout the hinterland, hitting fortified outposts, harrying Loyalists, and cutting vital supply lines to the coast.

Thomas Sumter, a wealthy planter on the Santee with a colorful if somewhat dubious past, had served with Richard Richardson in the Snow Campaign and as colonel of the 6th Carolina Regiment at Breach Inlet. Possibly bored with military inactivity and shaken by a family tragedy—all but one of his children died of smallpox—he resigned from the army and returned to his plantation in 1777. Sumter was living quietly at home with a surviving son and a crippled wife when he received news on 28 May of Charleston's capture. He left his home the same day accompanied by a faithful black servant, Soldier Tom, just a few hours before Banastre Tarleton arrived in his pursuit of Abraham Buford's luckless command retreating to its bloody fate at the Waxhaws. Tarleton burned Sumter's house after Sumter had ridden safely away. His name would become a rallying cry for men in both Carolinas as the fight continued against their British conquerors. Lacking material backing or support, Thomas Sumter rewarded his partisans with black slaves and provisions requisitioned by force from Loyalist or suspected Loyalist farmers and plunder taken at captured British strong points. This procedure was known as "Sumter's Law," a grimly amusing insight into the relentless nature of the war in the South. Always supremely aggressive, although occasionally guilty of carelessness and poor tactical judgment, Sumter was to fight seven set battles against his British and Loyalist enemies. At Blackstocks, South Carolina, commanding Georgia and South Carolina militia, Thomas Sumter met and stopped Banastre Tarleton and his regulars, a signal achievement in the southern war.

A second famous partisan leader was William Richardson Davie, the *beau sabreur* of the southern guerrilla leaders. Born into a Scottish family in Cumberland, England, he emigrated with his family to the colonies and was reared from the age of five in South Carolina. Because he carried out his civil and political life in North Carolina and retired to Landsford on the Catawba River in South Carolina, Davie is claimed rightfully by both states.

When Charleston fell, William Davie was at his home in Salisbury, North Carolina, recovering from a wound received at the battle of the Stono River where he had served as brigade major of Benjamin Lincoln's cavalry. When he had recovered from his injury, during the winter of 1780 William Davie was given authority by the General Assembly of North Carolina to raise a troop of cavalry and two companies of mounted infantry. The state, however, could not afford to furnish or equip this legion, so Davie, a successful lawyer in private life, disposed of a considerable estate and with his own funds raised and equipped the soldiers. Noted for dash and courage and as an excellent swordsman, by the end of the war Davie was reputed to have killed with his saber more of the enemy than any other officer in the American army.

The third great partisan, Elijah Clarke, moved from tidewater Virginia a few years before the Revolution to what is now Wilkes County, Georgia, at that time still a wilderness, and became a prosperous farmer. Clarke's deserved reputation as an effective and successful guerrilla commander has been overshadowed by those of Francis Marion, Thomas Sumter, and other more dramatic figures. A steady, reliable, and, when necessary, deadly fighting leader, Elijah Clarke made contributions to eventual victory in the South that merit high recognition.

After the British capture of Savannah in December of 1779, Georgia, the least populous of the southern states, seemed totally subdued by mid-February 1780. It was then that Elijah Clarke, a colonel in the Georgia militia, refused to accept the protection offered by the occupying forces and took the field with a growing partisan band, determined to reconquer his state. He had led his Georgians at Andrew Pickens's victorious battle of Kettle Creek in 1779 and was to serve well at Musgrove's Mill, McKay's Trading Post, the battle of Blackstocks, Long Cane, and Augusta. Clarke would fight until the British evacuated Georgia and South Carolina in 1782, commanding in that same year, with Andrew Pickens, the last and completely successful expedition against the still warlike Cherokee Indians.

With Savannah, Charleston, Beaufort, and Georgetown in British hands, King George's forces and their Loyalist allies advanced steadily from the coast into the middle and upper districts of Georgia and South Carolina, establishing strong outposts, patrol-

Figure 13.
Brigadier General Elijah Clarke

Figure 14.
William Davie, commissary general
for Nathanael Greene

Figure 15.
Brigadier General Thomas Sumter

ling the roads, and organizing the royalist elements in the backcountry. This was not achieved without bloodshed. Lieutenant Colonel George Turnbull of the Royal New York Volunteers, commanding the British garrison at Rocky Mount, South Carolina, sent out Captain Christian Huck, a Philadelphia lawyer who had come south as an officer in Tarleton's Legion, with 25 Provincial dragoons, 20 regular mounted infantry, and 60 South Carolina Loyalist militia. His assignment was to investigate continued reports of minor actions fought between American guerrillas and Loyalist militia detachments.

At dawn on 12 July 1780, Colonel William Bratton, Colonel Andrew Neel, and Colonel Edward Lacey with 260 South Carolina partisans attacked Christian Huck's camp at Williamson's plantation from three directions. Huck was shot dead in the first few minutes of the fighting and of his completely surprised men, 30 or 40 were killed and 50 wounded in the one hour of battle and a ruthless pursuit that followed. The partisans had one man killed and only a few wounded. The casualties from both sides were picked up by the attackers and brought to Colonel William Brandon's nearby farmhouse where Mrs. Brandon cared for all the injured with impartial solicitude.

The battle at Williamson's plantation was not important or large except that it demonstrated that a local partisan force could surprise and rout the Provincial regulars of Banastre Tarleton's Legion and the Royal New York Volunteers. This success cheered the partisans, and the backcountry began to catch fire.

During the same day, 12 July 1780, Colonel John Thomas beat off a Loyalist attack on his camp at Cedar Springs near the present Spartanburg, South Carolina. On the night of 13 July, Colonel John Jones of Georgia ambushed a Loyalist force at Gowen's Old Fort near the South Pacolet River and finally, during the morning of 16 July, Edward Hampton pursued and scattered the same Loyalist raiding party that had hit John Thomas's camp three days before. These were not big engagements, but they began to hurt. The British and Loyalists had lost more than 100 men in five days, while the American partisan casualties were less than half that number.

At the end of July, Colonel Thomas Sumter with 500 guerrilla fighters and no artillery moved against the British outpost at Rocky Mount, South Carolina. At the same time, William Davie with 40 of his dragoons and an equal number of mounted rifles carried out a coordinated operation against the British post at Hanging Rock, South Carolina. On Sunday morning, 30 July, Thomas Sumter arrived in position and sent a flag to George Turnbull demanding his surrender. Turnbull, a fighting New York Loyalist, replied that Sumter might come and take the post if he could, and the action began.

The British post was located on top of a hill near the west bank of the Catawba River at the mouth of Rocky Creek. It consisted of two stout log houses and a large clapboarded frame house, all three loopholed for musketry. Thomas Sumter did not know that Turnbull had ordered his men to construct a breast-high wall of heavy logs inside the frame house with clay packed in the space between the clapboards and the logs. It was impregnable to anything but artillery, and Sumter had no field guns. Three times the American partisans assaulted the houses, attempting to break in the doors, and three times they were beaten back, losing eight men killed, including Colonel Andrew Neel. A large granite boulder about 100 yards from Sumter's position and close enough to the smaller log house offered protection for someone to throw a firebrand at the house's roof. Colonel William Hill volunteered for the desperate venture and a young soldier, Jemmy Johnson of Fairfield, joined him. The two men's upper bodies were encased in crude armor made from thick bundles of pine lightwood bound together tightly with cords. Protected by these primitive corselets, Hill and Johnson raced the 100 yards of open ground to the boulder under intense fire from the three houses. Before they could ignite and hurl their firebrands, the defenders sallied out with the bayonet and drove the two back to the partisan lines. They just made it, with musket balls hitting the wooden armor and whistling around their ears. The two volunteers tried again, this time protected by a heavy covering fire from an advanced screen of riflemen. They reached the boulder, lit the brands, and threw them, successfully firing the shingles on the smaller log house. The walls of the nearby frame house had just begun to smoke when a heavy rainstorm suddenly blew in and extinguished the fire.

Thomas Sumter and his men, totally frustrated in their attempts to storm the post at Rocky Mount, called off the operation after an eight-hour battle and rode away. During their return march to Sumter's base at Landsford on the Catawba, the disappointed guerrillas met two parties of British and Loyalist soldiers coming up to relieve the threatened outpost. In the sharp little fight that followed, Thomas Sumter lost 20 men but killed 60 of his opponents, captured a few prisoners, and secured some good horses and muskets.

William Davie, meanwhile, had staged a bloody and successful ambush of a Loyalist unit in plain sight of the British strong point at Hanging Rock. Learning from his scouts that a patrol from that post numbering about 100 had stopped to rest at a farmhouse near the British position, Davie, undetected, placed his dismounted riflemen at the end of a lane leading to the house and part of his dragoons in the woods behind the house. The latter were ordered to carry out a mounted charge with the saber around the building and hit the surprised patrol retreating up the lane from the rifle fire. A second smaller detachment of horsemen was concealed in woods where Davie correctly surmised the enemy would run when attacked from two sides. Trapped suddenly between concentrated, aimed rifle fire from one end of the lane and a cavalry charge swinging around the house, the Loyalist patrol bolted in the direction William Davie had anticipated. They were caught by three attacks from three directions, the concealed dragoons galloping out of the woods and sabering the fleeing soldiers mercilessly. No prisoners were taken; all of the Loyalist fugitives were either killed or wounded and left on the field. The garrison at Hanging Rock, astonished and furious at an ambuscade successfully accomplished as they watched, beat desperately to quarters. William Davie rode away without losing a single man, and captured 100 muskets and sixty horses.

Shortly after Davie's exploit, Thomas Sumter received intelligence that the garrison at Hanging Rock had been weakened further by a detachment of 300 men sent to reinforce Rocky Mount after his attack on that post. Hanging Rock still was held by about 500 men. These included an element of Banastre Tarleton's Legion infantry, the Prince of Wales American Regiment, Colonel Thomas Browne's South Carolina Rangers, and Colonel Samuel Bryan's North Carolina Volunteers, a company of which had been badly cut up by William Davie a few days before. Major John Carden of the Prince of Wales Regiment was in overall command.

There were no fortified houses as there had been at Rocky Mount. The British instead were camped in the open, protected by earthworks and two fieldpieces. The entire front of the camp was covered by a deep ravine and a creek. The Prince of Wales American Regiment and some of Tarleton's Legion infantry held the right of the camp facing the ravine. Thomas Browne's Rangers and a second unit of legion infantry were posted in the center and Samuel Bryan's North Carolina Volunteers occupied the left, separated from the rest of the camp by a narrow tongue of woods extending from the forest behind.

Thomas Sumter had been given overall command of the 800 North and South Carolina partisans assembled for the attack by the officers of both state contingents. His plan was to ride straight toward the center of the British position, tether the horses out of range, and separate his force into three divisions, each division attacking dismounted a sector of the British encampment. The partisans struck Hanging Rock early in the morning of 6 August 1780. Unfortunately for Sumter's plan, his guides recruited from the local presumably Whig population missed the path and led the entire force too far to the right. All three divisions, charging together on foot, hit Samuel Bryan's North Carolinians camped on the British left. These, surprised and totally confused, fled through the woods to the center where Tarleton's Legionnaires and Browne's Rangers had beat to quarters, formed, and met the charging partisans with steady, disciplined fire. The center was overrun in turn and fell back on the Prince of Wales Regiment and the second element of Tarleton's infantry, also forming desperately under heavy point-blank fire. Colonel Thomas Browne with his Royal South Carolina Rangers almost changed the fortunes of the day by throwing his men into the tongue of woods separating the camps from whence he caught Sumter's partisans with a close flanking fire. Browne was forced to withdraw deeper into the forest by a furious attack of the still advancing Americans. This diversion, however, gave time for the unbroken unit of Tarleton's Legion and a remnant of the Prince of Wales Regiment, the latter almost decimated in the action, to go into a hollow square, bristling with bayonets and supported by the two fieldpieces. Strangely, Major John Carden, the British post commander, seems to have lost all self-control and turned over his responsibilities to a Captain Rousslet of Tarleton's Legion.

The shattered elements of the British garrison began to rally around and reinforce the soldiers in the square who stood firm and fighting hard, approximately in the area where John Carden's right originally had been stationed. Thomas Sumter did his best to organize an attack on this desperately forming position. Most of the undisciplined partisans, distracted and confused by their early easy victory and occupied in looting the captured portions of the camp, were totally out of control. William Davie, whose dragoons and mounted infantry were the best trained of the American force, observed a large party of the enemy again assembling near the central woods and swung his men through the forest behind it, completely routing a potential flank threat. That, however, was the only coherent American action in this part of the engagement.

Many of Thomas Sumter's partisans had loaded themselves with plunder, their ready ammunition was exhausted, and some already were drunk from captured rum. Sumter, unable to bring military order to a now chaotic operation, fell back to the tethered horses, mounted, and retreated with William Davie and his dragoons covering the column. The partisans marched away from Hanging Rock to the sound of British military music and three cheers for King George from the soldiers still holding the outpost they were ordered to guard. The Americans answered with three cheers for George Washington, but continued their retreat.

A small success on the road back to Sumter's base somewhat eased his failure to take Hanging Rock. The partisans suddenly met two companies of Tarleton's Legion infantry marching over from Rocky Mount. William Davie promptly charged these with the saber, dispersing them into the surrounding woods.

Whether Hanging Rock should be called a victory for Thomas Sumter and William Davie is open to question. British casualties were about 200, and partisan casualties, while never officially counted, seem to have been considerably less, possibly 20 killed, 40 wounded, and 10 missing. Sumter and Davie also captured 70 prisoners, 100 horses, and 250 stands of arms plus considerable stores and ammunition. The fruits if not the palms of victory clearly belonged to the American partisans.

On 16 August 1780, a few miles north of Camden, South Carolina, the new American army, commanded by Major General Horatio Gates, the hero of Saratoga, was utterly routed and almost destroyed by Lord Cornwallis. Two days later, at midday of 18 August, Banastre Tarleton, pushing relentlessly forward in the merciless summer heat with 100 dragoons of his legion and 60 light infantry, caught Thomas Sumter with 800 men, including 400 reinforcements sent to him by Horatio Gates before the battle of Camden, resting, bathing, and sleeping at his camp on Fishing Creek, thirty-eight miles from Camden. Tarleton swept through Thomas Sumter's vedettes and hit the camp before the surprised Americans could run to arms. Tarleton killed or wounded 150 of Sumter's men, captured 310 prisoners, and secured 800 horses, 1,100 stands of arms, 2 field guns, and 46 loaded wagons including 2 ammunition wagons. He also released 150 British prisoners taken by Thomas Sumter and Colonel Thomas Taylor in raids along the British supply line. Sumter escaped, riding a wagon horse bareback, leaving behind his hat, coat, and boots.

A savage and hot little action fought at Musgrove's Mill, South Carolina, on 17 August was a clear American victory but could not mitigate the double disasters of Camden and Fishing Creek. Learning that a strong body of Loyalists were posted at Musgrove's Mill on the south side of the Enoree River, Colonel Elijah Clarke with his Georgians, Colonel James Williams leading South Carolinians, and Colonel Isaac Shelby, who had joined Clarke with a contingent of wild frontier riflemen from the Watauga settlements in what is now Tennessee, determined to attack Musgrove's Mill. In the early morning of 18 August, 200 well-armed and well-mounted American partisans arrived about a mile north of Musgrove's Ford. Scouts sent across the river toward the mill clashed with a British patrol and rode back in haste with two wounded. Because surprise was out of the question, Clarke, Williams, and Shelby promptly took a defensive position half a mile back from Musgrove's Ford. In the meantime local people supporting the American cause came in to the partisans and informed their leaders that the British post had been strengthened recently by Lieutenant Colonel Alexander Innes with 200 Provincial regulars and 100 Loyalist recruits. The Provincials included a company of the Royal New Jersey Volunteers, a reinforced company of de Lancey's New York Brigade under Captain Abraham de Peyster, and about 100 mounted infantry of the South Carolina Loyalist regiment, part of Innes's own command. Colonel Daniel Clary with a strong force of local Loyalist militia also was there and the garrison at Musgrove's Mill exceeded 500. David Fanning, the famous North Carolina Loyalist partisan, also was at Musgrove's Mill when the action took place.

As soon as Elijah Clarke, Williams, and Shelby learned the enemy's numbers, they threw up a crude breastwork of earth, cut brush and logs, and waited for the expected attack. To test the British intentions, Captain Shadrack Inman of Georgia volunteered to take a mounted patrol across the ford and probe the enemy's position, provoking the British, if possible, to follow into the prepared ambush. Inman carried out his mission as planned and Alexander Innes came out with the infantry of his garrison and pursued the retreating Georgians. Some 200 yards from Clarke and Shelby's hidden defenses, Inman swung his command around, feinted toward the enemy center, then fell back in apparent confusion. Decoyed and oblivious of the waiting American partisans, Innes's infantry came forward shouting with drums beating the charge, to be met suddenly at 70 yards by concentrated rifle and musket fire. The Provincials and militia hesitated briefly, then, urged by their officers, advanced with the bayonet, driving Shelby's frontiersmen, whose rifles had no bayonets, from their position on the right of the breastworks. The American left, attacked at the same time, held, but Clarke seeing Shelby in difficulty threw his small reserve against the exposed British right flank. With the battle at a turning point, a retreating Watauga rifleman swung and shot Colonel Innes from his saddle. Spurred on by this sight and relieved by the flank attack, Shelby's men came back yelling, with rifle, hatchet, and knife. Several of their officers had fallen in the confused fighting, and the Loyalists began to waver. Clarke suddenly brought all of his command over the barrier in a wild, stabbing, shooting counterattack. The Loyalists stood and fought, then slowly fell back in good order on the ford. Pressed on all sides by the partisans, the Loyalist retreat became a rout, the brave Georgian Captain Shadrack Inman, whose daring maneuver had set up the defeat, being killed in the pursuit. The British casualties in the hard-fought little action at Musgrove's Mill were 63 dead, 90 wounded, and 70 captured, some 50 percent of the effectives engaged. The American loss was negligible, only 4 dead and 8 or 9 wounded.

With their demoralized enemy driven across the river, Clarke and Shelby pulled back their men into the comparative safety of the forest to rest briefly and consider the next move. The big British base at Ninety Six some twenty-five miles away seemed a logical objective. While Elijah Clarke and Isaac Shelby were planning an attack, a dispatch rider arrived from Colonel Charles Caswell with the news of Horatio Gates's terrible defeat at Camden. Caswell urged that all commanders still in the field get their detachments to safety before Lord Cornwallis's advancing army cut them to pieces.

Clarke, Shelby, and Williams realized they were in a dangerous position. Patrick Ferguson and George Turnbull had joined forces and were moving into a position to cut off retreat into North Carolina. When Lieutenant Colonel John Harris Cruger at Ninety Six learned of Innes's defeat at Musgrove's Mill, he was sure to march from that base with his crack New York Provincials. Cornwallis's victorious troops were fanning out over the countryside in pursuit of Gates's broken army. It was hammer and anvil with the Americans between, so the three commanders decided to move immediately, following backwoods trails, and try to join Colonel Charles McDowell's force lying at Gilberttown, North Carolina. Hurriedly mounting the 200 men and ordering the prisoners to ride double, one to every third American, the column rode to the northwest, with Patrick Ferguson, already apprised of the British defeat at Musgrove's Mill hard after them. On 18 August, the day Sumter's command was destroyed at Fishing Creek, Ferguson arrived one-half hour after Clarke and Shelby had broken camp, but his men and horses, pushed beyond endurance, were worn out and he regretfully called off the pursuit. The victors at Musgrove's Mill got safely away, Elijah Clarke returning to Georgia to raise more partisans and Isaac Shelby marching his men back over the mountains to the Watauga River. James Williams conducted the prisoners taken at Musgrove's Mill to Hillsboro, North Carolina, where remnants of the defeated American army were slowly assembling.

Elijah Clarke reappeared with 430 men on 14 September and invested a British-held post called the White House or McKay's Trading Post about a mile and a half west of Augusta, Georgia, defended by Thomas Browne with a mixed garrison of Loyalists and Cherokee Indians. Browne resisted all attempts to dislodge him until a British relief column from Ninety Six forced Clarke to raise the siege after suffering 60 casualties. Unfortunately, Clarke, in his haste to withdraw before he was caught between the defenders and the soldiers from Ninety Six, had to leave his wounded. The vindictive Browne, shot in both legs, ordered 13 of the hapless prisoners hanged in his presence and turned over the others to the Cherokees who tortured them to death. This action was to set the mood of intense hatred between Clarke and Browne that lasted throughout the war.

After this unsuccessful action Clarke took his 300 remaining men and the 400 women and children, the families of American partisans, on a two-hundred-mile march to safety among the settlers over the mountains on the Watauga and Nolichucky rivers.

On 21 September the irrepressible William Davie, in the midst of disaster, carried out another daring raid when he surprised and routed a detachment of Loyalist infantry and a unit of Tarleton's dragoons camped at Wahub's plantation, just across the Catawba River from Cornwallis's main camp about forty miles south of Charlotte, North Carolina. In his usual manner, Davie suddenly struck from two sides of the camp with a mounted charge, leaving 20 killed and 40 wounded on the ground. As he rode away with 96 captured horses and 120 stands of arms, his men could hear Cornwallis's army across the river vainly beating to quarters. One of Davie's men was wounded in the operation.

Again at Charlotte, North Carolina, on 26 September 1780 Davie with less than 200 men held up the entire advance guard of Cornwallis's army, checking and forcing back the cavalry of Tarleton's Legion. It was not until Cornwallis personally ordered forward the light infantry that Davie was driven from his position around the Charlotte Court House. In this action a handful of men led by a truly professional soldier successfully delayed a British army and inflicted considerable casualties before breaking off the engagement and retreating in good order. To be fair, Tarleton's Legion on this occasion was not led by the redoubtable Tarleton himself, who was temporarily out of action, down with yellow fever, but by his second in command, Major George Hanger.

After his return from the escort mission across the mountains, Elijah Clarke with Colonel John Twiggs commanded the Georgia contingent at the battle of Blackstocks on 20 November 1780. Three weeks later, 12 December 1780, Clarke and Colonel James McCall with only 100 veteran partisans surprised near Long Cane, South Carolina, a British column of 450 men marching from Ninety Six to clear the Long Cane area of guerrilla activity. Clarke, leading the advance, routed 200 Loyalist militia attached to the column, then hit the Provincial regulars forming for a counterattack. Clarke fell seriously wounded by the first British volley, and his men broke off the action to carry him to safety. Recovering slowly from injuries thought at first to be mortal, Elijah Clarke did not take the field again until he joined Henry Lee and Andrew Pickens during late May of 1781 in the successful attack on forts Grierson and Cornwallis defending British-held Augusta, Georgia.

Ten days before the action at Long Cane, 2 December 1780, Major General Nathanael Greene of Rhode Island had assumed command of American forces in the South, replacing the luckless Horatio Gates. The various partisan commanders thus came under his direction, and, at least in theory, the days of independent, uncoordinated actions were over. From July until December 1780 the partisans in South Carolina alone had inflicted on the British and Loyalist forces a loss of 1,200 killed and wounded with 1,286 captured. The American guerrilla fighters had sustained during the same period 497 killed or wounded and 320 taken prisoner. The men of the South had inflicted three times the number of casualties on their enemy as they suffered themselves. These figures, of course, include the brilliant raids and skirmishes of Francis Marion in the South Carolina low-country and the destruction or capture of Patrick Ferguson's force of 900 men at Kings Mountain on 7 October 1780 by riflemen from North Carolina, South Carolina, Georgia, and Virginia.

Partisan operations had compelled Lord Cornwallis to abandon his plan to invade North Carolina in 1780. By slowly bleeding the British, the partisans helped forge the first links in the chain of events that would lead to Cowpens, Guilford Court House, and Charles Cornwallis's surrender at Yorktown.

CHAPTER IX

The Battle of Kings Mountain, 7 October 1780

The battle of Kings Mountain fought in upper South Carolina on 7 October 1780 was an important step toward the eventual British defeat in the South. From the point of view of the military historian, it also is an extremely interesting engagement. At Kings Mountain, two approximately equal forces employing totally different battle doctrines met, and the formal eighteenth-century European method of land warfare gave way in the face of frontier American forest tactics based on accurate rifle fire and a flexible attack.

The reader must remember that the revolutionary war in the southern theater of operations was a savage, cruel civil conflict: brother against brother and neighbor opposed to neighbor. With the exception of Major Patrick Ferguson, who commanded the troops fighting under the British flag, all participants in the battle were Americans. Ferguson was a Scot, an officer in the British army, but his corps included 800 North and South Carolina Loyalist militia supported by 100 Provincial infantry from the middle states trained, equipped, and uniformed as British regulars. Patrick Ferguson's second in command was Captain Abraham de Peyster, a member of an old and distinguished New York family. Captain Samuel Ryerson, a New Jersey officer in Ferguson's command, claimed Dutch descent. Lieutenant Anthony Allaire, whose journal is one of the best sources for the action and its tragic aftermath, was a New York Huguenot.

The men who defeated Ferguson came from the farms and little towns of backcountry North Carolina, South Carolina, Georgia, and Virginia. A strong contingent of them were wild hunters out of the new Watauga, Nolichucky, and Holston settlements west of the mountains in what is now Tennessee.

Kings Mountain was a turning point in the American Revolution with a grim twist of irony: 900 Americans fighting with gallant desperation for strongly held loyalty to their king were doomed to be almost annihilated by 940 Americans equally dedicated to the freedom of their new homeland. Terrain and weapons were essential determinants in Ferguson's terrible defeat. Kings Mountain became a battlefield test of two military systems: the classic eighteenth-century European concept of close-order, disciplined volley fire supported by bayonet charges, opposed to precision-fire riflemen advancing from cover to cover in open order, falling back before the bayonet rushes, and returning

Figure 16.   Battle of Kings Mountain, South Carolina, 7 October 1780, by Robert Wilson

again to fight with the rifle from tree to tree as Ferguson's bayonet men, frustrated and weary, retreated uphill to their position.

The American partisans were armed chiefly with the long Deckhard or Dickert rifle, a muzzle-loading, flintlock piece of from 43 to 54 caliber. In the hands of a good rifleman, and the backwoodsmen at Kings Mountain were all excellent marksmen, the Dickert had an accurate killing range of about 300 yards. Using the greased patch system of reloading, the average rifleman could deliver one aimed shot a minute while an expert might fire two. The frontier rifle, however, remained essentially a hunting weapon and was too lightly constructed for successful use unloaded with a butt stroke in hand-to-hand fighting. Nor was it equipped for the standard socket bayonet; most of the partisans, after the Indian fashion, instead used hatchet and knife. This meant that the rifle had to be switched to the left hand or dropped for close work, a decided disadvantage against soldiers using musket and bayonet in a set field battle. Such a battle, however, Kings Mountain definitely was not. The British Provincial rangers serving at Kings Mountain and many of the Loyalist militia carried regular-issue smoothbore "Brown Bess" flintlock muskets weighing about 10 or 12 pounds and equipped with a socket bayonet. The muskets usually were of 75 caliber and loaded with buckshot plus a solid soft lead ball running about 14 to the pound. These bayonet-equipped muskets in the hands of steady soldiers became fearsome close-range weapons. A smoothbore is much faster loading than a rifle and a well-trained infantry soldier could discharge his musket three to five times a minute. An eighteenth-century musket, however, was a singularly inefficient piece with an accurate range of 88 to 90 yards and approximately a 9-foot error at 200 yards. Those among Patrick Ferguson's Loyalist militia not armed with the bayoneted "Brown Bess" were issued long knives with specially tapered wooden hilts that could be jammed into a rifle or fowling piece muzzle to form a crude plug bayonet. Obviously such an arrangement meant the weapon could not be reloaded without removing the bayonet, thus making it nothing but a combination club and spear as long as the knife was in place. No artillery was used in the battle by either side, and the American partisans had no saber-armed cavalry. They came to the battle mounted but dismounted in frontier fashion to fight on foot. Ferguson's cavalry consisted of 20 sword-armed horsemen, not enough to use as an effective shock force, which undoubtedly was one of the reasons he chose a thickly wooded hilltop as a battle position.

Weapons are stressed because the battle of Kings Mountain, or any other eighteenth-century battle, cannot be understood unless one comprehends exactly at what short range these people actually fought. Ferguson's men stood in their ranks and discharged disciplined volley fire on the order at an enemy shooting from cover at 200 yards or more, twice the accurate range the British muskets would carry (the American rifle had a killing range of 300 yards). Firing downhill is always difficult even with modern high-velocity weapons. If a muzzle is not depressed below an aiming point to compensate for the slope, a bullet will lift, and this is exactly what happened. Most of the volleys fired from the hill crest went over the heads of the frontiersmen moving up the slope, crouching behind trees, rocks, or bushes to take careful aim at the Loyalists silhouetted against the skyline.

When the Loyalists were given the order by Ferguson to charge with the bayonet, the terrain forced them to rush headlong down a steep incline, then fall back up the slope under constant aimed harassing fire. The partisans faded down the hill before the charges, moving easily in hunting shirt, leggings, and moccasins. When the enemy retreated, the partisans reloaded and followed from cover to cover, firing on targets of opportunity.

Why did Patrick Ferguson, a good and experienced soldier, choose a position impossible to defend against rifle-armed opponents using frontier forest tactics? No one really knows. It is true that he held the American backcountrymen in vast military contempt referring to them as "back watermen" and "mongrels." This sad underestimation of his enemy must have influenced his decision to select a seemingly impregnable position and make a stand even though Cornwallis with a British field army lay only thirty-five to forty miles away. A hard day's or night's march would have brought Ferguson and his command to safety and possible changed the course of history. The defeat at Kings Mountain and the loss of a splendid officer and some of his best light troops compelled Cornwallis to abandon the plan for an invasion of North Carolina.

Patrick Ferguson was aware that a large partisan force was closing in on him. Two deserters had come in to his camp and brought warning of the pursuit. He is said to have stated after he selected the final position that he was on Kings Mountain: he was king of that mountain and God Almighty could not drive him off it. This, of course, is pure arrogance, a facet of Ferguson's character that clearly contributed to the disaster, but, unhappily for him and his men, his denigration of the frontier fighting man was matched by his overestimation of the strength of his position. There was not even a proper water supply near the summit of Kings Mountain where he made his stand. The nearest spring lay more than halfway down the north slope and fell into partisan hands soon after the battle started.

What remains most puzzling is that Ferguson himself was an expert rifle shot and had invented and demonstrated to the British military authorities a superior and practical breech-loading flintlock military rifle equipped with a bayonet. While shorter and heavier than the American hunting rifle, it had an accurate killing range of over 200 yards, and Ferguson proved in England that he could deliver with this weapon five aimed shots a minute and hit a man-size target at 100 yards four times out of five. Only 200 of these excellent rifles were made during the revolutionary war. Rigid army conservatism and suspicion of "newfangled" inventions prevented their adoption by British forces, and apparently few were in the hands of his troops, even the crack 100 Provincials at Kings Mountain. Abraham de Peyster, Ferguson's second in command, seems to have used one and possibly some of the other officers had the breech-loaders. Patrick Ferguson carried his own special rifle. He had lost the use of his right arm from a wound received at the Brandywine, however, where, according to legend, Ferguson, lying in ambush, had spared the life of George Washington. The crippled right arm probably prevented the gallant major from using his favorite weapon at Kings Mountain. He was killed at the end of the action, charging on horseback the encircling partisans with a sword in his good left hand.

Major Patrick Ferguson presents an interesting study in leadership. He came from Scottish gentry and joined the British regular army at the age of fourteen when his father purchased him a cornetcy in the North British Dragoons (modern Scots Greys). A frail man with a driving spirit though physically ill through much of his life, he was forced to resign military service because of bad health. Pushed by an overriding ambition to be a soldier, he entered the army again in 1768 as a captain in the 70th Foot Regiment, invented and demonstrated his superior rifle, then volunteered for the American war. Ferguson did not attain his majority until 1779 at the age of thirty-four, old for an eighteenth-century major, a brilliant, ailing, bitter, very proud man, whose marked abilities and advanced-design rifle the authorities had chosen to ignore.

He was made inspector general of Loyalist militia in Georgia and the two Carolinas by Sir Henry Clinton and Lord Cornwallis in 1780, but Cornwallis never really trusted

Figure 17.
Major Patrick Ferguson, by Robert Wilson

Ferguson. He clearly was highly intelligent and a fine combat officer, but his commander feared Ferguson's willful, impulsive, and somewhat erratic personality. In 1780 Cornwallis wrote Lieutenant Colonel Nisbet Balfour, then British commander at Ninety Six, that he was afraid of Ferguson getting to the frontier of North Carolina and "playing some cussed trick," which Ferguson, of course, did proceed to do.

Another factor should be considered in the fateful choice of battle position, again related to Ferguson's background and nature. He was a keen sportsman and well-born Scottish gentleman, professionally frustrated, mistrusted, deeply ambitious, and therefore anxious for personal glory. He had become weary of running from men he considered to be immeasurably his inferiors whom he was quite sure would not stand up in battle to British-trained troops. He was aware that American militia had broken and run when faced by a bayonet charge at Camden and on several other occasions in the northern theater of operations. He expected them to break again. Ferguson did take the precaution of sending mounted couriers to Cornwallis only thirty-five miles away and to John Harris Cruger holding Ninety Six. His dispatch riders either were intercepted by partisan patrols or arrived too late for reinforcements to reach him. The fact remains that Ferguson chose to make a stand on a narrow, wooded hilltop and did not even bother to clear a field of fire down the surrounding slopes or throw up barricades and abatis with the plentiful timber readily available on all sides. He had time enough to accomplish these things before the attack. His failure to take precautions does not make sense, tactically or otherwise, but this is a question of human personality and its effects on events, military and otherwise.

To give him full credit, Patrick Ferguson seems to have had a personal affinity with frontier Americans. He looked down on them, socially and professionally, but he liked them, and they liked him. He would sit down and talk for hours with farmers whose loyalty to the crown had begun to waver and argue his case with humor, comprehension, and sympathy. Ferguson also was a chivalrous and humane man who would not tolerate acts of cruelty to women or children, even when men of their families were in arms against him. The result was that Loyalists, by conviction or conversion at his hand, flocked to the major's banner. These he armed and trained to fight as regular British soldiers. In an area other than the wilderness around Kings Mountain, on a battleground where classic European tactics were possible, he probably would have been successful.

Clinton and Cornwallis already had captured and garrisoned Savannah, Charleston, Beaufort, and Georgetown. They had won the battles at the Waxhaws, Camden, and Fishing Creek, while a growing network of fortified towns and outposts was being established to control conquered Georgia and South Carolina. Cornwallis, now British commander of the Southern Department, had decided that subjugation of North Carolina was not only essential to full pacification of Georgia and South Carolina but would lead to an eventual invasion and conquest of Virginia. Patrick Ferguson had been detached into the northwestern section of South Carolina and what is now Tryon County, North Carolina, to show the flag, intimidate the "rebels," raise and train Loyalist soldiers, and cover Cornwallis's western flank on his march into North Carolina.

Operating around Gilberttown, North Carolina, Ferguson had defeated the local leader, Colonel Charles McDowell, and driven him with some of his North Carolina militia over the mountain passes. McDowell and his men had taken refuge among the scattered frontier settlements in the transmontane area. Patrick Ferguson, following up his victory over McDowell, sent a verbal message by a paroled prisoner taken in the recent operation to the commanders of the frontier militia settled along the western waters of the Watauga, Nolichucky, and Holston rivers. The message staged that if the frontiersmen did not cease their opposition to British arms, he would march over the mountains, hang their leaders, and lay waste their country with fire and sword. This communication, added to the presence of McDowell and his desperate refugees, had exactly the opposite effect from that which Ferguson confidently expected.

The paroled prisoner who carried Ferguson's message was Samuel Philips, a distant relative of Colonel Isaac Shelby, who after the Revolution became governor of the new state of Kentucky and already had achieved considerable prominence as a leader on the southern frontier. When Shelby received the warning from Ferguson, he ordered his best horse saddled and rode fifty miles to carry the news to his friend, Lieutenant Colonel John Sevier, who commanded the militia in Washington County, North Carolina (now part of Tennessee). John Sevier was elected the first governor of Tennessee when that state was formed. The two men agreed to coordinate their actions, bring in all the support they could muster, and attack Ferguson before he could attack them.

The full force of the entire district was reckoned at 1,000 fighting men. Leaving half of these to guard the settlements against the still dangerous Cherokees, about 480 riflemen rode to the rendezvous at Sycamore Shoals on the Watauga River. Dispatch riders having been sent to western Virginia, Colonel William Campbell, a six-foot-two-inch redheaded Scot who carried his ancestral Highland broadsword, rode south to join the growing little army with 400 more riflemen. With Colonel Charles McDowell's 160 North Carolina refugee militia the column numbered over 1,000 men, all well mounted and most armed with deadly rifles.

The rendezvous at Sycamore Shoals must have been quite a sight. This was a people's army, and the women and children came with food and clothing for their men and to say good-bye to fathers, sons, and brothers marching to war. The southern frontier settlers were a deeply religious people who worshiped a stern and righteous God, and the prayers offered by the Reverend Samuel Doak were grim and appropriate. He preached from the Old Testament on Gideon's people rising against the Midianites and told the assembled riflemen to take as their battle cry, "The Sword of Gideon and the Lord." Very clearly, Ferguson and his men were seen as the Midianites.

This was a very informal, if deadly, little army, that rode without a supply column, each soldier carrying spare ammunition, clothing, and rations strapped behind his saddle. The men who followed Sevier, Shelby, and Campbell were big, shaghaired, rawboned southern frontiersmen, mean as rattlesnakes in a fight, schooled in savage, no-quarter Indian warfare where white flags had no significance and surrender meant torture followed by merciful death. This also was an army without uniforms, although a few of the officers had swords. Most of the soldiers wore linen hunting shirts, with buckskin leggings and moccasins. Broad-brimmed wool hats completed their eminently practical costume for campaigning in a hot and forested country.

On 26 September the men from over the mountains began their march, and on the second day two soldiers deserted—an all-too-frequent occurrence in the American Revolution—these being the same two who carried the news of the pursuit to Ferguson. When the frontier militia reached the eastern foothills on 30 September, they were joined by 350 troops from Wilkes and Surry counties, North Carolina, led by Major Joseph Winston and Colonel Benjamin Cleveland, the latter noted as a ruthless Indian fighter. Camped in a gap at South Mountain, the officers of the several detachments agreed on 2 October that Colonel William Campbell of Virginia should be overall commander of the expedition. This honor belonged properly to the senior officer, Colonel Charles McDowell of North Carolina, but he was sent instead to try to persuade the famous Daniel Morgan of Virginia to come south and lead the attack against Ferguson. Thus Charles

McDowell, whose flight to the Watauga settlements had sparked the operation, was absent when the battle took place at Kings Mountain, and his men were led by Major Joseph McDowell, the colonel's younger brother.

During the day of 4 October while the army waited at South Mountain 30 Georgians rode in behind Major William Candler and a Captain Johnston. These two officers were veteran partisan fighters who had served under Colonel Elijah Clarke, the famous Georgia guerrilla leader. Shortly thereafter Colonel Edward Lacey and Colonel William Hill joined the expedition with 100 South Carolinians, most of them from York and Chester counties. It was a tough and dedicated group of frontier fighters that marched from South Mountain to the selected prebattle assembly point at Saunders' Cowpens, the site of an even more decisive battle on 17 January of the next year. Here at the designated rendezvous Colonel Frederick Hambright, Colonel Joseph Graham, and Major William Chronicle came in with 60 volunteers from the Gilberttown and South Ford areas in North Carolina, while the disputatious, aggressive, and able Colonel James Williams joined the growing army with 60 more North Carolinians.

The combined force now almost 1,300 strong was assembled and its officers chose 940 of the best mounted and armed men to close in on Ferguson for the death hunt. These included 200 picked riflemen from Campbell's command, 120 under Shelby, 120 led by Sevier, 110 men following Cleveland, 90 with Joseph McDowell, and 60 under Winston. Edward Lacey and William Hill commanded their 100 South Carolinians, Hambright and Chronicle led 50 picked soldiers, and Candler's 30 Georgians formed part of James Williams's unit of 90 selected riflemen.

William Campbell and his column now rode toward Kings Mountain in anticipation of battle. The partisans already had received intelligence from a spy, Joseph Kerr, which pinpointed Ferguson's march route and probable position. Kerr, a cripple who used his physical condition to allay suspicion, had posed as a confirmed Loyalist and entered Ferguson's camps. There he obtained all the information needed to make a full report to the partisans of their enemy's movements and destination. To validate Joseph Kerr's information, Enoch Gilmer of William Chronicle's command carried out two scouting expeditions. Apparently Gilmer was an accomplished natural actor who easily persuaded local pro-British farmers of his confirmed Loyalist convictions. By prearrangement, during the second trip William Chronicle rode up with his men and "captured" Gilmer. Chronicle proposed to hang his "prisoner" from a tree by the farmhouse door, a prospect that terrified the women at the house. Seemingly persuaded by their frightened pleas, he consented to hang Gilmer elsewhere, so that his uneasy ghost might not haunt the place of execution. When they were out of sight the noose was thrown off and Gilmer related gleefully everything he had discovered concerning Ferguson's movements, thus preserving the clever scout's role as a Loyalist for future occasions. How Gilmer later was to explain his miraculous escape from death is not related. All news he gathered, however, pointed to Kings Mountain as the place to find Ferguson. A woman at a farm on the approach road to the mountain told Campbell's advance guard that she had sold chickens to Ferguson's men on the ridge at Kings Mountain. A young girl came out from another supposedly Loyalist homestead to watch the partisans ride by. She suddenly pointed to the now visible hills and called out, "Ferguson is up there." As the column neared the low mountain, several other Loyalist settlers were captured, brought in, and interrogated. They all said that Ferguson was on Kings Mountain.

The Kings Mountain range is only about sixteen miles in length, extending generally from the northeast in North Carolina southwesterly into South Carolina. The ridge where the battle was fought is in York County, South Carolina, about a mile and a half from the North Carolina line. It is some 600 yards long and about 250 yards wide from one base to the other. The top of the ridge itself is from 60 to 120 yards wide, tapering to the southwest, so narrow that even the musket of the period would carry easily at killing range across the battle area. The summit of the hill is about 60 feet above the surrounding country, and it was at the northeast or wide end of the ridge that Ferguson chose to stand and fight.

William Campbell's men rode in a fine drizzling rain throughout the night of 6 October, arriving at the base of the hill in the early hours of the morning of the 7th. About a mile from Kings Mountain the partisans dismounted and tied their horses, leaving behind a small guard. The battle would be fought on foot, and the attack force was divided accordingly into two columns that would move around the ridge on both sides and attack from all directions. William Campbell commanded the right flanking column of 470 men and Benjamin Cleveland the left of 440 men. Cleveland's and Sevier's forces would unite to complete the surrounding movement at the northeast end, while Campbell and Shelby were to close off all escape at the southwest, completing the encirclement.

Because of the difficult terrain and heavy forest, the backwoods riflemen were not discovered by Ferguson's pickets thrown out on the hill slopes until the Loyalists spotted the hunting-shirted riflemen advancing through the trees about a quarter of a mile away. The partisans had approached so close they could hear the British drums beating to quarters and Ferguson's famous silver whistle calling his men to battle stations.

Campbell and Shelby, coming up on two sides of the southwest ridge, were the first to enter the fighting, while the other frontier commanders still were working into position around the hill. At three o'clock in the afternoon of 7 October 1780, Campbell leading his Virginians is said to have suddenly shouted, "Here they are, my brave boys; shout like hell and fight like devils"—which the backcountry riflemen proceeded to do. They raised what has been called the "Tennessee Yell," a wild war shout probably derived from the terrible Cherokee war scream. In later, equally stirring times, its lineal descendant was to be immortalized as the "Rebel Yell." The author's grandfather, who served as a boy cavalry soldier under Fighting Joe Wheeler, taught the rebel yell to his Episcopal clergyman son, who in turn taught it to his sons. It is a most warlike and inspiring sound, having much the same effect on its users that bagpipes do on a Scottish Highland regiment moving into action. Captain Abraham de Peyster, a civilized, gently bred New Yorker and Ferguson's second in command, had heard the same high, keening battle cry at hard-fought Musgrove's Mill where he faced Isaac Shelby's riflemen for the first time. It is reported that he said, "These things are ominous, these are the damned yelling boys."

Ferguson's Provincial regulars and militia on his orders formed a rough square and fired disciplined volleys at the partisans moving up the slopes from tree to tree. Most of the volleys went over the heads of the crouching frontiersmen. Volley fire combined with directed bayonet charges was the classic European style of warfare, and Campbell's men were the first to receive an in-line bayonet charge. A few of the Virginians stood their ground with hatchet, knife, or clubbed rifle and were bayoneted where they fought. The rest retreated in good order down the hill, reformed, reloaded, and returned to the attack. While Ferguson's elite red-coated Provincial rangers were forcing back Campbell,

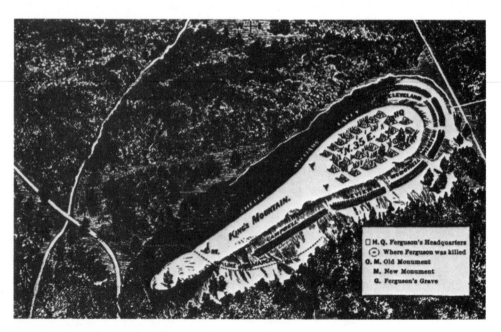

Figure 18.   Battle of Kings Mountain, South Carolina, 7 October 1780, from *The History of South Carolina in the Revolution, 1775–1780*, Edward McCrady (New York, 1901)

Figure 19.
Colonel William Campbell, by Robert Wilson

Shelby advanced with his contingent up the opposite side of Kings Mountain and brought the less disciplined South Carolina and North Carolina Loyalist militia under heavy fire. Ferguson swung his devoted Provincial company across the ridge and drove Shelby back and down with the bayonet. The summit of the ridge was bare of trees whereas the slopes were heavily wooded. The woods plus the steepness of the slopes impeded the downhill bayonet charges, but the cleared ridge made Ferguson's men, particularly the red-coated Provincials, clear targets to the riflemen firing from ranges the muskets could not reach.

As the circle tightened with the several partisan units moving into their assigned areas, Lacey and Hill with the York and Chester County men pressed up the northern slope to engage Ferguson's square from that side. At the same time Hambright and Chronicle led their men toward the crest of the northeastern side of the ridge. William Chronicle was killed by a musket shot while near the base of the mountain, but Frederick Hambright fought his way almost to the top, only to be beaten back by a bayonet charge led personally by Abraham de Peyster. With defense pressures directed elsewhere, Sevier on Campbell's right drove to the top of the ridge, pushing the left front of Ferguson's square in on the center. Cleveland had been impeded by swampy ground but, when he did come into position, added the weight of his contingent to Hambright's attack on the northeast sector. Winston also now came up on Hambright's left, and Joseph McDowell, filling a gap on the eastern slope, led his riflemen up and forward. James Williams, fractious to the last and still angry from an earlier altercation with Lacey and

Hill, at first refused to join the fight. Yielding to impulse, he suddenly shouted, "Come on boys, the old wagoner never yet backed out," and charged with his and Candler's 90 rifles up the slope in support of Shelby's embattled left. Williams was to fall mortally wounded at the very end of the action, one of the last fatalities at Kings Mountain.

Campbell and Shelby had borne the brunt of the fighting, having been driven back three times by desperate bayonet charges and nearly routed by the last Loyalist attack. Ferguson's preoccupation with these sectors of the action had permitted the encirclement, and as a partisan contingent was pushed back with cold steel, others would gain the ridge summit and shoot down the Loyalists in their ranks at point-blank range. When a bayonet charge fell back slowly to the crest, riflemen would follow, killing their enemy from behind cover with carefully aimed fire.

Finally, all the partisan units were in position and pressing up the slopes from every direction. The death circle was complete and Ferguson's corps, weary, discouraged, suffering heavy casualties, and running out of ammunition, began to waver. Ferguson had been wounded in the right hand but continued to ride on his horse from threatened point to threatened point, a clear target for enemy riflemen, encouraging his men with cool and desperate courage to continue the fight. A Loyalist militiaman raised a white flag and Ferguson rode over and cut it down with his sword. A second white flag went up at the other end of the square now pushed into a ragged circle and Ferguson rode over and cut that down too. Abraham de Peyster, more realistic, advised him to surrender, but Ferguson shouted that he would not give in to such a "damned set of banditti." Finally realizing that the day was lost, Ferguson apparently chose the ancient Celtic last mad measure of the sally, a do-or-die attempt to break a victorious enemy line by direct attack. With a few volunteers, among them Colonel Vesey Husbands of North Carolina and a South Carolina Loyalist officer, a Major Plummer, he led a mounted charge, sword swinging in his good left hand, in a vain attempt to force a breakthrough. Facing impossible odds the hopeless, if gallant, attempt failed completely. Ferguson and every man who followed him were killed outright or mortally wounded. It is claimed that at least 50 rifles were aimed at the Scottish major as he rode straight into the fire. Six or eight bullets hit him simultaneously and he toppled from his horse, to die a short time later. A stone at the northeastern end of the Kings Mountain ridge marks where he fell.

Captain Abraham de Peyster succeeded to the command and, knowing the battle was lost, raised a white flag and called for quarter. His enemies were men of the backcountry or savage hunters from west of the mountains. White flags meant nothing to them, and the massacre of helpless, beaten men continued until the partisans grew weary of killing. This was the way it was in Indian fighting. Some of the North and South Carolinians shouted "Tarleton's quarter," remembering the killing of the Virginians at the Waxhaws by Tarleton's dragoons for fifteen minutes after white flags were raised. The more responsible partisan officers tried to stop the shooting, beating down the rifles with their swords. Finally, Isaac Shelby, at the risk of his own life, rode up to within 15 yards of Ferguson's beaten corps and shouted, "Damn you, if you want quarter, thrown down your arms," and the surviving Provincials and Loyalist militia sullenly obeyed. By this time, they had been driven into a huddled group 60 yards long and less than 40 yards wide, surrounded by frontier riflemen on all sides. The main battle finally ceased after only an hour of fighting, from three to four o'clock of the afternoon of 7 October. Tragically, more killing still was to be done. A small unit of Loyalist militia that had been sent on a foraging expedition by Ferguson prior to the engagement heard the shooting and returned hastily. Seeing their comrades defeated and the partisans victorious, they opened fire. William Campbell, afraid that the survivors who just had surrendered might see this as an opportunity to make a break for freedom, ordered the men nearest him, who happened to be of James Williams's and Thomas Brandon's commands, to shoot into the prisoners as they stood massed together, helpless and weaponless. The partisans promptly obeyed this order and 100 more of Ferguson's men were shot down. The Loyalist foraging party got safely away, but not before James Williams was fatally wounded, probably by one of the retreating militiamen in the return fire.

The British losses at Kings Mountain were 119 killed, 123 wounded, and 664 captured out of 900 engaged. The partisan casualties, according to the official report, were 28 killed and 62 wounded from 940 taking part in the battle. Some reports state that Ferguson's body was defiled as it lay by the wild hunters from across the mountains. Since they were a savage, primitive lot, this dreadful fact probably is true. His enemies did, however, give Ferguson a proper burial. He lies under a big cairn of rocks at the base of the hill about 100 yards from a spring-fed trout stream, a proper resting place for a valiant Scottish gentleman who died bravely far from his homeland.

According to one story there were two women in Ferguson's camp who had followed his marches all the way from Charleston, a customary procedure in eighteenth-century armies. One, Virginia Sal or Salter, was killed early in the action and reportedly is buried with Ferguson under the cairn or more probably in one of the two common pit graves in which the Loyalist dead were interred. The other woman, Virginia Paul, survived the action and later made her way back to Cornwallis's army.

After the battle the badly wounded Loyalists were left to die on the deserted hilltop without water or medical aid. The unhappy prisoners, unwounded and walking wounded, then were marched for two days without food. The partisan army broke up, the South Carolinians and Georgians returning to their own areas of operations, the prisoners being taken into North Carolina. About a week after the engagement, while the Virginians and North Carolinians were camped some nine miles north of the present town of Rutherford, North Carolina, a complaint was made to Colonel William Campbell that certain of his Loyalist captives were robbers, assassins, and house burners, an accusation that could properly apply to both sides. A strange court, partly military and partly civil, was formed and twelve of the prisoners were tried and sentenced to death. Nine were hanged, including Colonel Ambrose Mills, whose main offense had been to command the North Carolina Loyalist militia at Kings Mountain. According to contemporary accounts, the condemned men died with great courage. The war in the southern backcountry was a very personal conflict, without mercy or even much consideration of basic justice.

Kings Mountain was the first significant military success after many American defeats, and when the news reached the North, it had a profound effect. General George Washington proclaimed it to the army in his General Orders as an important victory gained and a "proof of the spirit and resources of the country." Loyalist elements in North and South Carolina were thoroughly intimidated, supporters of the Revolution encouraged, and waverers swayed. Most important of all, Charles Cornwallis was forced to fall back into South Carolina and delay until the next year his projected invasion of North Carolina. The battle of Kings Mountain also set the scene for Nathanael Greene's arrival in the South, the formation of a new American army, an American military resurgence, and the signal victory at Cowpens on 17 January 1781. Kings Mountain thus could be called the first major step in the two-year campaign that led to Cornwallis's surrender at Yorktown and the final expulsion of the British from Georgia and the Carolinas.

CHAPTER X

The Battle of Blackstocks, 20 November 1780

John Rutledge, the refugee governor of South Carolina, writing on 6 October 1780 from his temporary headquarters at Hillsboro, North Carolina, issued a commission of brigadier general in the state militia to Colonel Thomas Sumter, who with his partisans was conducting raids against the British supply lines. Sumter was given command of all the militia in South Carolina with instructions to "embody" every man he could collect and hold this force in readiness to cooperate with Continental troops when these arrived. In the meantime, Thomas Sumter was to employ the militia to render the most efficient service possible to the beleaguered state. Governor Rutledge further advised that he wished all enemy outposts to be broken up and enemy columns throughout the country cut off from their bases and, if possible, destroyed. These were ruthless orders but this was a ruthless war, and Thomas Sumter, the Gamecock, was the man to carry them out. John Rutledge also appointed the great lowcountry partisan Colonel Francis Marion a brigadier general of the state militia, and the two famous guerrilla leaders were henceforth to command their men as part of an increasingly coordinated military effort to win back South Carolina and Georgia from the British.

On 7 October 1780 Major Patrick Ferguson and his entire corps of some 900 Loyalists were destroyed or captured at Kings Mountain, South Carolina. The action by partisan riflemen from Georgia, Virginia, and the two Carolinas checked successfully Cornwallis's first attempt to invade North Carolina. With a countryside aroused by the victory rallying against him and the guerrillas hitting his supply lines to Charleston, the British commander evacuated Charlotte, North Carolina, on 14 October and retreated into South Carolina. To complicate matters, Cornwallis contracted a severe case of malaria and Francis Lord Rawdon assumed direction of military operations in his place. Banastre Tarleton was sent ahead of the British and Loyalist regiments to scout with his dragoons for a proper wintering area. Winnsboro, South Carolina, was selected. The ill Cornwallis and his staff arrived and occupied the homes of wealthy American patriots. The troops camped in the buildings and on the grounds of a local school, Mount Zion Academy.

Horatio Gates, routed at Camden and about to be replaced by Nathanael Greene, tried to evolve a sound plan of action, using the troops that had gathered at Hillsboro after the defeat in combination with partisan groups still active in the field. He wrote, for example, to Francis Marion on 11 October and asked him to create some little diversion in the lower part of the state. Marion's answer was the skirmish at Black Mingo Creek where Colonel John Coming Ball and his Loyalists were routed. Horatio Gates then sent General William Smallwood to New Providence, North Carolina, to prepare for coordinated operations with Thomas Sumter. The redoubtable Brigadier General Daniel Morgan, who recently had rejoined the army from retirement on his Virginia farm, marched with a column on Hanging Rock, North Carolina, and William Davie with his dragoons and mounted infantry rode into the Waxhaws. Thomas Sumter was ordered to create a diversion between the Catawba and Broad rivers, while Francis Marion carried out instructions to keep the lowcountry up to the fall line (a range of high sand hills that once formed the ancient coastline) in wild confusion.

Just before Gates's replacement by Nathanael Greene, William Smallwood halted his march to join Sumter and waited for new orders. Thomas Sumter thus became an advanced spearhead of the American army marching with his command toward an encounter in the South Carolina backcountry.

The British still held the garrisoned outposts and major towns, but the sparsely settled hinterland increasingly belonged to the Americans. After Cornwallis had established his major operating base at Winnsboro, he sent an urgent request to Colonel George Turnbull of the New York Volunteers, now stationed at Camden, to send available mounted troops and drive Marion off the lines of communication to Charleston. Tarleton therefore was ordered into the lowcountry with most of his legion to conduct what proved to be a fruitless search and destroy campaign that never found the elusive Swamp Fox. Marion always stayed one jump ahead of his pursuers.

It was during Tarleton's absence from the upcountry that Major James Wemyss was ordered by Cornwallis to report to Winnsboro with his 63d Regiment. Wemyss just had completed a successful plundering expedition among the farms along the Pee Dee River and arrived with his men riding stolen horses and acting as mounted infantry. The letter detaching him from the Pee Dee area had stated that the "damned" Georgetown business (a raid by Marion) had altered totally the arrangements for Wemyss and the 63d. With Tarleton pursuing Marion, Wemyss and his regiment were needed at Winnsboro to counter Thomas Sumter, known from British intelligence to be moving again.

According to Horatio Gates's plan, Sumter was to threaten Winnsboro, forcing Cornwallis to order out his mounted troops to pursue him. It was hoped that this diversion might so weaken the British garrison that William Smallwood, with his few Continentals and all the North Carolina militia he was able to collect, could strike directly at Winnsboro and make the depleted British army fight at a numerical disadvantage.

Since William Smallwood had halted to wait instructions from the new commander due to arrive early in December, Thomas Sumter carried out his share of the assignment alone. Sumter knew that because Tarleton with the best enemy cavalry was a hundred miles away in the lowcountry chasing Francis Marion, he could operate with reasonable freedom. He therefore first made a sweep down the Sandy River to intimidate the numerous Loyalist families in that area and camped on 7 November at Moore's Mill only thirty miles from Cornwallis's headquarters. Major Wemyss, on patrol with his mounted infantry and 45 dragoons left behind by Tarleton, received intelligence that Sumter was near Moore's Mill and galloped into Winnsboro to report the information. Cornwallis gave Wemyss orders to attack Sumter's command as soon as possible. Tarleton had surprised the Gamecock at Fishing Creek, and perhaps he could again.

Late in the afternoon of 8 November the major marched up the road east of the Broad River with 45 dragoons under Lieutenant Moore Hovenden of Tarleton's Legion and the mounted infantry led by Lieutenant John Stark. Early on the same day, Sumter had captured and paroled a well-known Loyalist named Sealey, who had convinced his captors of his newly acquired revolutionary sentiments, and the Gamecock, in a hurry, let him go. The eloquent if deceitful Sealey made his way to the British column and offered to guide Wemyss and his command to Sumter's camping place. Wemyss, delighted to find such an efficient and vengeful agent, accepted Sealey's offer and assigned him and five selected dragoons the task of finding Sumter's tent and killing the partisan leader as soon as the planned attack began. The attack, however, had to be delayed because scouts sent out in advance returned and reported that Sumter and his men had broken camp. Local Loyalist information had placed the partisans five miles down the Broad River at Fish Dam Ford, so called because early inhabitants of the area, probably Indians, had built a crude stone weir across the current of the shallow stream to trap fish.

Sumter and his men, unaware of the closeness of the pursuit but operating in enemy country, established their bivouac and prepared for any eventuality. Colonel Richard Winn lay with his detachment near the riverbank to the left of the ford, while Colonel Thomas Taylor, also on the left, camped in the woods a short distance up from the stream. Colonels Edward Lacey, William Hill, and William Bratton placed their commands together on the right a few hundred yards inland from the ford, covering the approach road. Dismounted pickets were thrown out to guard against surprise and the partisans settled down for the night.

In the morning darkness Major Wemyss and his troops marching hard and fast blundered head-on into Sumter's screen. The pickets fired blindly into the British column and Wemyss, seriously wounded in the arm and leg, toppled from his horse, out of action before the fighting began. Lieutenant Stark of the 63d Regiment took command and, lacking knowledge of Wemyss's tactical plans, if any existed, gallantly if foolishly ordered a mounted charge in the dark against an unseen enemy. The riders galloping down the road to the ford were silhouetted against the scattered pickets' abandoned camp fires behind them and made excellent targets for the aroused partisans, who shot in natural enfilade positions from both sides.

In the confusion, Sealey and his five dragoon raiders rode straight through to Sumter's tent, set up right by the ford, probably one of the few tents in the encampment. Strange to say, Sumter still was deeply asleep, his orderly for reasons unknown having failed to wake him when the attack began, although it would seem the heavy firing should have accomplished that. Much the same thing had happened at Fishing Creek when Sumter's unsuspecting camp was hit by Tarleton, and the Gamecock, sleeping under a wagon, awoke in the middle of a cavalry charge and barely escaped on a saddleless wagon horse without coat, hat, and boots. Perhaps Sumter was a very sound sleeper, or possibly in accordance with time-honored South Carolina custom, he aided his slumbers with a few libations before retiring.

Before Sumter could rouse fully, dress, or buckle on weapons, the would-be murderers were upon him. He fought them off and, ducking under a tent flap, went over a rail fence and ran in his bare feet through a briar patch, without coat, hat, boots, or, on this occasion, trousers. Thomas Sumter spent the remaining hours of the night shivering in the November cold, under a cut-bank by the river. Early in the morning he found a stray horse and mounting bareback clung to the creature's neck. Sumter later claimed that the warmth of the horse's body probably saved him from freezing to death.

The wild mounted charge conducted in darkness naturally fell into disorder under the flanking fire and Lieutenant Stark, with some difficulty, pulled his troops back and reformed out of range. Cavalry tactics clearly were useless, so Stark dismounted his infantry and dragoons, formed a line with the dragoons on the right, and charged the partisan position frontally with bayonet, pistol, and saber. Colonel Taylor, stationed on the American left, met the full impact of the attack and was driven back toward the river. After discharging their pieces some of his soldiers were cut down or bayoneted where they stood. Taylor's men, however, had waited like veterans for the assault and volley fired on the command at ten paces before retreating in good order, Meanwhile, Colonel Lacey's detachment on the right came into action and poured a heavy flanking fire on the attacking British line from the protection of the woods, forcing the enemy to retreat in considerable disarray.

Lieutenant Stark, realizing that the action could not be continued without risking heavy losses and probably defeat, disengaged with commendable skill and rode away, leaving the British wounded in an abandoned cabin with a flag of truce and a warm fire. Among the 25 prisoners taken after the battle was the severely injured Major James Wemyss himself. The British lost 7 killed, the partisan casualties being 4 dead and 14 wounded. It was not a serious affair, but it hurt. When he received Stark's report, Cornwallis said with rueful and harsh humor that Wemyss obviously forgot he was an infantry officer and rode into battle. In any case, the skirmish had successfully located Sumter's column and the hunt was on. Cornwallis recalled Tarleton and his legion from their hapless pursuit of Marion and sent them with reinforcements after Thomas Sumter.

The latter, examining papers belonging to his prisoner Major Wemyss, discovered a list of houses burned during Wemyss's raid along the Pee Dee between Kingstree and Cheraw. Knowing that if his men saw the list the badly injured major would be summarily hanged or shot, Thomas Sumter, displaying unusual chivalry in this savage war, threw the papers in the fire. Wemyss eventually was exchanged and returned to England, but his wounds left him a cripple for life.

Tarleton, galloping up to Winnsboro on Cornwallis's order, met a series of couriers urging him to hasten his march. The dispatch riders also informed him that Sumter had been reported last at Hawkins Mill on the Tyger River with a thousand men. This last information happened to be true. Sumter had left Fish Dam Ford after the battle and ridden to Hawkins Mill on the Tyger, joined by volunteers as he marched, including 100 Georgia partisans led by Colonel John Twiggs, Colonel Elijah Clarke, and Majors William Candler and James Jackson. The Gamecock with his newly strengthened command began reconnaissance moves against British and Loyalist forces in the area. A force was detached to intimidate Loyalist farmers in the Lower Dutch Fork, the rich tongue of land between the Broad and Saluda rivers settled by industrious Palatine Germans and an important supply area for the British army. Colonel Thomas Taylor raided a depot at Summer's Mills, while 150 partisans rode to Brierley's on the Broad River to watch for any move by Major Archibald MacArthur waiting there with his Highlanders of the 71st Regiment for the arrival of Tarleton.

Banastre Tarleton and his legion joined MacArthur on 18 November. While the weary dragoons and mounted infantry were bathing and watering their horses at the river, Sumter's raiders rode up and opened long-range fire from the opposite bank. A dragoon horse went down and a soldier of the 63d Regiment, Wemyss's old command now under Tarleton, was slightly wounded. The British in reply brought up a 3-pounder "grasshopper," a light field gun of advanced design that could be handled by two or three men, and fired canister across the river. The partisans immediately broke off the engagement and rode away into the forest. To conceal the fact that the feared and hated legion had arrived, Tarleton first sent the red-coated Highlanders and the 63d Foot over the river on locally obtained flatboats. His dragoons and mounted infantry with their green tunics covered to conceal identity crossed that night by a ford three miles downstream.

Tarleton, moving fast on Sumter's trail, sent out mounted scouts well in advance of his column, who returned on the evening of 19 November with word that Thomas Sumter was marching in full force to attack a Loyalist-manned outpost at Williams's

Plantation. Tarleton then pushed up the bank of the Enoree River, camping late in the evening near the mouth of Indian Creek. During, the early morning hours of 20 November a soldier of the British 63d Regiment deserted, stole a horse, and made his way to the partisan camp. Sumter thus knew on 20 November that Tarleton with his legion, Archibald MacArthur's Highlanders, the mounted infantry of Wemyss's 63d Foot, and a detachment of royal artillery were on the march along the Enoree to cut the partisans off from the fords and drive them, hammer on anvil, against John Harris Cruger, waiting with a strong garrison at Ninety Six.

Since a continued retreat clearly would become increasingly dangerous and also diminish the usefulness of his original mission, the ever aggressive Sumter decided to halt and offer battle. He called in his colonels, and they all advised that a strong position be found and a stand made. This was a serious decision, pitting American partisan militia against British regulars and well-trained Provincials, but Colonel Thomas Brandon, operating in his own country, advised that a good place for a successful fight would be the nearby farm of Captain William Blackstock. This homestead was situated among the high wooded hills overlooking the Tyger River with stout log buildings and rail fences from which rifle and musket men could deliver fire. There also was a ford at the bottom of the hill behind the house with a road leading through the river swamp if retreat became necessary. The house site on its hill is still there, although the buildings disappeared long ago, and the wilderness has returned, but one may trace the old road to the abandoned ford and look down the now wooded slope up which Tarleton's men once charged.

The decision was made, and Sumter swung his command around, crossed the Enoree River, and marched toward Blackstock's farm. He left a small detachment under Patrick Carr at the ford of the Enoree to watch for and delay the pursuit if possible.

Tarleton broke camp before daylight and pushed rapidly forward. Late in the morning of 20 November, his scouts found Sumter's trail and the British commander ordered a forced march to strike Sumter before he could cross the Tyger. Carr, watching the ford, also had been assigned to hold and guard the prisoners captured at Fish Dam Ford and in Sumter's raids, because their presence with the main column would have impeded the move to Blackstock's farm. Tarleton's leading horsemen suddenly appeared and, storming through the ford, smashed into Carr's position. The partisans mounted and retreated precipitously without offering resistance or suffering casualties, but the dragoons cut down most of the Loyalist and British prisoners before they could identify themselves. Tarleton avoids admitting this tragic error in his memoirs, stating simply that his men charged Sumter's rear guard and defeated it with considerable slaughter.

The entire day of 20 November, Tarleton followed hard on Sumter's trail. About the middle of the afternoon, realizing that the infantry and artillery could not keep up the pace, he ordered them to follow at best speed and pressed forward with his legion dragoons, mounted infantry, and the mounted infantry of the 63d Regiment.

Thomas Sumter reached Blackstock's farm late in the afternoon of the same day and began to establish his battle position. His partisans, all experienced woodsmen, built fires and prepared meager rations of meat and meal, knowing that soldiers always fight better with full stomachs. While they were cooking and eating, Mary Dillard, the mistress of a farm six miles from Blackstock's, rode in. She had seen Tarleton's line of march and brought word that the British commander was advancing without infantry or artillery.

With the enemy approaching, Sumter had to make up his mind whether to fight or ford the Tyger and disband his troops with instructions to reassemble later at an agreed rendezvous, a customary tactic of partisan captains facing an admittedly superior enemy. On this occasion, time was too short before the pursuers arrived to make such arrangements. Sumter had 1,000 men, but no artillery. These soldiers, however, were veterans of almost two years of continuous partisan warfare. The original decision prevailed to give battle at Blackstock's farm where they stood, and dispositions were made accordingly.

The Blackstock house, barns, and outbuildings were one-storied and solidly built of logs. Situated on a low hill, they commanded a forty-to-fifty-acre pasture that sloped down to a shallow stream the British must cross to mount an assault on the partisans' position. Behind the house the land pitched sharply to the fast-running Tyger River and its swamp. About 200 yards to the right of the house lay a long ridge covered with a thick growth of hardwood and pine and to the left in front of the outbuildings at the top of the pasture was a strong rail fence about one-quarter of a mile long made of heavy saplings notched one on the other, an excellent defense for riflemen firing kneeling or prone. This fence formed one side of a lane leading to the house.

The road up from the ford went by the house on its right, continued down the slope, crossed the branch, and ran over a hill facing Sumter's position where Tarleton was to marshal his attack. After studying the terrain, Sumter selected as his command post a low wooded rise west of the house across the road coming up from the ford. Colonel Henry Hampton and his riflemen were ordered to occupy the log barns around the house. These buildings were unchinked, which permitted the soldiers to fire between the heavy logs as if they were loopholes. Down from the house and along the upper edge of the field were placed the 100 Georgia riflemen commanded by Colonel Twiggs. Below the forested ridge, and on Sumter's right, the Gamecock marshaled the troops under Colonels James McCall, William Bratton, Edward Lacey, Thomas Taylor, and William Hill, with Colonel Richard Winn commanding a reserve force to Sumter's left rear, behind the house and by the river. Captain William Blackstock was absent from home, serving with Colonel Benjamin Roebuck's regiment of South Carolina militia. Mary Blackstock rushed from her house and informed Sumter that she would not tolerate any fighting on her property, but the time had passed for such remonstrances. Tarleton had arrived and begun his dispositions, preparing for the attack. He was, as Daniel Morgan said later, a "down right fighter" and personally a very brave man, but he had 270 British dragoons and mounted infantry against 1,000 partisan militia, many armed with rifles. Since Tarleton's infantry and artillery contingents were still several hours behind his advance elements, neither side had field guns.

Tarleton's main objective should have been to fix Sumter in position and hold him there, preventing escape across the river until the British support troops arrived. Instead he chose to attack frontally a numerically superior force. Major John Money, commanding the 63d Regiment, was ordered to dismount his men and move against Colonel Twiggs and the 100 Georgians placed in an advanced position cross the field. Money swung his troops into line, fixed bayonets, and went forward. Sumter, with his usual impetuosity and confident in his superior numbers, ordered Colonel William Few with 400 militia to support Twiggs's Georgians and attack down the slope across the branch, uphill against the advancing 63d Regiment. The partisans, unaccustomed to set fighting, halted halfway to the stream and discharged a volley at too great a distance to effect any damage on their enemy. While they halted to reload, John Money with his 80 regulars hit them with the bayonet, driving 500 men back on Sumter's position. As the soldiers of the 63d swept up and forward, in the excitement of battle they advanced too far and came under precision fire from Henry Hampton and his riflemen shooting at 200 yards from the log outbuildings. As usual the partisans aimed at the epaulets and stripes. Lieutenants Cope and Gibson, junior subalterns in the 63d, both were killed outright. Major John Money, personally leading the charge sword in hand, crumpled mortally wounded as his soldiers neared the woods behind the Blackstock house, still pursuing the fleeing 500.

With the British clearly preoccupied in battle on the American left, Sumter galloped over from his command post and ordered Colonel Lacey to swing quietly through the woods on the right and flank Tarleton's dragoons sitting in their saddles watching the infantry fight. Lacey approached to about 50 yards from the British left unperceived and opened fire point-blank with buckshot on the unsuspecting horsemen. Some 20 troopers went down, but a Lieutenant Skinner rallied the Legion dragoons, attacked, and drove Lacey back with the saber.

Realizing that the action wavered in the balance, Tarleton ordered a cavalry charge uphill against a prepared infantry position with riflemen firing from cover. This does not reflect favorably on his tactical judgment, but caution never was Tarleton's outstanding virtue. Charging forward with Tarleton leading to support the 63d Regiment still stubbornly holding the ground won from Few and Twiggs, so many dragoons fell from concealed rifle fire that the road to the ford was blocked by the bodies of men and fallen chargers, the wounded, still targets, struggling back over their stricken comrades and kicking, screaming horses.

Tarleton ordered a general retreat, and his cavalry and the survivors of the 63d Reg-

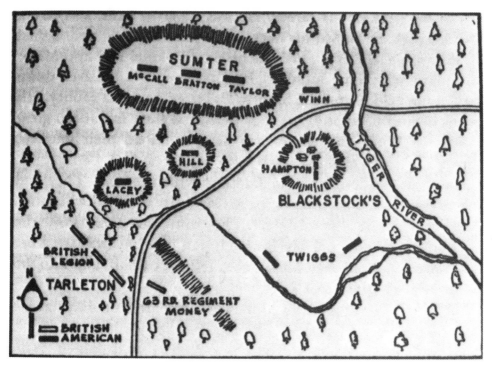

Figure 20.   Battle of Blackstocks, South Carolina, 20 November 1780, from *Gamecock* by Robert D. Bass

iment fell back in good order. As he retired with his men, completely disregarding his own safety, Tarleton swung from the saddle, picked up the unconscious John Money, slung him over the saddle bow, mounted, and carried the dying major back to the British lines in a hail of rifle bullets.

Sumter, who had ridden over to observe Colonel Lacey's flank attack on the British left, was returning to his command post on the central ridge. As reckless as Tarleton, he spurred to the American left where he could watch the dragoons and 63d withdrawing down the hill. A platoon of the 63d Regiment, grimly covering the retirement with ready loaded muskets, saw the mounted man wearing gold epaulets. The platoon halted, faced about, and fired a volley, all aiming at Sumter and the group of officers around him. A captain named Gabriel Brown was killed, but when Sumter saw the British swing into firing position he turned his right side toward the volley to protect his heart. Five buckshot raked across his chest muscles, one struck under his right shoulder, chipped his spine, and lodged under the left shoulder. Sumter reached his command post, still erect in the saddle, and dismounted, but one of his officers, Captain Robert McKelvey, was horrified to see a stream of blood running down his commander's back and splattering on the ground. He cried out that the general was wounded, but Sumter told him to be quiet. Since he could not move his right arm, he asked Colonel Henry Hampton to sheathe his sword for him, which Hampton did. Sumter then reassumed direction of the battle, but the bleeding would not stop and, calling Hampton to him, he asked that Colonel John Twiggs of Georgia, the next senior officer present, take command.

The partisans' field surgeon, Dr. Brownfield, was summoned. He and his assistants removed the general's uniform coat and shirt, turned him over on his face, and without anesthetics of any sort, dug the shot from under the left shoulder. Half-conscious, Sumter was placed in a crude litter of raw bull's hide, slung between two horses, and taken from the field and then across the ford to safety. Colonel Edward Lacey and 100 picked men went with him as a bodyguard. It is a commentary on the confused and bitter nature of the fighting in South Carolina, that Edward Lacey's father was a confirmed Loyalist.

Colonel John Twiggs, now in command, was a good officer and began promptly to exploit his considerable victory. As a result of two unsuccessful charges the British had left 92 dead and 100 wounded on the field, more than half of their force engaged. Colonel Twiggs picked up all the wounded of both sides and treated them impartially with as much humanity as time and means permitted. This fact is attested by Lieutenant Roderick McKenzie of the 71st Regiment in his "Strictures" on Tarleton's campaigns. McKenzie, who arrived later at Blackstock's farm when the infantry and artillery finally came up, was an on-the-scene observer. There were, however, only 3 American dead and 4 wounded, among them Thomas Sumter, so comparative losses were disproportionate. Tarleton, defeated for the first time in his sanguinary career, led the remnants of his command two miles from the battlefield and went into bivouac waiting for his reinforcements. He planned to attack again the next morning but John Twiggs disappointed him. With decoy camp fires left burning, the partisans abandoned their position during the night and quietly forded the river, leaving the field to the British.

Tarleton buried the dead of both sides, cared for the wounded, and reported a victory to Lord Cornwallis. He cited his own losses as 51 killed and wounded, but the partisan figure of 92 killed and 100 wounded seems to be closer to the fact. The Americans listed three killed and four wounded. Tarleton also excused an action of 270 men against 1,000 by saying that the 63d Regiment had been attacked and the fighting thus thrust upon him. Cornwallis wrote to him that he had no doubt the victory would be attended with good consequences for British affairs as it was with honor and credit to Tarleton himself. Cornwallis also expressed delight to hear that Sumter was in a position to give no further trouble because he had been the greatest plague for the British in that part of the country. Tarleton then sent a dispatch to his commander that stated his hopes for completing the destruction of all enemies in the district. He also wrote that Sumter was reported to be dead.

The battle of Cowpens, where Tarleton was to experience his greatest defeat, occurred less than two months later, on 17 January 1781. The importance of the battle of Blackstock's therefore lay in the fact that the dreaded "Bloody" Tarleton had been fought and checked by American militia, a fact that was to influence markedly the future course of the war in the South. Thomas Sumter survived his serious wound and took the field again in a few months.

CHAPTER XI

The Battle of Cowpens, 17 January 1781

The battle of Cowpens fought in upper South Carolina on 17 January 1781 well may have been the real turning point of the American Revolution. It was a culminating event, the dramatic end of a series of events that began with the savage defeat and death of Major Patrick Ferguson at Kings Mountain in October of the previous year, continued with Cornwallis's pursuit of Nathanael Greene across North Carolina and the British general's pyrrhic victory at Guilford Court House, and ended with the final siege and Cornwallis's surrender at Yorktown, Virginia. Cowpens also marks one of the few occasions when an American force met a British force of approximately equal numbers in a classic set battle on open terrain and Americans were the victors. On that day, without any question, the better army won, which makes Cowpens one of the most unusual and interesting actions of the war.

In addition to being a major American victory, Cowpens was a military encounter between two of the most colorful personalities of the revolutionary war: Brigadier General Daniel Morgan, famous leader of American frontier riflemen, and Lieutenant Colonel Banastre Tarleton, Cornwallis's dashing and ruthless commander of cavalry whose legion of light dragoons and mounted infantry was the chief British counter-guerrilla weapon in the southern theater of operations.

Daniel Morgan was born in 1736 of Welsh parentage, probably on the New Jersey side of the Delaware River. At the age of seventeen, this practically illiterate young man ran away from home and eventually wandered to the frontier of western Virginia, where he worked as a teamster, hauling supplies from Fredericksburg over the mountains. Living and working in the roughest of societies, Morgan was noted as a tough man among very tough men. As he matured he became a hard-drinking, hard-cursing brawler, adept in the eye-gouging, face-stomping technique of frontier fighting.

During the Seven Years' War, Morgan joined General Edward Braddock's army as a wagoner in the supply train on the march to Fort Duquesne. Surviving the massace of that army at the hands of the French and their Indian allies, he later antagonized a British lieutenant who struck him with the flat of his sword. Morgan promptly knocked the subaltern down, naturally was arrested, court-martialed, and sentenced to 500 lashes for striking an officer. These were administered so efficiently that his back was covered

Figure 21.
Brigadier General Daniel Morgan,
by Robert Wilson

Figure 22.
Lieutenant Colonel Banastre Tarleton,
by Robert Wilson

thereafter with deep scars and ridges where the whip tore the flesh away. It is a wonder that he survived such a punishment; many men who were so brutally lashed died. Morgan would say that the soldier assigned the task of administering the whipping had miscounted—only 499 instead of the sentenced 500 were given and the British government still owed him one. This single lash he applied in the opposite direction whenever his riflemen met the royal army.

When, after Braddock's defeat, western Virginia came under French attack, Morgan joined the army he hated and over the next six years, 1757 to 1763, developed a reputation as an expert woodsman and Indian fighter. The French and Indians had evolved a method of wilderness warfare which the British, except for a few special ranger units, never learned. In spite of his skill, Morgan was once ambushed by an enemy scouting party. His two companions were killed outright and he was hit in the neck and face by a musket slug that carried away all the teeth in his left lower jaw and scarred him for life.

Morgan therefore was an experienced soldier and a noted fighter well before the

Revolution. After the Seven Years' War he took up land near Battletown, Virginia, some ten miles east of Winchester. Legend has it that Morgan was at least partially responsible for Battletown's name—it was a rough tavern center where Morgan ruled as king of the fisticuff, gouge, and stomp set. Since there also is an old Virginia family named Battle, the town probably was founded by a member or members of that clan, but its more colorful, if legendary, origin has a certain appeal which bears repeating. Morgan married a local farmer's daughter, a strong-minded lass who proceeded to civilize him, and by 1771 he had become under her firm, stern guidance a respectable and reasonably prosperous frontier landowner. In the same year he was given a commission by the acting royal governor of Virginia as a captain in the Frederick County militia.

When the Revolution came in 1775, Morgan was selected to be captain of one of the ten rifle companies raised in Pennsylvania, western Maryland, and Virginia. He served with his 96 riflemen at the siege of Boston and was chosen by George Washington to accompany Benedict Arnold on the terrible march up the Kennebec River and across the Height of Land to Quebec. Morgan was captured in the unsuccessful attack on that city and exchanged late in 1776. Returning to the Continental army, he was promoted to colonel and given command by Washington of 500 picked riflemen.

With this soon-to-be famous corps, Morgan maintained a constant pressure on the British in the middle states until Washington detached him to the northern theater when "Gentleman Johnny" Burgoyne marched south from Canada. The American commander in chief told General Israel Putnam that the people in the northern army were so frightened by the Indians serving with Burgoyne that he was sending Morgan and his rifles to fight the savages in their own way. Morgan and Benedict Arnold successfully defeated Burgoyne, although Horatio Gates took and was given the credit, thus developing a reputation with Congress and self-delusions of military ability that later were to prove his undoing at Camden, South Carolina.

Morgan, who rightfully felt that his brilliant efforts at Quebec and Saratoga were largely ignored by the Continental Congress, became bitter and resentful. As a forty-four-year-old colonel he had asked for promotion from Congress—a request supported by George Washington—and that promotion had been denied. Morgan resigned from the army in disgust and went home to his farm near Battletown. After Horatio Gates was beaten and lost most of his army outside of Camden, Washington called on Nathanael Greene and Daniel Morgan to save the day in the South. Morgan agreed to accept a command post if he were made brigadier general. This request was granted, and he rode from Virginia to his day of glory.

The background of his adversary at Cowpens, the dashing Lieutenant Colonel Banastre Tarleton, was entirely different. Tarleton came from a wealthy, upper-middle-class family in Liverpool, England. The young man attended Oxford University and was destined for a legal career when the American Revolution began. He promptly applied for and obtained a commission in the cavalry, volunteering for service overseas in the rebellious colonies. A famous portrait of Tarleton painted after the war by Sir Joshua Reynolds catches the essential spirit of the man. It portrays him posing in his green dragoon uniform, a short, stocky, soldierly figure with finely chiseled, rather sensual features, his vanity and sense of drama evident on the canvas. According to one story, just prior to the army's sailing for North America, Tarleton in full regimentals and wearing a huge saber swaggered into a favorite London coffee house where he drew the weapon and brandished it over his head, proclaiming loudly all the dire punishments he intended for the ungrateful colonists of North America.

Tarleton proved to be a completely ruthless, if sometimes too impetuous, commander in the field, who understood instinctively the harsh but true fact that the only way to win a war is to defeat and, if possible, destroy the enemy. Placed in command of the British Legion, a mixed force of green-uniformed dragoons and light infantry recruited mainly from the Loyalists in the New York and New Jersey areas, he came south with Clinton and Cornwallis in 1779. As related earlier, Tarleton scattered Isaac Huger and William Washington's cavalry near Monck's Corner and at Lenud's Ferry on the Santee River in 1780. Shortly thereafter, he practically destroyed Abraham Buford's Virginia infantry at the Waxhaws. This last engagement was carried out with such ferocity that "Tarleton's quarter" became a byword in the Carolinas and set the tone of intense savagery that characterized the war in the South. This is the man who was to meet and be defeated by Daniel Morgan.

After Horatio Gates's rout at Camden, Nathanael Greene and Daniel Morgan were sent to the South with a mission to retrieve, if possible, the almost hopeless military situation in that theater of action. George Washington and his army were stalemated by Sir Henry Clinton in the North. The French alliance so far had brought no effective military help, and victory or defeat for the thirteen states hung in the balance, with the latter appearing far more likely.

Known Loyalist elements were strong in the South, a fact on which the British were relying to bring their southern campaign to a successful conclusion. If Georgia, the Carolinas, and Virginia could be conquered, pacified, and separated from New England and the middle states, there seemed small hope for independence. This was Sir Henry Clinton's plan and was adopted by his successor, Cornwallis, although Clinton believed, probably correctly, that Georgia and South Carolina were the key areas where complete victory must be achieved before any further moves could be made. Cornwallis on the other hand, considered the wealthy and populous state of Virginia the most important strategic objective, a decision that would lead him finally to Yorktown and surrender.

When Nathanael Greene took command at Charlotte, North Carolina, on 2 December 1780 he found only a shattered remnant of an army—the dispirited survivors of Camden and Fishing Creek. His Continental regulars did not exceed 1,100 and only 800 of these had arms and clothing fit for service. Some of William Washington's few cavalry soldiers were ordered back to Virginia because they were "too naked" to be given active combat duty. Since Cornwallis's troops outnumbered Greene's effectives by more than three to one, it seemed impossible that the American general could meet the whole British field army in a set battle and win. The British, however, were not concentrated at one or two bases but scattered among various towns and outposts in South Carolina and Georgia. There were garrisons at Savannah, Charleston, Beaufort, and Georgetown in the lowcountry and Camden, Ninety Six, Winnsboro, and Augusta in the backcountry with strongly held outposts including Fort Watson, Fort Motte, Orangeburg, and Granby Landing (the present Columbia) guarding the lines of communication. The British thus held the key towns and main roads, but the hinterland, the mountains, forests, swamps, and wild savannahs, belonged to the American partisans and therefore, potentially, to Nathanael Greene.

General Greene, with markedly inferior forces, now made what turned out to be an eminently wise, imaginative, and daring command decision. In the face of a superior enemy, he divided his small army and marched with one section from the Charlotte area, which was almost denuded of food supplies, to Cheraw in South Carolina. This move gave Greene abundant logistical support and placed him in a position to threaten Camden directly. He then sent Morgan with an independent corps of Continental light infantry, a detachment of militia, and William Washington's light dragoons around Cornwallis's left flank toward Ninety Six. Morgan's mission was to intimidate thoroughly all Loyalist elements in the general area and pose a threat to the strongly held British base at Ninety Six.

Greene also instructed Morgan to employ his limited forces against the enemy west of the Catawba River either offensively or defensively as his own prudence and discretion directed, acting always with great care and taking every precaution to avoid surprise attacks. Greene gave Morgan full command in his assigned area and instructed all officers and soldiers serving with the famous leader of riflemen to follow Morgan's orders.

Greene's instructions to Morgan are extremely interesting because they remain excellent advice to a guerrilla column operating through enemy territory in the twentieth century as well. Greene wrote that the object of Morgan's special force was to protect the part of the country in which it operated, annoy the enemy, "spirit up" the people, collect provisions, forage out of the way of the enemy, prevent plundering, and give receipts for whatever was taken, at least to all friends of the American cause. The late Mao Tse-Tung in his treatise on guerrilla warfare says, in effect, that the people are the water and the guerrillas fish that inhabit it. Greene and Morgan seem to have followed this concept.

Morgan was instructed further to fall back on Greene if he received information that the British were moving in force against his commander, who was lying with a weakened army at Cheraw. He must maintain a steady flow of intelligence concerning British movements back to Greene, something Cornwallis and Tarleton failed to do for each other during the latter's march to Cowpens.

A fortnight after Morgan's expedition began its sweep around Cornwallis's flank, information was brought to the American camp that a force of 250 Georgia Loyalists had crossed the Savannah River into South Carolina and were burning out patriot homesteads in the area between Ninety Six and Winnsboro. Morgan ordered William Washington with his dragoons supported by Major James McCall's unit of mounted South Carolina and Georgia militia to pursue and eliminate the Loyalist Colonel Thomas Waters and his raiders. Washington and McCall caught up with Waters at a small settlement called Hammond's Store. Striking by surprise from all sides they butchered the Loyalists. Waters and 60 men escaped by hard riding, but 150 Loyalist partisans were cut down by Washington and McCall's sabers and 40 more captured. Greene's instructions to "annoy" the enemy were being carried out with a vengeance.

Cornwallis lay at Winnsboro with about 3,500 soldiers. Major General Alexander Leslie was marching up from Charleston to reinforce him with 1,530 experienced troops, but by Cornwallis's order this force was moving by the old route via Nelson's Ferry to Camden, thus placing a deep river and impenetrable swamps between Leslie and the main army. Winter rains had been heavy. All streams were running in spate and the swamps were overflowing so that General Leslie's progress was slow and labored. The decision for the relief column to march by the swamp road was part of Cornwallis's overall strategy to mislead Greene as to British intentions and, at the same time, pose a threat to the American army at Cheraw.

Cornwallis, in the meantime, was in a dilemma. If he struck at Greene at Cheraw with his maximum available forces, Ninety Six and Augusta would be open to Daniel Morgan, now known to be at Grindall Shoals on the Pacolet River. Should he move instead against Morgan, the main British midcountry base at Camden would be exposed to an attack by Greene or the American general could join forces with Francis Marion and sever Cornwallis's communications with Charleston. The elimination of Waters's raiders by Washington and McCall at Hammond's Store and the rout of a Loyalist unit by a detachment of Morgan's force near Williams's Plantation had alarmed Cornwallis thoroughly, and he feared for the safety of Ninety Six. The British commander apparently did not know that Morgan had no artillery to breach that formidable post's fortifications. Cornwallis also must have been nagged by the memory of the dreadful defeat and destruction of Patrick Ferguson's corps at Kings Mountain in the previous October. This action had frustrated Cornwallis's first invasion of North Carolina, and nothing must happen to prevent the second march toward Virginia now in the planning stage.

Tarleton therefore was ordered on 1 January 1781 to lead out his legion of 550 men, dragoons, and light infantry, the 200-strong first battalion of the 71st Infantry Regiment (Highland Scots), and a detachment of Royal Artillery with a pair of the highly mobile 3-pounder "grasshopper" field guns—so called because these excellent little pieces literally jumped on their wheels when fired. The mission of these troops was to cross and advance up the west bank of the Broad River, find Morgan, and drive him over the Pacolet toward Kings Mountain where presumably Cornwallis and Leslie would be waiting to complete the entrapment.

Like so many British plans in the southern campaign, it was an excellent concept and should have worked except that Cornwallis inexplicably delayed his march and did not arrive in time to intercept Morgan after the battle of Cowpens. Tarleton lost that battle, even though he held all the tactical advantages including numerically superior cavalry and adequate artillery whereas Morgan had no field guns.

Tarleton, further reinforced by 50 troopers from the 17th Dragoons and 200 men (mostly new recruits) of the 7th Regiment (Royal Fusiliers), pushed on after Morgan. He found practicable fords over the swollen Enoree and Tyger rivers and on 14 January was brought three important items of information. First, Morgan held all the fords on the Pacolet. Second, Cornwallis had reached Bull Run (near the present Chester, South Carolina), and most important, General Leslie was out of the swamps and advancing rapidly to Camden. When he joined Cornwallis, the latter would have the power to crush Morgan and move on Greene.

Tarleton sent a dispatch rider urging his commanding officer to march with Leslie at all speed up the east bank of the Broad River. Tarleton meanwhile would force the guarded fords of the Pacolet and drive Morgan over the Broad into Cornwallis's and Leslie's waiting hands. Cornwallis instead detained Leslie in Camden, apparently to confuse Greene as to continued British movements, and it was not until 18 January, the day after the battle of Cowpens, that the British generals took the field. They were twenty-five miles south and east of Morgan's position instead of sitting on his escape route to Greene. Tarleton received no information at all of Cornwallis's movements from 14 to 17 January, a strange and tragic omission of vital combat intelligence during three key days. Tarleton, however, made a thorough reconnaissance of Morgan's outposts on the other side of the Pacolet and marched on 15 January toward the ford at the Old Iron Works, up the river from Morgan's positions. If the British crossed there, they could interpose a blocking force between the American column and Greene. Morgan, with his scouts carefully watching Tarleton's movements, swung his corps upriver to oppose the crossing. At nightfall, both armies bivouacked across the steam from each other. In the early morning hours of darkness, Tarleton broke camp and quickly marched downriver again, where he seized the lightly held lower ford and crossed before daybreak, just six miles from Morgan's main position.

When Morgan's scouts rode in with the news, he broke camp precipitately and fell back toward Thicketty (sometimes called Thickelle) Creek. Tarleton advanced rapidly to some log houses, built in the previous year by Patrick Ferguson, where he halted to permit the situation to develop before pressing on after Morgan's corps. One of Tarleton's patrols fanning out over the countryside discovered that Morgan had left his camp, so the British and Loyalist troops promptly marched forward and occupied the abandoned position. Morgan's retreat had been so rapid that they found half-cooked breakfasts still on the fires.

Tarleton's little army included his own green-uniformed British Legion of 550 men, dragoons and light infantry, brought up to strength with American prisoners captured at Camden—defection from both sides was a recurrent phenomenon in the American Revolution. There also were 200 infantrymen of the 7th Regiment (Royal Fusiliers), mostly young recruits, 50 red-coated horsemen of the 17th Dragoons, 200 veteran Highland Scots of the 71st Foot, and a detachment of blue-coated Royal Artillery, 50 strong, with two of the excellent 3-pounder grasshopper field guns. Tarleton's force thus numbered in excess of 1,000 well-equipped, generally well-trained regulars and Loyalist Provincials, as good a force as the British ever put in the field during the Revolution. There was also a small unit of Loyalist irregulars who played no significant part in the battle and therefore are not included with the line troops.

Morgan's corps, in spite of his written misgivings to Greene about the fighting qualities of his assigned militia, was one of the best small armies Americans ever fielded in any war. The regulars included 80 white-jacketed Continental dragoons led by Lieutenant Colonel William Washington of Virginia, a superb horseman and a born fighting man. There were some 300 light infantry of the Maryland Line, some of the finest Continental foot soldiers in the American regular army, commanded by that redoubtable Maryland gentleman Lieutenant Colonel John Eager Howard. The two companies of Virginia militia led by Captains Taite and Triplett were composed chiefly of veterans from the Continental line who had served out their enlistments. Former Continentals often were hired as substitutes by timid militia called up in a draft, so these Virginia units contained a large proportion of experienced soldiers. There also was a contingent of Georgians under Majors John Cunningham and James Jackson, all combat-tested partisans of Elijah Clarke's command. Clarke himself had been severely wounded and was not present at the coming action, but his people were, and they fought well. The force of North Carolina riflemen who followed Major Joseph McDowell had served at Musgrove's Mill and Kings Mountain and thus were veterans in the best sense of that word.

The rest of the militia in Daniel Morgan's corps were South Carolinians who rode in behind Colonel Andrew Pickens. He had kept the parole given after the fall of Charleston with scrupulous care until Loyalist barbarities in his own area forced him to revoke it. Pickens, a man of austere and meticulous honor, actually had gone to the British area commander and informed him face to face of his intended action. He then proceeded to revoke the parole and took the field with his old militia command. Andrew Pickens and his men having broken their paroles knew they could be hanged by the British if captured, a strong incentive to fight very well indeed. Because Morgan realized that his weakness in cavalry might be crucial in an engagement with superior enemy horsemen, a troop of 45 South Carolina and Georgia militia was formed, properly mounted, and armed with sabers. These augmented William Washington's 80 dragoons and were led by the now Lieutenant Colonel James McCall of the Ninety Six district. Although Morgan had no artillery to match Tarleton's two grasshoppers, many of the Georgia, North Carolina, and South Carolina militia were armed with rifles, a decided advantage in a long-range fire fight because these weapons in the hands of experts were deadly at 200 yards or better.

Tarleton's early morning crossing of the Pacolet River had forced Morgan to abandon his campsite and fall back on Cowpens near Thicketty Mountain. This was an open, partly wooded area where a local landowner named Hannah (sometimes reported as Saunders) had pastured and penned his half-wild cattle preparatory to a long overland drive to the market at Charleston. Cowpens also had been the gathering place for the riflemen who marched against Patrick Ferguson at Kings Mountain. It is described by contemporaries as an open, rolling woodland of first-growth pines and hardwoods, excellent country for cavalrymen but with very little cover for riflemen. The countryside has changed, and visiting the battlefield it is difficult in one's imagination to reconstruct the action, except that heavily wooded Thicketty Mountain still stands against the sky, looking just as it did to Morgan and his men two hundred years ago.

Morgan apparently did not decide to make his stand at Cowpens until the very last minute. He wrote to Greene on 15 January, just two days before the battle, that the enemy's great superiority in numbers and his own distance from the main army would enable Cornwallis to detach so large a force against him that action must be avoided for the safety of his troops. Morgan apparently came so close to despair that he seriously considered sending a dispatch to Greene requesting that he and his force be recalled from the field. Before any final decision was made, scouts galloped in with the word that Tarleton was only six miles away with 1,500 regulars. The figure was exaggerated, but it made up minds and provoked fast action by Morgan and his commanders.

Morgan thus was forced to fight where he stood, and he fought well. The battleground selected was almost perfect for his enemy and probably the worse place he could have chosen for his own army without artillery and greatly inferior in cavalry to the approaching British. The open mixed woodland with little underbrush was excellent terrain for sweeping, mounted attacks. There were no swamps or mountains on which Morgan could anchor his flanks, and the swollen Broad River ran full, fast, and deep only a few miles parallel to his rear. No prospect could be more disastrous to a beaten army attempting to cross such a river than to be caught in the process by the sabers of a superior cavalry. It is true that rain-deep creeks ran on both sides of the positions but these were only small watercourses that might slow down but could not stop a flanking movement.

Many years later Morgan tried to justify his selection of the Cowpens position by stating that his militia would have run if swamps on the flanks had presented such an opportunity. He also stated that he was sure that Tarleton, who preferred "down right fighting," would attack frontally and neglect the open flanks. Morgan even insisted that he would have welcomed an encirclement that could prevent the militia from running to their horses tethered behind the lines. This last opinion was based on the fact that all southern militia were, in essence, mounted infantry. They would not leave their horses behind, a pernicious and unmilitary habit which Morgan deplored because forage for the animals and food for the men presented a double supply problem. Also, the ready availability of rapid transportation could encourage thoughts of retreat before the shooting started. All of this, of course, is "after the fact" thinking to justify the selection of a battle position which did not need to be justified because Morgan won the engagement. It was true that American militia on occasion had broken and run before a British bayonet attack, but the Americans who fought at Cowpens were not the usual militia. Led by exceptionally fine field commanders, these men, hardened and honed to a fine edge by two years of savage conflict, came from fighting stock, a fact they had proved before and would prove again at Cowpens.

The truth probably is that Morgan offered battle at Cowpens because he could no longer run and had to make a stand. The British were hard on his heels, and a swollen river running deep and fast lay across his line of retreat. He also was in constant severe pain from his several ailments—and he was essentially a warrior. The old Battletown brawler decided to fight and that was that.

Morgan has been criticized for choosing an impossible position, but he commanded a picked force, one of the best small armies in American history, and his troop disposition was masterly, serving as a model for Greene's later disposition at Guilford Court House. The fact that Morgan won the battle successfully refutes all critics.

When Morgan finally determined to make a stand and gather all available forces at Cowpens, his decision also was influenced by the fact that Cowpens was well known and could easily be found by the militia, now steadily joining his forces. With Tarleton's cavalry patrols moving close behind, Morgan swung his corps toward Thicketty Creek leading to the rendezvous.

Tarleton wrote in his memoirs that patrols and spies were sent ahead to scout for the retreating Americans. Early on the evening of 16 January, Loyalist irregulars captured an American militia colonel who somehow had strayed away from the line of march. It has been conjectured that he might have solaced the forced retreat by repeated tipplings of "jugged courage" and thus happily bemused fell without a struggle into enemy hands. Whatever the reason for the wandering colonel, he was brought to Tarleton and interrogated. Tarleton immediately realized the necessity of staying close to Morgan and preventing him from crossing the Broad River now some ten miles away. American reinforcements also were reported on the way, and these must be checked and held before they could make a junction with Morgan's column.

When the command decision was made to fight at Cowpens, Morgan and his staff rode ahead with local guides and surveyed the planned battle area. They found a slope lightly forested in hardwoods and pines, possibly 150 yards long. This rose to a low ridge, dipped down to a shallow swale, and rose again to a higher ridge. Just behind the crown of the second ridge was a deeper gully in which cavalry might be concealed. The depth of the second draw was such that horsemen could rise in their stirrups and see all the way down the slope to the forest from which the British must come.

During the night of 16 January, volunteers rode up to Morgan's camp from the surrounding areas. Andrew Pickens came in with 150 mounted riflemen and others followed. Morgan, suffering intensely from rheumatism, sciatica, and hemorrhoids, apparently did not sleep at all. He moved instead among his tense men, stopping at each camp fire, telling a bawdy story, giving heart to his soldiers, preparing them for the ordeal ahead. Anyone who has been in an attack transport the night before a major landing or with a fleet moving up into action can imagine the scene. There is little chance to rest. The laughter is too ready and too boisterous; the hard, cold tension rises as the long hours to morning pass by.

Tarleton described the British approach march to the battle in his memoirs. At three o'clock in the morning of 17 January his pickets were called in and the column moved forward on the trail of the Americans. The baggage wagons were left behind, guarded by a small detachment from each unit. Three companies of light infantry supported by the legion infantry were stationed in advance. The Royal Fusiliers, the two fieldpieces with their crews, and the 1st Battalion of the 71st Regiment formed the center element while the cavalry of the legion, the 17th Dragoons, and mounted infantry followed as a rear guard. In broken and forested country an infantry advance guard is both quieter and more effective than mounted troops. If surprised, the foot soldiers can deploy and the cavalry, covered by infantry fire, will charge through with the saber to disperse the ambush.

The advance of the British in the dark across a country cut by ravines and swollen, muddy creeks naturally was slow. The British were guided by Loyalist woodsmen who knew the area, but they never ceased to wonder at the forest craft of the frontier Americans. Major George Hanger (Tarleton's second in command, who missed Cowpens because he had yellow fever) once stated that the Carolina backwoodsmen were more savage than the Indians and possessed all their vices but none of their virtues. He had known a Carolinian to travel two hundred miles through trackless forest guided only by the sun and stars to kill a man belonging to the opposite party. One British observer said that Tarleton had murdered more men and ravished more women that any other officer in the British army—he and George Hanger, a noted rake in his own right, made quite a pair.

An American night patrol was encountered in the early morning hours and Tarleton threw out an advance cavalry screen because Morgan now knew exactly where he was and no surprise was possible for either side. The troopers riding forward sighted the camp fires and reported that the Americans had halted at Cowpens. The British pushed forward, having marched all night, wet, muddy, weary, briar-torn, and breakfastless, to meet Morgan and, if possible, destroy him and his army. Tarleton commented enthusiastically on the "animation" of his officers and the continued "alacrity" of the soldiers. Tired and hungry, they still were tough, well-trained professionals and ready to fight.

An hour before sunrise, about six o'clock, Morgan's men were roused from their blankets and began preparations for the encounter. Breakfasts of corn cakes cooked the night before were eaten; baggage wagons were loaded in case of retreat and driven to the rear where they were concealed in the woods. The militia saddled their horses and tied them to the trees behind the battle position to facilitate rapid departure if this became necessary, and Morgan arrayed his forces.

Lieutenant Colonel William Washington's 80 dragoons supported by James McCall's 45 saber-armed Georgia and South Carolina mounted militia were stationed behind the second ridge in the deeper swale. Morgan deployed his veterans along the lower or first ridge. The experienced Virginia militia led by Triplett and Taite and a company of Georgians under a Captain Beale, some 140 men in all, were stationed on the right. The left was formed by the 300 Maryland Continentals, and the entire line of about 430 infantry was commanded by John Eager Howard of Maryland. About 150 yards down the slope were 300 South Carolina and North Carolina militia, many of them rifle armed, led by Andrew Pickens. They had been ordered by Morgan to wait for the enemy approach, then fire two aimed volleys at point-blank range. Pickens was then to retire in good order with his 300 militia across the face of the second line and around the left flank of the Marylanders, where he would re-form in the rear and return to the battle when needed. By this tactical arrangement Morgan was employing the always unpredictable American militia wisely, taking into consideration their well-known predilection to bolt in the face of a disciplined bayonet attack. He thus made a military virtue out of what could have become a calamity. Morgan also instructed Pickens's men that, if the British dragoons charged, every third man should fire while the others held fire and discharged consecutive volleys if the attack continued. This also would permit the first man to reload and continue the fire fight. The order went up and down Pickens's line: shoot at the epaulets and stripes, kill the officers and sergeants. At the very bottom of the slope, concealed by brush, broom sedge, and stunted trees, were 150 Georgia and North Carolina riflemen under Joseph McDowell and John Cunningham, with the same instructions—to kill officers and sergeants, then fall back through Pickens's line when the British advanced.

About eight in the morning, the Americans saw movement in the trees, and the British column debouched from the woods. Suddenly 50 dragoons trotted out, drew saber, and charged the 150 riflemen of the skirmish line. Tarleton was probing his enemy. The cavalry sweeping forward met a sudden, aimed fire from the riflemen concealed in the brush. Fifteen riders went down and the mounted attack faltered, falling back to the protection of the infantry moving into position. The two 3-pounder grasshoppers were advanced and showered the American skirmish line with canister. These, galled by the cannon fire, retreated as planned up the slope and joined Pickens's men, waiting for the main assault.

Figure 23.
Lieutenant Colonel William Washington

Figure 24.
Battle of Cowpens, South Carolina, 17 January 1781, from *A History of the British Army*, J. W. Fortescue (London, 1902)

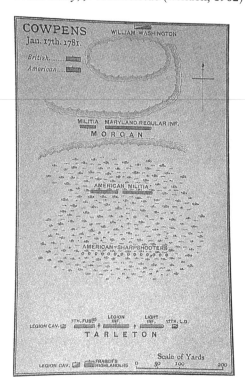

About 300 yards below Pickens's position at the bottom of the long slope and almost out of killing range Tarleton completed his formation, foot soldiers being ordered to throw down all equipment except muskets, bayonets, and ammunition. The light infantry moved to the right to equal the left of the American line. The legion infantry formed on their left with a grasshopper advanced between the two units. Then came the 7th Regiment (Royal Fusiliers) under Major Timothy Newmarsh. The second grasshopper was placed between the legion and the fusiliers. Fifty dragoons and a captain were placed on each flank of the British infantry line to cover these vulnerable areas and, as Tarleton said, threaten the enemy with encirclement. The first battalion of the 71st Highland infantry was placed 150 yards to the rear and a little to the left of Newmarsh's fusiliers. The reserve was formed of 200 horsemen, the dreaded sabers of the legion, stationed about 200 yards in the center rear of the main line.

The British and Loyalist regulars with drums beating, officers and colors in front, marched forward to the attack. Some of the new recruits in the fusiliers started firing in nervous reaction to the tension and well out of accurate musket range, but this was quickly suppressed. The scarlet, green, and blue line pressed up the slope in as good a formation as troops could move in open file.

Pickens's riflemen following orders commenced firing as soon as the British formations came within killing range. Their shooting was selective with the Carolinians and Georgians choosing as targets the soldiers wearing epaulets and stripes. Officers and sergeants staggered and went down; the attack wavered, its forward movement slowing. Pickens held his men long enough in the face of British bayonets to fire a second aimed volley, then began an orderly retreat to the left as instructed by Morgan across the front of the American line of regulars.

Tarleton, seeing the militia fall back and assuming the Americans were beginning to break as they had done at Camden, threw in the troop of 50 cavalry from his right flank. These galloped, sabers extended, against the last elements of Pickens's militia, which frankly bolted panicking the entire force. The Americans began to run for their horses tied behind the lines, a contingency Morgan had feared and done his best to avoid by wise orders and troop disposition. The story is told of a South Carolina militia lieutenant named Hughes, an extremely strong man, and notably fleet of foot who repeatedly outran his running men, and facing about struck right and left with the flat of his sword, commanding them to stand and fight or they would all be killed. Finally in a pine grove behind and to the right of Morgan's position, Pickens, a man of great courage, firmness, and presence, aided by Hughes and other officers, prevented the militia from getting to their horses, re-formed the line, reloaded rifles and muskets, and waited for orders.

As Tarleton's dragoons swept forward in a charge to accelerate what seemed to be the beginning of a rout, they were met by William Washington's white-coated horsemen, who suddenly swung out from behind the ridge around the now fleeing militia and smashed head-on into the pursuing British cavalry, driving them back in confusion. Washington then turned his men and cantered back to his position in the swale, covering in the process the last units of retreating militia.

Morgan's line of regulars and experienced militia had held their fire until all the militia cleared the front. As soon as this occurred, Tarleton's infantry, charging up the hill half-officered and badly out of formation, were met by a stunning volley. The British halted and for some ten minutes both lines exchanged volleys at point-blank range without faltering and with considerable casualties. Tarleton wrote afterward that the fire on both sides was "well supported" and produced "much slaughter."

His advance temporarily halted in a fire fight with the Americans, Tarleton trotted back and ordered MacArthur to lead his battalion forward and to the left, outflanking Morgan's right. The Highlanders moved out on the left oblique, pipes skirling a wild clan march. Seeing the Scots advancing, John Eager Howard ordered the Georgians and Virginians on the right of his line to face about, wheel to their right, about face, and confront the flank attack. Misunderstanding the order, they faced about and, instead of wheeling to form an angle in the line, marched straight to the rear. Seeing the militia on their right perform this maneuver, the Maryland Continentals did the same, and the entire line proceeded in good order up the slope. Morgan in great consternation rode up to Howard and demanded to know if his infantry was retreating. Howard replied that he was changing position to save his threatened right flank. Morgan wished to know if Howard were beaten and was asked if men who marched like that looked as if they were beaten. Morgan agreed and approved, telling Lieutenant Colonel Howard to continue the retrograde movement. Morgan would choose a second position; when the troops reached that point they were to face about and deliver volley fire.

Tarleton, believing quite naturally that the climax of the battle had come because the Americans seemed to be falling back all down the line, ordered his troops forward. Light infantry, the legion, Royal Fusiliers, and Highlanders all surged shouting after the Americans, charging with the bayonet to finish Morgan's army once and for all. Washington watching the attack from a position on the American left flank sent word to Morgan that the British, with many of their officers and sergeants dead or wounded, were coming on like a mob. When Morgan gave them one fire, Washington would charge from the flank with his cavalry. Morgan received the message just as Howard reached the bottom of the first shallow draw and started up the slope toward the second ridge. Morgan shouted to Howard, ordering him to face about, give the British one fire, and the day would be won.

At 7:45 in the morning, less than an hour after the engagement began, the Maryland Continentals, the veteran Virginians, and Georgians suddenly faced about and fired on order at ten yards, then went in with the bayonet. The disorganized British, blasted at point-blank range and minus half their officers, faltered, broke ranks, and ran. Tarleton wrote later that an unaccountable panic extended along his entire line: when British

Figure 25.   Battle of Cowpens, South Carolina, 17 January 1781, by Robert Wilson

soldiers attempting to surrender cried for quarter, the Americans, remembering as always the butchery at the Waxhaws, shouted "Tarleton's quarter," but Howard stopped the killing. Ordering the frightened enemy to lay down all weapons, he promised them good quarter, and the promise was kept.

Instead of surrendering, some of the light infantry and legion infantry ran down the road toward the Pacolet River. With his center disintegrating, Tarleton tried vainly to rally the beaten men. He also ordered the crack 200 dragoons in reserve to charge in support of the Highlanders still fighting grimly on the American right flank. The cavalry, caught up in the general panic refused to move and Washington, suddenly swinging around with his 125 horsemen, hit the retreating infantry and collected them as prisoners.

Tarleton, riding back to bring his unwilling cavalry into action by personal leadership, came under rifle fire from Pickens's militia which now appeared at the battle scene again on the American right flank. Tarleton's horse was killed and Robert Jackson, assistant surgeon of the Highland battalion, rode up and generously insisted that Tarleton take his mount, arguing that Tarleton's safety was of the highest importance to the entire army. The surgeon then tied a white handkerchief to his walking stick and strode coolly up to the victorious Americans. When challenged he replied that he was assistant surgeon of the 71st Foot, many of the men were wounded, and he came to offer his professional services.

On the American right, Archibald MacArthur and his Highlanders of the 71st Regiment fought on with hopeless courage. Pickens and the re-formed militia attacked them from one side, and they began slowly to fall back. Lieutenant Howard and the Marylanders moved in on the other flank, while the Georgians and Virginians charged into the middle. The fighting broke up into a confused melee. Howard shouted over the battle that quarter would be given and the Scots on MacArthur's order grounded arms and surrendered. The gallant Highland major offered his sword to Pickens, but 9 of the 16 officers attached to the heroic Scottish battalion lay dead or wounded.

With the battle already lost, Tarleton tried to bring his cavalry into action but only 14 officers and 40 men responded. The rest, almost 200 strong, fled the field. The Royal Artillery still fired its 3-pounders, but the Continentals rushed the guns and overran the position. All of the British artillerymen, trained professionals, fought their fieldpieces to the last and either were killed or wounded by the guns they served.

Tarleton riding with his 54 loyal horsemen to rescue the artillery was forced instead to retreat, and the American cavalry pursued him, Washington galloping some 30 or 40 yards ahead of his men. Tarleton seeing this turned his horse and with a few officers attacked Washington, who rose in his stirrups and cut at the dragoon on Tarleton's right, but the American's sword, parried by the British officer, broke short at the hilt. Washington's opponent swung his saber for the full backhand slash, but a young American named Collins came up at that moment and put a pistol ball in the British officer's shoulder. Another of Tarleton's dragoons struck at Washington, but the American cavalry had joined their commander and a Sergeant Major Perry parried the blow. Tarleton charged in swinging his saber but Washington blocked the cut with the hilt of his shattered weapon. Tarleton, now almost surrounded by white-jacketed American troopers, reined his mount around, hurriedly drew, and fired a pistol, wounding Washington's horse, then galloped away to safety. The battle of Cowpens was over.

In an hour of fighting Lieutenant Colonel Banastre Tarleton lost 100 dead, of whom 39 were officers. He also left in Daniel Morgan's hands 229 wounded, 600 prisoners including 27 officers, and two 3-pounder field guns, 800 muskets, 100 dragoon horses, and 35 wagons. The Americans collected the field music and the colors of the proud 7th Regiment, the Royal Fusiliers. The little American army suffered 12 killed and 60 wounded.

The retreating British dragoons racing to destroy their baggage wagons stationed behind the lines found that the assigned guards had taken the wagon horses and ridden to safety, but Loyalist irregulars who had not participated in the battle were pillaging the supplies. These men, presumably allies, were cut down ruthlessly by Tarleton's cavalry and the baggage burned before the Americans could capture it. On the next morning, Tarleton, having collected some 200 men, mostly dragoons, rode into the main British camp and reported his defeat to Cornwallis, who was some twenty-five miles from where he should have been.

Naturally, bitterness against Tarleton ran deep among the officers of the British army in South Carolina. They asked why he had attacked without consulting Newmarsh of the Royal Fusiliers and MacArthur of the Highlanders, both veteran officers and older men. In Charleston, Colonel William Moultrie, a prisoner since the fall of the city in 1780, noted that in discussing the defeat the British officers in the city were saying that it resulted from trusting such a command to an inexperienced boy. Stedman, the civilian commissary officer under Cornwallis, wrote that no other action during the entire period of the war reflected so much dishonor on British arms.

After ten days of recrimination Tarleton, perturbed and angry although apparently suffering no embarrassment, wrote to his commander requesting a court-martial to decide the blame and asking for permisson to retire. On 30 January, Cornwallis answered with a letter completely exonerating Tarleton, stating that the means he had used to bring the enemy to action were "able and masterly" and would ever do Tarleton honor. He also said that Tarleton's disposition of his force was unexceptionable and only the total misbehavior of the troops could have deprived him of the glory he justly was due.

Questions remain, however, that never will be answered. Why, for example, did Tarleton go into battle against a rested, fed enemy, waiting in position after the British had completed a twelve-mile night march through difficult terrain and then fought, perforce, on empty stomachs? Why did Cornwallis delay to grind corn instead of pushing up the other side of the Broad River to the Kings Mountain area where his army would have been in a blocking position? Why did Tarleton not use his superior cavalry in excellent cavalry terrain to outflank and envelop Morgan's position? There was no American artillery, so why didn't Tarleton use his two 3-pounder grasshoppers in preparation fire against the notably unsteady militia before the assault started? After the skirmish line of riflemen was forced to retire by a few rounds of canister, the field guns were not employed again until the very end of the action when the royal artillerymen desperately fought their guns until overrun. Why, finally, were no reports or information exchanged between Cornwallis and Tarleton from 12 through 16 January?

What was important was that two almost equal armies met on the field of battle and Morgan outfought Tarleton. It was a stand-up soldier's battle and the Americans won it because on that day they were the better fighting force. In his memoirs, Tarleton dispassionately admitted that his defeat at Cowpens must be ascribed either to the bravery and good conduct of the Americans, to the loose manner of forming which the king's troops always practiced in America, or to some "unforeseen event" that might terrify the most disciplined soldiers or "counteract the best concerted designs."

Probably the most important result of the battle of Cowpens was that again, as at Kings Mountain, Cornwallis suffered grievous losses and a serious weakening of his available forces just before a planned invasion of North Carolina and Virginia. He went ahead with the invasion notwithstanding, to his disastrous "victory" at the Guilford Court House in North Carolina and the final surrender of his army at Yorktown, Virginia. That British surrender may be traced directly to the series of bloody encounters in the two Carolinas during the twelve months prior to the final capitulation of the main British army in the southern theater of operations.

Charles Stedman, that prescient Loyalist observer, stated that "the defeat of His Majesty's troops at the Cowpens formed a very principal link in the chain of circumstances which led to the independence of America. Colonel Tarleton acquired power without any extraordinary degree of merit and on most occasions exercised it without discretion."

As General Cornwallis wrote to Lord Rawdon after the battle of Cowpens, "The late affair has almost broke my heart. . . ."

CHAPTER XII

Weapons and Uniforms

Knowledge of the ranges and capabilities of missile weapons employed by the forces engaged is essential to an understanding of the fighting concepts and tactics of the American Revolution. Otherwise, judged by modern standards, some of the actions make very little sense. The American Revolution was a transitional war; climate, terrain, and training based on applied experience produced changes and modifications in clothing and arms that were to affect profoundly the future development of organized warfare. Because this war was fought over great distances, in savage heat and equally savage cold, through wild or half-settled country, it was frequently difficult and often impossible to apply the formalized tactical concepts based on standard weaponry of eighteenth-century European conflict. Where these concepts could be applied, the British usually won. The war ended in an American victory, however. Thus the way it was fought and the weapons used deserve particular attention.

The basic weapon issued to a regular infantry soldier, whether British, French, German, or American, was a long-barreled (40 to 46 inches), large caliber (.65 to .80), heavy (8 to 12 pounds), flintlock, smoothbore, single-shot musket, equipped with a socket bayonet having a 14- to 19-inch blade. The bayonet fitted over the muzzle of the musket and locked into place on a barrel stud. The musket was loaded with a paper cartridge consisting of a measured quantity of black powder and a round, soft lead ball weighing about an ounce. The British .75 caliber musket fired a ball that ran 14 to a pound of lead. The French .69 caliber measured 22 balls to a pound of lead. If a lethal spread were desired, several buckshot could be and frequently were added to the solid

Figure 26. British Brown Bess flintlock musket with its original socket bayonet. Length: 4 feet 10 inches

slug. Francis Marion's South Carolina partisans preferred goose shot (number two's) for close work, a dreadful load that at point-blank range would tear a man apart.

To load such a smoothbore musket, the soldier took a paper cartridge which was tied at one end and twisted at the other, tore or bit off the twisted end, and tapped a small quantity of the powder into the flash pan with the cock at half cock or safety position. He then poured the remainder of the powder down the barrel, followed by the lead ball or a combination of ball and buckshot. The soldier could either leave the paper around the bullet or bullets to act as a gas shield or tamp it above the charge as a wadding. In either case, he rammed the full load down with his iron ramrod and seated it against the breech. The musket then was presented, the cock pulled to full cock, and the piece fired. So many steps and movements were necessary to ready a musket for firing that the soldiers learned each step by rote from drill manuals and drill sergeants. They then were trained to fire in volleys and on the order.

The solid lead ball discharged by these muskets theoretically would carry about 300 yards. Its accurate range was somewhere between 80 and 90 yards, and it was singularly ineffective against troops in open formation at over 150 yards. The big, heavy, soft lead slug with its low muzzle velocity (320 to 350 meters a second) had tremendous smashing and stopping power. At 100 yards or less, a man hit by such a bullet went down as if he were sledgehammered. A belly or lung wound usually was fatal and a smashed elbow or knee joint normally required an amputation. As to the military musket's accuracy, its bullet dropped vertically 5 feet over a distance of 120 yards from the muzzle. The French Charleville .69 caliber musket issued to many American troops during the last years of the war had a 9-foot error at 200 yards.

Colonel George Hanger, Banastre Tarleton's raffish second in command during the southern campaign in America, wrote in 1814 (*To All Sportsmen*) concerning the "Brown Bess" or English military musket:

> Brown Bess will strike a figure of a man at 80 yards. It may even be 100 yards, but a soldier must be a very unfortunate indeed who shall be wounded by a common musket at 150 yards provided his antagonist aims at him; and as to firing at a man at 200 yards with a common musket you may as well fire at the moon and have the same hope of hitting your object. I do maintain and will prove whenever called upon that no man was ever killed at 200 yards by a common musket by the person who aimed at him.

Lethal at close range with its heavy lead ball but hopelessly inaccurate at over 150 yards, this musket and its capabilities governed eighteenth-century infantry tactics. The famous linear formation was employed where infantry advanced to battle in column and deployed into a line two or three ranks deep for the actual engagement. Continental armies usually employed three ranks; the new American army fought in two ranks; the British abandoned the third rank as the revolutionary war progressed in favor of the two-rank formation. Behind the two or three ranks stood a single line of "file closers" who

Figure 27.   British Brown Bess musket

would replace casualties in the fighting ranks. Elite units, light infantry, and grenadiers, especially uniformed, armed, and trained, marched on the flanks of the regular line infantry. The flanks in open field warfare always were vulnerable to sweeping enemy attack and thus considered posts of honor. Field artillery was spaced along the front of the infantry line and cavalry formed either on the extreme flanks or in the rear. The mounted arm's missions were to exploit a victorious battle by charging a broken enemy with the saber, protect against flanking movements, or cover a retreat in case of defeat.

The infantry stood erect, shoulder to shoulder, and fired on command, with the second and third ranks firing separately. Very well-trained foot soldiers could deliver three to five volleys a minute. If dense battle smoke produced by the black powder loads began to obscure the field, the ranks would fire volleys on the order by platoons or battalions whenever and wherever the enemy formation might be seen, thus maintaining a constant running fire up and down the line. Since the muskets had no rear sights and often no front sights, individual infantrymen just aimed down the barrel and pulled the trigger on command. The tactical concept thus was to develop speed and a disciplined volume fire rather than accuracy.

An eighteenth-century classic set battle usually began when the lines were 600 to 300 yards apart. The artillery on both sides would commence firing with solid shot, canister, or powder-train fused shells. The latter were employed with the short, wide-mouthed field howitzers, the fuse being ignited by the gun blast. After a comparatively brief artillery exchange, one or both lines would move forward usually at the quick march, officers in front, drums beating, fifes squealing, national and regimental battle flags flying in the center of the formations.

At 100 yards or even as close as 50 yards, volleys were exchanged, three to five rounds a minute. This intense fire fight would continue point-blank until the commanding officer of one of the forces engaged (or the surviving senior officer) decided to order a bayonet charge. This usually occurred when the opposing side obviously had begun to wilt under the fire storm and a properly delivered attack with cold steel could win the day.

The essence of this kind of fighting (and one the Americans found difficult to learn) was fire discipline—troops so trained that they would stand unflinching and take heavy losses while delivering a greater volume of fire at greater speed than the enemy. When the fire fight had been accomplished successfully, the same troops must advance on the order and engage the enemy in hand-to-hand fighting with the bayonet. Battles of this nature required professional officers commanding long-term professional soldiers, trained in a brutally inflexible discipline and close order drill. Frederick the Great, king of Prussia in the middle eighteenth century, ordered his sergeants to bayonet from behind any soldier who showed signs of flinching in a fire fight.

To win a war conclusively, the main enemy forces or important elements of those forces must be met in open battle and defeated or, better, destroyed by death or capture. This the Americans did at Saratoga, Kings Mountain, Cowpens, and finally Yorktown, the last achieved with the help of a regular French army. George Washington's task and the task of other American field commanders was to train raw farm and village lads or wild backwoodsmen to face and fight British and German professional soldiers on equal terms in set battles—and win. That was a monumental assignment and not fully accomplished until after 1777 when instruction by such European advisers as Frederick von Steuben and actual combat experience finally permitted the Americans to field real armies. It should be remembered that in the first four years of war, Harlem Heights, Princeton, and Saratoga, with its forerunner, Bennington, were the only pitched battles of note won by the Americans against a civilized enemy. Harlem Heights was followed by Washington's defeat at White Plains and the loss of Forts Washington and Lee, while Princeton and Saratoga were offset by British victories at Germantown and the Brandywine. American forces at the most decisive action, Saratoga, outnumbered the British almost four to one.

The battle of Fort Sullivan, fought in 1776 near Charleston, South Carolina, also is justly celebrated as an American victory. It was, however, a defense action, fort against fleet, and thus not a pitched land battle.

The weapon for which America was famous—the long rifle—according to romantic fiction and legend enabled the stalwart patriots to face and ultimately defeat the hated red-coated invader. Unhappily for romance, this is not true. The average American soldier, whether Continental regular or state militiaman, was issued a smoothbore, bayonet-equipped musket. These weapons could be British .75 caliber Brown Bess muskets taken from captured British arsenals, picked up on the battlefield, or inherited from earlier colonial wars. Around 100,000 French .69 caliber Charleville and St. Etienne muskets were shipped from Europe to the American army during the war, and by 1781 soldiers of the Continental line were chiefly armed with these, as were many of the state militia. Some military muskets, however, like the Congress musket of .80 caliber, were manufactured in America during the war and issued to troops, but apparently never were produced in quantity. The long rifle, basically a civilian hunting weapon that could not mount a bayonet, was carried by special units, rangers, or rifle corps that operated as snipers, scouts, skirmishers, or a very mobile light infantry. The American partisans were

Figure 28.   British Brown Bess second model flintlock musket with a 42-inch barrel. This
was the standard weapon for British infantry in America during the Revolution. Length:
4 feet 10 inches

Figure 29.   French infantry musket produced at the St. Etienne arsenal. This was the type
used by French and American troops in the Revolution. Length: 5 feet 2 inches

Figure 30.   American flintlock rifle made in Pennsylvania and stocked in curly maple. A brass-
patch box with a lengthwise hinge is on the stock. Length: 5 feet

Figure 31.   German .80-caliber musket. This type of weapon was used by German
mercenaries in the Revolution. Length: 4 feet 10 inches

accompanied by rifle detachments, and the hunters from the transmontane settlements in
present-day Tennessee and Kentucky generally were rifle armed.

By 1770, the American rifle, developed by Pennsylvania gunsmiths from the jäger
rifle which their German forebears brought to the English colonies, could achieve an

accurate range of about 300 yards—more than three times that of a smoothbore musket. It had a barrel length of 39 to 49 inches, usually averaged between .40 and .60 caliber (.54 caliber was popular) with seven or eight grooves in the rifling. This rifle was loaded by pouring in a measured quantity of powder from a flask or horn, placing a greased leather or linen patch (carried in a hinged patch box set in the stock) on the rifle muzzle, seating the ball in the center of the patch, and ramming home ball, patch, and powder against the breech. The patch served as wadding, sealed against gas escape, cleaned the bore on the way down, and by filling the bore, forced the lead ball to engage the rifling, thus imparting an essential spin.

A .54 caliber rifle ball weighed about half an ounce, and this smaller bullet with a higher ratio of powder to ball than a smoothbore musket created a flatter trajectory. The long barrel firing a patched ball permitted almost complete combustion of the powder and thus produced greater range. The spin imparted by the rifling gave accuracy to the ball, while a notched rear sight and a blade or bead fore sight allowed precision shooting.

The American rifle weighed 7 to 8 pounds, considerably less than the average musket. It thus was a handy weapon for forest warfare or long-range campaigning. The rifle's limitations were that it took much longer to load than a musket and therefore had a slower rate of fire, one shot for every three fired by a musket. The American rifle, as already mentioned, did not mount a bayonet and its stock was too light for use as an effective club. Units armed with the long American hunting rifle without bayonets could not be employed efficiently in line of battle with troops volley firing the bayoneted musket. Rifles were very effective, however, in the hands of skirmishers or light, mobile forces operating in forested, swampy, or mountainous terrain.

The British army in the 1770s had no regular rifle corps, the Royal Rifle Brigade with its green uniform, Baker rifle (loaded using a greased patch), and long sword bayonet being organized later based on experience learned in the American war. During the Revolution the British employed instead riflemen forming the elite jäger corps attached to the German mercenary regiments serving in North America. These jäger rifles had short barrels ranging in length from 23.5 inches to almost 29 inches, were from .51 to .64 caliber, weighed between 6.9 and 9.8 pounds, and usually did not mount a bayonet. For hand-to-hand fighting the German riflemen were issued a basket-hilted hanger with a 22- to 30-inch blade. Backcounty southern Loyalist militia serving in local campaigns used their own hunting rifles.

A superior breech-loading, flintlock rifle equipped with a specially designed 25.5-inch socket bayonet was developed during this period by Major Patrick Ferguson of the British army—who, ironically, was destined to die at Kings Mountain, South Carolina, shot down by American riflemen.

A standard Ferguson had a 38.125-inch barrel and was of .65 caliber, although some officers' Fergusons were made with a 43-inch barrel and .69 caliber. The rifle weighed about 6.9 pounds and mounted a special 25.5-inch socket bayonet on a stud set under the barrel. The Ferguson had an excellent balance as a stabbing weapon with that bayonet attached. The rifle carried accurately around 250 yards, a shorter range than the American rifle, but, being a breech-loader, the Ferguson could be charged in the kneeling or even prone position. It also could be fired three to four times a minute. To load a Ferguson, the rifleman put the piece at half cock and swung the trigger guard,

Figure 32.   German flintlock rifle used by Hessian jäger riflemen during the Revolution. Length: 3 feet 8 inches

Figure 33.   British officer's breech-loading flintlock Ferguson rifle. Length: 4 feet 1.5 inches with a 25.5-inch bayonet, with a wide, flat blade

Figure 34.   Breech-loading Ferguson rifle, breech plug opened for loading. This rifle was presented by Patrick Ferguson to Captain Frederick de Peyster (1775–1776)

which served as a lever, almost a full turn. This dropped a detachable threaded breech plug, the base of which was formed by the trigger finial, exposing the interior of the breech. The soldier pushed in the bullet, depressed the muzzle so the ball would roll into the chamber, poured in the powder behind the ball, and, turning the trigger guard, re-screwed the plug. He then blew or brushed off the excess powder pushed up by the plug, primed the pan, and the rifle was ready to fire.

The obvious advantages of the Ferguson over the American or German rifles were the higher rate of fire and the fact that it mounted a bayonet. The soldier armed with a Ferguson did not have to stand exposed to enemy musketry while reloading, but was able to maintain a continuous fire from behind protection. Unfortunately for the British army in North America, the Ferguson never was adopted officially during the revolution-ary war; only a comparatively few ever saw action.

The field artillery of the period should be placed in two categories: long guns loaded with solid shot, bag shot, or canister and the shorter howitzers firing spherical, powder-train fused, explosive shells. The British, for example, used 3-, 6-, and 12-poun-der field guns and 4.5-inch, 5.5-inch, and 8-inch field howitzers. The French had 4-, 8-, 12-, and 16-pounder long field guns plus 6- and 8-inch field howitzers. The American army used whatever field guns or howitzers it could find in military arsenals or capture on the battlefield. Toward the end of the war, French artillery was supplied to the Amer-ican forces.

Any gun larger than a 16-pounder or howitzer bigger than 8 inches was considered a siege piece to be employed with the heavy shell-throwing mortars for attacking enemy fortifications or fieldworks. The little, short-range, brass coehorn mortar also was used in siege operations to throw small antipersonnel shells into the enemy's emplacements or approach trenches. The heavier guns and mortars could not be used successfully in field warfare because fifteen horses were needed to pull a 12-pounder into action. Six- and eight-horse teams were normal for the lighter guns and howitzers.

The field guns were loaded first with a flannel powder bag, then a round iron can-nonball was rammed down on top of the powder. The charge was ignited by a tube, either of tin or a quill, containing an inflammable composition. These tubes were placed in a vent on the breech of the gun and a port fire applied to the tube by a gunner when the order to fire was given.

The field howitzers and heavy siege mortars were shorter weapons with wide bores designed to throw explosive shells in varying trajectories. These shells were loaded with black powder and equipped with an open-ended wooden fuse, shaped like a truncated cone, filled with a combustible mixture of two ounces of nitre, one of sulphur and three of gun powder dust, thoroughly tamped. This fuse was driven with a wooden mallet (to avoid sparks) into an aperture in the shell left for that purpose and sealed with a special cement made from pitch, rosin, turpentine, and wax. The shells were loaded fuse up and the fuses ignited by the gun blast. With such a primitive and unreliable fuse mechanism,

Figure 35.   Eighteenth-century 12-pounder heavy field or siege gun on carriage

Figure 36.   Eighteenth-century 8.79-inch French heavy howitzer on carriage

Figure 37.   Eighteenth-century 4.5-inch light coehorn mortar on mounting.
This mortar fired an 8-pound shell and could be carried by two men.

Figure 38.   Eighteenth-century 16-inch French siege mortar on mounting.
This mortar, called a stone mortar, usually fired a metal basket filled
with explosive grenades for antipersonnel use

real air bursts were not possible, but the same effect could be obtained by deliberately firing ricochet shots in front of an enemy line, the shells bounding and exploding at about man height, hopefully in the middle of the hostile formation.

Both field guns and field howitzers also fired antipersonnel canister or bag shot, musket balls packed tightly in a tin container or coarse cloth bag. The can or bag held the balls together until they emerged from the gun muzzle when the load was released in a sudden lethal spread. The difficulty was that the canister and bag shot had effective ranges of 500 yards at best.

A 12-pounder field gun using solid shot had an extreme range of about 3,500 yards but an effective range of less than half that. The smaller field guns and the short howitzers had correspondingly shorter ranges. Because of these short and unreliable ranges field artillery usually began firing on an enemy at 800 to 600 yards and often much closer. Since all artillery of this period was smoothbore and, like the musket, singularly inaccurate at anything but comparatively short distances, it was employed accordingly on the battlefield. Eighteenth-century artillery firing point-blank at troops drawn up in shoulder-to-shoulder linear formation could be shockingly destructive. A 6-pounder traversed and fired on the oblique at a line of infantry might kill two or three men and wound four or five others with one load of canister. Here again, as in the musket volley exchange, only an intense and savage discipline would prevent troops from breaking under such terrible pressure. It is no wonder that green and inexperienced American militia faced for the first time by this artillery-musket combination in the hands of veterans panicked and ran on several momentous occasions.

To change the aim point up or down, a field gun or howitzer was raised or lowered by an elevation screw attached to the rear of the gun. The guns were traversed, in other words given deflection, by swinging the heavy trail around with hand spikes. To conduct this operation could take from two to six men, depending on the size of the piece. To handle a field gun or field howitzer, with its team of horses, two-wheeled ammunition limber, and gun with carriage, pulled as a composite unit, required a primary crew of five plus additional personnel to bring up ammunition, insert fuses in the shells, handle the horses, and carry out many other essential small jobs that made a well-trained gun team an effective unit. The basic crew of five was composed of a noncommissioned officer, a loader, a sponge and rammer man, a ventsman, and a firer. The noncommissioned officer commanded the detachment and layed (aimed) the piece. The loader inserted the powder bag and projectile (solid shot, canister, or shell) in the gun for the sponge and rammer man to ram home with his combined sponger and rammer. The ventsman thrust a sharp instrument like an awl down the touch hole or vent to prick the powder bag after it was loaded, thus ensuring ignition, while the firer placed the firing tube in the vent and stood by to discharge the gun with his port fire when the gun was brought on target and the command given. This port fire was a lighted slow match attached to a linstock, usually two bent iron match arms fastened on a wooden shaft two to six feet long. The more

Figure 39.   Eighteenth-century 6-pounder field gun on carriage

elaborate linstocks often had a spear blade mounted on the match end of the shaft to provide a defensive weapon for the firer.

After the gun was fired, the sponge and rammer man reversed his tool, dipped the sponge end in a ready bucket of water, and sponged out the barrel. At the same time the ventsman placed his thumb, covered with a leather thumb stall, over the vent to keep smoldering powder residue from exploding in the sponge man's face. The gun was now ready for the next discharge, and the loading process could be repeated.

Since the gun recoiled six or eight feet after each discharge, it had to be run up into battery again by muscle power (a 12-pounder weighed close to a ton) and the process repeated. A good gun crew could fire from three to five rounds a minute and support efficiently the fire pattern of the muskets.

An advanced design light 3-pounder field gun called the grasshopper because it jumped on its carriage when fired was employed by the British in the southern campaigns, usually in conjunction with mounted troops. Ready cartridges and projectiles were placed in compartments built into the trail, and the gun could be dismounted and carried on a stretcher by eight men with additional soldiers assigned to transport the carriage and wheels. While a four- or six-horse team was normal with the grasshopper, it could be pulled in an emergency by two horses. It was an excellent gun for mountain work or rough terrain, and it probably should be considered a step in the evolution of a truly mobile "horse artillery" capable of moving and maneuvering with cavalry or fast-moving light infantry.

Figure 40.   Eighteenth-century brass 3-pounder "grasshopper" field gun on display mount (weight 500 pounds with carriage)

Figure 41. Eighteenth-century 12-pounder naval gun on carriage with elevation/depression wedge under the breach

The American South with its broad savannahs and open pine forests was excellent cavalry country, and both sides used mounted troops extensively. Eighteenth-century British and American cavalry soldiers usually were armed with saber and carbine. Officers carried the saber plus a pair of pistols in saddle holsters, and some mounted units equipped all personnel with pistols. The lance, in the eighteenth century typically an eastern European weapon, is mentioned only once in southern fighting during the Revolution. Some of the mounted troops serving with the French army at Yorktown, Uhlan cavalry of the Duke de Lauzun's Legion, used the lance, but the fact that these men were Polish mercenaries undoubtedly explains its appearance.

A cavalry saber of the eighteenth century, whether straight or curved, had a single-edged blade between 31 and 37 inches long and weighed from 2 to 4 pounds. American sabers either were imported, captured, or of crude and simple domestic manufacture. Francis Marion's South Carolina partisans carried most effective heavy sabers made from plantation saw blades.

Figure 42.   British light dragoon saber with brass hilt. Blade length: 36 inches

Figure 43.   American or British infantry officer's short saber with yellow ivory grip and
brass lionhead pommel. Blade length: 27 inches

Figure 44.   Brass-hilted American saber with maple wood grip. Blade length: 33 inches

Figure 45.   American saber with brass hilt and dog or lionhead pommel. Blade length: 33
inches

Figure 46.   American saber with brass hilt and cherry wood grip. Blade length: 34 inches

Figure 47. American or British steel-hilted dragoon saber. Blade length: 37 inches

Figure 48.   Highland Scot backsword with basket hilt and fishtail grip. Blade length: 35 inches

Cavalry pistols differed considerably depending on the taste or wealth of the owner. The standard British military pistol was a single-shot, muzzle-loading flintlock of .56 caliber. French pistols were the same, but of .67 caliber. American officers and soldiers used what pistols they already possessed or could obtain. There were even some, like the long rifle, of American manufacture. Most pistols used by the American army, particularly in the later years of the war, were imports, probably from France.

The cavalry carbine often was a cut-down Brown Bess or Charleville with its barrel shortened to make it more handy for mounted use. Regular British carbines issued to cavalry, dragoons, artillery, light infantry, and some Highland Scot foot regiments had barrels varying from 28 to 42 inches in length and were standardized at .65 caliber. The light infantry, Highland Scot, and some heavy dragoon carbines were fitted with a barrel lug for bayonets. French cavalry carbines had a barrel of 30.75 inches and always were of .67 caliber. American horsemen used carbines of all descriptions, usually cut-down muskets, although French Charleville and St. Etienne carbines undoubtedly saw fairly general use in the closing phases of the Revolution.

Infantry officers' swords in all the armies differed with the taste and means of the owner. Some preferred the long, straight, slender small sword adapted only for thrusting. Most officers in the foot regiments carried the short sword or saber, light cut-and-thrust weapons, either straight or slightly curved, with a blade 25 to 30 inches in length and a guard on the hilt. The military hanger, a short single-edged cutting sword with a blade of around 25 inches, was issued to British sergeants and some grenadier regiments. In the French army, only grenadiers and sergeants carried these, but German jägers were equipped with hangers and most of the line units among the German mercenaries were issued hangers along with musket and bayonet.

All enlisted personnel in Highland Scot infantry regiments serving during 1776 in North America were given basket-hilted broad or single-edged back swords along with musket and bayonet. The swords proved useless in American forest warfare and ordinary soldiers abandoned them to use only musket and bayonet. The Scottish officers carried basket-hilted swords throughout the war. Some American militia, unequipped with bayonets, had short, 24-inch bladed hunting swords, similar to French and German hunting swords still used in those countries. The American frontier riflemen copied their Indian enemies and habitually carried a long, heavy hunting knife and tomahawk hatchet for hand-to-hand combat. Being natural knife and ax fighters, they were formidable antagonists in bush warfare.

The obsolete or obsolescent halberd, pike, and spontoon still were used for guard duty, trench or fort defense, or as junior officers' and sergeants' official equipment. These were shaft or pole weapons, the halberd being a combination ax and spear about 8 feet long including the blade, and serving as a sergeant's designation of rank. The spontoon was an officer's spear about 7 feet long including the blade; it also was a

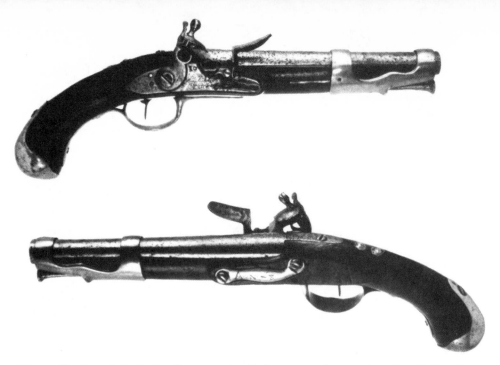

Figure 49.   French flintlock military pistol, with brass mountings, made at French Royal
Factory at Charleville. Length: 15.75 inches

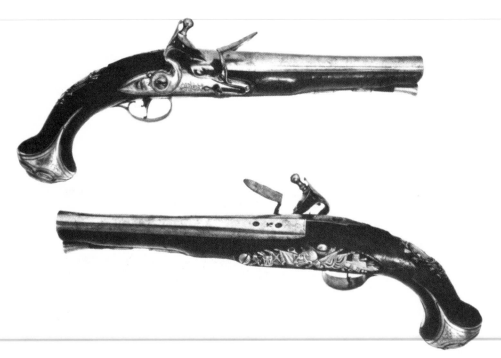

Figure 50.   British officer's flintlock holster pistols, sterling silver mountings. Length: 14
inches

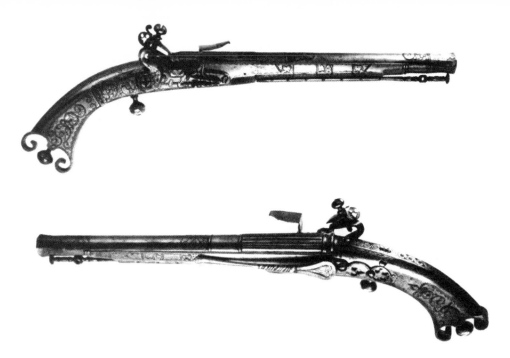

Figure 51.   British all-metal flintlock pistols carried by Highland Scot officers during the Revolution. Length: 16.5 inches

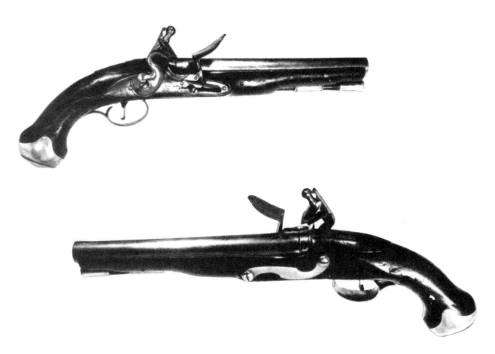

Figure 52.   Two views of a British light dragoon flintlock pistol. This weapon has a .65-caliber carbine bore and a 9-inch barrel. Length: 15.5

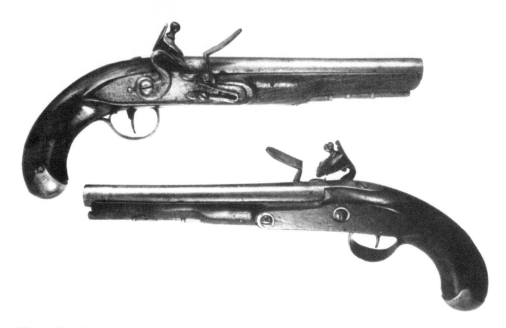

Figure 53.   American manufactured officer's flintlock holster pistols stocked in cherry wood. Length: 13.5 inches

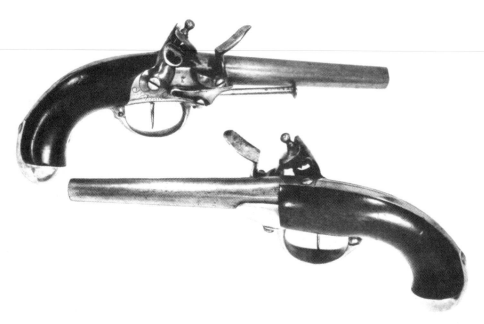

Figure 54.   French enlisted man's flintlock pistol, marked "St. Etienne" (French arsenal), brass furniture. Length 13.25 inches

Figure 55.   British flintlock rampart swivel gun. This is the type referred to in the text. Length: 54 inches.

Figure 56.   British .65-caliber light dragoon carbine with a 37-inch barrel. Length: 4 feet 4.5 inches

Figure 57.   British officer's flintlock cavalry carbine carried by light dragoons. This weapon had a 37-inch barrel. Length: 4 feet 5 inches

Figure 58.   German .75-caliber rifled carbine. Mounted Hessian troops carried this type of weapon during the Revolution. Length: 4 feet 3 inches

Figure 59.   British officer's fusil. Length: 4 feet 6 inches

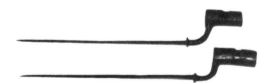

Figure 60.   American-made socket bayonet

Figure 61.   British socket bayonets. Top: bayonet
for Brown Bess infantry musket. Middle:
bayonet for officer's fusil. Bottom: short
bayonet for use with carbine

Figure 62.   French socket bayonets. Top: bayonet
for model 1763 Charleville infantry musket.
Bottom: bayonet for model 1746 Charleville
infantry musket

Figure 63.   American socket bayonets, crudely made,
the top bayonet having a very wide blade

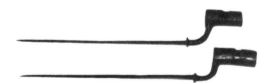

Figure 64.   Hessian socket bayonets made to fit
German infantry muskets

Figure 65.   British brass-hilted infantry sword. Blade length: 24.5 inches

Figure 66.   English hunting sword with silver hilt and ivory grip. Blade length: 27.5 inches

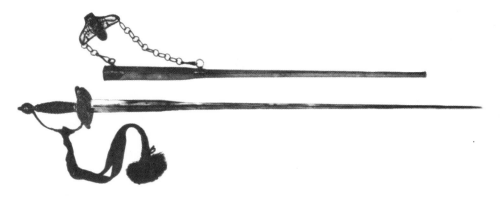

Figure 67.   British officer's silver-hilted small sword. Blade length: 35 inches

Figure 68.   Infantry hanger with steel hilt. Blade length: 26.75

symbol of rank in the foot regiments. The British and French officers in this period abandoned the spontoon in favor of the fusil, a lighter, shorter, smaller caliber officer's musket often made to individual specifications and equipped with a bayonet, which was far
better adapted to the rigors of American campaigning than the clumsy halberd or spontoon. Many British and French sergeants for the same reason carried musket or carbine
instead of the clumsy halberd. In a somewhat strange, archaic traditionalism, American
officers of foot regiments were required to carry spontoons throughout the war, as apparently did those in the German infantry regiments. How many harassed and practical
individuals saw fit to "lose" or "forget" their spontoons and carry fusil or carbine is
not reported in the sources. Pikes or trench spears in varying dimensions, probably hammered out by local blacksmiths, were used by the defending British garrison during the
siege of Ninety Six in South Carolina and would seem to have been issued for similar
operations in all theaters of the war by Americans and British alike.

Figure 69.   American fighting knife carried by   Figure 70.   Belt axes like those carried by American
        frontier riflemen in the Revolution   riflemen during the Revolution

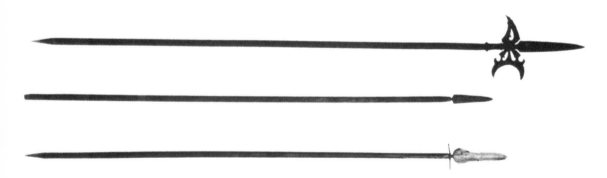

Figure 71.   Three pole arms with their shafts. Top to bottom: an American halberd, total
        length, 8 feet; an American pike, total length, 6 feet 9 inches; a British spontoon, total
        length, 7 feet

Figure 72. American Sergeant, 2d Maryland
Regiment Continental Line, 1778–1779

Figure 73. British Private, Light Infantry Company,
38th Regiment of Foot, 1775–1783

A thorough description of uniforms worn by American, British, French, and German troops serving in the Revolution cannot be given here. Brown was officiallly adopted by the Continental Congress as the color for American Continental uniforms on 4 November 1775. This was an eminently practical color for American warfare. On 2 October 1779, however, by authorization of the Continental Congress, George Washington fixed blue as the color for all branches of the American service with distinctive differences in lining and facings. Actually, the hunting frock made famous as the garb of rifle regiments was worn as field dress by most of the American army throughout the war. It could be made of deer leather, linen, or homespun and was dyed in various colors for various regiments. Hunting frocks all were cut in the same general pattern—a loose shirt reaching about 10 to 12 inches below the hips—but some had capes, cuffs, or fringes of a different color from the rest of the garment. The American soldier also wore long leggings or overalls of linen, undyed duck, or deerskin. Later in the war wool overalls were issued for winter use. These were shaped to the leg, fastened with four buttons at the ankle, and strapped under the shoe.

A broad-brimmed wool (for officers, beaver) hat, either cocked with distinctive bindings or worn brim down, was standard headgear for American troops. Some foot regiments still clung to their black leather caps and American (also British) cavalry usually wore leather, brass, or steel helmets mounted with bearskin and ornamented with long, flowing horsehair plumes.

Warfare in the rigors of heat, thorny underbrush, mosquitoes, chiggers, and ticks in the South progressively modified the fighting uniforms of British, Loyalist, and German forces serving in the area. The red wool uniforms of the British line regiments, the blue of the royal artillery, the green of Banastre Tarleton's Legion or John Simcoe's Rangers were worn in winter time, but during the hot summer months the British perforce were issued white linen or duck overalls and frocks. Even some of the Scottish regiments gave up their beloved kilts and adopted the long overall. (Modern-day hunters and fishermen from Virginia, the Carolinas, and Georgia would applaud such a sensible, practical, and necessary decision.)

British regiments in the South apparently still wore their bearskin or brass-fronted leather caps, although practicality may have again carried the day and the broad-brimmed hat, either cocked or with the brim down, replaced the traditional head protection during the heat of the summer. The Scots continued to wear their "bonnets," like the beret, a very good covering in any weather.

The stalwart, highly disciplined German mercenaries serving in the South seemed to have abandoned the knee-high leggings and wool trousers for lighter weight linen or duck overalls. Whether they continued to sweat stoically in their heavy dark blue wool jackets and falter on the long, hot summer marches under the weight of their tall brass caps is not reported.

The French, whose land service in the South was at Savannah, in September and October 1779 or during the same months in Virginia in 1781, did not suffer the full difficulties of southern campaigning. Their infantry at Yorktown for the most part wore the standard white wool jackets of the Bourbon armies with different colored facings for the several regiments. Since the siege took place during a Virginia autumn, the troops probably were issued the white linen breeches and long white canvas gaiters supplied for hot weather. (In winter, the French line regiments had white tricot breeches and black cloth gaiters.) One exception at Yorktown was the Royal Deux Ponts Regiment which had its own uniform of dark blue jacket and white breeches.

The French artillery wore dark blue jackets and breeches and the Pioneers were uniformed in dark blue jackets and red breeches. Officers' uniforms did not differ materially from those of the enlisted men except that they were made from finer cloth. All personnel in the line regiments wore a dark blue or black wool or beaver tricorne hat with a cockade and different colored pompom to designate the several units in the two battalions of a French regiment.

Figure 74. French Chasseur Corporal of the Soissonnais Infantry, 1780–1783

Figure 75. Hessian Fusilier, Regiment Knyphausen, 1776

Figure 76.   American Dragoon of Colonel E. M. Moylan's 4th Continental Regiment of
Light Dragoons, 1779–1781

The Duke de Lauzun's Legion of Polish and Irish mercenaries attached to the French army at Yorktown had sky blue tunics with yellow trousers for the cavalry and red trousers for the infantry. The mounted unit wore tall felt hussar bonnets, but the infantry apparently had the usual wool cocked hat of the line formations.

One may suspect that the pragmatic French, given a full taste of southern sun, rain, thorns, insects, snakes, and terrain, eventually would have adopted clothing more suitable to the region, weather, and general hardships of eighteenth-century warfare in the American South.

CHAPTER XIII

The North Carolina Campaign and Guilford Court House

In January of 1781 Charles Lord Cornwallis finally began to put into effect his grand strategic plan to subdue the rebellious southern colonies, by using occupied Georgia and South Carolina as bases for the conquest of North Carolina and Virginia. The plan was foredoomed to failure for several reasons. At Kings Mountain and again at Cowpens, Cornwallis had lost the best elements of his light armed infantry, essential units for warfare in a largely wilderness country. The ruthless partisan leaders of Georgia and South Carolina kept the field and restricted British control of the area to fortified towns, outposts, and the main avenues of communication. Cornwallis's great opponent, Nathanael Greene, was a master of the fighting retreat, and the expected military support from North Carolina and Virginia Loyalists never materialized in sufficient strength to affect seriously the eventual outcome of the campaign.

After Banastre Tarleton's savage defeat at Cowpens and Cornwallis's failure to overtake the retreating Daniel Morgan, the British commander on 25 January 1781 assembled his army at Ramsour's Mill on the south fork of the Catawba River. Since the loss of his light troops in two battles could be made up only by converting the entire infantry force into light troops, Cornwallis decided grimly to destroy all superfluous baggage and equipment. He set an example by ordering his own personal baggage to be destroyed with the rest. After spending two days at Ramsour's Mill resting his army and collecting flour, Cornwallis gave the order to march and the great pursuit of Nathanael Greene's retreating army across North Carolina began.

Morgan, falling back on North Carolina after his victory at Cowpens, camped at Sherrald's Ford north of the Catawba River and sent dispatches to General Greene informing him that the British had arrived at Ramsour's Mill in force and were pressing forward rapidly. Morgan also stated that he did not have sufficient troops to stop Cornwallis and therefore had requested General William Davidson to join him with all available North Carolina militia. Davidson marched into Morgan's camp on 26 January with 500 militiamen, and these were set to guard Beatty's and Cowan's fords on the Catawba River.

Cornwallis's advance guard reached the Catawba at Beatty's Ford on 29 January to find that heavy rains had swelled the river. The British were delayed for two full days in sight of the American camp fires until the waters subsided. During this halt it was decided to feint toward Beatty's Ford and force a crossing with the main army six miles downstream at Cowan's Ford. At one o'clock in the morning of 1 February, Lieutenant Colonel James Webster moved the 33d Foot to Beatty's Ford and opened a heavy artillery preparation fire on the North Carolina militia watching the shallow passage. Cornwallis meanwhile marched the six miles to Cowan's Ford, where the numerous camp fires in the darkness showed this crossing to be heavily guarded. Pushing to the river bank, Cornwallis ordered Brigadier General Charles O'Hara to throw his Guards Brigade across the ford which at this point was 500 yards wide. Into the swift, ice cold river marched the light infantry of the brigade, personally led by Lieutenant Colonel Hall. They waded across the ford, followed by the rest of the brigade and the other units in order, maintaining platoon formation as best they could against the hard sweep of the current. By the time they reached the middle of the stream, an American sentry saw the advancing column and fired at the lead elements. His alerted comrades soon joined him, and the fire from the American side became general. The Guards, ordered not to shoot until they gained the opposite bank, held fire. As they pressed forward out of the river, their commander, Lieutenant Colonel Hall, was killed by an American sniper. The light infantry of the Guards, dripping wet, half frozen, their commanding officer dead, formed line, delivered a rolling volley by ranks, and charged with the bayonet. The North Carolina militia broke and ran. General William Davidson, gallantly but vainly trying to rally his troops, was toppled by a snap shooting light infantryman as the North Carolinian swung into his saddle. Brigadier General O'Hara and Major General Alexander Leslie both lost their horses to the river current and almost were drowned themselves. Cornwallis's mount was hit by a stray bullet and fell dead as the general reached the other side of the river.

Once his whole force was across the stream Cornwallis ordered Banastre Tarleton to pursue the fleeing militia with his light dragoons. Colonel James Webster, having crossed at Beatty's Ford without significant opposition, rejoined the army with the 33d Regiment, and Tarleton's patrols swept the area. His scouts brought back word that the fugitives from the fords, supported by fresh militia units from Rowan and Mecklenburg counties, were assembling ten miles away at Tarrant's Tavern.

Cornwallis sent Tarleton, with his cavalry reinforced by the 23d Infantry Regiment, on a reconnaissance in force to probe and ascertain the strength of the gathering militia. Finding the North Carolinians drawn up across the road at Tarrant's Tavern and waiting to receive him, Tarleton ordered the cavalry forward in a mounted saber charge. His horseman attacked frontally, shouting the battle cry "Remember Cowpens," and swept through the American formation—some 400 strong—killing 40 or 50 and dispersing the rest.

Figure 77. Lieutenant General Charles Lord Cornwallis

Nathanael Greene continued to fall back, followed closely by the British. On 4 February the British army reached Salisbury, North Carolina, and learned that Morgan was only seven miles away, crossing the Yadkin River at Trading Ford. Tarleton's horsemen, Brigadier O'Hara's Guards, and Bose's Regiment of Hessian foot advanced over incredibly bad roads through rain and darkness in an effort to catch Morgan before he completed passage over the ford. The British reached Trading Ford at midnight to find that Morgan with the American rear guard had crossed the river earlier in the evening, taking all available flatboats with them.

The Yadkin continued to rise and again the British were delayed. After an enforced wait of several days, intelligence was received from Loyalist spies that Greene was marching to join Morgan at Guilford Court House. Since the North Carolina militia and reinforcements from Virginia had not yet joined Greene in any force, Cornwallis concluded that Greene would not risk a set battle against a superior enemy on the south bank of the Dan River.

The British general therefore pressed on with all expedition to get between the American army and the upper fords of the Dan, which runs along the North Carolina and Virginia border. When Cornwallis and his army on 15 February finally reached Boyd's Ferry on the Dan River, across the Virginia line, they found that the American army had passed the day before and, again, had taken all the flatboats with them. A few days before, on 9 February at Guilford Court House, Greene had regretfully accepted Morgan's resignation. The old fighter, suffering miserably from sciatica and acute hemorrhoids, simply could not keep the saddle any longer. Otho Williams of Maryland, a very good soldier, was given command of the light armed troops in his place.

The British army in its march to Boyd's Ferry had covered forty miles in twenty-four hours to find that Nathanael Greene had escaped. Disappointed, frustrated, and weary, Cornwallis marched by easy stages to Hillsboro, North Carolina, where he raised the royal standard and called by proclamation for all loyal subjects to rally in support of their king. Considerable numbers of these were responding to the call when Greene, who had learned of this movement and feared the effect of Cornwallis's proclamation, determined to cross the Dan from Virginia into North Carolina. He had been strengthened by a reinforcement of 600 Virginia militia under Brigadier General Edward Stevens, and on 21 February 1781, Lieutenant Colonel Henry Lee with his legion moved over the river from Virginia, followed on the next day by all of Greene's army.

About this time one of the more brutal incidents of the war in the South took place. Loyalist elements were stronger in North Carolina than in any other southern colony.

Figure 78. Lieutenant Colonel Henry Lee, by Robert Wilson

Figure 79. Major General Nathanael Greene, by Robert Wilson

Figure 80.   General Greene's Army, by Robert Wilson

Spurred by Cornwallis's proclamation, the old royal militia between the Haw and Deep rivers began assemblng under a Colonel John Pyle; Cornwallis detached Tarleton with 450 troops to meet and escort Colonel Pyle's militia to Hillsboro. Neither Cornwallis nor Tarleton knew that American intelligence, always better than British, already had brought word of the Loyalist rising. Greene sent Henry Lee and his legion, supported by two companies of Maryland Continentals with Andrew Pickens and his veteran South Carolina militia, to stop Tarleton and put down the Loyalists. In the course of several forays around the British positions Henry Lee had captured two of Tarleton's officers. He now forced these men to ride with his column on pain of death if they revealed his or their own identity when Loyalists were encountered. Lee's Legion wore a green uniform, and legion horsemen had helmets very similar to those of Tarleton's command. Henry Lee depended on this resemblance to complete the deception.

    The legion in green uniforms took the front of the column with the horse in the lead and Colonel Lee at the head. Lee's van officer, riding a few hundred yards in advance with the point, halted two well-mounted young countrymen who announced that they were delighted to meet Lieutenant Colonel Tarleton's command and had been sent forward by Colonel John Pyle to make contact if possible. They were brought to Henry Lee, who greeted them in his role of Tarleton with great cordiality and sent one young man back with two dragoons to carry "Tarleton's" congratulations and compliments to Colonel Pyle. Meanwhile, Andrew Pickens and the South Carolinians were concealed in a thick woods on the left of the road to support the planned operation. John Pyle arrived with his forces and drew up his some 400 men on the right side of the road to be reviewed and welcomed by "Tarleton." They calmly sat on their horses—400 mounted Loyalist militia with muskets, rifles, and fowling pieces slung on their shoulders. Henry Lee rode the entire length of the line with his dragoons behind him until he reached Colonel Pyle. Playing his role of the dashing British commander, Lee shook Pyle's hand warmly. At that moment, according to Henry Lee, the Loyalist left saw Pickens's men in the woods and began to fire (or, perhaps, prepared to fire). The entire American column turned on the Loyalists and sabered them where they sat, all or most of them with their weapons still slung. Some 90 were killed outright and 150 badly slashed. The survivors scattered into the woods and Lee did not pursue them.

The accounts are cloudy, and there might have been certain justifications for his action, as Henry Lee later claimed. The fact remains that most of the Loyalists clearly were totally deceived and cut down without a chance to defend themselves. Banastre Tarleton very properly was called "Bloody Tarleton" for his conduct and that of his command at the Waxhaws in 1780, when he almost wiped out Colonel Abraham Buford's Virginians. That, however, was a battle, which the Americans lost. The affair near the Haw River was pure butchery of unsuspecting men. The Loyalists in North Carolina, thoroughly intimidated by the killing only a mile from Tarleton's camp, did not come in to join the British army.

The country around Hillsboro had been almost exhausted of provisions, and the forward position of that town was considered too far from the Loyalist population between the Haw and Deep rivers for the British to protect their already frightened supporters. Greene's army also was across the Dan River and on the move, so Lord Cornwallis made the decision to retire from Hillsboro and take up a new position between the two rivers to be better able to cover the country and the people in his rear. The British army therefore abandoned Hillsboro and, passing the Haw River, camped on Alamance Creek. Unfortunately for Cornwallis, this retrograde movement was interpreted by the Loyalists in the area as a retreat, and, added to Colonel Pyle's disaster, further discouraged their active military participation with the royal forces.

As Lord Cornwallis retired, the American army pushed further into North Carolina, passed the Haw River near its source, and took station between Troublesome Creek and Reedy Fork. Nathanael Greene did not consider his force strong enough as yet to risk a general acton and therefore changed the position of his camp every night to avoid any possibility of a major encounter.

Cornwallis faced a hard decision. Because adequate provisions no longer were available for his army, he either must fight Greene and defeat him decisively or fall back on the Cape Fear River where supplies could be brought up by boat from British-held Wilmington. The latter decision would mean abandoning the Loyalists to the tender mercies of their Patriot neighbors, and only a real victory would encourage these same Loyalists to offer support. Hearing that the American light troops were posted carelessly near Reedy Fork, the British commander on 6 March pushed forward with all his army to attack the light elements, by surprise if possible. As usual, the Americans had word of the British advance and retired across Reedy Fork to Wetzell's Mill where they made a brief stand, but were dislodged with some losses by Lieutenant Colonel Webster's command. Greene did not come to his light troops' assistance, but retreated over the Haw River to wait for promised reinforcements.

Cornwallis, bringing up all his forces, camped at the Quaker Meeting House between the forks of Deep River. There he heard on 14 March that Brigadier General John Butler with a considerable body of North Carolina militia, a Virginia state regiment, 3,000 Virginia militia, and recruits for the Maryland Line regiments all had joined Greene, who now had a force of 9,000 to 10,000 men. Actually the American commander had only some 4,500 soldiers available for battle, while Cornwallis's effectives numbered slightly over 2,400. The odds against the British were still very heavy, indeed, and Cornwallis displayed supreme confidence in the quality of his men and in his own abilities to commit such a small army to the decision of battle.

The continued approach of Greene and the movements of his army, with the addition of strong reinforcements, apparently demonstrated a willingness to fight. In the evening of 14 March Cornwallis sent off his baggage to Bell's Mill on Deep River under the escort of Lieutenant Colonel John Hamilton and his North Carolina Loyalist regiment, 100 line infantry, and 20 of Tarleton's cavalry. At dawn on 15 March, the rest of the army, some 1,900 strong, began its move to Guilford Court House where Greene was reported to have taken post with all his forces.

About four miles from Guilford Court House the advancing British encountered Lee's Legion, some of William Preston's riflemen, and a few militia. These were attacked promptly by Tarleton's advance guard and, after a sharp fight, fell back in good order on the main American position, but Tarleton received a musket ball in his right hand. (The thumb and forefinger later were amputated.) To give Tarleton his proper due, he fought the battle of Guilford Court House with his mutilated hand in a sling and personally led a cavalry charge where he was slightly wounded, without a weapon and totally defenseless.

Nathanael Greene had chosen his position well at Guilford Court House, and his battle plan obviously was modeled on Daniel Morgan's at Cowpens. As Henry Lee, who fought there, wrote, the Guilford Court House itself was situated on the brow of a long, low hill, near the major state road to Salisbury. The slope descended for about half a mile, ending in a small valley with a brook running along the base, and Greene formed his battle lines up the slope, astride the road to Salisbury. Captain Anthony Singleton with two 6-pounders was stationed slightly in advance of the first line on the approach road the enemy must use, under orders to maintain his position until the fight became close and then withdraw promptly. Some yards behind the guns and placed on both sides of the road were the North Carolina militia under Brigadier Generals John Butler and Pinkertham Eaton. Three hundred yards up the slope in the woods was stationed the Virginia militia commanded by Brigadier Generals Edward Stevens and Robert Lawson. Robert Lawson's right flank and Stevens's left flank rested on the Salisbury road. The Continental infantry of four regiments were drawn up 400 yards to the rear of the Virginia militia in a field to the right of the road across a ravine. The two Virginia regiments on the right of the Continental line, led respectively by Colonels John Greene and Samuel Hawes, came under the overall command of General Isaac Huger of South Carolina. The two Maryland regiments on the left under Colonels John Gunby and Lieutenant Colonel Benjamin Ford were commanded by Colonel Otho Williams. Of these four Continental units, only John Gunby's 1st Maryland was composed entirely of veterans. The others were made up of new recruits stiffened by a handful of combat-experienced soldiers, but all the officers were veterans and, as Henry Lee says, "approved."

On the right of the first line of North Carolina militia, to guard its flank, were Colonel William Washington and his cavalry, Robert Kirkwood's battle-hardened company of Delaware infantry, and a battalion of Virginia militia riflemen led by Colonel Charles Lynch. Henry Lee with the cavalry and infantry of his legion, supported by the frontier rifles of Colonel William Preston and Colonel William Campbell, held the left of the North Carolinians. William Campbell was the same huge, redheaded Scot who was in overall command at Kings Mountain and led his Virginians on that bloody day with his ancestral Highland broadsword in hand.

In the rear of the American Continentals were placed two 6-pounders under Captain Samuel Finley; these plus Singleton's two advanced 6-pounders at the base of the slope composed the entire American artillery.

As soon as the approaching British came within range, Singleton opened fire as ordered on the head of the column with his two fieldpieces. This was answered promptly by the Royal Artillery under Lieutenant John MacLeod. While this brief cannonade continued, the British crossed the little stream and the different units deployed to the right and left, at the quickstep and with beautiful precision. The 71st Regiment with Bose's German mercenary regiment both commanded by Major General ALexander Leslie formed the right of the line. These were supported by the 1st Battalion of the Guards under Lieutenant Colonel Norton. The left included the 23d and 33d Regiments of Foot led by Lieutenant Colonel James Webster, supported by Brigadier General O'Hara with the grenadiers and 2d Battalion of the Guards. The light infantry of the Guards

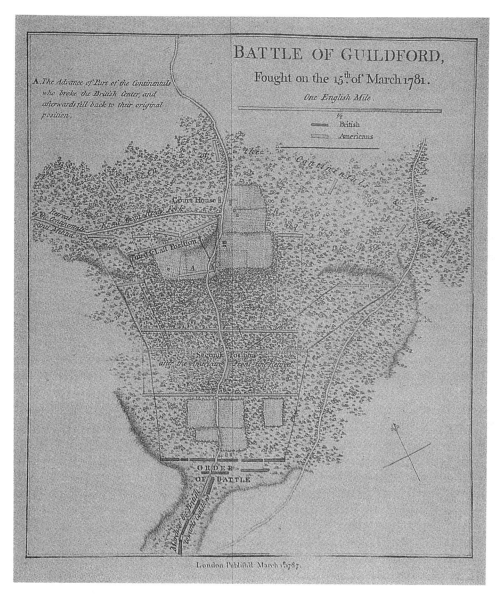

Figure 81. Battle of Guilford Court House, 15 March 1781, from *A History of the Campaigns of 1780 and 1781 in the Southern Provinces of North America*, Lieutenant Colonel Banastre Tarleton (London, 1787)

and the jäger riflemen were posted on the left of the artillery with the cavalry in column behind it on the road. These last three units constituted a corps of observation.

With the battle line formed, the British pressed steadily forward and up the slope without firing. The North Carolinians with William Campbell's riflemen and Henry Lee's light infantry were posted behind a long rail fence. At about 140 yards, too far for accurate musketry, the Americans delivered their first volley and then maintained a hot running fire up and down the line. The British continued a steady, cool advance without faltering. When Cornwallis's infantry came within point-blank range, the troops halted on command, delivered a smashing volley, and charged, shouting, with the bayonet. Except for a few brave individuals of Eaton's brigade who fell back, fighting, on the Virginians, the North Carolina militia suddenly panicked and fled the field. Henry Lee and William Campbell, their right flank exposed by the flight of the North Carolinians, pulled back into the woods on their left, battling desperately. William Washington, his left flank exposed by the same abrupt departure, retreated in good order to cover the Virginia militia on the right.

James Webster with his two regiments having routed the North Carolinians opposed to him, pushed up the slope and engaged the second line of Virginia militia. These men stood and fought magnificently, exchanging continuous close-range volleys with the British regulars and inflicting heavy casualties on their opponents. William Washington now threw Charles Lynch's Virginia rifles against the 33d Regiment on Webster's left; Webster changed front to meet this new attack. Charles O'Hara promptly brought up the grenadiers and 2d Battalion of the Guards to fill the gap, and Webster, attacking with the 33d Regiment supported by the light infantry of the Guards and the jägers, stopped Lynch's attack and drove back the Virginia riflemen. The 71st Regiment having come out of the woods on the right, General O'Hara brought the British center into line, attacked with the bayonet, and first Robert Lawson's and then Edward Stevens's Virginia militia were driven from the field, both units resisting stubbornly. Since General Leslie commanding on the British right had been obliged early in the fighting to bring forward his reserve, the 1st Battalion of the Guards, and commit them to battle, every unit in the British army except the cavalry now was engaged.

Because of the broken and wooded nature of the terrain, the battle had resolved itself into a series of almost separate engagements, but the British from right to left still pushed steadily up the slope.

James Webster, moving left and driving the Americans before him, crossed the ravine and temporarily gained the right of the four Continental regiments not yet engaged and unshaken 400 yards up the slope from the beaten Virginians. Their superiority in numbers and the weight of their disciplined fire forced Webster, separated as he was from the rest of the British army, to order his men back across the ravine to regroup on the other bank and join the units on his right.

As the British advanced, Lieutenant Colonel Stuart, commanding the 2d Battalion of the Guards, was the first to reach the open ground where the Continentals waited in their unbroken ranks. Stewart promptly attacked frontally the 2d Maryland Regiment stationed on the left of the Continental line, and the 2d Maryland, noted in former engagements for its steadiness but made up on this occasion chiefly of new recruits, suddenly broke and left the field in disorganized retreat, losing in the process Singleton's two 6-pounders which had been withdrawn successfully from their advanced position early in the battle. John Gunby of the 1st Maryland Regiment promptly swung his left against Stewart's Guards as they followed closely the routed 2d Maryland. William Washington, stationed with his cavalry in the rear of the Continental formation, sud-

Figure 82.   Battle of Guilford Court House, by Frank E. Buffmire (copied from a lost work by F. C. Yohn)

denly swung around Gunby's right flank and hit the advancing Guards with a savage saber charge. Stewart's command, suffering heavily, was forced back, and a Captain Smith of the 1st Maryland Regiment, leading his company with the bayonet against the retiring British, personally engaged Lieutenant Colonel Stewart and cut him down with his sword. Seeing that the attack was faltering, Cornwallis made a grim and terrible decision. He ordered Lieutenant MacLeod, who had moved his two guns up with the advancing British lines, to open fire with canister on the pursuing Americans through the ranks of the retreating 2d Guards Battalion. This brutal, point-blank fire further cut to pieces Stewart's men, but it effectively stopped Otho Williams's Marylanders and William Washington's cavalry, both units falling back to their former positions, but recapturing and taking with them the two 6-pounders.

The 71st Regiment moving from the right and the 23d Regiment coming up from the left linked in the center and Major General O'Hara, although severely wounded, rallied the broken remnants of the 2d Guards Battalion and brought these troops back into line. The three units advanced against the 1st Maryland Continentals and Washington's command, taking again the two 6-pounders and also capturing two ammunition wagons and two additional 6-pounders, which were all that remained of the American artillery. The 71st, fighting hard, pushed forward to an eminence near the courthouse itself and reached the left flank of the 1st Maryland Regiment and the Continental line. James Webster with the 33d Regiment, the light infantry of the guards, and the jägers attacked again across the ravine and forced back Samuel Hawes's Virginia Continentals and Kirkwood's Delaware company. In the severe fighting, James Webster, one of Cornwallis's most gallant and effective officers, fell mortally wounded at the head of his regiment, but his command successfully joined with the British center. Only the Virginia Continental regiment under Colonel Greene was still intact, and Nathanael Greene with Isaac Huger, realizing that a serious defeat could be avoided only by a tactical withdrawal and unaware that Henry Lee with most of his legion had fallen back from the woods and joined the American left, retired from the field in reasonably good order. The 23d and 71st Regiments with part of the cavalry were sent in pursuit, but Cornwallis, having suffered heavily in killed and wounded, soon recalled the pursuit and Greene retired unmolested, collecting his stragglers and broken units as he marched.

While the fighting in the center and on the American right took place, an almost separate battle had been fought through the woods on the American left. In this area, Brigadier General Alexander Leslie with the 1st Battalion of the Guards and the regiment of Bose under Lieutenant Colonel de Buiy had met fierce resistance from Henry Lee and William Campbell. The growth was so heavy that bayonets were of very little use and the Americans, using the trees as cover, made frequent stands. The British and Germans at times were engaged in front, flank, and rear, as bypassed American units returned to the action. At one point the guards battalion was almost broken. It had suffered grievously in attacking a low ridge against strongly posted Americans. No sooner were these driven from their position than other forces appeared on the British front and right flank and poured in a heavy and accurate fire. This action is reminiscent of Kings Mountain, and it must be remembered again that William Campbell had commanded at Kings Mountain and undoubtedly some of his riflemen at Guilford Court House had served there, too. The Guards had begun to break under the pressure when de Buiy came up on their left with his Hessian regiment. The Germans had not as yet suffered heavily, and Lieutenant Colonel Norton, commanding the guards, requested the Hessian commander to wheel his regiment to the right and cover the disorganized guards while their officers rallied them. This was accomplished successfully and the two units advanced together and drove away the Americans on their right. No sooner had they accomplished this when the Hessians and guards were hit from the rear by still another group of riflemen and were forced to march back over the same ground they already had passed to beat off the new attack. The action in the center and American right was over and Nathanael Greene already retiring from the field when the continued fire in the woods on the American left caused Cornwallis to dispatch Tarleton, who had come up with his supporting force, to find out if Alexander Leslie needed help. He arrived with part of his cavalry to discover the fighting virtually over and the roughly handled guards with the regiment of Bose standing in formation with ordered arms. A few determined American riflemen still maintained a long-range fire from behind trees. Tarleton, covered by a general volley from the guards and Hessians, cleared the area with a cavalry charge and the battle of Guilford Court House was over.

Cornwallis remained the victor on the field, but Nathanel Greene marched back in good order eighteen miles to the ironworks on Troublesome Creek where he promptly began to rally and reform his army. The British lost 93 killed, 413 wounded, and 26 missing, over one-fourth of their total forces engaged. Greene's losses totaled 78 killed and 195 wounded. As he wrote afterward to Thomas Jefferson, this was a "trifling loss" out of 4,500 men in the line.

The battle of Guilford Court House, fought on 15 March 1781, lasted just an hour and a half. Nathanael Greene was defeated, but he pulled his army back in good order before the climactic British attack and saved that army, thus displaying a rare order of cool battlefield leadership under very desperate circumstances.

Cornwallis and his gallant troops deserve only praise. Outnumbered two times over, they frontally attacked a greatly superior force in a prepared position and won. The fact that the victory was too costly, fruitless, and led inevitably to Yorktown and eventual surrender is part of Cornwallis's tragedy of command in the American war.

The Battle of Hobkirk Hill, 25 April 1781

After his grim pyrrhic victory at Guilford Court House, Cornwallis left 70 seriously wounded men under a flag of truce at the Quaker Meeting House and marched to the coast where a British garrison held the port of Wilmington. Here he rested his badly battered little army for eighteen days and then made one of the most fateful decisions of the entire war. Instead of continuing the campaign in North Carolina or returning to South Carolina either by land or sea, Cornwallis determined that the wisest course of action was to march north up the coast to tidewater Virginia where he could join his force to a strong corps that had been acting in that area from the beginning of 1781. These troops had been commanded first by Benedict Arnold, the traitor, now a brigadier general in the British army, and afterward came under Major General William Philips.

Cornwallis believed that such a move to threaten the wealthy and populous state of Virginia might draw Nathanael Greene back to the north. Cornwallis also apparently hoped that a vigorous military operation in Virginia and the possible reduction of that rebellious colony might be the most effective method of securing South Carolina and Georgia or reducing North Carolina. This decision, ironically, guaranteed that the hard-won victory at Guildford Court House would be followed by all the serious consequences of a decisive defeat.

Instead of marching north into Virginia to counter Cornwallis's move, as that general had hoped and planned that he might do, Nathanael Greene decided instead to move his operations back to South Carolina and acted immediately. Brigadier Generals Thomas Sumter and Francis Marion were informed by dispatch riders to assemble all their forces to cooperate with Greene's army, while Henry Lee was detached with his full legion of horse and foot to join Francis Marion and his partisans still striking viciously at British supply lines. During late April of 1781, Greene marched south from Deep River, North Carolina sending ahead instructions to Thomas Sumter and Andrew Pickens. The former was ordered to join his forces with Greene's army in the vicinity of Camden. Greene expressed a desire that Pickens would invest Ninety Six or, at least, prevent any reinforcement of Camden from that post.

Figure 83.   Francis Lord Rawdon, engraved by Stamier from a portrait by Sir Joshua
Reynolds

Francis Lord Rawdon, who had been given command in South Carolina by Cornwallis during the North Carolina campaign, had received no information of the British army's movements after Guilford Court House because his communications had been almost totally cut by the partisans. He was thus astonished to receive the intelligence that Nathanael Greene had marched back in force and was planning to attack his garrison at Camden, South Carolina. Following reports of the victory at Guilford Court House, he had confidently expected to hear that Greene's forces were destroyed or driven out of North Carolina and Virginia. Instead, the American general was marching against Rawdon in South Carolina and word came at the same time that Henry Lee and his legion had linked up with Francis Marion on the Black River. Lord Rawdon correctly judged Lee and Marion's operations as a diversion. Instead of sending reinforcements to Colonel John Watson watching partisan activities in the lowcountry, Rawdon recalled Watson and his entire command to Camden.

The absence of Henry Lee's Legion, some 300 horse and foot, and the fact that Virginia militia present at Guilford Court House remained in that state left Nathanael Greene with only about 1,200 effectives. He had expected Thomas Sumter to join him with all the South Carolina forces he could gather, but Sumter, something of a law unto himself, failed to do so. Lord Rawdon, however, had only some 900 men stationed at Camden, unless John Watson joined him in time, so the odds still were against the British.

Nathanael Greene did not believe his army strong enough to invest Camden, even against a garrison of 900 men. He placed his forces north of the town and waited for Lee, Marion, Sumter, and Pickens to join him. Stationed there, he still could use his superior forces in aggressive patrol actions to prevent the outnumbered British from collecting necessary supplies in the adjoining countryside. Hopefully, this tactic would eventually force Lord Rawdon to evacuate Camden and retreat to the coast. Then Nathanael Greene, reinforced by Lee and the South Carolina partisan leaders, could attack the British line of march and destroy them.

Nathanael Green now learned of the advance by Francis Marion and Henry Lee against Fort Watson, a strongly held post on the British line of communications to Charleston. He also received continuing intelligence reports of Colonel John Watson's march up the north bank of the Santee River toward Camden. The American general therefore decided to swing his army from its original position north of the town to the east side. This move would bring him closer to Marion and Lee, and also should block Watson's line of march up the Santee if that officer successfully eluded Francis Marion and Henry Lee. This change of post required Greene to pass Sandhill Creek which, with its tangled, wide, and difficult swamps, was totally impassable for the transport of artillery, wheeled baggage, and ammunition. Greene could march around the area and thus avoid the most difficult passages, but to do so would have taken twice the time he could afford to lose. The American general therefore placed his artillery and baggage wagons in the charge of Lieutenant Colonel Edward Carrington, his quartermaster general, with orders to retire north of Lynch's Creek, a naturally strong position. Carrington, with a small detachment of infantry to guard the guns and baggage, would remain there until Greene ordered him to rejoin. This being accomplished, the American army pushed directly through the swamps and took up a position east of Camden on the road leading from Camden to Nelson's Ferry, the route Nathanael Greene expected John Watson to follow and also the most direct road to Francis Marion and Henry Lee.

While stationed there, Greene received word that Marion and Lee's operations against Fort Watson were moving to a successful conclusion and that the cavalry of Lee's Legion had been detached to watch the movements of Colonel John Watson. In addition, a defensible passage on the Santee River road by the great swamp, which the British must traverse if Watson's route were maintained, was occupied by a force of infantry. Francis Marion and Henry Lee planned to join this blocking unit as soon as Fort Watson fell.

Since it seemed likely that Colonel John Watson would not soon reach Camden and might not get there at all, Nathanael Greene marched back through the swamps and again posted his army north of the town. Orders were sent to Edward Carrington to rejoin as soon as possible with the artillery and baggage. Greene then selected his position, Hobkirk Hill, a short distance from Camden and on the Waxhaws road. He was now closer to Carrington, who was returning with the guns and baggage wagons, and also in a more convenient location for the expected junction with Thomas Sumter and his upcountry partisans (which never took place). Hobkirk Hill commanded the country south to Camden and thus presented an advantageous battleground in case Lord Rawdon decided to leave his fortifications and attack. The latter was not expected because the American army was considered stronger than the Camden garrison. With such a possibility in mind, however, Greene's army bivouacked in order of battle. The regulars were stationed in line along the hill crest with their center on the Waxhaws road. Two hundred fifty-four North Carolina militia and William Washington's cavalry formed a reserve in the rear, and strong pickets were posted before the army, supported by patrols ranging in front and on the flanks. On 24 April dispatch riders came in with the news that Fort Watson had surrendered to Marion and Lee, and, late in the same day, prisoners captured in that operation were brought to Greene's camp. Among them were a few American soldiers who had been taken prisoner by the British previously and joined their captors (or so they claimed) because enlistment in the British army provided the best means to escape back to their friends. Specious or not, and desertion from both sides was common during the Revolution, these men apparently were received cheerfully and without question by their former comrades. One of the returned soldiers, a drummer in the Maryland Line, deserted back to the British during the night. Having watched Greene's dispositions, and being an observant young man, he gave Rawdon full and accurate intelligence of the American position, with the added information that Edward Carrington had not as yet come up with the artillery and baggage nor had Sumter arrived with reinforcements.

Rawdon, meanwhile, received a letter from Lieutenant Colonel Nisbet Balfour, the British commander in Charleston, with detailed news of Cornwallis's decision to move his operations into Virginia. In the same letter Cornwallis ordered Balfour to instruct Rawdon that he must abandon Camden and retire behind the line of the Santee River. American forces in strength between him and the coast made such a move impossible, and Rawdon further heard, to his great disappointment, that Colonel John Watson had been impeded by Marion and Lee and could not be expected to join him in time to support any immediate action against Greene.

From the deserter and American prisoners captured in patrol actions around the town, particularly during an American attempt to destroy the Camden Mill, Rawdon learned that Nathanael Greene's army was not so numerous as he thought, and that Edward Carrington had not rejoined with the artillery. This resolute young soldier (Rawdon was only twenty-six years old) promptly decided to attack before Greene's expected support arrived. Rawdon armed everyone in his command, musicians and drummer boys included, successfully fielding 840 infantry and artillery plus 60 Loyalist dragoons under Major John Coffin. On 25 April 1781, at ten o'clock in the morning, Rawdon marched out of Camden with two 6-pounders as his only artillery to strike a superior enemy holding a prepared position. The surrounding redoubts and the entire base of Camden were guarded only by resident royal militia and a few sick regulars.

Nathanael Green was posted on Hobkirk Hill, about two miles from the town defense lines. By keeping close to the swamps on the right of the Waxhaws road, the British successfully got into thick woods without being seen by American patrols. Making a wide circuit under cover of the forest, they drove in Greene's pickets on the left and advanced up the easiest part of the slope, thus depriving Greene's army of the principal advantage of its location on Hobkirk Hill. Either the British were fortunate or the American patrols careless, because Rawdon's column was not discovered until the light infantry of the Volunteers of Ireland, one of the best Loyalist regiments in the British army, suddenly struck out of the woods.

The pickets retreated in good order on Captain Robert Kirkwood, who, with the devoted remnant of his Delaware company, formed the immediate advanced support group for the left flank pickets, and the entire group fell back fighting.

During the brief interval permitted by Kirkwood's resistance, Nathanael Greene brought order out of confusion and formed his line of battle facing the enemy attack. This was accomplished although Greene was eating breakfast and his men cooking theirs when the attack began. The American order of battle was as follows. The two regiments of Virginia Continentals formed a brigade under General Isaac Huger. These were posted on the right of the road, the 4th Virginia commanded by Lieutenant Colonel Richard Campbell, the 5th led by Lieutenant Colonel Samuel Hawes. On the left of the road was the Maryland brigade of two regiments under Colonel Otho Williams, the 1st Maryland commanded by Colonel John Eager Howard and the 2d following Lieutenant Colonel Benjamin Ford. Colonel John Gunby was posted as second in command of the Maryland brigade. Fortunately for Nathanael Greene, Colonel Edward Carrington had arrived with the three 6-pounders and these, with a detachment of 40 artillerists, were placed in the center commanded by Colonel Charles Harrison. The reserve consisted of the North Carolina militia, led by Colonel Reade and the 87 cavalry of Lieutenant Colonel William Washington. These were stationed in the rear behind the center of the line. Greene also ordered the two center regiments, 5th Virginia and 1st Maryland, to close across the road and mask the two fieldpieces. Lord Rawdon was unaware that the American artillery had

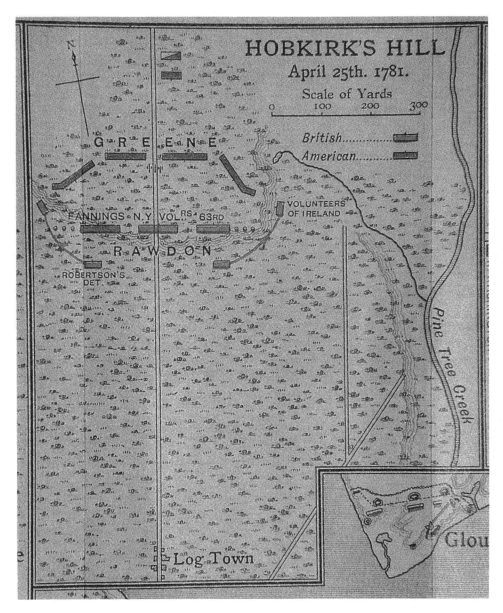

Figure 84.   Battle of Hobkirk Hill, South Carolina, 25 April 1781, from *A History of the British Army*, J. W. Fortescue (London, 1902)

arrived until the head of his main column emerged from the woods and was met by a shower of canister from the suddenly unmasked guns.

Rawdon, pushing the pickets ahead of him, pressed forward to engage Greene's army. The 63d Regiment of foot, British regular army, supported by the Loyalist Volunteers of Ireland, formed the right of Rawdon's line. The King's American Regiment, raised around New York, supported by Captain Robertson's detachment, held the left and Lieutenant Colonel George Turnbull's New York Volunteers the center of the British line. The South Carolina Provincial regiment and a cavalry troop of 60 New York dragoons marched in the rear as a corps of observation. Hobkirk Hill, like Kings Mountain and, later, Augusta and Ninety Six, was chiefly a battle of Americans against Americans.

Nathanael Greene, watching the steady approach of the British and Loyalists and seeing how narrow a front they presented, directed Richard Campbell commanding the 4th Virginia and Benjamin Ford with his 2d Maryland to advance and turn the enemy's left and right flanks respectively. The two center regiments of Virginia and Maryland Continentals were ordered at the same time down the hill to attack the British center with the bayonet as it came up the slope.

The American 6-pounders, well served by Colonel Charles Harrison and his artillerymen, for a few minutes disorganized and checked Rawdon's advance. He dressed his ranks, extended his front to meet the American flanking attacks, and came on firmly. Nathanael Greene's army outnumbered the British force by 300 men, and the Americans held a prepared position on a hill crest. It should have been an American victory, but one of those inexplicable chances of battle now occurred to change the fortunes of the day.

Isaac Huger, attacking down the slope with the Virginia brigade, was pushing the British left before him. William Washington, ordered to swing behind Rawdon's line and attack his rear, was carrying out instructions with his usual dash and élan. At this precise moment, the veteran 1st Maryland Regiment, the same unit that had driven Tarleton's infantry before it with the bayonet at Cowpens and forced back the guards battalion at Guilford Court House, broke and retreated. It had been among the finest regiments of the Continental line, and its conduct at Hobkirk Hill defies explanation.

As the 1st Maryland Regiment advanced against the British center in line with the 5th Virginia, two of its companies on the right became confused in their alignment and halted to re-form. Colonel John Gunby ordered the rest of the regiment also to halt and retire on the two companies, thus reestablishing the temporarily broken line of advance. It was a perfectly sensible and simple maneuver, but it turned out to be fatal. The British 63d Regiment, regular infantry opposing the Marylanders and seeing the retrograde movement, drove forward with a shout and the entire 1st Maryland Regiment, forgetting its previous heroic record, panicked and ran. Huger's Virginia brigade and the 2d

Maryland Regiment with Charles Harrison's artillery stoutly maintained the fight, but Colonel Benjamin Ford of the 2d Maryland was wounded and that unit also fell back, although in good order. Only the Virginians and Harrison's guns were left to hold the hill. Rawdon's right wing, pursuing the broken 1st Maryland, swung left and struck Samuel Hawes's 5th Virginia on their left flank, silencing the American guns in the process. Richard Campbell's 4th Virginia Regiment on Hawes's right, for inexplicable reasons, was suddenly infected by the unnerving American panic and fell back in disorder.

Nathanael Greene, seeing the day lost, ordered Hawes, with the only unbroken American regiment, to cover his retreat and retired from the field. The three 6-pounders were saved from British capture by manhandling them down the back slope and concealing them in thick bushes. Greene almost was taken prisoner as he personally helped to drag the guns to safety. Rawdon's advancing infantry missed the 6-pounders in the heat of the pursuit, and Washington, riding through the battlefield from his sweep behind the British lines, found them and pulled them back to Greene's army with his cavalry horses.

Unfortunately for Greene's original plan, Washington's sweep had been overly wide, and he came up too late to participate in the actual fighting. Washington only captured a few wounded British officers, but did bring in the 6-pounders and helped the 5th Virginia successfully to cover the retirement. Henry Lee credits him with stopping the pursuit by a furious saber charge against the British van, and he did return after Greene halted four miles away at Saunders Creek to carry out a reconnaissance. On that occasion, Washington, up to his old form, ambushed the 60 New York Provincial dragoons out on patrol, beat them soundly, and dispersed them. The next day, 26 April, Greene marched his bedraggled army up to Rugeley's Mill where he halted and made camp.

The losses in the battle were about even. Greene lost 132 killed and 136 wounded, captured, or missing. Rawdon suffered in killed. wounded, and missing between 257 and 269 men. Greene, however, with an aroused countryside from the coast to the mountains moving to assist him, could afford the losses and Rawdon could not. Like Cornwallis at Guilford Court House, Rawdon's victory won against a superior force proved barren. John Watson succeeded in evading Francis Marion and Henry Lee, arriving in Camden on 7 May and increasing Rawdon's force to some 1,200 effectives. Although the force was now roughly comparable to Greene's army, they were threatened by Thomas Sumter, Francis Marion, and Andrew Pickens operating in force. Fort Watson had fallen and other posts between Camden and Charleston were increasingly endangered. Supported by the presence of an American field army, the spirit of rebellion was rising throughout the state. Rawdon, therefore, decided to abandon Camden and all the country north of the Congaree River. He sent word to Lieutenant Colonel John Harris Cruger to evacuate Ninety Six and join Thomas Browne at Augusta, Georgia. Major Andrew Maxwell, the British commander at Fort Granby (now Columbia, South

Carolina) was directed to abandon his post and fall back on Orangeburg. Greene's patrols intercepted all of Rawdon's couriers and the messages never got through.

Lord Rawdon evacuated Camden on 10 May 1781, burning the jail, the mills, and a few private houses owned by prominent American patriots. He also took with him 500 Negro slaves and most of the Loyalist population of the town. Rawdon marched toward Nelsons Ferry on the Santee River, hoping to cross there and attack Francis Marion and Henry Lee besieging Fort Motte. After a one-day march Rawdon abandoned that idea and fell back on Monck's Corner, thirty-two miles inland from Charleston, with the hope that if reinforcements arrived he might be able to resume offensive operations.

Nathanael Greene had lost a battle and won a campaign. This progress of events paradoxically was to continue until the British finally were forced to leave Charleston, and the war in the South ended. It may truly be said that Greene never really won a clear-cut victory in the South against the British, although Eutaw Springs came very close to being a victory. He was destined, however, to conquer in the end, and that is the most important fact in any war.

After the evacuation of Camden on 10 May the British posts of Orangeburg, Fort Motte, and Granby fell to American attack on 11, 12, and 15 May respectively. Thomas Sumter invested and captured Orangeburg, with its entire garrison of 89 men and a considerable supply of very welcome provisions. After the fall of Fort Motte to Francis Marion and Henry Lee, Greene ordered Marion to march again into the lowcountry and hit Georgetown. Lee was instructed at the same time to move immediately against the important supply base of Fort Granby on the Congaree River.

General Sumter had planned to take Granby and even laid siege to that well-provided outpost. Believing its capture inevitable, he left Colonel Thomas Taylor there with a holding force and made his successful dash to Orangeburg. According to Hampton family tradition, it was during these operations around Granby that Colonel Richard Hampton, a noted horseman and swordsman, on a mounted scouting foray surprised and cut down with his saber a British vedette about to give the alarm.

Henry Lee, marching hard from Fort Motte, arrived before Granby during the early morning hours of 15 May. Fort Granby had been established on the south bank of the Congaree near Friday's Ferry and was well fortified with parapet, abatis, and a deep ditch or fosse. Protected by the river on one side, it was reasonably open to assault on the other three, but the garrison of 350 men under Major Maxwell, an officer in the Prince of Wales Regiment and a Maryland Loyalist, could put up a stiff resistance from the well-built earthworks. Since Lord Rawdon still might return in force, it was believed necessary to take the fort as soon as possible.

Lee therefore promptly began to erect a battery for his one 6-pounder on the edge of the woods to the west of Granby. The morning remained exceedingly foggy, allowing completion of the battery and placement of the gun in position before the garrison observed the accomplished fact. As soon as the fog lifted, Captain Finley commanding the gun fired one round shot over the fort's parapet, thus summarily announcing the American presence and utterly confusing the defenders. Lee's infantry advanced promptly with the bayonet, cutting off the enemy pickets and moving up to within assault distance of the works. Having been informed by local intelligence of Maxwell's weak and avaricious nature, Lee sent Captain Joseph Eggleston of the legion to conduct negotiations. Maxwell was only too glad to comply with the surrender demand on the condition that private property should be retained by the possessors without investigation of title. The Hessian officers assigned to the fort insisted that they keep their horses. To facilitate matters, Lee agreed, and the capitulation was duly signed. According to these terms, the garrison would be permitted to return to Charleston as prisoners of war until exchanged and the Loyalist militia were to be treated in the same way as the regulars. Lee would also provide an escort to protect the prisoners and their property from other less scrupulous Americans.

Before noon of 15 May the garrison of 340 soldiers, of whom 60 were regulars and 280 militia, marched out behind Major Maxwell with two pieces of artillery, all personal possessions, and two covered wagons loaded with the plunder taken from the surrounding countryside. Public stores, mostly ammunition, liquors, and salt, came into Lee's hands to be turned over as soon as possible to Greene.

Sumter, who had expected to capture Fort Granby and use its accumulation of ill-gotten wealth to reward his partisans in accordance with his principle of "Sumter's Law," was profoundly annoyed by Lee's bloodless victory. This attitude would complicate American command arrangements, an unfortunate development in an otherwise increasingly hopeful military situation.

CHAPTER XV

The Capture of Augusta and the Siege of Ninety Six

Francis Lord Rawdon had defeated Nathanael Greene at Hobkirk Hill on 25 April 1781. As happened so often, Greene lost an engagement but successfully extricated the American army from potential disaster and, aided by circumstances and the movement of events, in due course attained his objective. In the closing years of the war, it might be said very truly of both Cornwallis and Rawdon "that the stars in their courses fought against Sisera." To use a slang phrase, it was impossible for the British any longer "to win and stay even." With the upcountry and midlands of South Carolina in almost total disaffection, Rawdon was unable either to exploit his victory or maintain an advanced position. The British commander therefore determined to fall back on the coast and establish defensible lines based on Charleston. On 10 May Rawdon evacuated Camden after burning most of his stores, baggage, and even the personal belongings of some of the inhabitants. He also fired the jail, the town mill, and other buildings that might be useful to the Americans. Rawdon left behind some 31 wounded American prisoners taken at Hobkirk Hill and 61 British wounded, including 3 officers, all hurt too badly to be moved by wagon or carriage. Rawdon wrote to Cornwallis from Monck's Corner on 24 May that the situation in the province made it necessary to withdraw from the backcountry and assemble whatever troops could be collected at the point where he had taken station.

Fort Watson, Orangeburg, Fort Motte, Fort Granby, and Camden all had fallen into American hands by 15 May, Orangeburg and Granby without a single American casualty. This meant that those posts connecting Camden, Ninety Six, and Augusta with Charleston and Savannah now were in American hands with heavy loss for the British in stores, provisions, ammunition, and weapons essential to a continued prosecution of the war in South Carolina. The British hold in the South was eroding rapidly.

Francis Marion, as ordered by Nathanael Greene, marched on Georgetown and arrived before that town on 5 June. He promptly began regular siege approaches, but the British garrison evacuated Georgetown by sea on 6 June and sailed to Charleston. Marion moved in, leveled the defense works, and occupied Georgetown in another bloodless American victory. In forays fanning out over the lowcountry he successfully cut off a large percentage of British supplies, particularly salt, a most important commodity which His Majesty's forces were now totally lacking. British lines were contracting inexorably; the only posts up from the coast still held were Ninety Six and Augusta. The British, however, could strike and strike hard. During Marion's absence with his brigade on the Quinby Bridge and associated operations, a South Carolina Loyalist named Manson appeared off Georgetown on 2 August with an armed vessel. He effected a landing under cover of his ship's guns, dispersed the few militia defenders, burned forty-two houses, and withdrew without opposition.

After his decision to retire from Camden, Rawdon had sent dispatch riders to John Harris Cruger at Ninety Six, instructing him to abandon that base and fall back across the Savannah River to Augusta, Georgia, where the doughty Loyalist Colonel Thomas Browne lay behind strong entrenchments. These dispatches all were intercepted by Greene's patrols, and Cruger continued to hold his position, fortifying and strengthening Ninety Six with desperate haste.

Nathanael Greene selected Augusta as his first objective and sent Lieutenant Colonel Henry Lee with his legion and Brigadier General Andrew Pickens with the South Carolina militia to strike across the Savannah River where Thomas Browne defended the Augusta area with three forts, Galphin, Cornwallis, and Grierson. On the march toward the river Henry Lee sent out a strong reconnaissance party under Captain Ferdinand O'Neale, who discovered that the annual royal present to the Indians had arrived at Fort Galphin, about twelve miles below Augusta on the north bank of the Savannah. This gift consisted of considerable quantities of powder, ball, small arms, liquor, salt, and blankets.

On the morning of 19 May, Lee brought his forces around Galphin. He then ordered a detachment of mounted militia assigned to his command to advance openly on the fort's gate, knowing that the British and Loyalist garrison held the local citizen soldiers in absolute contempt and probably could not resist the temptation to sally out and drive them away. A selected unit of legion infantry was brought up under cover of the surrounding forest and concealed on the edge of the woods with orders to rush the fort from the opposite direction as soon as most of the garrison came out in pursuit of the militia. The defenders reacted just as Lee thought they would. His concealed light infantry rushed the open gate and Galphin fell into American hands with the loss of only one man, who died of sun stroke. The British casualties, not including the entire garrison of 126 which was captured, amounted to only three or four killed and a few wounded, while the present to the Indians, stored in the fort, made a welcome addition to American supplies.

During the evening of 21 May, Lieutenant Colonel Lee crossed the river and pushed on to Augusta with his reinforced legion. He arrived there to find that Andrew Pickens, with the South Carolina militia, and Elijah Clarke, leading his Georgians, already were closing in on Forts Cornwallis and Grierson, the two British posts defending Augusta. Pickens had ordered the construction of a small artillery emplacement about midway between the forts which commanded both works. Colonel Thomas Browne who commanded all British forces in upper Georgia held Fort Cornwallis, a strongly built work on the river bank in the center of town garrisoned by 320 Provincial regulars with two pieces of artillery. These were supported by 200 Negro slave laborers who loyally maintained the fortifications even under fire. Half a mile up the river across a narrow creek swamp lay Fort Grierson, named for its commander, Colonel Grierson, with a garrison of 80 Loyalist Georgia militia.

The three American commanders, Pickens, Lee, and Clarke, camped with their men in the woods west of the town, decided on a plan of attack and selected the weaker Fort Grierson as the first objective. If Colonel Grierson could be forced to abandon his position, he and his militia might be intercepted and destroyed as they tried to fall back on Fort Cornwallis.

On 23 May the assault on Fort Grierson was launched. Andrew Pickens and Elijah Clarke with the South Carolina and Georgia militia attacked the fort on its north and west; Major Pinkertham Eaton of North Carolina with his battalion passing along the north side of the swamp approached the work from the south; Henry Lee with the infantry and artillery of his legion moved along the swamp on its southern margin parallel with Eaton, ready to support the North Carolinians or check Browne if he ventured a sally to save Grierson. The legion cavalry under Captain Joseph Eggleston was posted in the woods south of Lee with orders to fall on Browne's rear should he advance against Lee.

As soon as Colonel Browne observed Henry Lee's movements along the southern margin of the swamp, he advanced from Fort Cornwallis with a strong force and two field guns. Lee and Browne exchanged a long-range and comparatively ineffective cannonade and Browne retired again behind his fortifications. Fort Grierson fell quickly to the combined attack. Many of the garrison were killed, wounded, or captured and Colonel Grierson was shot by one of Clarke's Georgians apparently after surrendering. A few survivors made their way to Fort Cornwallis under cover of the river bank. The war in this area had been fought with unparalleled ferocity on both sides, and Colonel Grierson, noted for his cruelty, was another victim of this "no quarter" mentality. The three American commanders tried to discover the murderer and punish him, but he never was found. American casualties at Fort Grierson were comparatively light. Unfortunately, among them was Major Pinkertham Eaton, the promising young officer from North Carolina.

South of the swamp where its creek flowed into the river was a large brick mansion house belonging to a prominent Loyalist. Here Lieutenant Colonel Lee took post with his legion while Pickens and Clarke stationed the militia in the woods on the left of Fort

Figure 85.
Brigadier General Andrew Pickens,
by Robert Wilson

Cornwallis. The best approaches to the British work were studied and entrenching tools assembled from Fort Galphin and surrounding farms or houses. Fort Cornwallis was located near the Savannah River, and its banks afforded a reasonably secure passage for the besiegers. It therefore was decided to break ground near the river and extend the American siege lines around the fort to its left and rear.

Meanwhile, Colonel Browne, an able and dedicated soldier, continued to strengthen his works as best he could. He had refused contemptuously to negotiate with the Americans, but now permitted one of the British officers captured at Fort Grierson to enter Fort Cornwallis under a flag and return to the American lines with medicines and other items needed for badly wounded prisoners taken in the same operation. Browne acted as though he still was dealing with Elijah Clarke instead of Lee and Pickens; Browne and Clarke were mortal enemies with good cause. They had fought each other for two years with unrelieved bitterness and naturally no trust existed. When Browne discovered that Andrew Pickens and Henry Lee were directing the operation, communications were established between besieged and besieger that eventually would lead to an honorable British surrender.

Since the area around the fort was a completely flat river plain without any natural elevations on which American artillery could be placed with advantage, it was determined to build a Maham Tower such as Marion and Lee had done at Fort Watson. Seeing the American lines advance, Browne decided to impede their progress by sallies out from Fort Cornwallis. Just before midnight on 28 May, a picked British assault force suddenly hit the trenches by the river and drove the surprised American guards out of their position. The support under a Captain Handy came up and, after a brief but savage bayonet fight, rewon the trenches and the British withdrew to their fortifications. During the next night Browne ordered a second attack against the same sector of the American lines. This was met and driven back by Captain Michael Rudolph of the legion, who personally led his bayonet men and cleared the trenches with vicious hand-to-hand combat. On 30 May the timbers arrived for the Maham Tower and construction was begun that evening, concealed by an old house. The framework was filled in as the tower rose with fascines, earth, stone, or brick rubble to add the necessary solidity to the structure.

Realizing that their opponent would try to destroy the tower, Pickens and Lee double-manned the lines in this key area, specifically designating one company of muskets to guard the tower. That same night Browne struck for a third time, launching one assault against the river quarter and personally leading an elite unit of his garrison against Pickens's militia, who were holding the lines in the rear of Fort Cornwallis. Captain Rudolph met and defeated the attack by the river and Captain Handy, commanding the troops designated to watch the still uncompleted tower, left one company behind to guard that structure and swung his men around the fort where Pickens's militia were being driven out of their trenches by Browne's bayonets. In this section of the lines, after furious close fighting with cold steel and heavy losses by both sides, Browne retreated in good order to the fort and the siege continued.

The British commander, understanding fully the danger a completed tower presented to his position, determined that it must be destroyed. He therefore had a platform erected in an angle of the fort directly opposite to the Maham Tower on which were mounted two of his heaviest pieces of artillery. These opened on the tower, but work continued even under fire, and on 1 June the tower was finished, overlooking the British parapet. An apron was constructed behind the tower, up which a 6-pounder could be dragged and mounted on the platform, firing through an embrasure cut in the heavy logs that had been placed to form a defense on top. At dawn on 2 June the gun was in position and orders were given to begin counterbattery fire against the British guns which were maintaining a steady cannonade. By noon of that day, both of Browne's fieldpieces were dismounted and the interior of the fort raked except for the sector nearest to the tower which could not be reached and those areas protected by heavily built traverses.

Colonel Browne still would not consider surrender. He sent a Scottish sergeant pretending to be a deserter who informed Lee that he knew where the British powder magazine was located. Red-hot shot properly directed might reach and blow it. Apparently, the Scottish sergeant's job was to gain Lee's confidence and then fire the house in front of the tower, hopefully taking the tower with it. After considering the matter further, Lee became suspicious and ordered the "deserter" removed from the tower gun platform and placed under guard. Thomas Browne, frustrated in this attempt, then sallied out unimpeded and burned two of four empty log houses lying outside the fort's perimeter. The American commanders were puzzled why two houses had been spared and planned to use the larger one, which had a second story, as a rifle position to cover the planned general assault. A party of Pickens's best riflemen were selected to occupy the house before daylight on 4 June to cover the attack scheduled for nine in the morning. About three o'clock on that same morning, the Americans were wakened by a violent explosion that destroyed the house. Browne had driven a sap from the fort under the selected rifle position, laid a mine, and blown it. Fortunately, the men had not yet taken up their positions, so there were no casualties. Lee wrote that the guards watching the British works reported that fragments of the house were tossed 30 or 40 feet in the air.

At nine o'clock the American columns were brought into position for the assault, but Pickens and Lee, hoping to prevent further bloodshed, sent yet another letter pointing out that the final blow was about to be struck. Would the British commander consider an honorable submission instead? Browne again replied adamantly that he would defend the post to the last. Lee and Pickens delayed their attack to await developments, aware that Browne's position was becoming increasingly hopeless. Later the same day, a British officer came from the fort with a flag and negotiations were commenced for a formal surrender. Because 4 June was the king of England's birthday and Browne's pride would not permit him to surrender on that day, Lee and Pickens set 5 June as the date for submission. Their conditions were accepted and the British garrison brought down its flag and marched out at eight in the morning of 5 June as stipulated in the surrender agreement. The defeated troops laid down their arms, and Captain Rudolph marched in, occupied Fort Cornwallis, and raised the American flag over the conquered works. Augusta and its defenses were in American hands. Because the war in Georgia had been waged without mercy by both sides, Pickens and Lee, remembering Colonel Grierson's murder, feared for Thomas Browne's life. He undoubtedly had been guilty of unpardonable cruelty to the patriot population and was understandably hated, but he also was a brave soldier who had surrendered on honorable conditions after a bitterly fought and skillful defense. Colonel Browne and a few of his officers therefore were paroled and sent to British-held Savannah with a strong infantry escort ordered to guard Browne and his companions until they reached safety, a mission accomplished successfully. Before Thomas Browne left with his escort, he inquired about his Scottish sergeant, the pretended deserter, stating that the man had acted as a soldier under orders. Pickens and Lee magnanimously released the overjoyed sergeant (who had expected to be executed), and he was permitted to accompany the paroled British officers to Savannah.

While the siege of Augusta was in progress, Nathanael Greene began his operation against the strong British base at Ninety Six. He marched from his camp at Friday's Ferry (at the present Columbia, South Carolina) and, taking the direct route, arrived before Ninety Six on 22 May. Greene's entire effective force, not including locally raised militia, numbered only 1,000. Francis Marion and his brigade were in the low-country watching the area from Georgetown to Charleston. Thomas Sumter was on detached service, patrolling the country south and west of the Congaree River, while Andrew Pickens, Elijah Clarke, and Henry Lee had invested the forts at Augusta. For the time being, General Greene had only his small army of regulars to initiate siege operations designed to force the surrender of a heavily fortified and strongly garrisoned position.

The town of Ninety Six was given that name because it lay exactly ninety-six miles from Keowee, the chief town of the Cherokee Indians. Beginning as a trading post, it had developed over the years into the principal settlement of the Ninety Six district, that territory lying between the Saluda and Savannah rivers. This was (and is) a green, fertile, rolling country and during the late eighteenth century had the largest white population of any district in South Carolina. When the British recovered most of the state after the battle of Camden in 1780, they established a strong post at Ninety Six, the apex of a triangle with Camden lying about 107 miles to the east and Augusta 59 miles south and east. These fortified towns watched the upper regions in two states and served as operations bases for expeditions into the backcountry, while maintaining British communications with the coast through a chain of fortified outposts.

Before the war Ninety Six had been guarded by a simple ditch and palisade as a protection against the Indians. After the town was established as an important base in 1780, the British garrison strengthened the original defenses considerably. Lieutenant Henry Haldane of the Royal Engineers, who also was an aide-de-camp to Lord Cornwallis, arrived and directed the construction of even more sophisticated works. The result proved so defensible that, even with the help of Pickens and Lee, Greene was unable to take the position either by siege or assault.

The British commandant at Ninety Six who successfully defended the town was Lieutenant Colonel John Harris Cruger, a New York Loyalist of distinguished family background and connections. His garrison included 350 Provincial regulars—150 men from the 1st Battalion of de Lancey's New York Brigade and 200 soldiers from the 2d Battalion of Allen's New Jersey Volunteers. There also were some 200 Loyalist South Carolina militia recruited by General Robert Cuningham and commanded by a Colonel King. Only one British regular was stationed at Ninety Six, Lieutenant Barreté of the 23d Regiment. About 100 Loyalist families had come in to Ninety Six as refugees, and a labor battalion of slaves maintained the fortifications.

Figure 86.
Lieutenant Colonel John Harris Cruger,
by Robert Wilson

On learning that Greene's army was marching toward Ninety Six, John Harris
Cruger advised the South Carolina Loyalist militia to escape on horseback to Charleston.
There was not food enough to feed so big a garrison during a long siege, and the known
bitter enmity of the anti-British southerners to their Loyalist neighbors would complicate matters should the fort surrender. Colonel King and his men, however, proudly
refused to leave what they considered a post of duty. Instead, they turned their excellent
horses into the woods and remained to support the garrison and await the trial of battle.

Lieutenant Henry Haldane, Cornwallis's engineering officer, had arrived at Ninety
Six about 5 December 1780 and found the fortifications in much better state than he had
expected. Haldane surveyed the post and recommended two additions to the defenses,
marking their best locations on the ground. He indicated the proper line for an abatis (a
planned tangle of tree trunks, sharpened branches, and stakes) 30 yards from the ditch
and urged the construction in an area adjoining the eastern corner of the town stockade
of an earthern fort in the form of an eight-pointed star protected by a dry ditch and
abatis. He believed that these works would make the fort both respectable and convenient for the garrison. Lieutenant Haldane also worked out a secret code which he presented to the commander at Ninety Six to facilitate correspondence with Charleston.

The Institute of Archaeology and Anthropology at the University of South Carolina is in the process of investigating the British works at Ninety Six and all the evidence that remains of Nathanael Greene's siege approaches. One still may walk the tree-grown parapet of the star fort and go down into the shallow pit, the remains of the unsuccessful well the thirsty defenders tried to sink during the siege. With some exceptions, current archeological findings validate the contemporary accounts of the operation.

The star redoubt was a defense work in the classic style laid down by the Marquis de Vauban and other European military engineers with eight points and sixteen salient and reentering angles protected by a fraise of pointed stakes, a dry ditch, and an abatis. A stout wooden platform permitting cannon to be fired directly over the parapet was constructed to cover the angle where the defenders expected the main attack. Although details of the defenses for the star fort's parapet are not available, it is probable that the British military engineers followed the model used at Fort Motte and Fort Granby. At these two posts, the earth parapets were fronted and retained by a pen or crib of heavy logs laid horizontally to prevent solid shot or shell from demolishing simple earthworks and using plentiful available material instead of the masonry reinforcement used in Europe. If Fort Motte may be an example, a closely set row of strong wooden stakes about five feet high was placed vertically behind the parapet at Ninety Six to retain the earth and provide a regular firing position. Below the stakes were three firing steps of logs laid horizontally to permit the musket or rifleman to aim and discharge his weapon, then step down under cover to reload.

The star fort at Ninety Six was defended by 150 Provincial regulars and 50 South Carolina militia commanded by Major Joseph Greene. As the strongest sector of the works, it also contained most of the ammunition and provisions to last out a siege.

To complete his defense perimeter, John Harris Cruger had his black labor battalion dig a ditch around the entire town and throw up the earth against the original stockade to form, with an abatis, a proper solid fortification high enough to protect the garrison and provide firing positions wherever needed. The town jail at the opposite end of the town from the star fort, the only masonry building in Ninety Six, was enclosed by a regular earth and log hornwork, thus constituting an internal strong point overlooking the shallow ravine west of the town through which a small stream ran, the only water supply available to the inhabitants of the garrison. The fortified brick jail could serve as a last defense area into which the garrison might retreat if the star fort and town were taken by assault.

Modern archeological research supports the evidence of the written sources that two sturdy blockhouses were constructed to guard the north and south gates of the town. Covered trenches or caponiers connecting the star fort with the town defenses provided protected communications to various key points within the fortifications. To guard internal troop movements against plunging artillery fire, traverses (heavy log and earth shelter barricades) were set up in the star fort and various other areas wherever Cruger and his engineers considered them necessary.

Because the stream was the only water supply, an outlying fortification was erected near the brow of the hill across the ravine to the west of the town to supplement the water defense provided by musketmen firing into the ravine from the jail. This smaller fort has been excavated and proved to be a hornwork protected by a ditch 8 to 10 feet wide and from 3 to 4 feet in depth. The work was built around two reinforced log barns (the south and north barns) which served as bastions, the area inside the fort being approximately 80 by 200 feet. In contrast to Forts Motte and Granby, the stockade posts extended above the earth parapet with a firing step behind the upright posts, thus giving the hornwork its name the "stockade fort." A posthole for a light swivel gun has been found by the excavators near the west end of the south barn. This swivel obviously was placed to fire down the west ditch as well as cover the southeastern and southern approaches. There probably also was an abatis to impede assault and perhaps a

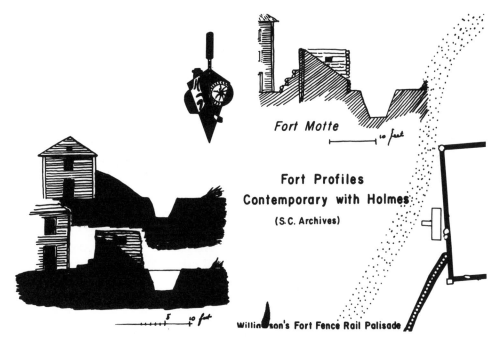

Figure 87.   Fort Profiles: Fort Granby, South Carolina, and Fort Motte, South Carolina, 1780–1781. The defenses undoubtedly are similar to those constructed by the British at Ninety Six

fraise of sharpened stakes fixed in the parapet and pointing downward. The stockade fort lay across the ravine about 100 yards from the west parapet of Ninety Six and was connected with the town by a covered way or caponier, broken only where the stream came through. A captain with an infantry company garrisoned the stockade fort, also called Holmes Fort.

For artillery, John Harris Cruger originally had two 3-pounders and some light swivel pieces. He anxiously requested Cornwallis to send him two 6-pounders, which were dispatched without a military escort and captured by an American militia patrol. Subsequently a third 3-pounder, an antique brass weapon, arrived from British headquarters with a load of entrenching tools, so three 3-pounders were the only guns Ninety Six could mount against its besiegers.

Thus the British fort at Ninety Six awaited Nathanael Greene's attack, garrisoned by 550 resolute men with adequate ammunition and food but a makeshift water supply. The fort's able commander, John Harris Cruger, was determined to hold his position at all costs. He was supported in this decision by his wife, Ann DeLancey Cruger, who stayed with him until the siege began and then refused to go as a refugee to Charleston, residing instead with Major Greene's wife at a nearby farm throughout the operation. This action was marked by flashes of gallantry. Greene, having discovered their presence, treated Mrs. Cruger and Mrs. Greene with complete courtesy and placed a guard over the house to ensure their safety.

On 22 May 1781 General Greene arrived with his army before Ninety Six and promptly began siege operations. The Americans camped in four areas around the town, 427 Maryland and Delaware Continentals, 421 Virginia Continentals, 66 North Carolina militia, and 60 men assigned to Captain Robert Kirkwood's scout detachment who also were from Delaware. Lacking enough men to establish a regular investment, Greene, following the advice of his engineer, Thaddeus Kosciusko, decided to hit the strongest point in the fortifications. He correctly reasoned that the capture of the star fort would be followed inevitably by the fall of Ninety Six. Somewhat to Cruger's surprise, the Americans established a three-gun battery within 130 yards of the star fort and opened their first trench only 70 yards away. Modern archeologists have been able to trace Greene's parallels and trench lines because, over the course of two hundred years, fallen leaf and pine needle humus have filled them, thus making the earth entirely different from that of the surrounding area. The latter is a red clay that packs and bakes in the summer heat to a general consistency of cement. Colonel Kosciusko, superintending the siege operations, said it was like digging through soft stone.

Digging of this sap so close to a regular fortified position was against all the basic principles of siege warfare. Cruger immediately constructed a gun platform in the salient angle of the star fort nearest to the besiegers and, mounting all three of his artillery pieces, opened a heavy fire supported by musketry from infantry manning the parapet on

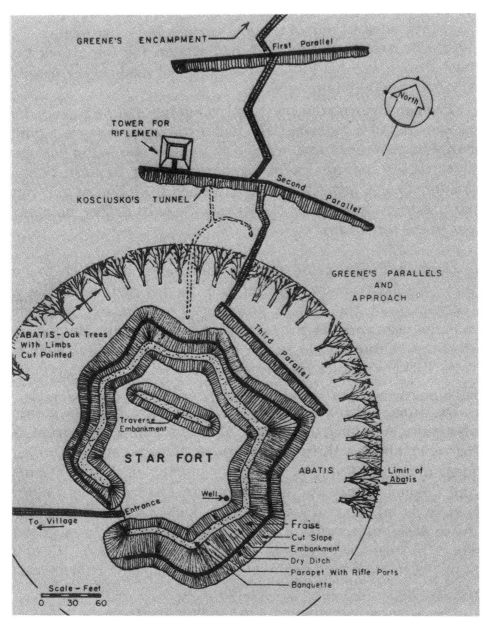

GREENE'S ENCAMPMENT

First Parallel

North

TOWER FOR RIFLEMEN

Second Parallel

KOSCIUSKO'S TUNNEL

GREENE'S PARALLELS
AND
APPROACH

ABATIS - Oak Trees
With Limbs
Cut Pointed

Third Parallel

Traverse
Embankment

STAR FORT

ABATIS

Limit of
Abatis

Well

To Village

Entrance

Fraise
Cut Slope
Embankment
Dry Ditch
Parapet With Rifle Ports
Banquette

Scale — Feet
0   30   60

Figure 88.   Star Fort at Ninety Six, South Carolina, and Nathanael Greene's approaches, 22 May–19 June 1781

Figure 89.
Colonel Thaddeus Kosciusko,
by Robert Wilson

23 May. Lieutenant John Roney of de Lancey's New York Volunteers led out a sortie of 30 picked men and rushed the American sappers. The sally group bayoneted everyone who did not scramble back to safety while a working party of Loyalist militia and black slaves destroyed the American works and carried off all the tools. Greene's losses were comparatively heavy, but Cruger had only one casualty, Roney, who was mortally wounded in the combat flurry and carried, dying, back into the fort.

The entire sortie was so well timed, planned, and executed that the British assault team was back inside the fortifications before American reinforcements arrived on the scene.

Having learned a lesson, Greene withdrew his forces to a more respectful distance and began new siege approaches, still directed at the star fort. Two block batteries were set up about 300 yards from the objective and personnel were trained in siege craft under cover of a ravine. American fatigue parties furnished by detail from the line regiments and working from dawn to dusk under the direction of Kosciusko and his assistant engineer, Captain Dalzien, on 27 May completed the first parallel about 220 yards from the star fort and erected during the same day a 20-foot-high battery just 140 yards away from the star fort's parapet. The first parallel was about 4 feet wide and 3 feet deep, protected along its lip by fascines (wooden stakes bound together) and gabions (wicker baskets filled with earth). It extended about 60 yards and deprived the garrison of adequate cover for a flanking attack on the American positions, also blocking the Island Ford road to any reinforcements that might arrive from that direction.

On 30 May the American sappers completed a fleche about 100 yards from the British fort. This often is referred to as the second parallel but actually was two trenches constructed to meet at a point directed toward the enemy works. It provided communications, flanking fire in two directions against a sally, and an advanced gunnery position. Two or three additional one-gun batteries were also established to support the enfilade fire. By 3 June, Greene's labor details had begun to work on a third parallel less than 60 yards from the star redoubt, and Colonel Cruger noted on the same day that his fresh provisions were giving out and the garrison must start on the salt provisions, which might last a month if the besieged managed with care.

Greene drove his sappers and work parties to finish the third parallel around the British abatis. The defenders, seeing the American works push inexorably forward, directed an intense fire from the star on the labor details as they pushed the trench along, working behind a rolling wooden shield or mantelet. To counter this fire, General Greene ordered a Maham Tower to be built near the third parallel and about 30 yards from the star fort. This reportedly was raised about 40 feet high and constructed either of logs notched and laid lengthwise or possibly of stacked gabions and fascines. It probably was made of both materials, with the earth-filled gabions placed in layers inside the log pen to strengthen it against artillery fire. American riflemen manned the tower's firing platform on 3 June and shot down any defender who showed his head above the parapet. Cruger, undaunted, raised the parapet of the star fort 3 feet by laying sand bags with loopholes for musket fire, but the artillery mounted on the exposed platforms could not be used during the day under the sniping from the tower, so the British commander dismounted the guns and remounted them every night. Cruger tried to burn the tower with red-hot shot in the dark hours, but the village lacked proper furnaces for heating the shot and the logs were green. This attempt failed, and the tower remained a constant and dangerous menace. The garrison in the star fort erected, however, a traverse 16 feet high which gave some protection to men moving from sector to sector inside the works.

With the tower in position and the American trenches being pushed forward, Greene sent a formal summons to the fort demanding a surrender. Colonel Otho Williams, Greene's adjutant, went forward under a flag and requested permission to present the surrender demand to Cruger. The British officer of the day, a Lieutenant Stelle, refused to call Cruger but accepted the written demand for a capitulation which informed the garrison that Lord Rawdon's retreat from Camden to Charleston and the capture of all the British posts on the Wateree, Congaree, and Santee rivers left the beleaguered garrison no hope. Greene demanded an immediate surrender and warned Cruger against the folly of continued resistance. Since the garrison at Ninety Six had suffered only one officer killed and eight soldiers wounded, Cruger's position was hardly perilous and he rejected what he considered an insulting demand.

Greene, rebuffed by Cruger, then tried other means to bring the garrison to terms. Arrows tipped with burning pitch were shot into the town to burn the wooden houses, but Cruger successfully countered this move by having the shingles of all the structures torn off. The trench lines moved each day toward the star fort, while the garrison continued its forays against the besiegers, one raid from the redoubt destroying the movable wooden mantelet that protected the workmen in the advanced sap from musket fire. The American batteries, however, advancing with the lines, successfully dismounted the British 3-pounders that had fired at night from the star fort's gun platforms, thus depriving the garrison of its only artillery.

An event now occurred that infuriated the British defenders. The siege of Augusta had ended with an American victory on 5 June and Henry Lee sent the prisoners taken there to Greene at Ninety Six before they were marched to Salisbury, North Carolina, and confinement. Lee says in his *Memoirs* that it was a mistake—the escort officer sent to Greene with the British prisoners from Fort Cornwallis took the wrong route, the road that passed by Ninety Six. According to the contemporary Loyalist historian Charles Stedman, they were marched by in view of the garrison with drums beating and the British flag reversed. Colonel Cruger ordered his garrison to fire on the column, which it did, but fortunately no one was injured. Lee severely reprimanded the escort officer, but the incident merely hardened the resolve of the defenders, particularly the South Carolina Loyalists, who feared the vengeance of their fellow South Carolinians serving with Pickens and Lee.

Lee arrived on 8 June with his forces from Augusta, and Andrew Pickens came in with the militia somewhat later the same day. Greene now had sufficient strength to push his siege forward to a hoped-for successful conclusion. Greene and Kosciusko had concentrated the attack on the strongest point in the fortifications, the star fort, neglecting the post's Achilles' heel, its water supply. Lee was directed to commence regular approaches against the stockade fort on the hill west of Ninety Six that guarded the stream while Greene continued the main attack against the star.

During the night of 9 June two sorties were made by two strong assault groups from the garrison. One of these units came out from the sally port behind the star fort and entered the American advanced trenches, penetrating to a battery of four guns. These would have been knocked out if hammers and spikes had been brought along to spike the vents. The raiders, however, discovered the mouth of a mine that was being pushed from the third parallel under the curtain of the star redoubt. By placing barrels of gunpowder under the fort's wall, sealing the mine, and igniting the powder by a fuse from the advanced trench, a breach could have been blown and a way opened for an American assault. The British sortie found Colonel Kosciusko making a night inspection of the mine and almost captured him. The gallant Pole escaped but in his hurried departure received an "inglorious" wound that made it difficult for him to sit a horse with ease during the next several weeks.

Henry Lee had opened regular siege approaches against the hornwork guarding the stream. The second sortie of 9 June hit his trenches, bayoneted several soldiers, and captured the commanding officer of a covering party. They retired safely, but Lee was so angered by the opposition that he sent a sergeant named Whaling with nine volunteers to burn the stockade. This was done during daylight on 12 June under cover of a "dark, violent storm" without rain. The sergeant led his special assault group carrying bundles of combustibles and crawling on their bellies from cover to cover. They made it to the ditch and were reaching up to ignite their fire bundles placed at the base of the stockade on the parapet when sentries discovered them. The sergeant and five men were killed outright in the ditch but four men escaped unhurt in a hail of bullets.

Greene, in the meantime, had completed the third parallel and the American sappers had brought two approach trenches up to within six feet of the ditch around the star. The tunnel for the mine also had only a few feet to go until it reached the British fort. Greene sent an urgent appeal to Pickens to send a few barrels of gunpowder to blow the British works because the sappers would be under the enemy ditch by the next night or following morning. Greene's intelligence had informed him that Rawdon had marched from Charleston on 7 June with a strong column to relieve Ninety Six. Speed therefore was absolutely necessary if the town were to be taken.

The evening of 12 June a farmer named Hugh Aikens was seen riding along the American lines south of the town, talking affably with the officers and soldiers on duty. Very little attention was paid to him because he was a known resident of the area and friendly visitors from the countryside were permitted to visit the siege lines and observe the operation. When Aikens reached the road leading directly into Ninety Six, he suddenly spurred his horse and galloped at full speed toward the town gate. The nearest American sentries fired at him but missed and Hugh Aikens rode for Ninety Six, waving a letter over his head. The garrison on watch in that sector opened the big gate quickly and let him in, and he delivered the message to Cruger that Rawdon had arrived at Orangeburg about one hundred miles away and was marching to relieve Ninety Six with reinforcements newly arrived in Charleston from abroad.

This good news, greeted with wild cheers by the garrison, naturally inspired the British to hold against all attack until help came. That, however, was becoming increasingly difficult. Henry Lee had driven his lines to within a few yards of the hornwork and established 6-pounders in batteries, thus bringing the outlying redoubt and the stream in the ravine under direct triangular artillery fire. By 17 June it was obvious to Cruger that the hornwork no longer was tenable, and the British garrison was evacuated during the night without loss, using the caponier into the town.

The sufferings of the garrison from thirst now became extremely severe. A well had been laboriously dug inside the star fort (the excavation is still there) but no water was found. The stream lay within pistol shot of the American besiegers, so water could not be procured during the day. In the night, naked Negroes from the labor battalion were sent to the stream with buckets in the hope that their movements might not be seen. In this way a scanty supply of water was maintained, but it became clear that the defense of Ninety Six under the increasing pressure could not be maintained. Cruger, a most determined man, refused to be discouraged or to consider surrender because he knew Rawdon was approaching as speedily as possible.

Three fresh regiments of infantry had arrived at Charleston from Ireland on 3 June. Selecting only the crack flank companies (light infantry and grenadiers) of these regiments, Rawdon marched from Charleston on 7 June and was joined at Monck's Corner by the British units stationed there. He now had a total of 2,000 effectives with whom he pressed forward toward Ninety Six as swiftly as the intense heat would allow, the troops from Ireland still in their heavy red wool uniforms suffering terribly under the South Carolina June sun.

Greene was informed of Rawdon's departure from Charleston on 11 June and promptly detached his cavalry under William Washington with orders to join Thomas Sumter. The two commanders were instructed to move out in front of Rawdon and impede his march as much as possible. From this time on Greene had steady intelligence of Rawdon's approach and, realizing that it probably would be impossible to reduce Ninety Six by regular siege operations before the relief arrived, decided to risk a general assault. The third parallel was completed, and the approach trenches were within a few feet of the ditch. The assault would be directed at the star fort, and on the morning of 18 June all American guns that would bear on target laid down a heavy preparatory cannonade. At noon two assault groups moved forward to the attack, the leading elements equipped with hooks fastened on long handles to pull down the sand bags on the parapet. American riflemen on the tower platform and stationed with the advanced batteries maintained a steady aimed covering fire while the Virginia and Maryland Continental brigades manned the third parallel and fired volleys by platoons.

Lieutenant Colonel Richard Campbell of Virginia with a picked detachment from the Virginia and Maryland brigades had overall command of the attack on the left with Lieutenant Isaac Duval of Maryland and Samuel Selden of Virginia personally leading the assault team. Lieutenant Colonel Henry Lee directed the attack on the right with Captain Michael Rudolph commanding a unit of the legion infantry and Kirkwood's Delawares. At twelve noon as planned, on the second cannon shot, the attack began. Major Greene, holding the star fort, had supplied the garrison with trench spears hammered out by the town blacksmith, and these were piled in readiness against the parapet. He ordered the garrison to fire one musket volley and then meet and break the assault on the parapet with bayonet and spear. The ditch was twelve feet deep, but the first wave of the American attack partially filled one sector with fascines and standing on these began to pull down the sand bags with their hooks. Once the ditch was filled and a breach made, Greene could send in the Continentals, take his losses, and overwhelm the defenders. A desperate counterattack was the only answer, and Major Greene ordered two sortie parties of 30 volunteers each to leave through the sally port at the rear of the star and, staying under cover of the ditch, circle the fort from opposite directions and strike the Americans on both flanks. These 60 men, led by Captain Thomas French of New York and Captain Peter Campbell of New Jersey, suddenly charged from both sides the Americans assailing the parapet and, using the bayonet only, killed or wounded some 40 of the attackers. Lieutenant Duval and Lieutenant Selden were among the casualties.

   The force of the assault had been broken and Greene, knowing that his regulars were inferior in number to Rawdon's approaching column, called off the operation on the

Figure 90.   The final American assault on the Star Fort at Ninety Six, South Carolina, 18 June 1781, by Robert Wilson

evening of 19 June. He had sent off his baggage already, and the American army raised the siege of Ninety Six and marched away, crossing the Saluda River during the late afternoon of 20 June.

The American losses during the investment numbered 147 Continentals killed, wounded, or missing with Captain George Armstrong of Maryland being the only regular officer killed in the twenty-seven-day siege. The militia casualties at Ninety Six were not reported, but Captain Joseph Pickens, the brother of Andrew Pickens, died in the operation. The British lost 27 killed and 58 wounded, but Lieutenant John Roney who led the first sortie was the only officer killed.

The Americans, convinced, as Greene wrote Francis Marion, that Ninety Six was on the eve of surrendering, marched off mortified and disappointed. Greene sent dispatches to Sumter, communicating to that independent commander his route of retreat, and, at the same time, ordering William Washington to rejoin him with his cavalry. Since Washington and Sumter had failed in their assignment to delay Rawdon, they also had no reason to rejoice.

Rawdon arrived at Ninety Six with 1,800 foot and 150 horse after a grueling forced march of fourteen days in the hottest season of the year, his troops lagging and dropping from heat exhaustion. This had been quite a feat because, to evade Sumter and Washington, he had followed a longer route rather than the direct road to Ninety Six. He was greeted by the garrison with exhilaration, but promptly pushed on after Greene with 800 foot and 60 horse. The rest of his command, utterly fatigued by the terrible march, was left with Cruger at Ninety Six to evacuate the town and fort that had been defended for so long and so bravely. Rawdon had offered the local Loyalist population two choices. If they would stay and hold the fortified base, he would leave a garrison and support it when he could from Charleston. If, however, they were unwilling to remain, he would abandon Ninety Six and provide haven for the South Carolina Loyalists and their families within the Charleton enclave. The Loyalists chose the latter for obvious reasons. They knew the Americans would return and feared the vengeance of their former friends and neighbors. The British commander therefore gave orders to destroy what fortifications could be destroyed quickly and assigned Cruger the task of escorting the refugees to safety.

Greene's siege of Ninety Six thus ended in failure and retreat, but his objective had been attained. The last strong British base in the upcountry was evacuated after a brave and successful defense. Despite winning battles, the British lines were slowly being forced back on Charleston.

Lee wrote later that if Greene had attacked the stream defenses first and cut the water supply, Ninety Six would have capitulated with few casualties. This opinion is probably correct, but Colonel Kosciusko, a classically trained European military engineer, believed, in accordance with that training, that a fort must fall if its key defense work is taken. The fact was, of course, that Cruger and his command refused to surrender and continued to fight for twenty-seven days until help arrived. Cruger, therefore, remains the real hero of the operation. The ultimate tragedy of Ninety Six is that Cruger and all his valiant garrison, with the exception of one British regular officer, were Americans, and so were their besiegers.

CHAPTER XVI

Quinby Bridge, 17 July 1781

The battle of Quinby Bridge fought on 17 July 1781, some eighteen miles south of Monck's Corner, South Carolina, was not a big engagement. On this occasion a stubborn British defense beat back every American attempt to drive Lieutenant Colonel James Coates and his 19th Regiment from their position at Quinby Plantation, and a frustrated Thomas Sumter finally broke off the action and withdrew. When the fighting ceased, the British column continued its planned retirement on Charleston. The battle of Quinby Bridge, however, typifies the slow, inexorable military pressure that gradually drove the British into an ever-decreasing perimeter around the port city. The royal armies and their Loyalist supporters could and did win single engagements up through the late summer of 1782, but it became increasingly clear by the end of 1781 that, with the forces available, they could not win the war in the South.

Lieutenant Colonel James Coates with his 19th Regiment and a unit of 150 mounted infantry of the South Carolina Loyalist Rangers had been sent to guard the British post at Monck's Corner about thirty miles from Charleston. If Coates were forced to retire, there were three roads he could take. The main route joined the Dorchester road at Eighteen Mile House, crossed the Goose Creek Bridge, proceeded by the Quarter House, an old tavern, at the beginning of Charleston Neck, and continued on to the town itself. A second road went east of the western branch of the Cooper River, ran near Biggin Church, and passed Fair Forest Swamp via the Wadboo Bridge. From Wadboo Bridge there were two possible routes. One followed the Cooper River, crossing its eastern branch at Bonneau's Ferry. The other swung even further east and crossed Quinby Creek over Quinby Bridge near the plantation of Richard and Thomas Shubrick. Both roads terminated at Hobcaw Point on the main river about four miles upstream and across from Charleston. A British garrison at Dorchester and a small detachment at the Quarter House Tavern could watch any military developments that might occur and guard the line of communication. Thomas Sumter, placed in overall command of a special force operating in the Monck's Corner area, had these outposts, Monck's Corner, Dorchester, and the Quarter House, as his major objectives. He led his own partisans supported by Henry Lee's Legion and Francis Marion's brigade. Greene also had ordered Sumter to lose no time and to push the campaign night and day to allow the British no rest.

As soon as intelligence reached Lieutenant Colonel James Coates that Sumter was moving in force against the British positions, he crossed the west branch of the Cooper River and took station at Biggin Church, a sturdy brick building already fortified to meet such a contingency. All the supplies gathered at Monck's Corner were removed at the same time and stored in the church. The bridge crossing Biggin Creek, a tributary of the Cooper, permitted the British to maintain contact with Monck's Corner, while a bridge over Wadboo Creek could be used if Coates retreated down the east bank of that branch of the Cooper River.

Sumter assembled his forces for an attack against James Coates's position at Biggin Church and sent out a contingent to destroy Wadboo Bridge and cut off that avenue of escape. He reported later to Greene that this mission had been accomplished, including the sinking of two British schooners moored near the bridge. Colonel Peter Horry with elements of Marion's brigade and a contingent of Sumter's riflemen also was moved up to within three miles of Biggin Church, where, at about five o'clock on the afternoon of 16 June, his camp was hit suddenly by Major Thomas Fraser, leading mounted South Carolina Loyalist Rangers. Horry's men, taken completely by surprise, fell back and regrouped, and Colonel Edward Lacey's rifles with steady aimed fire checked Fraser's charge. Thomas Fraser broke off the engagement and fell back on James Coates's position at Biggin Church. During the same day an unidentified group of American partisans, probably one of Sumter's units, tried to force Biggin Bridge but were driven back by Coates's pickets. When Henry Lee and Wade Hampton arrived with their troops to support Sumter, they were thoroughly angered to find the key bridge still in British hands. They had to fight their way across.

Having achieved his purpose of confusing and delaying the American advance by these diversionary actions, James Coates, obviously informed by his scouts of Sumter's raid, sent a working party to repair Wadboo Bridge. He then set fire to Biggin Church, leaving all stores and baggage in the building, and marched off during the night of 16 June, crossing Fair Forest Swamp and Wadboo Bridge unhindered.

Sumter did not know that the British had left Biggin Church until in the darkness his scouts saw the burning building. This was about three o'clock in the morning, and Sumter promptly roused the sleepy soldiers and ordered them out in full pursuit, leaving behind his one piece of artillery, a 6-pounder, because it might delay the infantry. Lee and Hampton led the chase past Wadboo Bridge and discovered from tracks of men and horses that the British column apparently had divided. Coates had decided to send his mounted Rangers to Charleston via the Bonneau Ferry road. The 19th Regiment swung to the left after leaving Fair Forest Swamp and took the route leading to Quinby Bridge. Coates, it seems, did this because he believed horsemen might not be useful in a retreating action through swampy and heavily wooded terrain. Perhaps he hoped to divide the pursuit, which is exactly what happened. Wade Hampton rode off on the trail of the

South Carolina Rangers, while Lee, joined by Francis Marion's cavalry, followed the 19th Regiment. The South Carolina Rangers moved faster than Hampton expected and crossed Bonneau Ferry, securing all available boats on the other side. Having failed to stop the Rangers, the Americans had to overtake James Coates and force him to fight before he could cross and destroy Quinby Bridge behind him. The creek could be passed easily only at this point unless a wide detour were made upstream, which would further delay the pursuers.

About a mile to the north of the bridge, Lee overtook Coates's rear guard, about 100 men of the 19th Regiment under Captain Colin Campbell, escorting almost all the regimental baggage. After a brief and frightened show of resistance, the entire rear guard surrendered in spite of their captain's frantic efforts to rally them. These were mostly new recruits, freshly arrived with the three regiments sent as reinforcements to Rawdon.

Coates, unaware of the loss of his rear element, crossed Quinby Creek with the main force and prepared to destroy the bridge as soon as Campbell arrived with the baggage. Planks were pried or cut loose and a howitzer set up on the southern end to cover the working party detailed to complete destruction after the rear guard and baggage had passed. Since he naturally thought that Captain Campbell was covering his retreat, John Coates was completely surprised when Lee and Marion's cavalry appeared, riding hard for the bridge. Most of the British infantrymen still were on the long causeway leading from the bridge to higher ground or moving in close-order line of march up the narrow path beyond the causeway. Coates ran down the causeway, desperately trying to form a line of defense supporting the howitzer. At this crucial moment, Captain James Armstrong, leading the first section of Lee's cavalry, approached the northern end of the bridge. If he had rushed the crossing immediately, the British might have been routed. Instead Armstrong halted his troop and sent a rider back to Lee for instructions. Lee's angry reply was that the cavalry must attack without regard to circumstances, which Armstrong promptly did, galloping across the bridge at the head of his section, the loosened planks slipping into the creek under the hooves of the charging horses. The howitzer, with portfire lighted and just about to be applied, was rushed before the piece could be fired while most of the British infantry scrambled from the causeway and out of the path, running toward the shelter of the plantation house. Armstrong's headlong charge had dislodged some of the planks in the center of the bridge, but Lieutenant George Carrington leading the second section of Lee's cavalry took his people across, again at the full gallop, jumping the gap in the center and closing up with Armstrong. Lieutenant Colonel Coates, temporarily separated from his men, placed his back against one of the few supply wagons that had kept up with the main column and, drawing his sword, defended himself against Captain Armstrong's saber slashes.

The third section of legion horse under Captain O'Neale came up but hesitated at the growing breach, and Hezekiah Maham, leading Marion's cavalry, passed O'Neale's contingent and stormed over the bridge. Maham's mount went down, hit by musket

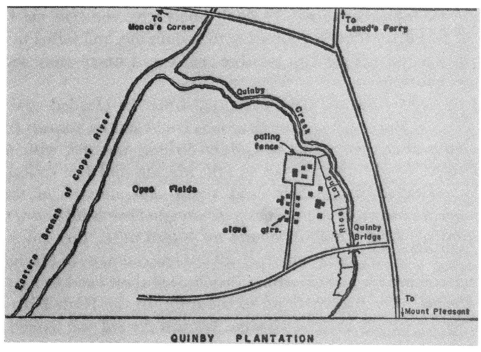

Figure 91.   Battle of Quinby Bridge, South Carolina, 17 July 1781, from *Gamecock* by Robert
D. Bass

fire from the growing British resistance, but Captain James McCauley commanding Marion's first troop took his men over the dangerous gap and joined Armstrong and Carrington on the causeway where soldiers of the 19th Regiment, rallying around their
embattled commander, were putting up a stiffer fight. Two of Henry Lee's dragoons
were killed in the desperate hand-to-hand conflict around the howitzer and several were
seriously wounded. Lee came up and joined Maham in directing repairs to the bridge
under growing small arms fire. With Lieutenant Colonel Lee's Legion were two surgeons, Dr. Irvine and Dr. Skinner. Irvine was noted for his reckless disregard of danger
when treating wounded in the field. Skinner had the reputation of being timid and always
staying well behind the fighting. The two men did not like each other and Skinner constantly criticized his colleague for rashness. At Quinby Bridge, Dr. Irvine, as usual, was
riding between Lee and Maham at the head of the column. He was wounded by musket
fire and sent back for treatment to the surgeon's field station where Dr. Skinner, to
punish Irvine's temerity, refused to treat the valiant surgeon's serious gunshot wound
until all the other injured had been tended. Contemporary reports state that Skinner's
conduct made a very poor impression on the soldiers.

Armstrong, Carrington, and McCauley, now cut off from reinforcements by the shattered bridge, fought their way through the British infantry on the causeway and wheeling to the left up the stream successfully brought their surviving men into the protection of the surrounding forest. Lieutenant Colonel Coates, relieved of immediate pressure, gathered his scattered regiment and fell back dragging the recaptured howitzer across the open fields to the house and outbuildings of the Shubrick plantation, a relatively short distance downstream.

The Shubrick home, a large two-storied structure, was surrounded by barns, outbuildings, and slave quarters with a sturdy rail fence enclosing the mansion itself and the usual kitchen and flower gardens. Coates, having successfully pulled his soldiers back to the house area, reorganized the demoralized regiment with commendable coolness and drew it up before the house in a hollow square, bristling with bayonets, the rescued howitzer covering the front of the formation. Other musketmen were deployed along the rail fences or stationed at the house windows. Having disposed his troops in as strong a position as possible, he waited for the inevitable American attack.

Lee, frustrated in his attempt to repair the bridge adequately and give immediate support to Armstrong, Carrington, and McCauley, marched the remainder of the cavalry up Quinby Creek where Francis Marion joined him with his infantry and the infantry of Lee's Legion. The two commanders then forded the stream, moved down through the woods, and advanced to the edge of the open fields lying around the plantation. There they halted and carefully reconnoitered the British position. Having decided after the reconnaissance that Coates was too strongly posted to warrant an attack with their available forces, Lee and Marion stopped all operations and waited for Sumter to come up with the rest of the little army.

Thomas Sumter marched in with his infantry late in the afternoon and, with his customary violent aggressiveness, promptly ordered an immediate general attack. He had arrived without the 6-pounder field gun, an essential for any operation against a prepared position, especially when the enemy had artillery—the shell-throwing howitzer rescued at the bridge. Both Marion and Lee protested the decision, insisting that Sumter wait until Captain Singleton could bring up the 6-pounder. Sumter, the "Gamecock," ignored them and the assault was launched forthwith. The cavalry was stationed in reserve to cover any possible retreat. Sumter's own brigade, with the exception of 45 men under Colonel Thomas Taylor, advanced on the right by the rice fields along the creek and occupied the slave cabins. From the protection these offered they maintained a largely ineffective long-range fire on the mansion and the buildings and fences surrounding it. Taylor was ordered to attack with his 45 men the fences on the British left, bringing him as he went forward under direct fire from the British muskets. Taylor reached the fence, but a bayonet charge led by Captain Scerett forced him to abandon the position and fall back, again across the open field. Francis Marion stationed on the far left with his own and Lee's infantry advanced across the field to cover Taylor, taking heavy losses as he came. Marion also reached the fence and ordered his men to lie down and fire under the scant cover of the rails and palings, rising only to load. Here they remained and fought until all their ammunition was exhausted, when Marion, protected by the growing darkness, withdrew in good order. Early in the engagement the British had retired into the house and picketed garden where they maintained an active defense until night fell. The entire action had lasted about three hours, but the honors rested with John Coates and his 19th Regiment. The British had rallied after the surprise at the bridge, retreated to the house, and held the post against heavy attack. Sumter broke off the action at sundown and, sending back a cavalry detachment to bring off the dead and wounded, retired across the now repaired bridge and camped about three miles away from the battlefield. Armstrong, Carrington, and McCauley had rejoined the main force so the commanders were able to take stock of their respective losses.

Sumter planned to renew the assault in the morning after Captain Singleton arrived with the 6-pounder, but it was an angry army that made camp that night and dissension broke out immediately. Sumter was blamed for ordering an attack without artillery and exposing Marion's and Taylor's men unnecessarily while not supporting them properly from the rest of his brigade posted in the shelter of the slave quarters. Colonel Taylor was particularly irate, and Marion, thoroughly disgusted, moved off during the night with his badly hurt brigade. Lee followed the next morning, marching back to Greene's headquarters in the High Hills of the Santee leading his entire legion, without informing Sumter that he planned to do so. His army thus weakened, Sumter decided not to renew the battle and fell back across the Santee River. Coates, after holding his position until he was sure the Americans did not plan to return, continued his retirement to Charleston whence reinforcements were moving up to his support.

The battle of Quinby Bridge had ended in an American failure, with comparatively heavy losses for Sumter's force, and in humiliation, recriminations, and anger against the overly impetuous Gamecock. The numbers actually engaged in the fighting are not definitely known but seem to have been in the neighborhood of 500 to 600 on each side. The American losses at the bridge and around the house were around 60 killed and wounded. Lieutenant Colonel John Coates reported 6 killed and 38 wounded although he obviously did not include the 100 men of the rear guard captured by Lee during the approach march to the bridge. The partial destruction of that bridge by Coates which prevented Lee from committing his main force of cavalry in time to take advantage of British confusion, the 19th Regiment's stubborn defense of Quinby plantation, and Sumter's poor judgement and bad generalship combined to lose a battle for the Americans, but the country north of Charleston was progressively being abandoned. The British high command, even with the three new regiments that had arrived as reinforcements, did not possess an adequate replacement potential. Any loss of trained personnel—the 145 casualties suffered at Quinby Bridge—became increasingly serious. The mouth of the net was closing and the long war dragging to its finish.

CHAPTER XVII

The Battle of Eutaw Springs, 8 September 1781

The battle of Eutaw Springs fought on 8 September 1781 is claimed as a victory by both sides. Tactically, the honors belong with the British because Lieutenant Colonel Alexander Stuart commanding British and Loyalist forces held the field and Nathanael Greene broke off the action and retired in comparatively good order. The engagement, however, was one of the most hotly contested in the entire war. Both British and American casualties were heavy, and Greene came very close to winning the battle. In the long view, Eutaw Springs must be considered an American strategic victory because Stuart was forced by his heavy losses and a hostile countryside to retreat from Eutaw Springs and fall back on the increasingly smaller British-held enclave around Charleston. Eutaw Springs also was the last major battle fought in South Carolina. While it clearly should be judged a British tactical victory, a defeat of an American army in the field never was sufficient to establish royal control over any area in the South. To accomplish this, the American armies had to be destroyed, all partisan raiders successfully eliminated, and the country totally pacified. These three necessary objectives were never accomplished, and Greene, who did not win a major battle in the southern campaign, was destined to emerge as the unquestioned victor in the Carolinas and Georgia.

After General Greene retired with his army from Ninety Six and Rawdon ordered that post evacuated, the American general marched to the High Hills of the Santee to rest and rebuild strength. The weather had become so intensely hot that hostilities temporarily were suspended. The British commanders, harassed and worn by their attempted defense of a vast semiwilderness area without sufficient troops, were progressively forced to abandon the greater part of South Carolina. British control after Ninety Six was confined within the three great rivers, Santee, Congaree, and Edisto, and, as the year of 1781 progressed, these last holdings shrank to a much narrower compass. There were the usual skirmishes, raids, and one minor, if bloody, encounter in July at Quinby Bridge where it crosses Quinby Creek about eighteen miles from Monck's Corner, South Carolina.

A tragic note was added to an already bitter war by the hanging of Colonel Isaac Hayne on Rawdon's order just before the latter's departure to Englad because of ill health. Rawdon with the ship in which he was traveling were captured by the French

Admiral Count François Joseph Paul de Grasse, which adds a further ironic note. Hayne, a wealthy and respected planter, had been given his parole after the fall of Charleston in 1780. He later made a declaration of allegiance to the king when Brigadier General James Patterson, the British commandant in Charleston, refused to let Hayne leave the city unless he did so. Hayne complied because his wife and children were gravely ill with smallpox and he felt that he must return to the plantation and care for them. The declaration of allegiance was made, however, on the assurance that Hayne never would be asked to bear arms against his countrymen. After the British were driven successfully from his home area (Hayne Hall was about four miles from Jacksonborough, South Carolina), Colonel Hayne, believing that British expulsion freed him from his declaration of allegiance, took up arms again in the American cause. He was captured by Major Thomas Fraser leading a detachment of mounted South Carolina Loyalist Rangers, who surprised Hayne's camp on Charleston Neck. Taken to Charleston, Hayne was imprisoned, condemned, and hanged on 4 August 1781. He died bravely, on the scaffold, and his death, instead of intimidating the South Carolinians, roused them to fury and thus for the British was totally counterproductive. Hayne was a symbol, a martyr to his cause, and angered and outraged men flocked to join the forces of Greene and the several partisan leaders.

After the retirement of Nathanael Greene's army to the High Hills of the Santee, the British field army under the command of Lieutenant Colonel Alexander Stuart moved out of the Charleston area and marched inland, taking post near the junction of the Congaree River with the Wateree, some sixteen miles from Greene's encampment, but these miles were mostly flooded swampland. The American general, meanwhile, was reinforced by a brigade of North Carolina Continentals and, on 28 August (according to Charles Stedman, 22 August), after the waters began to drop, Greene marched down from the High Hills of the Santee to offer battle to Alexander Stuart. The Americans proceeded up the northern bank of the Wateree, crossing near Camden. From there, Greene moved his army south and west to Friday's Ferry on the Congaree where he was joined by General Andrew Pickens with militia from the Ninety Six district, and also a small force of recently raised state troops led by Lieutenant Colonel William Henderson of the South Carolina Line.

When Stuart received intelligence that Greene was on the march, the British commander fell back to Eutaw on the Charleston road about forty miles from the confluence of the Congaree and Wateree. This move was made to protect his line of communications with the coast and also to meet a convoy of provisions coming up from Charleston.

Greene crossed the Congaree and advanced toward the new British position by slow degrees, thus giving time for Brigadier General Francis Marion to join the American army with his brigade from the Georgetown area. The junction of the two commanders took place at Henry Laurens's farm on 7 September a few miles from Eutaw. At four in the morning of 8 September, Greene and Marion broke camp and marched to attack the British, lying some seven miles away. At six o'clock that morning, two deserters from Greene's army came to Stuart with word that the Americans were not far away and moving to the attack. Unfortunately for the British, this report was not credited, and the two men were arrested and placed under guard. As usual, American intelligence from a generally friendly countryside was far better than British information. Greene knew exactly where Stuart was posted, but the latter remained completely unaware of the American approach, in spite of the warning given by the deserters. Stuart even sent out an early morning foraging party of 300 or 400 unarmed men protected by a small escort to dig sweet potatoes to feed his hungry army. This operation was to take place in fields alongside the very road down which Greene was marching.

The Americans were advancing in two columns with artillery at the head of each. Lieutenant Colonel Henry Lee with his legion cavalry rode in advance, while William Washington covered the rear with the Virginia Light Horse. About eight in the morning, four miles from the British camp, Captain James Armstrong of Lee's Legion, leading a scout force, reported the approach of what was thought at first to be the van of Stuart's army. Lee halted and drew up his legion infantry across the road with the cavalry stationed in open woods on the right and William Henderson's South Carolina state troops posted in thick woods on the left. As soon as the British foraging party appeared, Lee attacked the head of the column with his infantry, the legion cavalry swinging around to the rear to cut off escape. The unarmed rooting party escaped by scattering and running into the nearby woods, and the cavalry escort promptly rode off at full speed, but several of the infantry escort were killed in the American attack, and 40 were captured with their captain. The alarm had been given; Stuart hastily beat to quarters and pushed artillery up the road to delay the American advance. Lee, with the forward elements, requested support from General Greene, and Colonel Otho Williams, the adjutant general, brought up Captain William Gaines at the full gallop with two 3-pounder field guns. These unlimbered and answered the British fire, and during this artillery exchange both armies formed for battle.

Greene's first line was composed of the South Carolina and North Carolina militia. The North Carolinians under Colonel Francis Malmedy, a French nobleman in American service, formed the center with the South Carolinians in equal detachments on the right and left. Brigadier General Francis Marion commanded the South Carolinians on the right and Andrew Pickens the left. Colonel William Henderson, leading the South Carolina state troops, held the left flank of the first line, and Lieutenant Colonel Henry Lee with his legion of horse and foot covered its right.

The Continental regulars were drawn up as the second line, with the North Carolinians in three battalions on the right commanded by General Jethro Sumner. These battalions were led, respectively, by Colonel Ashe and Majors Armstrong and Blount. Two battalions of Virginia Continentals under Lieutenant Colonel Richard Campbell composed the center, the battalions commanded by Major Sneed and Captain Thomas Edmunds. The veteran Marylanders in two battalions formed the left. Colonel Otho

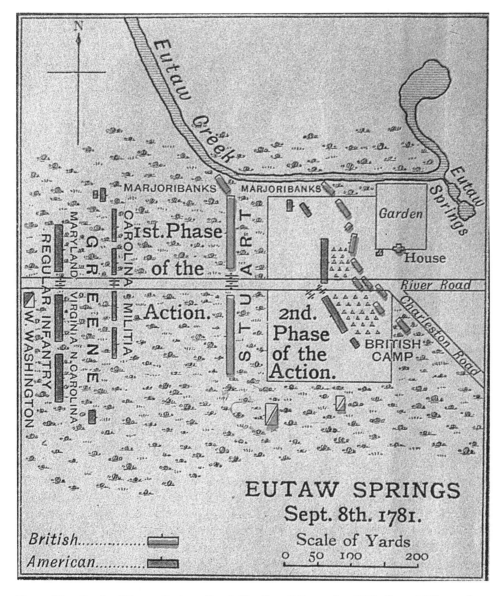

Figure 92.   Battle of Eutaw Springs, South Carolina, 8 September 1781, from *A History of the British Army*, J. W. Fortescue (London, 1902)

Williams led the Maryland regulars, with Colonel John Eager Howard and Major Henry Hardman commanding the battalions. Captain William Gaines with his two 3-pounders moved on the road in the center of the first line. Captain Browne's (according to Lee, Captain Finn's) two 6-pounders holding the same order followed with the second line. Lieutenant Colonel William Washington, commanding Baylor's Regiment of Horse and Captain Robert Kirkwood's experienced Delaware Continental infantry composed the reserve with orders to march under cover of the woods. The entire American army mustered about 2,100 effectives, not the almost 4,000 reported by Stuart to Cornwallis after the action.

Stuart drew up the British army, also numbering about 2,300 men, in one line a few hundred yards in front of his camp with tents left standing in the haste of the movement. His own 3d Regiment of foot, the Buffs, composed the right with its flank resting on the Charleston road. Lieutenant Colonel John Harris Cruger, with the remnants of three good Loyalist battalions—a unit of de Lancey's New York Brigade, the New Jersey Volunteers, and the New York Volunteers—held the center, while two veteran British infantry regiments, the 63d and 64th, were posted on the left. Major John Marjoribanks, with three light infantry companies and three companies of grenadiers composing together one battalion, was posted slightly in advance to the right of the Charleston road with his right flank resting on steep-banked Eutaw Creek and his left, covered by a thick hedge, reaching back in an oblique to the right flank of the Buffs on the road. Marjoribanks's battalion included six flank companies of the three regiments from Ireland which Rawdon had led to the relief of Ninety Six. Two pieces of artillery were stationed on the Charleston road between Marjoribanks and the 3d Regiment, the other two British guns being posted on the road that ran by Patrick Roche's plantation and went to the parishes of St. Johns and St. Stephens. This forked off from the Charleston road and passed through the British left wing. Major John Coffin, commanding the small British cavalry force, mostly Loyalist horsemen raised in Charleston, was placed with his mounted contingent and a reinforcement of infantry behind and in support of the British left. The British were drawn up in wooded terrain, but not far in Stuart's rear lay an open field bounded on the north by Eutaw Creek running out of a deep ravine just behind the battle area—the site of the famous Eutaw Springs. A strongly-built, two-storied brick house, with outbuildings and a palisaded garden stretching to the stream bank, commanded the cleared land. The British camp was pitched on the open ground south and west of the house. As the American lines advanced against the waiting British, skirmishers from the two opposing armies met in a flurry of musket fire and then fell back as artillery on both sides engaged in a hot, point-blank exchange. Captain Gaines's two 3-pounders were dismounted and a British 4-pounder also was put out of action.

The American first line pushed forward, shouting, into a steady disciplined fire, taking its losses without faltering, the militia in the center pressing the attack like veterans.

Figure 93.   Battle of Eutaw Springs, 8 September 1781. Engraving by J. B. Longacre from the painting by T. Stothard

General Greene wrote after the battle to Steuben that the conduct of the South Carolinians would have graced the infantry of the great king of Prussia. It should be remembered, however, that these were not inexperienced recruits, but war-hardened partisans following Francis Marion and Andrew Pickens, leaders they knew and trusted.

The North Carolina militia in the center, unfortunately, did not merit the same accolade. These were chiefly new men called up for the campaign and commanded by Colonel Malmedy, a foreign officer personally unknown to his soldiers. The 64th Regiment, British regulars, supported by some of Cruger's Loyalists, suddenly counterattacked with the bayonet, and, after a brief stand, the North Carolinians were pushed back in confusion, forcing the rest of the American first line to retreat in sullen good order, still fighting savagely. Greene immediately ordered the North Carolina Continentals under Brigadier General Sumner to fill the gap caused by the militia's recession. These came up splendidly in line with Henderson's state troops on the left and Lee's Legion infantry on the right, and the Americans advanced again, pushing the stubborn British slowly before them.

The American left wing, led by Lieutenant Colonel William Henderson, was engaged frontally with the 3d Regiment and also suffered severely from an oblique flanking fire from Marjoribanks's light infantry and grenadiers stationed on the British right across the Charleston road. As he led his men forward, Henderson went down badly wounded, and the South Carolinians, demoralized by the loss of their leader, began to waver. Lieutenant Colonel Wade Hampton, the second in command, displaying cool battlefield leadership, rallied the state troops and, leading them personally, continued the attack.

The fighting became intense along the entire line and the militia in the center, temporarily bolstered by the arrival of Sumner's command, retired from the battle with empty ammunition pouches. Sumner's North Carolina brigade of Continentals, unable to sustain the disciplined British volley fire, also fell back, and Stuart's left swept forward with the bayonet. This was the crisis of the battle. Greene, who had held back his best troops, the Virginia and Maryland Continentals, threw them in with orders to take the field with the bayonet.

The Virginians and Marylanders moved forward in perfect order and at the double, officers in front. When they came within 40 yards of the British line, the Americans halted, delivered one crashing volley, and went in with the steel. The fighting was so close that American Continentals and British regulars were found lying dead, mutually transfixed by each other's bayonets after the battle. Lee with his legion infantry swung around the exposed British left flank and attacked in that sector. The British left and center, under the intense pressure on front and flank, began to give way and finally broke, retreating into the open field around the brick house. Major Coffin, still not engaged, withdrew the British cavalry into the woods on the left of the field, while John Marjoribanks, with the unbeaten right wing, held his ground and covered the British retirement with steady aimed fire. As Stuart's disintegrating left and center fell back, Major Sheridan of the New York Volunteers with a detachment of his command occupied the brick house—a natural fort in the middle of the battlefield. Lieutenant Lawrence Manning of Lee's Legion, the ancestor of the present South Carolina family of that name, hotly pursuing Sheridan, almost forced his way with some of his men through the house doors. Sheridan's New York Volunteers bodily thrust the Americans out and barred the door, then, taking positions at the windows, maintained a steady fire in all directions from their muskets and a few light swivels they had brought in with them.

John Marjoribanks still maintained his position on the right, and Lieutenant Colonel Stuart, having pivoted his demoralized troops on the unbeaten right wing, was frantically attempting to form a new line facing south and west toward the abandoned camp. Greene, realizing that Marjoribanks must be dislodged, ordered William Washington with the reserve to force a passage where the British position rested on Eutaw Creek. The dashing Virginia cavalry leader promptly obeyed, galloping forward with the cavalry, his personal red banner, "Tarleton's Terror," carried behind him. Not waiting for Wade Hampton or Robert Kirkwood, who had been ordered to support him with their infantry, Washington frontally charged Marjoribanks's position, but could not force his way through the thickly growing dwarf jack oaks protecting the British flank companies. Wade Hampton came up and Washington swung his horsemen left to try with Hampton a breakthrough by the creek bank around the British right. In the process of carrying out this maneuver, he exposed his command to a devastating side fire from the British flank companies posted in and behind the oak thicket. Washington and all but two of his officers were brought down and the wounded Washington was captured. Kirkwood arrived with the veteran Delawares, joined Hampton's state troops and Washington's survivors, and the combined force drove Marjoribanks from his protecting oak trees in desperate short-range fighting. Marjoribanks, however, pulled back without breaking and formed a new line with its rear to the creek and its left stationed around and in the palisaded garden. There the gallant major continued to resist successfully all American attempts to dislodge him while Stuart re-formed his battle line, anchored on Marjoribanks unbroken right wing.

The British had fallen back in the pivoting movement through their own camp, abandoning tents and equipment to the pursuing Americans. The only logical explanation for what occurred next must rest on the basic training of all American forces in the Revolution. Except for a very few crack units, such as Henry Lee's Legion, the necessary military discipline did not go very deep. As the Continental officers charged through the tents into the open field, they came under intense raking fire from the house. The same officers also discovered that most of their men, obviously thinking the battle won, had broken ranks and were looting the British encampment, apparently concentrating in consuming, on the spot, the provisions, particularly quantities of rum found among the supplies. Only Lee's Legion infantry, fighting from behind the protection of an outbuilding on the far right of the American line, with Hampton's and Kirkwood's commands on the far left, remained under control. Most of the other units in Greene's advancing line now fell into complete disorganized confusion.

Marjoribanks on the British right and Major Coffin with his cavalry on what had been Stuart's left, both watching the situation develop, promptly launched attacks on the two American flanks. Nathanael Greene apparently still was unaware of the growing demoralization of his army and ordered Lee to counterattack Coffin with his Legion cavalry. According to Lee, Greene had detached a majority of Lee's cavalry to support William Washington's ill-fated charge and the legion horsemen still were scattered. Only one section responded under Captain Armstrong, and Major Coffin, charging with the saber, drove the depleted unit back without much difficulty.

General Greene, now realizing the extent of the confusion, determined that he could save his army only by retiring in as good order as possible from the field. The order was given and the officers, gaining a measure of control over some of the men, began the withdrawal. This was not to be unhindered. Major Coffin, carried away by his victory over Lee, attacked the soldiers still scattered among the tents. Fortunately for Greene, Wade Hampton had been ordered to cover the retreat. Collecting a few horsemen and followed by his infantry, he countercharged Coffin and drove him off in vicious hand-to-hand fighting. In the course of pursuing the defeated British, Hampton and his men advanced too far and came under heavy fire from Sheridan's men in the house and Marjoribanks's battalion, still dug in around the palisaded garden. Hampton fell back on the retreating American army, and Marjoribanks sallied out and seized the two American 6-pounders and two British 6-pounders taken when the Continentals overran the British line. Greene had brought up all four guns to batter the brick house into submission, but the fieldpieces had been placed in battery too near the house, and all the gunners were killed or wounded by Sheridan's men firing from the windows. Marjoribanks, with his own battalion supported by Sheridan's New York Volunteers, then charged out from his position and drove those Americans remaining on the field into the protection of the woods, where Wade Hampton had reorganized his command and was protecting the withdrawal. Tragically, Marjoribanks, the only real hero of the battle, was mortally wounded in this last attack and was carried, dying, by his men into the protection of the garden.

A battle that should have been an American victory had ended with Alexander Stuart holding the field but far too crippled to follow up his advantage. Greene delayed long enough to collect his wounded, leaving behind only those men who had fallen near the house, and made arrangements with Stuart to bury the dead. Greene also left a strong covering force under Wade Hampton and marched away to Burdell's seven miles up the road, where his battered forces could rest and lick their wounds.

Stuart remained in position at Eutaw the night after the battle and all the following day, then withdrew slowly to Charleston with his badly hurt little army, abandoning the area to American occupation, as happened so often in the southern war.

For the number of men engaged, the losses on both sides were heavy. The British suffered 85 killed, 350 wounded, and 257 missing, for a total of 692. This was over one-quarter of the men engaged. Greene reported casualties of 251 killed, 367 wounded, and 74 missing, also a total of 692, slightly more than one-third of the whole. The American capture of over 200 prisoners in the attack that broke the British left and center before the fiasco of the camp occurred accounted for the disproportionate number of missing from Stuart's army.

Both sides claimed a victory, but Stuart undeniably controlled the field after Greene's retirement. Greene, however, regrouped and reorganized at Burdell's and followed Stuart's retreat on Charleston, slowly driving the British defense forces into a small holding perimeter around the port city. Again, as at Guilford Court House and Hobkirk Hill, Greene eventually would possess all the advantages of a major victory.

If palms are to be awarded at Eutaw Springs, they belong chiefly to the British army, to John Marjoribanks, and Majors Sheridan and Coffin, the three men who saved the day for Alexander Stuart. Wade Hampton was unquestionably the outstanding American officer on that bloody and crucial occasion.

CHAPTER XVIII

The Yorktown Campaign—
First Phase

Three days after his calamitous victory at Guilford Court House, Lord Cornwallis retired slowly toward Cross Creek, leaving 70 of the most seriously wounded at the nearby Quaker Meeting House under a flag of truce. Cornwallis's army had to move because they had no tents, the baggage having been destroyed before the pursuit of Nathanael Greene, and food was almost exhausted. The British commander hoped that a settlement of Loyalist Scots at Cross Creek would furnish provisions and give shelter to his many sick and injured. Cross Creek lay on a branch of the Cape Fear River about one hundred miles from Wilmington, North Carolina, thus a line of communications might be opened by water from Cross Creek to the British base on the coast. On the day his march began Cornwallis issued a proclamation announcing Greene's defeat and calling on all loyal subjects to rally around the king's standard. He offered protection of their persons and property to all "rebels" who came in, surrendered their arms, and took the oath of allegiance. This done, they would be permitted to return home on military parole, all obligations for service completed.

As so often happened in the South, Cornwallis's ringing pronouncement had little or no effect, and Greene's regrouped army followed closely on the heels of the British march. There was no major fighting although skirmishing occurred between the light troops, but the presence of an American army in strength dampened thoroughly any enthusiasm for the British cause among the surrounding population. If the British really had won a major battle, why were they falling back on the coast with an American army moving behind them? Greene had other objectives in mind and broke off his pursuit at Ramsay's Mill on Deep River, leaving Cornwallis to march unimpeded during the last few days of the movement.

When the British arrived at Cross Creek they found the Scots loyal and helpful, but very few recruits joined the army. The new post, however, proved a complete disappointment. Provisions for horses and men were exceedingly scarce. The river was too narrow and its banks too steep for loading and unloading. With the exception of the Scots at Cross Creek, who had been mercilessly persecuted by their rebellious neighbors, most of the people in the surrounding area were bitterly hostile to the British cause. Cornwallis clearly could accomplish nothing by remaining there. In hope of finding adequate food and better medical care, Cornwallis led his army to Wilmington, arriving at that town on 7 April 1781. During the march, Lieutenant Colonel Webster died of wounds received when he led the last victorious charge at Guilford Court House, and Lord Cornwallis wrote on 23 April a most compassionate letter of sympathy to the young officer's father, the Reverend Dr. Webster of Edinburgh. Such examples of thoughtfulness show why he inspired loyalty among soldiers who followed him through wilderness terrain across great distances and fought courageously, often against very great odds.

Shortly after Cornwallis arrived in Wilmington, North Carolina, he learned that Greene had marched south by the direct road to Camden, South Carolina. The British commander faced a choice of difficult alternatives, all of them dangerous. If he marched immediately toward South Carolina, he feared he could not arrive in time to intercept Greene, and the fate of the big British base at Camden would then already be decided. Depleted by sickness, desertion, and the heavy losses suffered at Guilford Court House, Cornwallis could field only 1,435 men, an inadequate force to resume active campaigning in the Carolinas. To remain at Wilmington with the summer heat approaching would endanger the health of his remaining troops. To return by land down the coastal road to Charleston seemed a fruitless and perilous course of action because it would be a journey through a wild country cut by the great river swamps and threatened by Francis Marion and his partisans across and along the line of march. If the army traveled to Charleston by sea, a long delay waiting for transports and escort vessels would be inevitable. An ocean trip could result in the loss of all or most of the cavalry and artillery horses, a frequent occurrence on sea voyages in the eighteenth century because the animals, stabled below decks, broke their legs if any heavy weather were encountered. Furthermore, the British considered a move by sea to be an admission of fear compared to an overland march and thus a disgrace.

After considerable thought and discussion with his officers, Cornwallis concluded that the best course of action was to march north to Virginia. There he could join his battered army to the strong corps operating out of Norfolk and on the York and James peninsula under Major General Philips. It was hoped that this move might draw Greene back from South Carolina to defend wealthy, populous, and vulnerable Virginia. Cornwallis still believed that a campaign to subjugate that rebellious state would be the best means of conquering the rest of the South.

On 7 May, Major General Philips received a letter from Cornwallis informing him of his decision to march north and proposing Petersburg, Virginia, as a point of rendezvous for the two forces. Unfortunately for Cornwallis, Philips, a very able man whose advice might have changed the course of events, contracted a fever and died just four days after his army reached Petersburg. Benedict Arnold succeeded him in command.

In his movement north Cornwallis pushed forward with very little opposition except for a few minor skirmishes which his army won. The British, however, antagonized the countryside by inflicting unnecessary savagery on the local population of Halifax, Virginia. The two men responsible, a sergeant and a private of dragoons, were convicted of rape and robbery, court-martialed, and executed, but this prompt punishment failed to ameliorate the ill feelings. The junction of the two armies took place on 20 May, and Cornwallis assumed command of the combined force.

The Marquis de Lafayette, a young French aristocrat, had been placed in command of the small American army watching General Philips. Lafayette had judged correctly that the British intended to occupy Petersburg and tried by forced marches to reach the town first. Philips beat him in the race, and Lafayette retired, recrossing the James River and taking up a position on the northern bank between Richmond and Wilton.

Cornwallis's plan was to force a fight with Lafayette, defeat him, and then destroy all American stores within reach. The British commander would then fall back on the coast and wait for instructions from General Sir Henry Clinton, the British commander in chief stationed in New York. Cornwallis's army in Virginia, already greatly superior in numbers to the opposing Americans, now was further strengthened by two additional British regiments of foot and two battalions of German mercenary infantry sent by Clinton from New York.

As soon as a report of British reinforcements reached him, Lafayette retreated northward to meet General Anthony Wayne, who was marching south through Maryland with 800 men of the Pennsylvania Line sent by George Washington to support the operations in Virginia. (Lieutenant Colonel Henry Lee suggested that Wayne's 800 should have been called "the Irish Line" because most of them were Irish—and they were a rough, aggressive, disorderly lot.)

The British followed Lafayette as far as Hanover County, destroying public stores wherever they found them. Cornwallis, however, was unable to catch the fast-moving marquis and finally gave up the chase, turning his attention to a more attainable goal.

The General Assembly of Virginia was meeting in a guarded session at Charlottesville to vote to raise taxes and militia and to increase the regular forces of the state to meet the British attack. Lieutenant Colonel Banastre Tarleton, still presenting the image of the dashing cavalry leader despite his reverses in South Carolina, was detached by Cornwallis with 180 horsemen of his legion and 70 mounted infantry of the 63d Regiment with orders to strike at Charlottesville and surprise the legislators. Tarleton started his movement immediately and on the way captured twelve wagons loaded with arms and clothing destined for Greene's army in the South. Tarleton burned these wagons, rode swiftly on, and crossed the Rivanna at the base of Charlottesville hill. He charged across the stream, captured or scattered the guards watching the ford, swept into town, and seized seven members of the assembly. Governor Thomas Jefferson, warned at his home of Tarleton's approach, barely escaped into the mountains. Tarleton also found and destroyed at Charlottesville 1,000 new muskets and 400 barrels of gunpowder plus

Figure 94.   Marquis de Lafayette,
by Robert Wilson

several hogsheads of tobacco and packets of clothing, the latter intended for the Virginia troops that were to be raised. The British cavalry commander then rode down the Rivanna River to rendezvous with Colonel John Simcoe of the Queen's Rangers and coordinate movements with him.

Simcoe had been sent by Cornwallis at the same time he detached Tarleton to attack General Frederick von Steuben, George Washington's German drillmaster, who was reported to be at the Point of Fork on the James River guarding a considerable quantity of stores with a strong force of eighteen-months men and militia. The Point of Fork is where the Rivanna and Fluvanna rivers meet the James. On hearing from prisoners captured on the line of march that Steuben already had transported the stores to the south side of the Fluvanna and planned to cross there with his entire detachment, Simcoe pushed forward as swiftly as possible. He arrived too late to stop von Steuben's crossing, but captured about 30 men, the last to leave. All stores and the main body of troops were safely on the other side and Steuben had taken the available boats with him. Simcoe therefore decided to use what today would be called psychological warfare by making such a convincing demonstration with his rangers on the opposite bank of the river that the Americans would think his force to be the advance guard of the whole British army. The ruse succeeded beyond all expectations. Frederick von Steuben retreated the next day in great haste, abandoning most of the stores he had been assigned to guard.

Four British hussars carrying their saddles, carbines, and sabers and accompanied by 28 infantrymen crossed the river in several small canoes they found. The hussars had been instructed to capture stragglng horses the Americans might have left behind and then to ride down and take station on the road Steuben had followed. If an American patrol should come back up the road to check on the pursuit, the four hussars were ordered to raise a shout and charge with the saber, pretending to be an advance element of Cornwallis and a full British field army. This happened exactly as planned. A patrol was encountered, the four hussars charged, and the Americans fell back rapidly on their main column, reporting to von Steuben that a "powerful" British advance was hard on his heels. He prudently hurried his march and continued on for twenty miles before camping for the night.

The Marquis de Lafayette meanwhile had been joined by Anthony Wayne and his 800 Continentals. Together they recrossed the Rappahannock River and marched on the track of the British army falling back on Williamsburg. On the road they were joined by von Steuben and his men fleeing Simcoe, and the combined force pressed forward. There was a brief and savage little encounter a few miles above Williamsburg between Simcoe, leading his Queen's Rangers supported by some German jäger riflemen, and Lieutenant Colonel Butler of the Pennsylania Line commanding American riflemen and a small force of cavalry. The engagement was indecisive, although Lafayette claimed the advantage in his report.

On 21 May 1781 George Washington left his army in position outside of New York watching Clinton, traveled to Connecticut, and conferred with Admiral de Barras and the Count de Rochambeau, respectively commanding French naval and land forces in North America. The three determined that the combined French and American armies would strike hard—either an attack on New York or an operation at a designated point in the Chesapeake Bay area. The selected target would be hit as soon as Admiral de Grasse arrived with a strong French fleet from the Caribbean. Washington wrote Congress a full report of the conference, but the express courier carrying the letter was captured in the Jerseys by a British patrol and this very important information fell into Sir Henry Clinton's hands. He naturally became alarmed for the safety of New York and promptly dispatched a message to Cornwallis in Virginia instructing him to detach certain units and send them by sea to New York at his earliest convenience. This was a direct order, and Cornwallis prepared to comply. He knew, however, that a detachment of these troops would leave him insufficient forces to remain at Williamsburg facing a strongly reinforced Lafayette. Cornwallis therefore decided to cross the James River and retire on Portsmouth, Virginia, where he could have access to the sea and support from the Royal Navy. An express was sent to Sir Henry Clinton in New York, stating that Cornwallis would comply immediately with the requisition and informing his commander in chief of the reasons for the planned withdrawal to Portsmouth.

On 4 July the British army marched from Williamsburg and camped on the higher ground covering the ford and causeway that led to the island of Jamestown. Lafayette, mistakenly thinking that the main British army had crossed the river, determined to attack what he believed to be only a rear guard. Cornwallis apparently had hoped the young and impetuous marquis would be so misled and therefore held his troops in battle readiness, instructing his pickets to fall back before the American approach with the appearance of alarm and surprised confusion. This was the battle of Green Spring, named for the plantation near which it was fought. The American army had to cross a causeway flanked by marshes in order to attack a prepared British position, and Lafayette walked into a trap. The sharp, bloody action that ensued on 6 July ended with an American repulse. The retreating Americans could not be pursued, however, because the engagement took place just before sunset. If daylight had lasted one more hour, the Marquis de Lafayette might have suffered a very serious defeat. Instead, he withdrew safely from his ill-conceived venture—a frontal attack on a strongly posted enemy—across a narrow causeway flanked by half-flooded marshes. The British lost only 5 officers wounded and 70 enlisted personnel killed and wounded. The American casualties in killed, wounded, and captured were about 300.

The morning after the battle of Green Spring, Cornwallis's army crossed the James River without interruption. The units designated for embarkation to New York were sent forward to Portsmouth, and the rest of the British army marched there by easy stages. The troops were on board ship and ready to leave when an order came from Sir Henry Clinton countermanding the sailing. Intelligence had been received from dispatches intercepted at sea by alert frigate patrols of the intended arrival off the American coast of a powerful French naval force. This fleet would sail from the West Indies during the summer of 1781 and coordinate its operations with the French warships already at Newport, Rhode Island. General Clinton therefore instructed Cornwallis to establish a defended post and anchorage to protect British ships of the line, either at Old Point Comfort or Yorktown. The British commander in chief also expressed in the strongest possible terms his intention of holding the Chesapeake area in the face of the French threat and said that in due season he would send to Virginia all the troops that could be spared from other assignments.

After receiving these instructions, Cornwallis ordered his engineers and the officers of naval units stationed in the area to survey Old Point Comfort as a possible base. They studied this location and reported that military works established there would neither command the entrance to Hampton Roads nor secure ships of the royal fleet lying at anchor in the Roads. Cornwallis decided that the best choice would be to fortify Yorktown on the York River and Gloucester just across that river, the only places under his control capable of affording the necessary anchorage and protection for major war vessels.

During July 1781 a series of British mischances and mistakes began which ultimately led to Cornwallis's surrender at Yorktown. Admiral Mariot Arbuthnot, who had handled fleet operations brilliantly during the siege and capture of Charleston in 1780, sailed for England on 2 July, leaving Rear-Admiral Thomas Graves in command at New York. Graves promptly wrote Admiral George Rodney, British naval commander in the West Indies, of the expected arrival on the American coast of a strong French fleet from the West Indies. Rodney dispatched to New York on 7 July the *Swallow*, a fast sloop, bringing word that British naval reinforcements had orders to make the Chesapeake Capes as swiftly as possible and move from there up to New York. He requested that Admiral Graves place frigates with the latest information on station along the coast to facilitate the passage of the support squadron.

Rodney heard on 7 July that the French Admiral de Grasse was standing in with his fleet at Cap François, Haiti, and sent a dispatch vessel to inform Sir Peter Parker, the commander of British naval forces at Jamaica, of enemy movements. On 1 August, however, pleading ill health, Rodney departed for England, probably to deposit the loot he had won at St. Eustatius, and thus Rodney, one of Great Britain's most aggressive and skillful sea commanders, was not present at the battle of Yorktown and the Capes of the Chesapeake. Because Rodney later defeated de Grasse at the Saints Passage in 1782, one may speculate whether the issue would not have been different in the fighting off the Capes if Rodney had been there instead of Graves.

The British naval command in the West Indies had received false intelligence that de Grasse had dispatched fourteen ships of the line to the Chesapeake area. The same report stated that the French admiral with the remainder of his fleet would escort a large merchant convoy to France. Admiral Sir Samuel Hood therefore was ordered to sail for the Chesapeake Capes with fourteen ships of the line. He promptly sent the brig *Active* to inform Admiral Graves of his movement, but *Active* and *Swallow*, the sloop dispatched earlier by Rodney, both were lost to enemy patrol action. Admiral Graves remained ignorant of current developments in the West Indies and sailed from New York hoping to intercept a troop convoy from France presumed to be destined for Boston. Graves missed the convoy and returned to New York on 28 August. Awaiting him were duplicates of *Swallow's* and *Active's* dispatches that had been sent in other fast ships. He learned the same evening that Admiral de Barras, the French naval commander at Newport, Rhode Island, had sailed south on 25 August with his full division.

Sir Samuel Hood moved slowly up the coast with his frigates scouting each possible French landing point and finding nothing because de Grasse, who had started north five days earlier than Hood, proceeded even more slowly and was sailing behind him. Hood finally arrived off New York and reported in to Admiral Graves. As the senior officer present, Graves took command and on 31 August sent five ships of the line and a 50-gun ship, all that could be made ready in time, across the New York bar to join Hood, waiting with his division outside. The entire fleet of nineteen ships of the line with supporting frigates sailed immediately for the Chesapeake. Sir Henry Clinton had just received valid information that Washington and Rochambeau had left the New York area and were marching south to rendezvous with Admiral de Grasse, coming up from the West Indies with a full flotilla of transports and warships. He also was bringing 3,300 good regular troops from Haiti and other French islands in the West Indies to reinforce Lafayette. Since Washington and Rochambeau were leading 4,000 French regulars and some 2,500 American Continentials, American and French forces in Virginia mustered more than 14,000 men, over three times the number of Cornwallis's defending British troops at Yorktown and Gloucester.

Admiral de Grasse had sailed from Cap Francois on 5 August with twenty-eight ships of the line and escorting frigates. He passed through the old Bahama channel between northern Cuba and the Bahama banks and anchored on 20 August (the day after Hood arrived off New York) in Lynnhaven Bay, just within the entrance of the Chesapeake. As soon as his fleet was secured, an officer sent by the Marquis de Lafayette boarded the flagship and briefed de Grasse on the general situation. The French admiral immediately detached four ships of the line to block the York River and sent several frigates to convey the Marquis de St. Simon with some 3,000 French troops up the James River to reinforce Lafayette. At the same time, Washington and Rochambeau, having led Clinton to believe that an attack on New York was imminent, were marching south to join Lafayette around Yorktown with 6,000 regulars.

In the morning of 5 September, a French scout frigate patrolling outside the capes sighted topsails and signaled to de Grasse that a fleet was steering toward the bay. At first, the French were hopeful that the approaching ships were Admiral de Barras's squadron coming from Newport. As soon as the ensigns flying on the lead units could be distinguished, it was clear that instead they were the combined divisions of Graves and Hood: two 98-gun vessels, twelve 74s, one 70, and four 64s, as well as supporting frigates—the scouts and light cruisers that accompanied all eighteenth-century navies. To meet these ships, the French had one magnificent warship, the *Ville de Paris*, a three-decker of 104 guns, which carried de Grasse's flag, three 80-gun ships, seventeen 74s, and three 64s. In sum, the British had nineteen ships of the line and the French twenty-four (four French ships were blocking the York River).

From Cape Charles on the north to Cape Henry on the south, Chesapeake Bay at its entrance is about ten miles wide. The main channel in the eighteenth century ran between Cape Henry and the Middle Ground, a shoal about three miles north from the cape. When the French scout frigate first sighted the British fleet, it was steering on a southwest course for the entrance of the main channel with the wind from the northeast. The British were under foresails and topgallants only and formed into a line of battle as they approached the entrance.

Figure 95. The French fleet coming out of the Chesapeake Bay around Cape Henry, 5 September 1781

The French, in a bad anchorage and with a north-northeast wind, could not get under way until the ebb, when they began to drop down to the bay entrance on the outgoing tide. Some of the big ships had to make several tacks to clear Cape Henry, so the French line was late in forming and had not closed up completely in battle formation as they moved out into the open sea beyond the Capes.

Admiral Graves, on the *London*, sighted the first French units standing out from the entrance and flew the signal to form into a column on an east/west line. When the signal was executed, the British ships would be sailing in line, close hauled out to sea, on the opposite tack from which the fleet currently was heading and on the same tack the French were heading. Admiral de Grasse's van, about three miles away, veered a point or two southward. Shortly thereafter, Graves's signal was executed and the British ships, wearing together, came about on the new tack. Admiral Hood's division, which had been the leading group as the British approached the entrance, now became the rear element as Graves's fleet headed out to sea, roughly paralleling the French advance. Graves then flew the signal ordering all his ships to be brought to, which meant they came to as complete a stop as was possible for a full rigged sailing vessel and waited for the French

Figure 96. The English fleet attacks the French fleet coming out of the Chesapeake Bay, 5 September 1781

center to come abreast the British center. The two lines were almost parallel, but the British with five fewer ships did not extend to the rear of the French, who just had cleared Cape Henry.

Admiral Graves at this time proceeded to make the classic tactical error that would condemn Cornwallis to surrender at Yorktown. Graves already had ordered his fleet to wear and form in line of battle heading out to sea. This meant that each ship followed the next exactly astern at regular intervals. A new signal instructed the van ship, *Shrewsbury*, to turn to starboard and head toward the enemy. As each ship followed the leader in succession, the British line approached the French line on an oblique angle. The same signal was repeated twice, so the British angle of approach became more pronounced as the two fleets came within effective gun range. The result, of course, was that only the first twelve British ships actually engaged the enemy. Seven ships, the rear element of the British line, did not engage at all. According to the usual interpretation, Admiral Graves's adamant and unimaginative maintenance of the battle line guaranteed that a naval force inferior in numbers would fight a superior force with less than two-thirds of the weaker fleet committed to battle.

It would seem that the signal to maintain the line remained flying on *London* until, finally and belatedly, the signal for "close action" was hoisted. The latter had been flown briefly once before, but Admiral Graves apparently felt that his ships were not properly extended to turn and bear down on the enemy and had brought it down and sent up the "in line" signal again. Admiral Hood commanding the rear division finally was able to sail down on the French in late afternoon when the second signal for "close action" went up. As the British approached, de Grasse ordered his line to bear south, and Hood never was able to engage. Firing ceased just after sunset and the French came about and sailed back into the bay.

Richard W. Hale, Jr., writing in the *Proceedings* of the Massachusetts Historical Society (Volume 71, 1953–1957) presents a different approach to the battle of the Capes. He exonerates Admiral Graves and places the blame on poor communications, believing that Admiral Hood did not understand the flag hoist Graves had flying. There is considerable evidence to support Hale's concept. The British system of flag signaling at sea still was in the process of development. Sir Home Popham's Marine Vocabulary, which employed the new alphabetical flags along with the numeral flags already in use, was not introduced in the fleet until 1800. The Marine Vocabulary gave an admiral the means to hoist an unambiguous signal to meet the various contingencies of maneuver or battle.

According to Hale, Graves was a resolute, fighting admiral, trained in aggressive ship-to-ship action by Admiral Richard "Black Dick" Howe, one of England's most distinguished naval leaders. Howe favored engaging an enemy line on a slanting (lasking) approach with each attacking unit keeping an even line of bearing so no one ship might move dangerously out ahead of the others. In this way the advancing line could deliver fire on the approach and crash through the opposing line at almost regular intervals, each ship as it passed firing a double broadside, the starboard raking the vessel on the right through her bows, the port raking the ship on the left through her stern ports. After crippling the enemy in this way, single ships could be engaged with overwhelming force and captured. This was the theory of naval warfare Graves brought to the Chesapeake. *London*'s log indicates that Graves flew "engage the enemy" constantly throughout the action and hoisted "line ahead" only twice for short intervals.

Rodney, on the other hand, drilled his captains to sail in very close order, using the classic line ahead ordained for the Royal Navy since the end of the seventeenth century by the Duke of York's Fighting Instructions. Rodney, however, believed the rigid line ahead could be used offensively as well as defensively. He favored charging an enemy line with his line, crashing through its center, each British ship as it passed delivering port and starboard broadsides on the enemy units directly on the left and right. In this way the middle elements of an enemy formation could be smashed and the line broken and scattered while remaining vessels could be destroyed or taken by concentrated attack.

According to Hale's article, Graves flew the signal for "engage the enemy" and began with his five ships the lasking approach following Richard Howe's doctrine. Hood on *Barfleur*, who had been serving with Rodney in West Indian waters, interpreted the signal to mean "approach the enemy in line ahead." He therefore did not begin a lasking attack but remained in line ahead as did the commanders of his fourteen ships. Graves, puzzled, angry, and desperate, seeing the chance to attack the French fleet before all of its units emerged from the bay slipping away, summoned a frigate to take a message ordering Hood to conform to the signal. By the time the frigate arrived at *London* all twenty-four of the big French ships had rounded Cape Henry, and the opportunity to strike a decisive blow had passed.

For whatever reason—whether Graves mishandled the action or Hood misunderstood a signal—the French fleet was not defeated, although the losses on both sides were comparatively heavy, the British suffering about 346 and the French about 200 killed and wounded. Graves considered renewing the action on the next day, but several of his van ships were so badly damaged by French gunfire (one later had to be abandoned and burned) that he decided not to do so. The British admiral maintained station off the Capes until 9 September and finally sailed back to New York without accomplishing anything further, to the complete and frustrated rage of Admiral Hood. Hood believed that after firing stopped at sunset, Graves should have tried to beat de Grasse into the bay to block both his return and de Barras's arrival. Although the British were somewhat crippled aloft (the French always fired on the uproll to bring down mast and rigging), most of Graves's batteries were intact. If the British had sailed into the bay ahead of de Grasse, a defense order could have been taken at anchor (the ships were worn on spring lines) to bring the broadsides to bear. Cornwallis then would have been covered, and the British army eventually could have been evacuated by sea and saved.

Instead, although the indecisive action fought off the Capes was not truly a French victory, it condemned the British field commander at Yorktown to withstand without relief a siege against overwhelmingly superior numbers and guns. Yorktown was destined to be lost—the crucial and calamitous defeat for British arms in America.

CHAPTER XIX

The Yorktown Campaign—
Second Phase

On 14 August 1781 a letter was received at George Washington's headquarters outside of New York from Admiral de Barras, the French naval commander at Newport, Rhode Island, stating that Admiral de Grasse was sailing for the Chesapeake from the West Indies with twenty-nine ships of the line (actually there were only twenty-eight) and 3,300 regular troops drawn from the San Domingo garrisons, including the crack infantry regiments, Agenois, Gatinais, and Touraine. De Grasse very clearly had no plans to operate in New York waters and wrote Barras that he would remain off the North American coast no later than 15 October.

The truly stupendous task facing Washington was to concentrate all available ground forces, French and American, 450 miles south of the main army bases. If this movement of two armies were not accomplished in exactly sixty-one days the opportunity to inflict a decisive defeat on the British with massive French help would be lost. The capture of New York and destruction of Sir Henry Clinton's army must wait. The allied armies would march to Virginia.

George Washington decided to allot 2,500 men for the march south, leaving the remainder of the army, one regiment of artillery, Sheldon's Dragoons, and seventeen small regiments of infantry behind to guard West Point and the Hudson River defenses. All the French troops were to be assigned to the expedition. The Marquis de Lafayette, already operating in Virginia, was sent orders to prevent Cornwallis from evacuating the Yorktown area and retreating into North Carolina. To assist him in accomplishing this formidable task, Lafayette was authorized in the same dispatches to keep Anthony Wayne and his 800 Continental infantry, instead of their being sent to reinforce Nathanael Greene in South Carolina. Admiral de Barras was persuaded to cancel his plan for an attack on Newfoundland with his naval squadron and supporting troops. He promised instead to cooperate with Washington and the Count de Rochambeau, commander of French land forces in North America. Rochambeau was preparing to sail on 25 August to join de Grasse, bringing in his ships French heavy siege artillery and salted provisions for the allied armies.

To persuade Clinton and British intelligence that the troop movement was directed against Staten Island and New York, French troops in position near Chatham were directed to set up bake ovens a usual preparation for siege warfare, while work details began ostentatious improvements on the roads running toward British lines.

On 19 August the armies broke camp and marched to King's Ferry. General William Heath remained in the Highlands with his depleted force to watch Clinton in New York. During 20 and 21 August, the American army crossed the river to the Jersey shore, over 4,000 French regulars following four days later. The two forces joined and marched in three columns, ostensibly toward Chatham, but on 30 August, they turned south and headed toward Princeton and Trenton, the old battlegrounds of an early war. The crucial movement to the Chesapeake and Yorktown at last was under way.

On the morning of 1 September an express rider brought word from General Heath to George Washington that a British fleet, the combined forces of Admirals Graves and Hood, had sailed from New York harbor with some twenty ships of the line, enough to overwhelm Barras if they intercepted him. Clinton, successfully deceived at first of Washington and Rochambeau's real destination, had learned the truth, and the expedition against Cornwallis at Yorktown might be doomed to frustration and failure. If Graves and Hood reached the Chesapeake before Admiral de Grasse, Cornwallis could be relieved and either supported or evacuated as circumstances dictated.

Just south of Chester, Pennsylvania, on 5 September a dispatch rider from Lafayette brought word to Washington that Admiral de Grasse had reached the Chesapeake with twenty-eight ships of the line and 3,300 troops. The new French reinforcements gave Lafayette sufficient strength to prevent Cornwallis from escaping by land. Admiral de Grasse's fleet already in position blocking the entrance to Chesapeake would cut off all possibility of relief by sea.

Between 14 and 24 September the combined armies came in by land and sea to concentrate at Williamsburg, Virginia. As soon as Washington arrived, he went down to the lower Chesapeake and visited de Grasse on his flagship, the *Ville de Paris*.

It was clear that the American and French armies in the Virginia theater of war now held a clear numerical advantage over the British. In addition to the French fleet with its naval personnel, there were 7,800 French ground troops and 8,845 Americans, the latter including Lafayette's and Wayne's forces plus 3,200 Virginia militia, the largest contribution to the war ever made at one time by that state. More French regulars than American Continentals were serving at Yorktown, a fact often forgotten in accounts of the war.

Cornwallis's army mustered some 7,000 effectives, regulars, and well-trained Provincials, with sixty-five cannon. Most of this artillery consisted of light field-pieces essential to open field fighting but not very useful for counterbattery fire against enemy siege guns. The only heavy artillery were the 18-pounders taken off the frigate *Charon* that had been brought up the river for safety along with the sloop of war *Guadeloupe* and other lighter naval units when de Grasse entered the bay. Cornwallis's inner defense lines around Yorktown were reasonably strong with ten redoubts and fourteen batteries. Douglas Southall Freeman's *George Washington* (volume 5, chapters 21–23) gives an excellent description of the British and allied works around Yorktown. According to Freeman, to guard his works Cornwallis had established an outer defense line anchored on steep-banked Yorktown Creek southwest and west of the town, swinging around to a shallow water course, Wormeley's Pond and Creek, south and southeast of Yorktown. With the allied forces available the line might be turned on the British left, but this would place the attacking forces too far from Yorktown. If the assault were directed against the British right, it would come under direct short-range fire from the British batteries with resultant heavy casualties. The open fields between the deep ravine of Yorktown Creek and the water meadows above Moore's Mill on Wormeley Pond were about half a mile wide, but a redan and three British redoubts established between the two creeks gave fire cover to the area. The American and French reconnaissance teams reported to their respective commanders that the inner earthworks around the town itself did not seem to be very strong and probably enclosed too large an area to be defended by Cornwallis's forces. Two advanced redoubts had been thrown out on the British left near the river, both defended by fraise and abatis and one with a surrounding ditch or fosse. These, however, were not connected with each other by works of any sort and lay about 400 yards in advance of the main town lines.

Across the river at Gloucester, Tarleton commanded the British defenses with cavalry and mounted infantry plus a small contingent of regular line infantry. Cornwallis planned that Gloucester should be the escape route to the north if escape became necessary.

The siege began on 28 September when the Americans moved into position on the British left and the French on the British right with lines extending from Wormeley Creek to the York River above Gloucester Point. To the astonishment of both armies, an early morning scouting party on 30 September discovered that the British had abandoned their outer line of defenses except for the two advanced redoubts on the left. Both British and American officers later strongly criticized this move on tactical grounds, but Cornwallis believed that he had excellent reasons for the decision. Clinton had sent assurances through the allied blockade that he would send a powerful relief force from New York on or about 5 October. With the comparatively limited number of troops under his command, Cornwallis felt that he could prolong the siege by contracting his lines and holding until the expected help arrived.

The Americans and French now pushed the siege forward vigorously. The abandoned British works were occupied and ground broken for the first approach trenches on 30 September. Across the river the Duke de Lauzun with his legion, reinforced by Virginia militia, was assigned to watch and contain Tarleton, and it was there that the first battle action took place.

On 3 October a strong British foraging party, led out at daybreak by Lieutenant Colonel Thomas Dundas, was returning to Gloucester with wagons and pack horses loaded with Indian corn. As they moved back toward the fortified area, dragoons of the rear guard observed mounted American militia following them and halted in a screen of trees to set an ambush. The militia, apparently suspicious, fell back, and the British wagons with their mounted infantry escort were almost to the Gloucester lines when a Lieutenant Cameron, patrolling with a dragoon contingent in the rear, reported that the Americans were advancing again, this time in force, and help was needed. Shortly afterward, a long column of dust and the sky blue uniforms of French hussars riding in advance came into sight.

Figure 97.   British officers on the ramparts at Yorktown, Virginia, by Sidney King

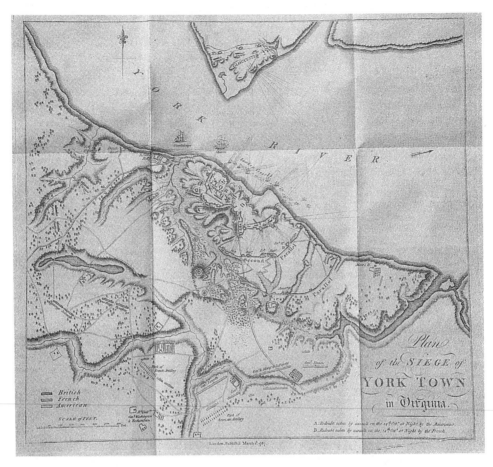

Figure 98.   Plan of the siege of Yorktown, Virginia, 28 September–19 October 1781, from
A History of the Campaigns of 1780 and 1781 in the Southern Provinces of North America,
Lieutenant Colonel Banastre Tarleton (London, 1787)

A section of Tarleton's Legion cavalry, reinforced by a detachment of the 17th
Dragoons and some of John Simcoe's veteran troopers, were ordered out from Gloucester under Tarleton's personal command to check the pursuit and cover the retreat of the
supply wagons. These horsemen with the mounted wagon escort formed in the woods
while Tarleton rode forward with Lieutenant Cameron and his contingent of dragoons
to reconnoiter the approaching French and Americans. Brigadier General de Choisy, the
field commander, ordered a general advance, and the French cavalry charged Tarleton
and his reconnaissance party. A Polish uhlan, one of the 35 lancers attached to Lauzun's
mercenary legion, thrust his lance into a British dragoon's horse, and the wounded

beast lunged against Tarleton's mount, throwing both horse and rider to the ground. The British cavalry rear guard waiting in the woods galloped out to save their leader, and the two cavalries met head-on, but these horsemen were just as battle hardened and experienced as Tarleton's and would not be forced back. Tarleton, who had found a riderless horse in the melee, remounted and ordered his bugler to sound a general retreat. The British dragoons retired in good order behind the mounted infantry of the wagon escort which had dismounted, formed a battle line, and checked the French pursuit with disciplined volley fire. Tarleton's cavalry rallied behind the musket line and returned to the attack with the saber, but the French horsemen fell back behind their own infantry and American militia units moving up into action. Somewhat to the astonishment of both the British and the French, a select Virginia militia battalion, commanded by Lieutenant Colonel John Francis Mercer, met and checked the British mounted charge with cool steadiness. After five years the Americans—Continentals and militia alike—were becoming real soldiers. Tarleton called back his attack and retreated into the Gloucester works. It was his last engagement in the American war, a somewhat ironic ending to a bloody and dashing battle record.

During the night of 6 October the first allied parallel was opened on the British left at about 600 yards. Admiral de Barras had arrived with his squadron on 10 September bringing the heavy siege artillery. These were loaded and dragged up for emplacement with whatever local horses and oxen could be obtained; on George Washington's direct request American officers lent their spare mounts to facilitate the operations. At the same time the British in Yorktown were killing horses they no longer could feed or turning the weak and hungry creatures out to shift for themselves between the lines.

Throughout the nights of 4, 5, and 6 October the British had maintained a steady cannonade to impede, if they could not prevent, the opening of the parallel. Washington and Rochambeau saw no point in wasting good ammunition until all was ready; thus allied guns did not return the fire. Also on 5 October, the day before the first parallel was opened, dispatches had been received from Nathanael Greene in South Carolina telling of the hard-fought battle of Eutaw Springs. Although the British held the field at Eutaw Springs, shortly after the engagement they had abandoned their position and fallen back, badly shattered, on Charleston. Encouraged by this news from the South Carolina front, the allies continued the siege of Yorktown.

As Freeman states, the first parallel ran from the bank of the York River approximately 600 yards from the advanced redoubt on the British far left to just east of the head of Yorktown Creek. This line was never more than 800 yards from the British positions at any point, a good artillery distance but well out of musket or rifle range.

There had been very few American and French casualties from the British cannon fire and on 7 October, in accordance with proper eighteenth-century military custom at the beginning of a formal siege, the American light infantry marched into the completed entrenchment with drums beating and colors flying. This was a far cry from the confused and amateurish American operations around Boston in 1775.

Rochambeau instructed the French under General St. Simon on the British extreme right to dig a narrow support trench next to the river just west of the mouth of Yorktown Creek. A redoubt was established here, protected from British raids by the steep-banked stream. It mounted seven field guns, four siege mortars, two howitzers, and two 24-pounder long guns to meet and neutralize the British star redoubt across the creek.

Both armies began work on six redoubts and batteries defending the first parallel and continued without interference from the British lines. The French established several batteries and by noon of 9 October the Americans had emplaced heavy mortars on the extreme right that could bring that sector of the British lines under high-trajectory shell fire. With most of the guns in position the French were given the honor at three in the afternoon of the same day of beginning the cannonade and bombardment. It was taken up all around the siege line and continued during that entire night. By the next morning two more French and two American batteries were completed and a total of forty-six guns and mortars joined in a half-circle of steady fire.

The Duke de Lauzun and Brigadier General de Choisy, watching Tarleton in Gloucester, discovered a British raiding force in six flatboats attempting to make a landing around the right flank. The French light field artillery aided by St. Simon's 24-pounders from the redoubt across the river forced the British to return to Gloucester Point. That key outpost, closely invested by the French army and supporting American militia, was in perilous condition. Tarleton's and Simcoe's troopers had been forced to kill some 1,200 starving horses, which meant that the British cavalry and mounted infantry were no longer an effective force, and cavalry would be essential if it became necessary to break out. Although British morale was beginning to erode under the increasing pressure, Cornwallis still believed that he could hold the town until the expected help from Clinton arrived.

During the full day of 11 October allied guns continued a mounting and aggressive cannonade while British fire noticeably decreased. Observers could see that parapets and embrasures on Cornwallis's line had suffered considerable damage. That night two of the British frigates on the river hoisted anchor and began to maneuver. The suspicious French promptly turned the guns of St. Simon's big redoubt on the moving ships. *Guadeloupe* got safely behind a point of land, but *Charon* was set on fire by red-hot shot and burned to the water's edge. The smaller British naval units also in range tried to escape, but others were set on fire, and by morning several more vessels had been destroyed. The French artillerists were highly professional.

Two more French batteries of three 24-pounders each were operative by 11 October, and the allied command with most of the artillery in position determined that a second and closer parallel must be established as soon as possible. The two strong outlying redoubts on the British extreme left must be taken by direct assault if a second parallel were to be successfully completed. The allied engineers' answer to this problem was to drive a trench from the first parallel on an angle toward the redoubts and throw up an epaulement or strong point at the end of the new trench in line with the advanced British redoubts. When finished, the strong point would cut the attack distance to the first redoubt by almost half—about 300 yards. A low ridge of ground gave some protection to the workers as they labored steadily through the night hours of 11 October. The British, however, suspected something and brought the French sector from which the trench extended under heavy artillery fire, which was answered by a furious French countercannonade. An American wrote after the battle that he never had seen a more beautiful or tremendous sight, the French shot and shell going over in one continuous blaze the entire night.

By the morning of 12 October the trench was finished and the soldiers were moving up under cover to start the epaulement. Work on this strong point was pushed forward rapidly and by early morning of the fourteenth the British redoubts had been so damaged by artillery fire that an assault on both advanced positions was planned for the next day. Major General de Viomenil was given the honor of attacking the near redoubt with a picked French force, while Alexander Hamilton, at his own request, had command of the American assault group assigned to hit the redoubt overlooking the river.

About seven o'clock on the evening of 15 October allied batteries ceased fire and the two attack forces moved forward in the growing dark against their objectives. Suddenly small arms fire came from the redoubt on the allied left. The French had been discovered. Then fire spurted from the redoubt by the river. Alexander Hamilton's assault group also had been seen, and the hope of surprise in both cases was lost. The French and Americans, however, drove forward with the bayonet and successfully took the assigned redoubts, the French either capturing or killing some 120 defenders. John Laurens with a picked detachment swung around to the rear of the strong point that Alexander Hamilton was attacking frontally, and the overwhelmed British garrison of 45 surrendered.

The British promptly turned on the captured redoubts every gun that could bear, but working parties came through the fire and within forty-five minutes the French and Americans had thrown up walls of earth facing the British lines high enough to protect the triumphant attackers. French support troops and engineers suffered heavily, however, from British artillery fire as they moved up to the new redoubt through the still uncompleted trench.

Later in the morning of 16 October elements of the New York brigade marched into the work captured by Hamilton with drums beating and colors flying. The British, in no mood for traditional display, answered this ceremony with a heavy artillery fire, but the allies now were in rifle range of Cornwallis's lines and marksmen on both sides maintained a constant, accurate, and killing fire.

French and American artillerists soon emplaced two howitzers in each of the captured works, forcing the British garrison to endure a close-range shelling along with the sniper fire. The working parties, digging night and day, pushed the American line to the river and with the new French works the two captured redoubts were incorporated in a second parallel only 300 yards from the British positions. Cornwallis and his army had been hemmed in on three sides, and only the river offered a possible avenue of escape.

The British command, fully aware that the opening of a second parallel would mean that the already half-ruined works on their left could not stand for many more hours, had resorted to the last expedient of besieged and desperate men—the sally. About four o'clock in the morning of 16 October, a few hours before the New York brigade occupied the captured redoubt, a picked force of 350 British assault troops, the 80th company of grenadiers from the guards, with a unit of light infantry led by Lieutenant Colonel Lake and Major Thomas Armstrong, hit the junction of the French and American lines. They pushed into a sector of the second parallel where the workers had been withdrawn from the two uncompleted batteries to dig elsewhere along the line. The raiders found a small detachment of the Agenois regiment fast asleep; they killed or wounded several men and drove forward to the French sap, a zigzag communication trench leading to the first parallel. Here they were challenged by an alert American artillery battery. "Push on, my brave boys," shouted the British leader, Lieutenant Colonel Lake of the guards, "and skin the bastards." Fortunately for the allies, the Count de Noailles happened to be near at hand with a strong covering patrol. He attacked with the bayonet in the dark and after a few minutes of confused fighting the British retreated, leaving behind seventeen allied casualties and six damaged artillery pieces, their touch holes spiked with bayonet points. The raiders suffered seven casualties of whom five were captured, but the spiking had been done in the dark and in a hurry. The allied guns were only partially damaged and back into service within a few hours. As Cornwallis later reported to Clinton, after this honorable but unavailing adventure, the allied forces so consolidated their positions that the defenders could not show a single gun without immediate counter battery fire. To make matters even more difficult, British artillery ammunition was almost exhausted.

Only two choices remained. Cornwallis could either surrender Yorktown or evacuate the town and try to get away across the river. He decided characteristically to try the latter, and sixteen large boats were prepared for the attempt, scheduled for ten o'clock on the evening of 16 October.

Cornwallis planned to abandon all unnecessary baggage and to leave a small detachment to surrender the town with a letter addressed to General Washington asking his consideration for the sick and wounded remaining behind. The British commander hoped to transfer his infantry and artillerymen without being noticed in the darkness across to Gloucester, join Banastre Tarleton's garrison, attack the French and American besiegers by surprise, and fight their way to freedom.

All these arrangements were made in complete secrecy, and the movement went undetected. The light infantry, most of the guards, and part of the 23d Regiment landed at Gloucester. At this very critical time for the British, a violent wind and rainstorm suddenly came up and drove several loaded boats down the river, so there was no way to get additional troops across. Clearly, a total evacuation that crucial night was impossible. Cornwallis grimly ordered back from Gloucester those units that already had crossed, but even this movement was forced to wait until the morning of 17 October, when the storm-driven boats finally straggled back upstream.

At daybreak of 17 October, the allied batteries opened with more than one hundred field guns, howitzers, and mortars in position for a steady cannonade and bombardment, ripping and blasting the British earthworks. The British replied with a few small mortar shells which did very little damage. As Cornwallis later reported to General Clinton, the only artillery ammunition still remaining were one 8-inch mortar shell and about one hundred small antipersonnel coehorn mortar shells. All other solid shot and shell had been used up in the siege and many of the guns dismounted by allied fire. Finally, the heartsick British commander determined that he must capitulate. His numbers were sadly diminished by wounds and illness, and Clinton had not kept his promise to come to Cornwallis's rescue. The allies could take the town by direct bayonet assault anytime they chose to do so.

Somewhere between nine and ten o'clock in the morning of 17 October American officers watching the British lines through the smoke and explosions of the bombardment saw the red coat of a drummer standing on the shattered parapet of the most southerly British hornwork. He held himself erect, facing the fire storm, and he was beating the parley. The cannonade was so intense they could not hear the drum, but messengers were sent running, and all firing suddenly ceased. A British officer then came out before the defenses and waved a white handkerchief. American officers went forward to meet him and, after covering his eyes, brought him back through the lines to General Washington. His blindfold was removed, and he presented a letter to the American commander. It was a message from Lord Cornwallis asking that all hostilities cease for twenty-four hours while terms of surrender for Yorktown and Gloucester might be discussed and settled.

American, French, and British officers met at the Moore House (still standing) about half a mile behind the first parallel to decide the terms. These were harsh but honorable and correct. All British military and naval personnel were to be surrendered as prisoners of war. Officers and seamen of the Royal Navy would become French prisoners, the army, American prisoners. Officers of both services could keep their sidearms and personal possessions. They would be permitted to go on parole to Great Britain or any American area in British possession. As an added courtesy, a fast sloop of war was provided to carry Cornwallis's dispatches under a flag to New York.

The formal capitulation took place on 19 October 1781, thirteen days after the first siege parallel had been opened. Cornwallis surrendered 7,157 soldiers, 840 sailors, and 80 camp followers, but there were 2,000 sick and wounded in his hospitals. The people of the neighborhood were invited to watch the ceremony, and a considerable number attended. The Count de Rochambeau's French regulars, elegant in their smart white uniforms, lined the west side of the road on which the British were to march. The Americans, battered and many of them ragged, lined the east side in two ranks, uniformed Continentals in front, hunting-frocked militia behind.

The British in their red uniforms and the German mercenaries in blue came marching down the road from Yorktown, stepping in time to a slow march, "The World Turned Upside Down." A magnificently uniformed British officer, Brigadier General Charles O'Hara of the Guards, who had followed Cornwallis through all of his southern campaign, rode with his mounted staff at their head. When the British general reached the two groups of mounted officers, American and French, he began to address Rochambeau, who with generous courtesy pointed across to George Washington. O'Hara apologized politely for his mistake and explained to Washington that he represented Lord Cornwallis, who was not well. Washington replied with equal politeness that, this being the case, O'Hara should consult his deputy, General Benjamin Lincoln, the same officer who had surrendered the entire American army of the Southern Department to the British at Charleston, South Carolina, in 1780—the world was indeed turned upside down.

Benjamin Lincoln was offered Cornwallis's sword, which he refused and returned to O'Hara, explaining to the brigadier that the French hussars in their sky blue tunics and yellow trousers had formed a mounted circle around a nearby field. The British were to enter this circle in order by regiment, lay down their arms, and march back between the French and American lines. After being cased the British and German flags were borne past the American and French battle standards that floated high and proud. In the eighteenth century a defeated army customarily played a march of the conquerors during a surrender ceremony as a chivalric gesture. At Yorktown, George Washington demanded English or German music in sardonic return for the British demand at the capitulation of Charleston that the drums of the humbled "rebels" should "not beat a British march." The melancholy operation finally was over. Sullen, resentful men marched into the circle, presented arms, laid down muskets, bayonets, and cartridge boxes, then sadly filed out. Afterward the allies could rejoice together over a victory where losses had been comparatively light for both armies: a total of 75 killed and 199 wounded.

Yorktown would prove to be the deciding engagement of the American Revolution. The royal forces were contained in small enclaves around New York, Wilmington, North Carolina, Savannah, and Charleston, and the last effective field army had been lost. The British government, occupied with a general European war, could no longer maintain an effective military presence in the former thirteen colonies. The conflict, however, would continue with sporadic savagery for over a year until peace was finally concluded on 3 September 1783.

After the capture of Yorktown, the British were treated with all the military amenities of a graceful period in history. Brigadier General O'Hara was invited to dinner with George Washington and Rochambeau and proved a most affable guest, poised and courteous, his conduct befitting an officer of the guards, whether victor or vanquished. The defeated officers were entertained with considerable ceremony in both American and French officers' messes. The Count de Rochambeau even offered Lord Cornwallis, a member of his social and military caste, a personal loan to tide him over his current difficulties. In spite of these stilted courtesies of a formal era, however, Yorktown was lost and the British cause in America with it.

CHAPTER XX

Why the British Lost the War in the South

By the time the British high command in London and New York decided in 1778 to transfer major military operations from the North to Virginia, the Carolinas, and Georgia, they already had made a serious psychological error in their long-range southern strategy.

In 1776 the great warrior tribes of the South occupied much of their ancient lands from the mountains to the Mississippi River. These were not primitive, wandering folk but settled peoples with comparatively complex social systems. They could field thousands of warriors, and most of the tribal fighting men by the mid-eighteenth century were armed with muskets. Extended contact with the white men, however, had in no way changed the cruel nature of Indian warfare. The acquisition of new weapons and the ever-present fear among all the eastern Indian tribes of continued white encroachment actually added further and more sophisticated dimensions to that warfare.

The Cherokees, the nearest of the big tribes to the British settlements, still held their territories in northern Georgia and upper South Carolina. Through the work of two very able royal agents, John Stuart and Alexander Cameron, the Cherokees in 1776 remained firm supporters of the British government.

On 3 October 1775 John Stuart wrote to General Thomas Gage, the British commander in Boston, that he opposed using the Indians for indiscriminate attacks on anti-British elements in the South. He would employ them to aid in executing a concerted plan or to act with their Loyalist neighbors. This message and its bearer, a confirmed Loyalist named Moses Kirkland, were captured and the letter published by order of the Continental Congress to demonstrate that the British were willing to use savages against the rebellious colonists, which was true. John Stuart and Alexander Cameron had already arranged for the Cherokees to hit the southern frontier from Virginia to Georgia as a diversion in support of a British amphibious assault on the coast. Such an attack occurred on 28 June 1776 when Admiral Sir Peter Parker and General Sir Henry Clinton mounted a joint operation against Charleston's island defenses.

The Cherokees struck along the entire southern frontier on 1 July, two days after the British had been repulsed by Charleston's defenders. With so many of South Carolina's defenders tied down at Charleston, if Parker and Clinton had been successful, the Cherokee coordinated assault would have been far more effective. The Indian operation was replete with the usual surprise attacks on outlying homesteads, the torture and massacre of defenseless old men, women, and children. The Cherokees were punished terribly by a punitive expedition launched later in the summer and fall of 1776 by the two Carolinas, Georgia, and Virginia which shattered tribal fighting power. The southerners of the back-country, however, held the British responsible for loosing the horrors of Indian warfare on the frontier. Many waverers who otherwise might have remained neutral or even served the British actively therefore undoubtedly were influenced to support the cause of independence.

The British decision to move their main military effort southward was based on sound strategic reasoning, and why they had not done so earlier in the war is difficult to understand. Pro-British feeling was strong in the South, and Loyalist leaders had been imploring the British for several years to make a major effort there, promising effective military support when such a move took place.

Saratoga, fought in 1777, had been the first and last big American victory in the North, but Canada remained safely in British hands. New York and its environs were strongly held by the king's forces, and the royal fleet maintained a reasonably tight blockade along the coast of the thirteen rebellious colonies. British raiding parties hit northern ports and American military depots so hard that George Washington was at times almost in despair. He warned the Continental Congress in 1779 that it might be necessary to dissolve his army and stop active warfare for a year until the country and American fortunes could recover with the help of active military aid through the French alliance. After almost four years of war without a decision, a general apathy toward the conflict permeated the population of the thirteen states.

Clinton, therefore, was justified in believing that the war in the North was at a stalemate that could end only in a British victory. All he had to do was hold New York, continue his raids, conquer and occupy the South while maintaining a naval blockade on northern ports, and the North inevitably would surrender.

Clinton thought Georgia and South Carolina were the key to control of the South. If Savannah and Charleston were in British hands, British forces cooperating with the Loyalist elements could fan out and occupy both states. These Loyalists, organized and trained by British officers, would be used to defeat and hold down their rebellious breth-ern. After Georgia and South Carolina were occupied and pacified, the waverers and neutrals could be brought over and the two provinces used as a secure base for operations against North Carolina and Virginia. It was a good, even wise, plan in general concept and might have succeeded except for incredible British blundering and an equally incred-ible failure to establish unity of command and command planning. It has been stated that one monument which a grateful nation should erect is a memorial to the British generals who won the Revolution for us.

The first part of the overall concept was executed by the British with smooth efficiency. Savannah, Georgia, was taken on 29 December 1778 and its American defenders dispersed with light losses and little difficulty. Colonel Archibald Campbell, the British commander in this operation, was not only an excellent soldier but a wise, high-minded, and honorable gentleman. His treatment of the American prisoners taken in the fighting and his understanding attitude toward the Georgians of all political convictions influenced many to come in to swear allegiance and enlist in the Loyalist units being formed. Unfortunately for the British cause and fortunately for the American, Campbell relinquished his command to superior officers who were far less perceptive. Three weeks after the victory, Major General Augustine Prevost arrived at Savannah with reinforcements from British Florida. He promptly assumed direction of the fighting and sent Colonel Campbell upriver to Augusta, which he seized and garrisoned. Posts were established throughout the state and by the middle of February 1780 Georgia appeared to be completely under British control.

A strange and interesting commentary on the war in 1779 and the attitude of many southerners to the long, weary, indecisive struggle was the offer made by the city of Charleston to Prevost when he arrived before its land defenses with 3,000 men in May of 1779. On this occasion the port city, so gallantly defended against the British attack in 1776, proposed to remain neutral for the duration of the war. Prevost scornfully refused the offer and demanded an immediate surrender. Nothing happened because General Prevost had bypassed the American army in his march north and learned that Benjamin Lincoln, the American commander in the South, was pushing up the Savannah road with superior forces. Prevost withdrew across the Sea Islands to Savannah, but the neutralist attitude of Charleston justified British expectations.

Almost a year later on 12 May 1780 Charleston fell to a joint assault by Clinton leading a British army cooperating with royal fleet units under Vice Admiral Mariot Arbuthnot. It was a beautifully executed operation following the classic European doctrine of siege craft. General Lincoln and the entire American army of the South were captured with the city.

Clinton had insisted as part of the surrender terms that all the defenders and the citizens of the city should be considered prisoners of war. The Continental regulars and their officers were to be confined. The militia and citizens having submitted on parole would be allowed to return to their homes. Shortly after the fall of Charleston, Andrew Williamson and Andrew Pickens commanding South Carolina militia at Ninety Six surrendered to the British under these terms, taking parole for themselves and their men as prisoners of war. Joseph Kershaw, the militia commander at Camden, South Carolina, surrendered himself and his troops with the same conditions. A similar offer was made by Henry Clinton to the people at large: come in and swear allegiance with full pardon and serve loyally with the king's forces against the rebels or take parole as prisoners of war. Many persons, especially in the coastal area where the British power lay, accepted the latter terms. Some swore allegiance and joined Loyalist military units.

In spite of assurances to the contrary by pro-British leaders, Loyalists willing to fight for the British against their own people never were so numerous or enthusiastic as the British high command had been led to believe. When this fact became obvious, Clinton realized that the terms he had imposed—of prisoners of war on parole—allowed many of the very people whom he wished to convert and recruit to remain permanent neutrals, legally permitted to sit out the war, taking neither side. If his plan to use the loyal people of South Carolina to help subject and control their revolutionary neighbors, friends, and relatives were to be successful, all the men safely on parole must be made liable to recruitment. Using this line of reasoning, Clinton on 3 June 1780 committed an error of judgment as large as that of encouraging a Cherokee attack on the southern frontier. He issued a proclamation declaring that all inhabitants of the province who were prisoners on parole should, from and after 20 June 1780, be freed and exempted from all such paroles and be reinstated to all the rights and duties of citizens and inhabitants. The same proclamation further stated that all citizens so described who did not return to their allegiance and a due submission to his majesty's government should be considered as rebels and enemies of that government and be treated accordingly.

All those who had taken parole after the fall of Charleston considered that their duty was performed and they could spend the remainder of the war quietly at home. The South Carolinians and Georgians had surrendered honorably under conditions honorably offered. Now the British commander had broken his pledge and men on parole were ordered by proclamation to take up arms against their own people or be considered rebels and treated as such. As Charles Stedman, the contemporary Loyalist observer says, "It was not long before the seeds of discontent appeared which, when fully matured, produced a counter-revolution in the minds and inclinations of the people as complete and as universal as that which succeeded the fall of Charleston."

Having issued his proclamation, Clinton returned to his command base in New York leaving Cornwallis with about 4,000 British and Loyalist regulars to complete the final subjection and organization of a South Carolina beginning to boil with resentment. Feelings among the inhabitants, particularly the Scots-Irish settlers in the Waxhaws, already were raw because of the conduct of that dashing and ruthless British cavalry commander, Banastre Tarleton. Lieutenant Colonel Tarleton correctly believed that the best way to win a war is to destroy both the enemy's forces and his will to fight, but he sometimes carried this military conviction to the point where it became counterproductive.

On 29 May 1780, just after the fall of Charleston, Tarleton pursued and caught at the Waxhaws in South Carolina Lieutenant Colonel Abraham Buford retreating northward with the 3d Virginia Regiment and the remnants of William Washington's cavalry. Tarleton's dragoons charged through the bewildered and scattered Virginians, many calling for quarter, and sabered them without mercy. Of Buford's command 263 were either killed outright or badly wounded and captured. Charles Stedman writes, "The King's troops were entitled to great commendation for their activity and ardour on this occasion, but the virtue of humanity was totally forgot." The local inhabitants were at first appalled and then infuriated. "Tarleton's quarter" became a watchword, as the British would grimly discover at Kings Mountain and Cowpens. Banastre Tarleton's action at the Waxhaws also set the tone for the fighting to come.

Many settlements in South Carolina separated by the great river swamps were so isolated that the war had hardly touched their lives. Now it came to them as it had to the Waxhaws. Some British field commanders, such as Major James Wemyss of the 63d Regiment, considered all dissenters from the Church of England to be real or potential rebels. James Wemyss burned the dissenting church at Indian Town in what was then St. Mark's Parish because he considered all Presbyterian churches to be "sedition shops." Again, at the Waxhaws, British troops on patrol burned the house and books of the Presbyterian minister to the Scots-Irish community.

In a few short months the British had thoroughly antagonized and in many cases forced into open rebellion men who would have been quite content to remain at home as paroled prisoners of war. In the same period the British managed to shock, anger, and estrange large elements of Scots-Irish Presbyterians and Welsh Baptists by attacking their churches, the very center of settlement life. The ruthless brutality of Tarleton undoubtedly created a sense of fear, although most South Carolinians and Georgians simply became angry and vengeful.

The hard, dour, Scots-Irish Calvinists, the Welsh Baptists, the Huguenot and English planters now took the field with Francis Marion, Thomas Sumter, Elijah Clarke, and William Davie. It was impossible to intimidate by fiat or force men schooled in the ultimate harshness of Indian warfare and frontier life whose immediate forebears in the wars of Europe and the British Isles had manned the walls of Enniskillen, Londonderry, or La Rochelle and advanced through the Boyne waters with Marshal Schomberg.

Many persons in the Carolinas and Georgia still supported the royal cause for personal advantage or, in most cases, honest political conviction. Here again, the British high command in the South was guilty of blundering miscalculation. The only chance of British success lay in a steady, methodical subjugation and organization of Georgia and South Carolina. It was not enough to defeat Patriot armies in the field and establish a network of garrisoned outposts. Those already loyal to the British cause must be encouraged and protected while the people as a whole had to be convinced of the inevitably of British victory, and the latter never was accomplished.

Lieutenant Roderick McKenzie of the British 71st Highland Regiment, who served with courage and distinction through most of the fighting in the South, wrote in August of 1781:

> We cannot with reason expect those that are loyal will declare their sentiments until they find us so strong in any one place as to protect them after having joined. Our taking post at different places, inviting the Loyalists to join us, and then evacuating those posts and aban-

doning the people to the fury of their bitterest enemies, has deterred them from declaring themselves until affairs take a decisive turn in our favor. We shall then find the people eager to show their loyalty. While the issue remains doubtful we should not expect it.

Cornwallis was to find this all too true as he marched through North Carolina in pursuit of Nathanael Greene. Loyalist farmers would ride into his camp, express their support in warmest terms, and then ride home again.

The failure of the British to establish unity of command and command planning has been cited as another reason for their failure in the South. The same failure had occurred in early campaigns in the North. The excellent strategic concept of cutting New England, the center of rebellion, away from the middle colonies by a pincer movement from Canada and New York had ended in the British catastrophe of 1777 at Saratoga where John Burgoyne lost an entire army. Sir William Howe, the British commander in New York, decided to capture Philadelphia instead of moving in force to support and link up with Burgoyne's southward march.

Sir Henry Clinton correctly believed that Georgia and South Carolina were the keys to victory in the South. Charles Lord Cornwallis, who succeeded Clinton as commander in chief in the southern theater, believed instead that wealthy and populous Virginia was the key to a sound southern strategy—seize and control Virginia and the rest of the South could be conquered with comparative ease. Unhappily for a British chance of victory, George Lord Germain, the secretary of state for American colonies in London, agreed with Cornwallis.

After Clinton returned to New York following the fall of Charleston, Cornwallis acted according to his convictions. His first attempt to invade North Carolina was checkmated by the savage defeat of Patrick Ferguson at Kings Mountain on 7 October 1780. This action destroyed an important element of Cornwallis's light troops, and he fell back to winter quarters in Winnsboro, South Carolina. On 17 January 1781, at Cowpens in South Carolina, Banastre's Tarleton's command was smashed by Daniel Morgan. Again Lord Cornwallis lost valuable and essential units for the necessary fast-moving campaign. In spite of two grim lessons (British field commanders consistently underrated American fighting ability even after they were taught otherwise by experience), Cornwallis advanced into North Carolina, leaving Georgia and South Carolina inadequately garrisoned and patrolled, the general population turning against their conquerors, and the southern partisans holding the hinterland and rampaging along the British supply lines.

On 15 March 1781 Cornwallis met Nathanael Greene and won the pyrrhic victory of Guilford Court House in North Carolina. He then made his final and fatal error. After falling back to the coast at British-held Wilmington with his badly hurt and battered army, Cornwallis decided to move his main operations from Wilmington up to the Petersburg area of Virginia where a strong British force already was stationed. He did this without consulting Clinton, his commander in chief, who later bitterly condemned Cornwallis's decision. When Cornwallis marched north, Nathanael Greene marched back into South Carolina, and the war in the South essentially was lost by the British even before the final siege and capture of Yorktown on 19 October 1781.

After the comparatively easy captures of Savannah and Charleston, the British thus committed one serious error after another. They overestimated the number of Loyalists who would flock to their aid. They antagonized thoroughly the very people on whose eventual support they must depend if victory were to be achieved. Operating on the plan to subjugate southerners by using other southerners, the British precipitated in 1780 one of the most ferocious civil wars in history, where kinsman fought kinsman and neighbor betrayed neighbor. Loyalties in this war became totally confused and desertions from both sides remained a constant debilitating factor.

As Brigadier General Samuel Griffith says in his introduction to a translation of Mao Tse-Tung's *On Guerrilla Warfare*: "Historical experience suggests that there is very little hope of destroying a revolutionary guerrilla movement *after it had survived the first phase and has acquired the sympathetic support of a significant segment of the population* [emphasis added]."

As it became increasingly clear that the British could not protect their adherents or control the hinterland, an ever-growing number of southerners supported the partisans who kept the war alive in the South. Only a handful of British officers ever understood or tried to understand the men they fought or learned to fight effectively in a land of intense summer heat and incapacitating diseases, vast swamps and forests, wide, deep, and unbridged rivers, and the impenetrable laurel thickets of the southern mountains. Here was a natural country for guerrilla warfare and an almost impossible terrain for classic European operational concepts.

Both sides made blunders, but the British mistakes could not be remedied. When they failed to subjugate Georgia and South Carolina and win over by force or persuasion the majority of the people, the British lost not only the war in the South but the final and best chance to subdue the thirteen colonies. The British did not evacuate their last stronghold, New York, until 25 November 1783 after the signing of the peace treaty, but the climactic Franco-American victory in the South at Yorktown, Virginia, in 1781 assured American independence.

Chronology of the Revolution 1775–1783

Lexington, Massachusetts   19 April 1775

The first shots of the American Revolution were fired. Lieutenant Colonel Francis Smith of the 10th Foot and Major John Pitcairn of the Royal Marines, leading a column of 700 British soldiers sent home from Boston by General Gage to destroy military stores at Concord, exchanged fire with American militia on Lexington Green. In the first blood shed in the Revolution, 8 Americans were killed and 10 wounded.

Concord, Massachusetts   19 April 1775

Lieutenant Colonel Francis Smith and Major John Pitcairn destroyed the stores at Concord. On their line of march to Boston they were harassed by American sniper fire. Reinforced by Brigadier General Hugh Percy and his 1st Brigade, the British continued their retreat under heavy pressure, finally reaching Charlestown in safety. British regulars had been defeated by American militia.

Capture of Fort Ticonderoga, New York   10 May 1775

Ethan Allen and Benedict Arnold with some 83 raiders captured British-held Fort Ticonderoga without firing a shot. Possession of the fort proved of inestimable value because the artillery taken from Ticonderoga enabled George Washington to carry out a successful siege of Boston and force British withdrawal from that town.

Bunker Hill and Breeds Hill, Massachusetts   17 June 1775

After suffering almost prohibitive losses, 2,500 British regulars attacking frontally drove 1,200 American defenders from their fortified positions on Bunker Hill and Breeds Hill dominating the Charlestown Isthmus.

George Washington Assumes Command of the   3 July 1775
Continental Army

George Washington of Virginia, appointed commander in chief of the new American Continental army by the Continental Congress on 15 June 1775, assumed command of that army on 3 July, with headquarters at Cambridge, Massachusetts.

Ninety Six, South Carolina   10–21 November 1775

Major Andrew Williamson and Major James Mayson with South Carolina Patriot militia were besieged in a stockaded fort erected at Savage's Old Fort near Ninety Six by Loyalist forces under Major Joseph Robinson and Captain Patrick Cuningham. Both sides suffered casualties, and the indecisive fighting ended in a truce called on the evening of 21 November.

Great Bridge, Virginia   11 December 1775

At Great Bridge, Virginia, commanding the road to Norfolk, Colonel William Woodford with 700 Virginia Patriot militia supported by 200 North Carolinians attacked and routed royal Governor Dunmore and his almost 500 British regulars and Loyalists. Norfolk later was burned by Virginia Patriot militia and largely destroyed as a center of Loyalist sympathy.

Great Canebrake, South Carolina   22 December 1775·

Colonel William "Danger" Thomson with 1,300 rangers and militiamen at the Great Canebreak on the Reedy River surprised and captured most of a Loyalist force operating in the area. Its leader, Captain Patrick Cuningham, deserted his men and escaped, riding a barebacked horse, to the Cherokee Nation.

The Snow Campaign, South Carolina   23–30 December 1775

After the successful December campaign against the Loyalists of the upcountry, Colonel Richard Richardson's Patriot militia marched back to the Congaree River impeded on most of their route by fifteen inches of snow. The troops suffered heavily from exposure and frostbite. The operation was known thereafter as the Snow Campaign.

Attack on Quebec, Canada   1 January 1776

Benedict Arnold of Connecticut and Daniel Morgan of Virginia, after a grueling march up the Kennebec River and over the Height of Land, joined Richard Montgomery in an attempt to capture Quebec. Sir Guy Carleton successfully defended the town against the American attack. Montgomery was killed, Arnold wounded, and Morgan with most of the Kennebec column was captured. Canada remained safe from American attack for the rest of the war.

Moore's Creek Bridge, North Carolina   27 February 1776

Colonel Richard Caswell and Colonel Alexander Lillington commanding North Carolina militia were attacked frontally across Moore's Creek Bridge by Loyalist Highland Scot settlers led by Brigadier General Donald McDonald. The Scots were defeated and routed with heavy casualties, a key American victory in the early stages of the southern fighting that assured that royalist elements would not dominate North Carolina.

Boston, Massachusetts, Evacuated by the British   17 March 1776

Sir William Howe evacuated Boston, Massachusetts, and sailed north with his entire army in 170 ships to Halifax, Nova Scotia, after a siege of a year's duration. George Washington's American Continental army occupied the town.

The Battle of Three Rivers,   8 June 1776
Quebec Province, Canada

General John Sullivan, commanding the dispirited American army in Canada after the defeat at Quebec, ordered Brigadier General William Thompson to attack the British position at Three Rivers. Sir Guy Carleton and General John Burgoyne with superior forces drove back the Americans, mostly Pennsylvania troops, who left behind 25 dead and 200 prisoners. British losses were very light.

The Defense of Sullivan's Island, South Carolina   28 June 1776

Colonel William Moultrie with his South Carolina troops successfully defended the palmetto log and sand Fort Sullivan guarding the entrance to Charleston harbor against the attack of a British fleet under Sir Peter Parker. During the same operation Colonel William Thomson frustrated a flanking movement on Sullivan's Island by British troops commanded by Sir Henry Clinton advancing across Breach Inlet from Long Island.

The Cherokees Attack the Southern Frontier   1 July 1776

Incited by the royal agents John Stuart and Alexander Cameron, the powerful Cherokee Nation struck along the entire southern frontier killing men, women, and children and burning backcountry settlements. The Indian attack was meant to be coordinated with the attack on Fort Sullivan, but the great distances involved with resultant poor communications frustrated British planning.

Lyndley's Fort, South Carolina   15 July 1776

A group of Patriot settlers who had taken refuge in Lyndley's Fort near Rabon Creek in Laurens County, South Carolina, were attacked by Indians and Loyalists, some of the latter dressed as Indians. Reinforced by 150 militia, the settlers beat off and routed the attackers.

Seneca, South Carolina   1 August 1776

Colonel Andrew Williamson, leading a punitive expedition against a band of Cherokees commanded by Alexander Cameron, was ambushed in the early morning of 1 August by superior Indian forces. Williamson's men retreated in confusion but the day was saved for his little army by Colonel Leroy Hammond, who with a few followers led a mounted charge that checked the Indian advance. Francis Salvador was killed in this action, the first Jew to die for American freedom.

Tugaloo River, South Carolina   10 August 1776

The Cherokees were defeated by Andrew Pickens, whose contingent suffered no casualties in a skirmish on the Tugaloo River. After the fighting the Indian towns of Estatoe and Tugaloo were razed to the ground.

The Ring Fight, South Carolina   August 1776

Andrew Pickens, leading a scouting party of 25 men, was surprised and surrounded by some 200 Cherokee warriors. Forming a circle, Pickens and his scouts loaded and fired in turn, successfully holding off a hand-to-hand attack until Joseph Pickens, Andrew's brother, arrived with a volunteer rescue force.

Tamassy, South Carolina   12 August 1776

Andrew Williamson and Andrew Pickens leading the full expeditionary force met and defeated a large Cherokee war party near the Indian town of Tamassy. Both sides suffered casualties, but the Indian losses were twice those of the South Carolinians. The town of Tamassy then was burned.

The Battle of Long Island, New York   27 August 1776

Sir William Howe with 20,000 British troops, supported by royal fleet units under his brother, Admiral Richard Howe, landed on Long Island and defeated George Washington and his army of about 10,000 effectives. Washington and most of his army escaped by boat the night of 29–30 August under cover of a fog.

Harlem Heights, New York   16 September 1776

Nathanael Greene and George Clinton led 1,800 Americans in a two-hour sharp but limited engagement against British and Hessian regulars. The British were checked and driven back to their main lines. The losses were roughly equal.

The Black Hole of the Coweecho River,   19 September 1776
North Carolina

Colonel Andrew Williamson's column was ambushed by the Cherokees about nine miles south of the present town of Franklin, North Carolina, in a steep, wooded gorge of the Coweecho River known as the "Black Hole." After suffering heavy casualties the South Carolinians attacked frontally and cleared the pass.

Valcour Island, New York   11 October 1776

Benedict Arnold operating on Lake Champlain with a makeshift fleet of two small armed schooners, two sloops, four galleys, and eight gondolas fought for seven hours a superior British squadron under Sir Guy Carleton. The latter included one ship, two schooners, a floating battery, one big gondola, twenty gunboats, and four armed long-boats. Arnold was defeated but escaped during the foggy night with his remaining ships. The action so delayed Carleton that he called off operations against strongly fortified and American-held Ticonderoga at the foot of the lake because of the lateness of the season. The famous naval historian Alfred Thayer Mahan considers that Valcour Island saved the Revolution by upsetting the British timing and giving the Americans a chance to gather their forces.

White Plains, New York   28 October 1776

British and Hessian regulars numbering 4,000 attacked 1,600 Americans holding Chatterton's Hill near White Plains. The Americans were driven from the hill although the British suffered 300 casualties to the American 200. The main American position was not hit for reasons the British commander, Sir William Howe, never explained.

Fort Washington, New York   16 November 1776

Colonel Robert Magaw, American commander at Fort Washington on the upper end of Manhattan Island, after a brief and not too spirited defense, surrendered Fort Washington with its garrison of more than 2,800 men to General Wilhelm von Knyphausen, commanding the German mercenaries in British service.

Fort Lee, New Jersey   20 November 1776

Lord Cornwallis with 4,500 regulars captured American-held Fort Lee on the New Jersey side of the Hudson River and took 100 prisoners. Nathanael Greene, commanding the fort, was warned by a deserter, offered no resistance, and abandoned the position with most of the garrison, leaving all stores, munitions, and artillery behind.

Battle of Trenton, New Jersey   26 December 1776

On Christmas night George Washington crossed the ice-laden Delaware River with 2,400 men and eight guns. At eight o'clock on the morning of 26 December, he surprised at Trenton, Colonel Rahl's Hessian brigade stationed in the town, supported by 50 jägers, 20 British dragoons, and an artillery detachment. The Hessians lost 32 men killed including Colonel Rahl and 886 men taken prisoners. The Americans lost 2 men (frozen to death on the march), and 2 officers and an enlisted man were wounded. It was a brilliant stroke following a series of defeats.

Princeton, New Jersey   3 January 1777

After his success at Trenton George Washington marched on Princeton, New Jersey, where he ran head-on into Charles Mawhood's brigade acting as the British rear guard. Mawhood was routed and pursued, suffering 273 casualties. The Americans had 40 killed and 100 wounded. It was a small but clear-cut victory for Washington.

Treaty of Dewitt's Corner, South Carolina   20 May 1777

After suffering a succession of defeats and burning of many of their towns east and west of the mountains with destruction of all food supplies, the Cherokees sued for peace. American casualties among the South Carolina, North Carolina, Virginia, and Georgia troops involved were in the low hundreds. The Indians lost over 2,000 killed and ceded most of their lands east of the mountains.

Oriskany, New York   6 August 1777

Colonel Barry St. Leger with a British column, later supported by two small battalions led by Sir John Johnson and Iroquois warriors under the Mohawk chief Joseph Brant, struck inland from Oswego on Lake Ontario and invested American-held Fort Stanwix between the Mohawk River and Wood Creek. A rescue expedition of 800 American militia commanded by General Nicholas Herkimer was ambushed by Brant. They beat off the attack and retreated, but Nicholas Herkimer died later of his wounds.

Battle of Bennington, Vermont   16 August 1777

General John Burgoyne during his march south detached Lieutenant Colonel Baum with 374 Brunswick mercenaries supported by some British regulars, Loyalist Provincials, and Iroquois Indians. Their mission was to capture Bennington, Vermont, where food, munitions, and draft animals were thought to be assembled. General John Stark with 1,500 American militia struck Baum's force and killed or captured all but 9 of his Brunswickers. Baum died in the action and his Indians fled the field. Colonel Breymann, coming to Baum's rescue with 642 men and two guns, also was attacked by Stark, now reinforced by Seth Warner and almost 400 men. Breymann suffered 80 casualties and lost his two guns. Stark and Warner in the two engagements had some 30 killed and 40 wounded.

Fort Stanwix, New York   23 August 1777

After Herkimer's militia retreated with their wounded commander, St. Leger reestablished the siege of Fort Stanwix. Major General Benedict Arnold was sent by General Schuyler with 1,000 men to raise the siege. He spread false rumors ahead of his march vastly overstating his numbers. St. Leger's Indians and Loyalists accordingly deserted him, and he was forced to retire, the siege ending on 23 August.

The Battle of the Brandywine, Pennsylvania   11 September 1777

George Washington met Sir William Howe on the Philadelphia road at Chadds Ford along Brandywine Creek. Outnumbered and outgeneraled, Washington and his army, after a hot, well-sustained action, retreated in comparatively good order, but it was an American defeat. American casualties were estimated at 900 killed and wounded, while the British suffered 90 killed and 468 wounded or missing.

The Battle of Saratoga, New York   19 September–17 October 1777

After a hard-fought action on 19 September at Freeman's Farm and a thorough defeat on 7 October at Bemis Heights, General John Burgoyne, his retreat progressively cut off by superior American forces, on 17 October surrendered at Saratoga his entire army of British regulars and German mercenaries. Burgoyne's army by this time numbered less than 4,000 effectives. Major General Horatio Gates, the American commander, received the surrender. This very important victory effectively and permanently stopped British attempts to cut off New England from the middle states via the Hudson Valley.

Action at Paoli, Pennsylvania   21 September 1777

After Washington's retreat from the Brandywine the British followed the retiring American army. At one o'clock in the morning of 21 September, Major General Charles "No Flint" Grey hurled three British battalions using the bayonet only on Anthony Wayne's camp at Paoli. The Americans were caught completely by surprise and suffered 300 casualties with 100 men captured. The Americans called it the "Paoli Massacre," but it was a successful British night attack carried out with dash and skill.

Battle of Germantown, Pennsylvania   4 October 1777

After Sir William Howe captured and occupied Philadelphia on 26 September 1777, his main force of 9,000 men was stationed in and around Germantown. George Washington attacked the British lines in the early morning hours of 4 October. Six companies of British regulars, holding Justice Benjamin Chew's strong stone house in the middle of the battle, delayed the American advance. Washington's attack was progressing well when the American troops, confused and running out of ammunition, suddenly panicked and retreated from the field. Anthony Wayne later said, "We ran away from victory."

The French Alliance   6 February 1778

After months of diplomatic maneuvering by Benjamin Franklin and other American representatives in France, a treaty was signed by the Continental Congress with that country making available French ships, troops, and increasing military supplies to aid in the war with Great Britain. This alliance assured American independence.

Valley Forge, Pennsylvania   Winter of 1777–1778

The sufferings of the American army in the camp at Valley Forge during the winter of 1777–1778, sick and lacking food, proper clothing, or shelter, still stirs anger and compassion. Two very important facts emerge from the ordeal: the towering moral figure of George Washington, who stayed with his army and held it together, and the arrival of the Prussian drillmaster, General Baron Frederick von Steuben. Under his strict and professional supervision the American army began to learn to stand up to British and German regulars in a set battle.

The British Abandon Philadelphia   18 June 1778

Without the necessary reinforcements to hold Philadelphia independent of support from New York, Sir Henry Clinton, the British commander, determined to abandon the city and remove his army to New York by an overland march. Clinton believed that Philadelphia was too far from the seacoast to depend on the royal fleet and evacuation was a military necessity.

Battle of Monmouth Court House, New Jersey   28 June 1778

The hard-fought drawn battle of Monmouth Court House ended with about equal casualties on both sides. The British commander, Sir Henry Clinton, retired the night after the battle and Washington held the field. Washington, however, blamed General Charles Lee's indecisive behavior, disorderly retreat, and failure to obey orders as the main reasons why Monmouth Court House was not a clear-cut American victory. Lee was suspended from command for twelve months. Monmouth Court House also was the last major set battle between American and British regular forces fought in the northern theater of the war.

Kaskaskia, Illinois   4 July 1778

Lieutenant Colonel George Rogers Clark, a Virginian, with 175 volunteers, captured British-controlled Kaskaskia, the town's French inhabitants surrendering without firing a shot. Vincennes and Cahokia also submitted, and the territory was organized as the county of Illinois in the state of Virginia.

British Capture of Savannah, Georgia   29 December 1778

With the war at a stalemate in the North, the British planned a southern strategy. A British fleet sailed up the Savannah River and landed Colonel Archibald Campbell with 3,000 crack British regulars and Provincials below Savannah, Georgia. This little army attacked and defeated the American General Robert Howe, attempting to defend the town with 700 Continentals and militia. Savannah fell the same day.

Port Royal Island, South Carolina   3 February 1779

General William Moultrie with 300 American troops (mostly from General Stephen Bull's Beaufort, South Carolina, militia) met and defeated Major Gardiner with a strong detachment of British and Provincial soldiers from the Savannah garrison. The British were trying to establish an advanced base for a planned march into South Carolina.

Kettle Creek, Georgia   14 February 1779

Colonel Andrew Pickens, Colonel John Dooly, and Lieutenant Colonel Elijah Clarke with South Carolina and Georgia militia at Kettle Creek, Georgia (near the present city of Washington), pursued, caught, and defeated soundly a strong force of North Carolina Loyalist militia marching to join the British at Augusta. The Loyalist commander, Colonel Boyd, was mortally wounded in the action.

Vincennes, Indiana   24 February 1779

The British lieutenant governor of Detroit, Colonel Henry Hamilton, marched with 250 Loyalists and Indians and recaptured Vincennes. George Rogers Clark raised a force of 130 men at Kaskaskia, half of them French, and marched through flooded country to Vincennes. Hamilton's Indians fled, and Clark bluffed him into surrendering to a force no bigger than his own.

Briar Creek, Georgia   3 March 1779

At Briar Creek down the Savannah River from Augusta, Colonel Mark Prevost with 900 British regulars and Provincials severely defeated with heavy loss some 1,500 Americans under General John Ashe. These had been sent by Benjamin Lincoln, now commanding American forces in the South, to retake Augusta.

Prevost's Siege of Charleston,   11–13 May 1779
South Carolina

General Augustine Prevost advanced from Savannah with a strong British army and invested Charleston on 11 May. After minor skirmishing on the town's approaches, Prevost received word of Benjamin Lincoln's approach with the American army of the South and withdrew from Charleston during the night and early morning of 12 and 13 May, retreating south via the Sea Islands.

Battle of the Stono River,   20 June 1779
South Carolina

One of the hottest actions of the war in the South took place on the north side of
the Stono River, just south of the present town of Rantowles. General Lincoln, following
General Prevost's retreating army along the coastal route, engaged a British rear guard
under Lieutenant Colonel John Maitland at Stono Ferry. The battle was indecisive and
Maitland withdrew safely, but casualties were heavy on both sides.

Stony Point, New York   16 July 1779

General Anthony Wayne of Pennsylvania commanding 1,200 men of the new elite
American light infantry carried out a successful surprise night attack using the bayonet
only against the British post at Stony Point. The Americans suffered only 15 killed and
83 wounded, among them Anthony Wayne, but the British had 133 casualties with 543
captured.

Battle of Newtown, New York   29 August 1779

Two dreadful massacres of the white settlers in the Wyoming Valley of Pennsylvania
and the Cherry Valley in New York occurred in July and November of 1778. The attack
on the Wyoming Valley was led by the Loyalist Colonel John Butler, his son Walter, and
Sir John Johnson, leading Loyalists and some Indians. The Cherry Valley Massacre was
carried out by Joseph Brant and his Iroquois. An American expeditionary force led by
Generals John Sullivan and James Clinton moved into Indian territory, burning villages
and crops as they marched. At Newtown, near the present city of Elmira, 1,500 Loyalists
and Indians were beaten and routed by the Americans. Forty towns were burned during
this campaign, and the power of the Iroquois was broken, although they remained actively hostile throughout the war. A second attack against the Indians, also in August, of
600 men marching from Pittsburgh under Colonel Daniel Brodhead burned towns and
crops belonging to the Senecas, thus avenging the massacres.

American Expedition to Castine, Maine   July–August 1779

In July of 1779 Massachusetts, acting alone, sent 1,000 militia under Generals Sol-
omon Lovell and Peleg Wadsworth to attack 600 British and Canadian troops under
General Francis McLean holding Castine, Maine. The Americans came by sea under the
escort of armed vessels commanded by Commodore Dudley Saltonstall. The Massachusetts force was put ashore on 25 July, but all attacks on Castine were beaten off by the
British defenders. The arrival of a small British naval squadron under Sir George Collier
forced the Americans to lift the siege. Saltonstall's fleet was run up the Penobscot River,
beached, and burned, and the Americans struggled home through the wilderness. George
Washington referred to the misadventure as "that unfortunate expedition."

Paulus Hook, New Jersey   19 August 1779

Major Henry Lee of Virginia carried out a surprise attack on the British-fortified outpost at Paulus Hook. The British casualties numbered 50 with approximately 150 taken prisoner. This was a minor but successful operation.

French and American Siege of   16 September–19 October 1779
Savannah, Georgia

Major General Benjamin Lincoln with an American army of over 3,000 effectives allied with a French army of some 4,000 troops supported by a powerful French fleet, the French army and navy under the command of Admiral the Count d'Estaing, invested Savannah. An attempt to take the town, defended by Major General Augustine Prevost with 2,500 British regulars and Provincials, failed with heavy casualties for the attackers. D'Estaing sailed away with his army, and Lincoln marched back to Charleston.

Sir Henry Clinton's Siege of Charleston   29 March–12 May 1780
South Carolina

Major General Sir Henry Clinton invested Charleston, South Carolina, with formal siege approaches in March 1780. Admiral Mariot Arbuthnot ran the forts at the harbor entrance on 8 April and brought the guns of the royal fleet on the city, and Major General Charles Lord Cornwallis closed off all escape across the Cooper River. When Clinton's advanced siege parallels reached assault distance, Benjamin Lincoln on 12 May surrendered the town and his entire army.

Monck's Corner, South Carolina   14 April 1780

Lieutenant Colonel Banastre Tarleton and Major Patrick Ferguson surprised and routed General Isaac Huger and Lieutenant Colonel William Washington's American cavalry guarding Biggin Bridge over the Cooper River near Monck's Corner. The bridge then was carried by the British and Provincial troops with the bayonet, and American militia stationed on the other bank were beaten and scattered.

Lenud's Ferry, South Carolina   6 May 1780

Banastre Tarleton, riding hard as usual, again surprised Colonel Anthony White with the remnants of the American cavalry at Lenud's Ferry on the Santee River. The Americans were defeated and dispersed.

The Waxhaws (Buford's Massacre), South Carolina   29 May 1780

Colonel Abraham Buford retreating northward with Virginia Continentals after the fall of Charleston was overtaken by Lieutenant Colonel Banastre Tarleton and his Loyalist Legion. Tarleton charged and Buford tried to surrender after the first American volley but in the confusion some of his men still resisted. The Loyalist dragoons and supporting light infantry ignored the flags of truce and sabered or bayoneted 113 Continentals while wounding 150, a total of 263 casualties out of 350. It was known thereafter to the Americans as Buford's Massacre.

Charles Lord Cornwallis Assumes Command of   5 June 1780
the British Army in the South

Sir Henry Clinton sailed from Charleston, South Carolina, to New York on 5 June 1780 leaving Charles Lord Cornwallis with some 4,000 regulars and Provincials to complete the conquest of the southern states.

Ramsour's Mill, North Carolina   20 June 1780

At Ramsour's Mill approximately 400 Patriot militia fought about the same number of Loyalist militia. Both sides suffered comparatively heavy casualties, and the action was indecisive. Since the Loyalist rising was premature and against explicit instructions of the British commander, Lord Cornwallis, it hurt the British cause in the Carolinas by disorganizing and discouraging more opportune and better planned action by British sympathizers.

Williamson's Plantation, South Carolina   12 July 1780

Colonel George Turnbull, commanding the British post at Rocky Mount, South Carolina, dispatched the Loyalist Captain Christian Huck with a strong detachment to scout and check if possible the rising anti-British reaction in the upcountry. Colonels William Bratton, William Hill, Edward Lacey, Andrew Neel, and Captain James Mc-Clure, all of Thomas Sumter's command, surrounded and surprised Huck's force camped at Williamson's Plantation (the present Brattonsville). The Loyalists were routed and Huck was killed in the action.

Cedar Springs, South Carolina   12 July 1780

Colonel John Thomas, commanding the Spartan regiment of South Carolina Patriot militia, was warned by his mother of a Loyalist plan to attack his camp. She accidentally heard the news while visiting her Patriot husband imprisoned at Ninety Six and rode sixty miles to bring the information. When the Loyalists attacked Colonel Thomas's camp at Cedar Springs (just south of the modern Spartanburg), they ran into a prepared ambush and were soundly beaten.

Gowen's Old Fort, South Carolina   13 July 1780

Colonel John Jones of Georgia, leading Georgia Patriot militia to join Colonel Charles McDowell in North Carolina, surrounded and attacked the camp at Gowen's Old Fort of a party of Loyalists pursuing Colonel John Thomas. The Loyalists surrendered without serious resistance. Gowen's Old Fort was located not far from the South Pacolet River and the Spartanburg-Greenville County line.

Horatio Gates Assumes Command of Southern   25 July 1780
Army, Buffalo Ford, North Carolina

At Buffalo Ford on Deep River, North Carolina, Major General Horatio Gates, appointed by the Continental Congress, assumed command of the reconstituted American Army of the Southern Department and began his ill-fated march to Camden, South Carolina, and disaster.

Rocky Mount, South Carolina   30 July 1780

Thomas Sumter arrived with a strong force before the British post at Rocky Mount held by the Loyalist Lieutenant Colonel George Turnbull. Summoned to surrender, Turnbull refused, and Sumter launched his attack. The main fortified area was a frame house internally reinforced by logs and clays. An almost successful attempt to fire the frame house by hurling fire brands on the roof of an adjacent building was frustrated when a summer rainstorm extinguished the flames. Sumter retreated but lost a valued officer, Lieutenant Colonel Andrew Neel, killed in the action. Seven of Sumter's soldiers also were killed.

Hanging Rock I, South Carolina   30 July 1780

Lieutenant Colonel William Davie ambushed three companies of Colonel Samuel Bryan's North Carolina Royalists within sight of the strong British post at Hanging Rock. Most of the Loyalists were killed or wounded, and Davie with his victorious Patriot North Carolinians retreated, bringing with them the weapons and horses of the defeated enemy. The British garrison at Hanging Rock was too startled by the sudden attack to intervene.

Hanging Rock II, South Carolina   6 August 1780

Thomas Sumter and William Davie with 800 American partisans attacked the strongly held British post at Hanging Rock, garrisoned by 1,400 men under Major John Carden. After fighting for three hours and inflicting heavy casualties, Sumter lost control of his force which had begun looting the British camp. Sumter then withdrew, leaving the post in British hands. William Davie, who had maintained control of his men, charged and dispersed a British relief column coming from Rocky Mount.

Capture of British Convoy, Kershaw County,   15 August 1780
South Carolina

   Colonel Thomas Taylor of Sumter's command attacked and captured Colonel Matthew Carey and his entire command at Carey's Fort on the Wateree River opposite Camden. In the same operation Taylor captured a supply convoy coming from Ninety Six.

Battle of Camden, South Carolina   16 August 1780

   Horatio Gates with his American Army of the South and Lord Cornwallis commanding the British forces in South Carolina fought a "meeting" battle near Gum Swamp and Sanders Creek on the Old Waxhaws Road a few miles from Camden. Gates's army was defeated and routed, although Baron de Kalb and his Maryland and Delaware Continental troops on the American right resisted to the end. Gates fled the field, but de Kalb was mortally wounded.

Fishing Creek, South Carolina   18 August 1780

   After the Battle of Camden, Cornwallis sent Banastre Tarleton with a picked force of 100 dragoons and 60 infantry after Thomas Sumter, known to be operating north of Camden. Tarleton caught Sumter and his 800 men completely by surprise resting by or bathing in the river. Sumter escaped but 150 Americans were killed and many wounded. The supply convoy and prisoners taken by Thomas Taylor were recaptured or released.

Musgrove's Mill, South Carolina   18 August 1780

   In one of the hottest small fire fights of the war in the South, Colonel Isaac Shelby with his detachment of frontier riflemen, Colonel Elijah Clarke of Georgia, and Colonel James Williams of South Carolina decoyed the Loyalist Colonel Alexander Innes from his post at Musgrove's Mill to attack their force, ambuscaded across the Enoree River in a strongly held position. Innes fell into the trap and his recently reinforced garrison was badly beaten. Innes fell, seriously wounded, and Captain Shadrack Inman of Clarke's Georgians, the real hero of the operation, was killed.

Nelson's Ferry (Great Savannah),   25 August 1780
South Carolina

   Francis Marion, camped at Nelson or Neilson's Ferry on the Santee River north of Eutawville received information that 150 American prisoners taken at Camden were bivouacked for the night at Thomas Sumter's plantation, Great Savannah. Marion attacked, captured the British escort, and released the prisoners who refused to join him but continued to Charleston and internment.

Blue Savannah, South Carolina   4 September 1780

Francis Marion, retreating from a superior force of Loyalists led by Major Micajah Ganey and Captain Jesse Barefield, led them into a trap at Blue Savannah in Marion County where he severely defeated them.

Siege of McKay's Trading Post near   14–18 September 1780
Augusta, Georgia

Elijah Clarke invested the British-held McKay's Trading Post near Augusta, Georgia, held by Colonel Thomas Browne with his Loyalist forces and a detachment of Cherokee warriors. The arrival on the scene of a relief column from the British garrison at Ninety Six forced Clarke to raise the siege. Browne, wounded in the action, took revenge by hanging American prisoners taken in the operation or turning them over to the Indians who tortured them to death.

Wahub's Plantation   21 September 1780

Lieutenant Colonel William Davie surprised a detachment of Banastre Tarleton's Legion camped across the Catawba River from Cornwallis's main army. After inflicting heavy casualties and capturing horses and equipment, Davie withdrew safely while the main British army vainly beat to quarters on the other side of the Catawba.

Benedict Arnold's Treason   September 1780

In September of 1780, General Benedict Arnold, the American commander at West Point, New York, tried to betray that strong post to the British for £10,000. Foiled in this attempt by the capture on 23 September of British agent, Major John André, carrying incriminating papers, Arnold fled to the British whom he served thereafter as a brigadier general.

Charlotte, North Carolina   26 September 1780

Colonel William Davie with about 150 American soldiers supported by a few local volunteers all stationed in ambush around the Charlotte courthouse fought and held up for some minutes the advance of Tarleton's Legion cavalry. (Tarleton was ill, and his famous corps was under the command of Major George Hanger.) Colonel Webster's regular British infantry and the infantry of the legion came up and forced Davie to retreat in good order.

Black Mingo, South Carolina   28–29 September 1780

Having learned that the Charleston Loyalist Colonel John Coming Ball, with a strong force, was camped at Shepherd's Ferry on Black Mingo Creek, Francis Marion attacked with his partisans at midnight of 28 September, driving Ball and his Loyalists into the swamp. Colonel Ball escaped, but Marion captured his fine horse, which he renamed "Ball" and rode throughout the war.

Kings Mountain, South Carolina   7 October 1780

The British officer Major Patrick Ferguson, with a force of around 800 North and South Carolina Loyalists supported by 100 of his Provincial rangers, was surrounded and attacked at Kings Mountain by approximately the same number of frontier militia from North Carolina, South Carolina, Virginia, and Georgia. Most of the Americans were armed with the deadly long rifle. Ferguson died in the action, and almost all of his command were killed, wounded, or captured. This was a real American victory and one of the turning points in the Revolution.

Tearcoat Swamp, South Carolina   25 October 1780

Francis Marion surprised Colonel Samuel Tynes and his Loyalists in their camp by Tearcoat Swamp where Tynes was assembling British sympathizers from the surrounding area. Tynes and his men were routed and scattered although Tynes escaped, to be picked up later by a special squad which Marion sent to find him.

Fishdam Ford, South Carolina   9 November 1780

With information that Thomas Sumter was operating in York and Chester counties, South Carolina, Cornwallis sent Major James Wemyss with his 63d Regiment and 40 dragoons of Tarleton's Legion on a search and destroy mission. Having located Sumter's camp at Fishdam Ford on the Broad River, Wemyss led a mounted night attack, but the attack was checked and thrown back with casualties by the alerted Americans. The British retreated leaving their wounded, including Major Wemyss, who was hit in the first fire. Thomas Sumter, surprised in his tent by a special British murder squad, escaped, but did not take part in the battle.

The Battle of Blackstocks, South Carolina   20 November 1780

Banastre Tarleton, pursuing the retreating Thomas Sumter, pushed forward with his cavalry and mounted infantry, leaving his slower infantry and artillery to follow at their best speed. Sumter, meanwhile, had determined to make a stand at the farm of William Blackstock overlooking the Tyger River. Tarleton with an inferior force frontally attacked the strongly posted Americans and was beaten back with heavy casualties. The Americans lost only 3 killed and 4 wounded but among the latter was Thomas Sumter. Colonel John Twiggs of Georgia assumed command of the Americans and retreated that night with his little army across the Tyger leaving the field to Tarleton, who claimed victory.

Nathanael Greene Assumes Command of the   2 December 1780
Southern Army, Charlotte, North Carolina

Major General Nathanael Greene of Rhode Island assumed command of the American Army of the Southern Department replacing Horatio Gates. Making his temporary headquarters at Charlotte, North Carolina, Greene began to make plans for a renewed offensive against Lord Cornwallis in South Carolina.

Long Cane, South Carolina   12 December 1780

At Long Cane, Colonel Elijah Clarke and Colonel James McCall with 100 men engaged over 400 Provincials and Loyalist militia from Ninety Six under Lieutenant Colonel Isaac Allen. The American partisans were beaten but Clarke and McCall both were wounded, the former seriously.

Halfway Swamp and Singleton's Mill,   13 December 1780
South Carolina

At Halfway Swamp, Major Robert McLeroth with his 64th Regiment escorting Loyalist recruits to Camden was attacked by Francis Marion and his partisans. McLeroth drew up his men in a field east of the road and negotiated. It was decided that a mass duel would be fought between selected teams from each side to decide the issue. McLeroth used the delay to get his troops on the road without Marion's knowledge. A later attempt to trap McLeroth's column up the road at Singleton's Mill failed when Marion's men discovered all the Singleton family was down with smallpox and left the area hurriedly.

Mutiny of the Connecticut Line   25 December 1780

Two regiments of the Connecticut Line stationed near Morristown, New Jersey, angered at the lack of food and no pay for five months, mutinied and assembled on the parade ground. A veteran Pennsylvania regiment summoned in the crisis forced them back to quarters. The ringleaders were arrested, and the mutiny collapsed.

Hammond's Store, South Carolina   30 December 1780

Brigadier General Daniel Morgan, operating by Nathanael Greene's orders with a strong force in upper South Carolina, sent Colonel William Washington with 75 Continental dragoons and about 200 mounted militia led by Colonel James McCall to attack a contingent of some 200 Georgia Loyalists, led by Colonel Thomas Waters, which had been raiding the area. Washington and McCall surprised Waters and his force at Hammond's Store, and in a seven-mile retreating action the Loyalists suffered 150 casualties with 40 men captured.

Mutiny of the Pennsylvania Line   1 January 1781

Poorly fed, ill clothed, and unpaid for a year, the Pennsylvania Line regiments in camp at Morristown, New Jersey, rebelled under the leadership of their sergeants, and marched toward Princeton. Cooler heads prevailed, some of the grievances were redressed, and order was established. By 29 January, however, half the Pennsylvania veterans whose enlistment had expired were discharged.

The Battle of Cowpens, South Carolina   17 January 1781

Brigadier General Daniel Morgan at Saunders Cowpens in upper South Carolina met and soundly defeated Lieutenant Colonel Banastre Tarleton and his army of British regulars and well-trained Provincials. The forces were about equal but the American army on that day was the better army and won. The British losses, particularly in light troops, were very heavy, and Cowpens should be considered the real turning point of the Revolution. The royal forces never fully recovered from this disaster.

Mutiny of the New Jersey Line   20 January 1781

Following the action of the Pennsylvania regiments, the New Jersey Line of three regiments stationed at Pompton, New Jersey, also mutinied. George Washington no longer would tolerate such conduct and ordered General Robert Howe of South Carolina with veteran New England troops to put down the rebellion, which Howe did. Twelve of the mutineers were selected as a firing squad and forced to execute two of their ringleaders. The mutiny then collapsed.

Georgetown, South Carolina   24–25 January 1781

Francis Marion, coordinating an attack on Georgetown with Lieutenant Colonel Henry Lee and his legion, captured the town and the British commandant, Colonel George Campbell. British forces, however, continued to hold out in a strong redoubt and several other buildings. Marion and Lee were forced to withdraw without achieving their objectives—destruction of the royal garrison and occupation of Georgetown.

Cowan's Ford, North Carolina   1 February 1781

Lord Cornwallis, advancing into North Carolina in pursuit of Nathanael Greene's retreating army, crossed the Catawba River running in winter spate and routed the North Carolina militia defending the crossing. The militia commander General William Davidson was killed by a British light infantryman as he tried to rally his broken command.

Tarrant's Tavern, North Carolina   1 February 1781

After the forcing of the Catawba fords, Banastre Tarleton with his cavalry reinforced by the 23d Infantry Regiment was sent by Cornwallis to scout the strength of the gathering American militia. Finding a force of about 400 North Carolina militia drawn up across the road at Tarrant's Tavern, Tarleton charged them with the saber, killing 40 or 50 and dispersing the rest.

The Haw River, North Carolina   25 February 1781

Some 400 North Carolina Loyalists under Colonel John Pyle moving to reinforce Cornwallis's army were intercepted by Lieutenant Colonel Henry Lee and his legion masquerading as Banastre Tarleton and his legion. The Loyalists mounted and with weapons slung were drawn up to be reviewed by the supposed Tarleton when Lee suddenly ordered a saber attack. The unsuspecting Loyalists were butchered, 90 being killed and 150 wounded. Though morally inexcusable, the action kept the Loyalists in the area thoroughly intimidated.

Wiboo Swamp, South Carolina   6 March 1781

Wiboo Swamp was the first engagement in a series of savage retreating actions which Francis Marion conducted to obstruct the advance of the British column led by Colonel John Watson. At Wiboo Swamp, Gavin James, a private in Marion's brigade, single-handedly held a narrow causeway until Marion and his partisans could withdraw safely into the swamp.

Mount Hope Swamp, South Carolina   March 1781

At Mount Hope Swamp, Colonel Hugh Horry of Marion's brigade fought a successful delaying action against John Watson to cover Marion in his carefully planned fighting withdrawal.

Lower Bridge of the Black River,   March 1781
South Carolina

Captain William McCottry, commanding Francis Marion's riflemen, prevented Colonel John Watson from crossing the partially destroyed bridge over the Black River. Watson suffered such heavy casualties from the long-range and deadly accurate rifle fire that he was forced to call off the operation and fall back with his many wounded on the coast.

Snows Island, South Carolina   March 1781

While Francis Marion was occupied with John Watson, Colonel Welbore Doyle carried out a pincers movement with a second British column against Marion's headquarters at Snows Island on the Pee Dee River. After a stiff and bloody skirmish, Doyle captured the island. Its defenders under Colonel Hugh Ervin destroyed all the carefully hoarded supplies and ammunition before they abandoned the position.

The Battle of Guilford Court House,   15 March 1781
North Carolina

Cornwallis, attacking with an inferior force Nathanael Greene's much stronger army holding a prepared position at Guilford Court House, drove the Americans from the field. The British suffered such heavy losses in this pyrrhic victory that the royal army was forced to fall back on the coast. Greene retreated in good order, regrouped, and followed Cornwallis, then swung south and marched back to South Carolina. Cornwallis rested briefly at Wilmington, North Carolina, and decided to move his operations to Virginia.

Sampit Bridge, South Carolina   28 March 1781

Sampit Bridge was the last in the series of actions between Marion's brigade and Colonel John Watson's column that had begun at Wiboo Swamp on 6 March. At Sampit Bridge, Marion, following Watson's retreat, attacked and badly cut up his rear guard as it forded the Sampit River, the bridge already having been partially destroyed by the partisans to impede the British as they retired.

Fort Watson, South Carolina   15–23 April 1781

Henry Lee with his legion again joined Francis Marion's partisans on 14 April, and the two leaders marched with their combined forces against the British post, Fort Watson, established on a high Indian mount at Wright's Bluff on Scott's Lake, an arm of the Santee River. Without artillery the Americans could not take the strongly defended position until, following a suggestion of Major Hezekiah Maham of Marion's brigade, a tall log tower was erected manned by riflemen and overlooking the British stockade. Unable to answer the rifle fire or stop an impending assault, the British commander, Lieutenant James McKay, surrendered.

Hobkirk Hill, South Carolina   25 April 1781

The Battle of Hobkirk Hill fought just north of Camden, South Carolina, during the morning hours of 25 April ended in a British victory. Francis Lord Rawdon advancing from Camden with some 950 men drove Nathanael Greene and his army of approximately 1,200 from the ridge they occupied. An inexplicable panic among the soldiers of the veteran 1st Maryland Continental Regiment spread to the rest of the army and forced Greene to withdraw from the field. The casualties were about equal, 268 Americans and between 257 and 269 British killed, wounded, and missing.

Fort Motte, South Carolina   8–12 May 1781

The British had fortified with earthworks, a stockade, and a ditch the plantation home of Rebecca Motte. The garrison was commanded by Lieutenant McPherson of de

Lancey's Corps. Henry Lee and Francis Marion invested the fort and finally forced its surrender by gaining Mrs. Motte's permission to burn her home. The roof was ignited either by fire arrows or a ball of burning pitch and brimstone hurled in a sling by one of Marion's men. McPherson surrendered the position.

Lord Rawdon Evacuates Camden, South Carolina   10 May 1781

Although Lord Rawdon was the victor at Hobkirk Hill, Greene's army and an aroused countryside made his position at Camden untenable. He therefore destroyed Camden's fortifications and abandoned the town, thus surrendering the area by default to Nathanael Greene.

Orangeburg, South Carolina   11 May 1781

Thomas Sumter arrived before the British post at Orangeburg held by 80 troops. Sumter demonstrated so strongly before the town that the garrison surrendered without fighting.

Fort Granby, South Carolina   15 May 1781

On the evening of 14 May, Henry Lee arrived before Fort Granby, an important British post on the Congaree River. Under cover of darkness and a heavy fog, Lee had a battery erected commanding the fort at point-blank range. When morning came, after one warning shot over the stockade, Major Andrew Maxwell, British commander at Granby, surrendered on terms without fighting and marched away, taking all his acquired plunder with him.

Fort Galphin, South Carolina   19 May 1781

Fort Galphin had been established on the South Carolina side of the Savannah River downstream from Augusta. Captain John Rudolph of Lee's Legion under Henry Lee's orders invested the fort in which the annual royal presents to the Indians had been stored. The fort surrendered after a short resistance, 180 British prisoners being taken and all the Indian goods falling into American hands.

Lord Cornwallis Assumes Command of   20 May 1781
Combined British Forces in Virginia

On 20 May 1781 Charles Lord Cornwallis assumed command of the combined British forces in Virginia at Petersburg replacing the American traitor, Brigadier General Benedict Arnold, who had succeeded Major General Philips when the latter died of fever.

Siege of Ninety Six   22 May–19 June 1781

On 22 May Nathanael Greene invested the strong British post at Ninety Six defended by Lieutenant Colonel John Harris Cruger and a garrison of Provincials supported by South Carolina Loyalist militia. Even after Henry Lee and Andrew Pickens joined Greene following the capture of the British forces defending Augusta, Georgia, Cruger refused to surrender. He fought on until the news arrived of the imminent arrival of Lord Rawdon marching from Charleston with a British relief column. Nathanael Greene on 19 June raised the siege and marched away.

Tarleton Strikes Charlottesville, Virginia   4 June 1781

Lieutenant Colonel Banastre Tarleton struck Charlottesville, Virginia, with a surprise cavalry raid and seized seven members of the Virginia General Assembly. Governor Thomas Jefferson was warned and barely escaped into the mountains.

Augusta, Georgia   5 June 1781

Henry Lee with his legion and supporting troops crossed the Savannah River, joining Andrew Pickens and Elijah Clarke commanding respectively South Carolina and Georgia militia in an investment of Fort Grierson and Fort Cornwallis defending Augusta. Grierson fell to the Americans on 23 May and Lieutenant Colonel Thomas Browne, Elijah Clarke's old opponent, surrendered Fort Cornwallis on 5 June, after the American siege approaches and an artillery mounting Maham tower made his position untenable.

British Evacuate Georgetown, South Carolina   6 June 1781

British forces, unable to maintain a proper defense of Georgetown, South Carolina, against increasing American pressure, abandoned the town and evacuated by sea to Charleston.

Lord Rawdon Relieves Ninety Six, South Carolina   21 June 1781

Lord Rawdon arrived at Ninety Six on 21 June with a strong column and relieved John Harris Cruger and his weary defenders. Rawdon's infantry, many of them new arrivals from Great Britain and still in wool winter uniforms, were so fatigued by the march from Charleston in June heat that a proper pursuit of Greene's retreating army could not be effected.

Williamsburg, Virginia   26 June 1781

A savage little engagement was fought near Williamsburg, Virginia, on 26 June 1781 between John Simcoe's Queen's Rangers supported by a small force of German jäger riflemen and Lieutenant Colonel Thomas Butler leading elements of the Pennsylvania Continental Line with some American cavalry. The action was indecisive, but the Marquis de Lafayette, commanding American troops, claimed the advantage in his report.

Green Spring Plantation, Virginia   6 July 1781

At Green Spring Plantation, the Marquis de Lafayette attacked with the American forces under his command what he thought was a British rear guard. It was, instead, Cornwallis's full army camped on the high ground overlooking the causeway and ford leading to the island of Jamestown. The Americans advanced into a prepared trap across the narrow causeway flanked by marshes. Lafayette suffered heavy casualties but managed to pull back safely just before nightfall. Only the growing darkness prevented a British pursuit and an even greater disaster for the demoralized Americans.

Biggin Church, South Carolina   16 July 1781

Major Thomas Fraser, commanding a mounted unit of the Loyalist South Carolina Rangers, attacked by surprise Thomas Sumter, Henry Lee, and Francis Marion's camp near Biggin Church. Colonel Edward Lacey and his riflemen of Sumter's command broke the Loyalist attack by rifle fire and Fraser retreated.

Quinby Bridge and Shubrick's Plantation   17 July 1781

American forces under Thomas Sumter, Henry Lee, and Francis Marion captured Lieutenant Colonel James Coates's rear guard and baggage and forced Quinby Bridge. Coates abandoned the bridge and retreated with his 19th Regiment to the Shubrick plantation house across Quinby Creek where they beat off all attempts of the Americans to dislodge them.

Burning of Georgetown, South Carolina   2 August 1781

A British raiding party arriving from Charleston by sea landed at Georgetown, scattered its few American defenders, and burned several houses near the waterfront. They then retreated in good order and departed again by sea.

Execution of Colonel Isaac Hayne   4 August 1781

Colonel Isaac Hayne, believing that American occupation of the area on which his home and plantation were located freed him from his declaration of allegiance to the British made after the fall of Charleston in 1780, took up arms again for American freedom. He was captured on Charleston Neck while leading a raiding party by Major Thomas Fraser of the Royal South Carolina Rangers and his command. Hayne later was tried, condemned, and hanged by the British for treason. In death he became a martyr and his name a rallying cry for his fellow South Carolinians.

George Washington Marches South   19 August 1781

Having received word that the French Admiral the Count de Grasse would arrive off the Chesapeake with a powerful fleet in early September, George Washington decided to march south from the New York area with the combined American and French armies that had been watching Sir Henry Clinton in New York. On 19 August the Americans began the long march, followed four days later by the Count de Rochambeau and his French regulars.

De Grasse Arrives off the Chesapeake   20 August 1781

Admiral de Grasse arrived from the West Indies off the Chesapeake Bay with 28 ships of the line and 6 escorting frigates. He also brought some 3,300 French regulars.

De Barras Sails from Newport,   25 August 1781
Rhode Island

Admiral de Barras sailed from Newport with a support squadron of the French fleet carrying a powerful bombardment train and additional troops to support the operation against Cornwallis, who had fortified and was holding in strength Yorktown, Virginia.

Admiral Thomas Graves with Admiral   31 August 1781
Hood's Reinforcement Sails from New
York for the Chesapeake

Admiral Thomas Graves and Admiral Samuel Hood with 19 ships of the line and 4 frigates of the Royal Navy sailed from New York for the Chesapeake.

Battle of the Capes or Lynnhaven Bay,   5 September 1781
Virginia

Admiral Thomas Graves with 19 ships of the line engaged Admiral de Grasse's French fleet of 24 ships of the line off Cape Charles and Cape Henry, the entrance to Chesapeake Bay. The fighting was indecisive, and Graves returned to New York leaving Cornwallis and his army besieged by Washington and Rochambeau.

The Burning of New London, Connecticut   6 September 1781

Benedict Arnold, leading a British amphibious attack against New London, Connecticut, burned the town and killed or wounded most of the garrison at Fort Griswold. The American commander, Colonel William Ledyard, died in the action. The royal fleet maintained the ability to strike where and when it pleased from New York to Canada throughout the war.

The Battle of Eutaw Springs,   8 September 1781
South Carolina

In the battle of Eutaw Springs, Nathanael Greene's army in the first phase beat the British and drove back most of their line in near rout. Major John Marjoribanks, commanding British flank companies, held out in a brick house and fenced garden on the British right. The British under Alexander Stuart regrouped and counterattacked, driving the disorganized Americans from the field. The numbers engaged and losses were roughly equal.

Loyalist Raid on Hillsboro,   12 September 1781
North Carolina

A strong force of North Carolina Loyalists under the command of Hector MacNeil made a surprise attack on Hillsboro and captured 200 American prisoners. These included Governor Thomas Burke of North Carolina, his Council, two Continental colonels, and several other officers. MacNeil and his column also released 60 Loyalist prisoners. MacNeil was killed in a skirmish with American militia as he retired from Hillsboro after the raid.

The Siege of Yorktown, Virginia   28 September–17 October 1781

On 28 September the American Continental army under the personal command of George Washington and the French army led by the Count de Rochambeau invested Yorktown, Virginia, where Lord Cornwallis lay behind fortifications with his British, Provincial, and German mercenary army. This was a classic siege with successive parallels and saps driven toward the British lines. On 17 October after an unsuccessful attempt to escape across the river, the British beat a parley and sent an officer to discuss terms of surrender.

Gloucester, Virginia   3 October 1781

A British foraging party sent out from the fortified post of Gloucester across the York River from Yorktown was pursued by the Duke de Lauzun's Legion of Polish and Irish mercenaries supported by Virginia militia. Banastre Tarleton commanding at Gloucester rode out with his dragoons to cover the retreat and in the ensuing fight was unhorsed but escaped unharmed. It was the last action in America of the dashing British leader of cavalry.

Cornwallis Surrenders at Yorktown,   19 October 1781
Virginia

Brigadier Charles O'Hara of the Guards led out Yorktown's British garrison and surrendered to Washington and Rochambeau 7,157 soldiers including 2,000 sick and wounded in the town's hospitals, 840 sailors, and 80 camp followers. George Washington was victorious at last. Fighting continued for another year, but the loss of the army at Yorktown doomed the British war effort in North America to defeat.

Clouds Creek, South Carolina   17 November 1781

Colonel William "Bloody Bill" Cuningham with 300 Loyalists attacked by surprise an American Patriot militia group some 30 in number led by Captain Turner and camped at Clouds Creek in Edgefield County. Only two of the Patriots escaped, the rest being slaughtered.

British Evacuation of Wilmington,   ca. 18 November 1781
North Carolina

Major Craig commanding the British garrison at Wilmington, North Carolina, unaware of Cornwallis's surrender at Yorktown, held his position until ordered by General Alexander Leslie to evacuate by sea to Charleston, South Carolina. The garrison and resident Loyalists completed the operation by 30 November.

Hayes's Station, South Carolina   19 November 1781

Bloody Bill Cuningham attacked Colonel Hayes, fortified in his home with a small force of Patriot militia. Hayes refused to surrender and Cuningham fired the house, forcing the defenders to surrender. Cuningham then personally killed in cold blood Colonel Hayes and 14 of his captured men. Two already had died in the fighting.

Wambaw Creek, South Carolina   14 February 1782

Colonel Benjamin Thomson, a brilliant Loyalist cavalry leader from Massachusetts, came to Charleston, South Carolina, in the last months of the war and organized a force from the remnants of various British and Provincial units. With these men he defeated Marion's brigade at Wambaw Creek in a hard-fought minor engagement.

Tydiman's Plantation, South Carolina   25 February 1782

Following up his victory at Wambaw Creek, Benjamin Thomson on the next day, 25 February, in a hot little battle again defeated Marion's brigade.

British Evacuation of Savannah, Georgia   11 July 1782

General Alured Clarke and his British garrison at Savannah, Georgia, evacuated the town and departed by sea, having held the position since Savannah's capture on 29 December 1778. General Anthony Wayne then marched in with his American Continentals and occupied Savannah.

Fair Lawn Plantation, South Carolina   29 August 1782

Fair Lawn Plantation was Francis Marion's last engagement of the war and a British victory. On this occasion, Major Thomas Fraser's Royal Dragoons charged and broke through Marion's position. Marion retreated in good order, but the British won the day.

Skirmish at the Combahee River,   27 August 1782
South Carolina

Lieutenant Colonel John Laurens, a distinguished young officer of a famous South Carolina family who had served with George Washington in the North, was ambushed by 140 British soldiers foraging for rice on the north bank of the Combahee River. With the alternatives of surrendering or fighting, Laurens led his men at the charge against the ambush and was killed in the action.

Last Campaign against the   16 September–17 October 1782
Cherokees

Brigadier General Andrew Pickens of South Carolina and Colonel Elijah Clarke of Georgia with 414 men marched against the Cherokees who, under the leadership of a Loyalist, Colonel Thomas Waters, were again raiding the frontier settlements. Waters escaped but Indian towns along the Chattahoochee River were burned. On 17 October several chiefs came in and made a temporary treaty agreement. This was ratified later at Augusta by the governor of Georgia.

British Evacuation of Charleston,   14 December 1782
South Carolina

On 14 December Major General Alexander Leslie, commanding British forces in South Carolina, withdrew his troops from the advanced works on the Charleston peninsula and marched them down to Gadsden's wharf at the foot of what is now Calhoun Street, where the soldiers were embarked. At eleven o'clock in the morning on the same day American troops led by General Anthony Wayne occupied Charleston.

Evacuation of New York and Brooklyn   25 November 1783

At one o'clock in the afternoon the British forces holding New York marched to their boats at the East River wharves and evacuated New York. Brooklyn was evacuated on the same day. The Americans occupied the lower part of New York, and George Washington with Governor Clinton entered the city. A provisional peace treaty with Great Britain already had been ratified by Congress on 15 April.

Appendix

The British Attack on Fort Sullivan, South Carolina
28 June 1776

AMERICAN FORCES

COMMANDING OFFICER
Major General Charles Lee
COMMANDER AT FORT SULLIVAN
Colonel William Moultrie

Continentals

2d South Carolina Regiment: Colonel William Moultrie (Muster—413)
3d South Carolina Regiment (Rangers):   Colonel William Thomson (Muster—ca. 330)
North Carolina Continentals: Lieutenant Colonel Clark (Muster—ca. 200)
Virginia Continentals:*   Colonel Peter Muhlenberg (Muster—ca. 700)

Artillery

Detachment from 4th South Carolina Regiment: (Muster—22)

State Troops and Militia

South Carolina State Troops: Colonel Daniel Horry (Muster—200)
Raccoon Company of Riflemen: Captain John Allston (Muster—50)
Detachment of South Carolina Militia: (Muster—50)

Total Muster

ca. 1,965

*Only 500 Virginia Continentals were present for the defense of the city. Muhlenburg's 700 must have included additional North Carolina or South Carolina regulars sent from the city garrison, probably all or part of Thomas Sumter's 6th Regiment assigned by Charles Lee on 8 June to support William Thomson at Breach Inlet on Sullivan's Island.

Casualties

Killed—12
Wounded—25

BRITISH FORCES

COMMANDING OFFICER, NAVAL FORCES
Admiral Sir Peter Parker

Ships

Bristol (50 guns): Captain John Morris
Experiment (50 guns): Captain Alexander Scott
Active (28 guns): Captain William Williams
Solebay (28 guns): Captain Thomas Symonds
Acteon (28 guns): Captain Christopher Atkins
Syren (28 guns): Captain Tobias Furneau
Sphynx (20 guns): Captain Anthony Hunt
Friendship, armed vessel (22 guns): Captain Charles Hope
Ranger, sloop (8 guns): Roger Willis
Thunder, bombship: James Reid
St. Lawrence, schooner: Lieutenant John Graves

Casualties

Killed and wounded—ca. 219

COMMANDING OFFICER, LAND FORCES
Major General Sir Henry Clinton

Regular Army

(Muster—2,200)

Royal Marines and Boatman

(Muster—600–700)

Total Muster

ca. 2,800–2,900

The First Battle of Savannah
29 December 1778

AMERICAN FORCES

COMMANDING OFFICER
Major General Robert Howe

Continentals

Georgia Continentals: Lieutenant Colonel Samuel Elbert (Muster—150–200)

Militia

Georgia and South Carolina Militia: Brigadier General Isaac Huger (Muster—500–550)

Casualties

Killed—83
Wounded—11
Captured—ca. 453

BRITISH FORCES

COMMANDING OFFICER
Lieutenant Colonel Archibald Campbell

Regular Army

71st Regiment of Foot (Highland Scots):   Lieutenant Colonel Archibald Campbell
Four battalions of German mercenaries

Artillery

Detachment of Royal Artillery

Provincials

One battalion, North Carolina Royalist Regiment: Colonel John Hamilton
One battalion, South Carolina Royalist Regiment: Colonel Alexander Innes
New York Volunteers

Total Muster

ca. 3,000

Casualties

Killed—7
Wounded—19

The Siege of Savannah
24 September 1779–19 October 1779

AMERICAN FORCES

COMMANDING OFFICER
Major General Benjamin Lincoln

Continentals

1st Brigade: Brigadier General Lachlan McIntosh (Muster fit for duty, 21 September 1779—387)

2d Brigade: Brigadier General Isaac Huger (Muster fit for duty, 21 September 1779—409)

Artillery

Five 4-pounders
South Carolina Regiment of Continental Artillery: Colonel Barnard Beckman (Beekman?) (Muster—72)

Militia

1st Brigade: Brigadier General Lachlan McIntosh (Muster fit for duty, 21 September 1779—541)

Charleston Militia:

2d Brigade: Colonel Maurice Simons (Muster fit for duty, 21 September 1779—227)

Light Troops: Lieutenant Colonel John Laurens (Muster fit for duty, 21 September 1779—175)

Casualties

Continentals: Killed and wounded—250
Militia: Killed—1; Wounded—6

Total Muster of American Troops engaged—2,307

(This does not include 278 reported sick, 60 on "command" ["special duty"] and 23 on furlough who may have rejoined before the battle.)

SOURCE: The above information is copied verbatim from the "Return of the Troops under the Command of Major General Benjamin Lincoln, 21 September 1779," contained in the Benjamin Lincoln Papers preserved in microfilm at the South Carolina Archives. It lists units but does not give the muster for cavalry and attached troops. These include Temple's Dragoons, Pulaski's Legion of horse and foot, Colonel Horry's Dragoons, Captain Snipe's militia horse, and Captain Elliot's "Independent Company" (probably mounted). Pulaski's Legion on garrison duty at Charleston on 27 July mustered 172 effectives including ca. 70–73 infantry, so the entire cavalry force could not have numbered more than 400 to 500 sabers. (Pulaski led 200 in the cavalry attack.) The 1st, 2d, 3d, 5th, and 6th South Carolina Continental regiments are listed as present at Savannah plus the Georgia Continental brigade. Since the latter numbered only 137 (probably commanded by Lieutenant Colonel Samuel Elbert), it may have been brigaded with the South Carolinians and thus should be included with the "Return" of 21 September. Even with the Georgians counted separately, the entire muster, including sick, men on furlough or detached duty, and the estimated cavalry, adds up to a maximum of 2,805.

Edward McCrady in his *History of South Carolina in the Revolution* (reprint, Columbia, S.C., 1972), vol. 1, p. 407, states that Lincoln's forces came to about 4,000. This number is taken from William Moultrie's *Memoirs of the American Revolution* (reprint, New York, 1968), p. 41. McCrady (p. 413, note 1) also cites two Virginians, Lieutenants Parker and Walker, among the wounded at Savannah (*South Carolina and American General Gazette*, October 27), and on page 413 quotes Marshall's *Life of Washington* (vol. 4, p. 134), which states that Virginia dragoons and infantry were detached by Lincoln to Augusta after the siege of Savannah was lifted. According to the Lincoln Papers (023) there were 361 Virginia infantry under a Colonel Mason still present with Lincoln's army on 6 June. Whether these, plus additional Georgia militia, were with the American forces during the siege cannot be stated with any assurance. It would seem probable from the "Return" of September 21 that Lincoln's army numbered closer to 3,000 than 4,000.

FRENCH FORCES

COMMANDING OFFICER
Admiral Charles Count d'Estaing

Regular Army

Regiments are not listed, but the French land forces present at the siege of Savannah are estimated at 3,500 to 4,000 regulars. The French and American allies mounted 53 pieces of artillery and 14 mortars. Since the Charleston regiment of artillery had only five 4-pounders, most of the ordnance clearly was French.

Casualties

Killed—244
Wounded—584

FRENCH SHIPS OF WAR

Ships of the Line

1st Division: four 74-, one 66-, and two 64-gun ships
2d Division: four 74-, one 64-, one 54-gun ships and d'Estaing's flagship *Languedoc*, mounting 120 guns
3d Division: one 80-gun ship, *Tonnant*, three 74-, one 70-, three 64-, and one 50-gun ships

Frigates

One 38-, five 36-, and one 18-gun frigates

Ships captured from the British in the West Indies

One 60-gun ship of the line, *Experiment*, two 20-, and one 18-gun ships (probably light frigates or corvettes) plus two privateers of 10 guns each. The French battle fleet off Savannah numbered altogether twenty–five ships of the line including the two captured British vessels, ten frigates and corvettes, and two armed privateers.

BRITISH FORCES

COMMANDING OFFICER
Major General Augustine Prevost

Regular Army

16th Regiment of Foot: Lieutenant Colonel Glazier
71st Regiment of Foot (Highland Scots):   Lieutenant Colonel Maitland
Two regiments of German mercenaries

Artillery

Including naval battery—ca. 100 guns, howitzers, and mortars mounted on Savannah defenses

Royal Marines

A detachment of Royal Marines

Royal Navy

Sailors of the Royal Navy manning the naval battery

Provincials

South Carolina King's Rangers: Captains Raworth and Wyley
South Carolina Dragoons: Captain Tawse
New York Volunteers
de Lancey's Brigade (one battalion):   Lieutenant Colonel John Harris Cruger
North Carolina Royalist Regiment: Lieutenant Colonel John Hamilton

Militia

South Carolina Loyalist Militia: Lieutenant Colonel Thomas Browne
Georgia Loyalist Militia: Major James Wright

Naval Forces

Armed brig, *Germaine*, stationed on the river above the town as flank guard for right of British
    lines

Total muster of British Troops engaged—ca. 2,500
Casualties

Killed—7
Wounded—19

Siege and Capture of Charleston, South Carolina
7 March–12 May 1780

AMERICAN FORCES

COMMANDING OFFICER
Major General Benjamin Lincoln

Continentals

1st Regiment of South Carolina Continentals (Muster—231)
2d Regiment of South Carolina Continentals (Muster—246)
3d Regiment of South Carolina Continentals (Muster—259)
1st Regiment of North Carolina Continentals (Muster—287)
2d Regiment of North Carolina Continentals (Muster—301)
3d Regiment of North Carolina Continentals (Muster—162)
1st Regiment of Virginia Continentals (Muster—336)
2d Regiment of Virginia Continentals (Muster—306)
3d Regiment of Virginia Continentals (Muster—252)
1st Detachment of Virginians (Muster—258)
2d Detachment of Virginians (Muster—232)
Attached Virginia officers (Muster—46)
Light dragoons (Muster—41)
Georgia Continental officers (Muster—5)

Artillery

157 guns in battery
South Carolina artillery (Muster—93)
North Carolina artillery (Muster—64)
Charleston Battalion of Artillery (Muster—168)
Cannoniers, manning town batteries, probably militia (Muster—167)
General staff (Muster—6)
Engineer staff (Muster—6)

Militia

1st Battalion of Charleston militia (Muster—352)
2d Battalion of Charleston militia (Muster—485)
South and North Carolina militia (Muster—1,231)

French and American sailors: serving with the city
defense forces (Muster—ca. 1,000)

A French company (cited by Moultrie) (Muster—43)

Total Muster of American and French Forces engaged—6,577
Casualties

Killed—89
Wounded—138
Captured (including civil officers and prisoners)—ca. 6,662–6,684*

BRITISH FORCES

COMMANDING OFFICER
Major General Sir Henry Clinton

Regular Army

Light Infantry (Muster—800)
Grenadiers (Muster—900)
7th Regiment of Foot (Muster—400)
23d Regiment of Foot (Muster—400)
33d Regiment of Foot (Muster—450)
42d Regiment of Foot (Muster—700)
63d Regiment of Foot (Muster—400)
64th Regiment of Foot (Muster—350)
Hessian Grenadiers (Muster—1,000)
Royal Artillery (Muster—200)
Guides and Pioneers (Muster—150)

Provincials

Queen's Rangers (Muster—200)
Fanning's Corps (Muster—100)

*This number is Edward McCrady's computation and also   *South Carolina in the Revolution*, vol. 1, p. 510).
includes the 1,000 sailors (Edward McCrady, *History of*

British reinforcements from Savannah, Georgia
Regular Army

71st Regiment of Foot (Highland Scots):   Major Archibald McArthur
Light Infantry: Major Graham
A detachment of dragoons

Provincials

British Legion (horse and foot):   Lieutenant Colonel Banastre Tarleton
American Volunteers: Major Patrick Ferguson
New York Volunteers: Lieutenant Colonel George Turnbull
South Carolina Royalists: Lieutenant Colonel Alexander Innes
North Carolina Royalists: Lieutenant Colonel John Hamilton

Total Muster of British reinforcements from Savannah—ca. 1,750
(including Tarleton's 250 dragoons)
Reinforcements received from New York

Charles Lord Cornwallis and Francis Lord Rawdon

Total Muster—ca. 3,000

Total Muster of British Forces engaged*—ca. 12,000
Casualties

Killed—78
Wounded—189

BRITISH NAVAL FORCES

COMMANDING OFFICER
Admiral Mariot Arbuthnot

Ships of the Line

Europe, 64 guns; *Russell*, 74 guns; *Robuste*, 74 guns; *Defiance*, 64 guns; *Raisonable*, 64 guns;
Renown, 50 guns; *Romulus*, 44 guns; *Roebuck*, 44 guns

---

*Edward McCrady, *A History of South Carolina in the Revolution*, vol. 2, p. 435, states that the British State Papers Office puts the effective number of British troops besieging Charleston at 12,847. This, however, would include command group, officers, doctors, surgeons, commissariat, and other auxiliaries of various descriptions. It also may be doubted if the round numbers cited by Henry Carrington, *Battles of the American Revolution* (New York, 1876), pp. 493–94, for several of the regiments listed are correct. They must represent an approximation, as Carrington points out.

Frigates

Blonde, 32 guns; *Perseus*, 32 guns; *Camilla*, 20 guns; *Raleigh*, 28 guns; *Redmond*, 32 guns; *Virginia*, 28 guns

Casualties

Killed—14
Wounded—15

The Battle of Camden
16 August 1780

AMERICAN FORCES

COMMANDING OFFICER
Major General Horatio Gates
Colonel Otho Williams, adjutant general

Continentals

Major General Johann deKalb; 1st Maryland Brigade: Major General William Smallwood;
    2d Maryland Brigade: Major General Mordecai Gist; Delaware Regiment:
    Lieutenant Colonel Vaughn (Muster—ca. 900) Armand's Legion: Colonel Charles
    Armand (Muster—60 horse and 60 foot)*

Artillery

Seven 6-pounders: Captain Singleton (?) (Muster—100)

Militia

One brigade North Carolina militia: Brigadier General Richard Caswell (Muster—1,800)
One brigade Virginia militia: Brigadier General Edward Stevens (Muster—700)
One company Virginia state troops serving as light infantry: Lieutenant Colonel Charles
    Porterfield (Muster—100)
One troop of South Carolina volunteer mounted infantry (Muster—ca. 70)

*The 60 dragoons of Armand's Legion plus the 70-odd   Horatio Gates possessed.
mounted South Carolina volunteers were the only horse

Total Muster of American Forces engaged (with officers)—ca. 4,100

(Only approximately 3,052 of these were actually fit for duty and saw action.)

Casualties

Killed, wounded, and captured (including officers)—ca. 683–733

BRITISH FORCES

COMMANDING OFFICER
Lieutenant General Charles Lord Cornwallis

Regular Army

23d Regiment of Foot: Lieutenant Colonel James Webster
33d Regiment of Foot
Two battalions (five companies) of the 71st Regiment of Foot (Highland Scots)
Artillery

Four 6-pounders and two 3-pounders: Lieutenant McLeod (?)

Provincials

British Legion (mixed cavalry and mounted infantry):   Lieutenant Colonel Banastre Tarleton
Volunteers of Ireland: Colonel Francis Lord Rawdon
Royal North Carolina Regiment: Lieutenant Colonel John Hamilton
North Carolina Volunteers: Colonel Samuel Bryan

Total Muster of British Forces engaged—2,239

Casualties

Killed—68
Wounded—245
Missing—18

APPENDIX

The Battle of Kings Mountain
7 October 1780

AMERICAN FORCES

COMMANDING OFFICER
Colonel William Campbell

Militia

Virginia militia: Colonel William Campbell (Muster—200)
North Carolina militia: Colonel Benjamin Cleveland, Major Joseph Winston, Major Joseph
   McDowell (Muster—260); Colonel Frederick Hambright, Major William Chronicle
   (Muster—50); Colonel James Williams (Muster—60)
South Carolina militia: Colonel Edward Lacey, Colonel William Hill (Muster—100)
Georgia militia: Major William Candler (Muster—30)
*Frontier militia from across the mountains:** Colonel Isaac Shelby, Lieutenant Colonel John
   Sevier (Muster—240)

Total Muster of American Militia engaged—ca. 940

Casualties

Killed—28
Wounded—62

BRITISH FORCES

COMMANDING OFFICER
Major Patrick Ferguson

Provincials

One company Ferguson's Corps:** Major Patrick Ferguson (Muster—100)

---

*The transmontane militia from the settlements on the Watauga, Nolichucky, and Holston Rivers was raised in an area still, at that time, part of North Carolina. After the Revolution these "across the mountains" areas provided a population nucleus for the new states of Tennessee and Kentucky.

**Ferguson called this detachment of 100 men "Rangers" but they were uniformed in red coats, not green, and equipped with smoothbore musket and bayonet rather than the rifle. These Provincials were recruited among the Loyalist elements in New York and New Jersey.

Militia

North Carolina militia: Colonel Ambrose Mills (Muster—ca. 430–450)
South Carolina militia: Probably Major Daniel Plummer (Muster—ca. 320–356)

Total Muster of British Provincials and Loyalist
Militia engaged†—850–902

Casualties††

Killed—119
Wounded—123
Captured—664

The Battle of Blackstocks
20 November 1780

AMERICAN FORCES COMMANDING OFFICER
Brigadier General Thomas Sumter

Militia

South Carolina militia: Colonel Thomas Brandon, Colonel William Bratton, Colonel Henry
    Hampton, Colonel William Hill, Colonel Edward Lacey, Colonel James McCall, Colonel
    Thomas Taylor, Colonel Richard Winn (Muster—ca. 800–900)
Georgia militia: Colonel John Twiggs, Colonel Elijah Clarke, Major William Candler, Major
    James Jackson (Muster—ca. 100)

Total Muster of American Troops engaged—ca. 900–1,000

Casualties
Killed—3
Wounded—4

†Two hundred Loyalist North Carolina and South Carolina militia commanded by a Colonel Moore were absent from the battle on a foraging expedition and returned to exchange a few volleys after the main fighting was over. James Williams was killed at this time.
††Accounts of Ferguson's casualties differ widely, ranging from 119 to 225 killed and from 123 to 263 wounded and left on the field. The accounts of the number of prisoners taken varies from 664 to 731. Since all sources generally agree that the opposing forces were about equal in numbers and the Americans mustered around 940, the list of casualties and prisoners which brings Ferguson's little army to 906 is here accepted. This is the number given by Anthony Allaire, a Loyalist officer serving with Ferguson and a survivor of the battle.

BRITISH FORCES

COMMANDING OFFICER
Lieutenant Colonel Banastre Tarleton

Regular Army

Mounted infantry of the 63d Regiment of Foot: Major John Money (Muster—80)

Provincials

Dragoons and mounted infantry of British legion: Lieutenant Colonel Banastre Tarleton
(Muster—190)

Total Muster of British Troops engaged—270

Casualties

Killed—92
Wounded—100

The Battle of Cowpens
17 January 1781

AMERICAN FORCES

COMMANDING OFFICER
Brigadier General Daniel Morgan

Continentals

Light infantry of the Maryland Line: Lieutenant Colonel John Eager Howard (Muster—ca.
290)

Virginia Cavalry

Lieutenant Colonel William Washington (Muster—80)

Militia

Virginia militia: Captain Taite; Captain Triplett (Muster—ca. 100)
Georgia, North and South Carolina militia: Colonel Andrew Pickens; Major Joseph
McDowell; Major John Cunningham; Major James Jackson; Captain Beale (Muster—
ca. 490)
McCall's Georgia and South Carolina mounted infantry: Lieutenant Colonel James McCall
(Muster—45)
Total Muster of American Forces engaged—ca. 1,005

Casualties

Killed—12
Wounded—60

BRITISH FORCES

COMMANDING OFFICER
Lieutenant Colonel Banastre Tarleton

Regular Army

7th Regiment of Foot (Royal Fusiliers): Major Timothy Newmarsh (Muster—200)
71st Regiment of Foot (Highland Scots): Major Archibald McArthur (1st Battalion
Muster—200)
17th Regiment of Dragoons (One troop Muster—50)
Royal Artillery two 3-pounder "Grasshoppers" (Muster—50)

Provincials

British Legion: Lieutenant Colonel Banastre Tarleton Cavalry (Muster—200) Infantry
(Muster—350)
Total Muster of British Forces engaged* :—1,050

Casualties

Killed—ca. 100
Wounded—229
Captured and missing—600 (including wounded)

---

*They also seem to have been 100 or possibly 150 Loyalist militia who took no part in the battle.

The Battle of Guilford Court House
15 March 1781

AMERICAN FORCES

COMMANDING OFFICER
Major General Nathanael Greene

Continentals

Maryland Brigade: Colonel Otho Williams, Lieutenant Colonel John Eager Howard; 1st
    Maryland Regiment: Colonel John Gunby; 2d Maryland Regiment: Lieutenant
    Colonel Benjamin Ford (Muster—ca. 632)
Delaware Regiment: Captain Robert Kirkwood (One company Muster—ca. 80)
Virginia Brigade: Brigadier General Isaac Huger; 4th Virginia Regiment: Lieutenant
    Colonel John Greene; 5th Virginia Regiment: Lieutenant Colonel Samuel Hawes
    (Muster—778)
Henry Lee's Legion: Lieutenant Colonel Henry Lee; Legion infantry (Muster—82)
    Legion Cavalry (Muster—62); Virginia cavalry: Lieutenant Colonel William
    Washington (Muster—90)

Artillery

Captain Anthony Singleton, Captain Samuel Finley; Four 6-pounders (Muster—ca. 100)

Militia and State Troops

North Carolina Brigade of two regiments: Brigadier General John Butler, Brigadier General
    Pinkertham Eaton (Muster—ca. 1,000)
Virginia Brigade of two regiments: Brigadier General Edward Stevens, Brigadier General
    Robert Lawson (Muster—ca. 1,200)
North Carolina Rifle Corps: Colonel William Campbell, Colonel William Preston, Colonel
    Charles Lynch (Muster—ca. 60)
Virginia Rifle Corps: (Muster—ca. 340)

Total Muster of American Forces engaged—4,384–4,444
(the second number is Nathanael Greene's official return two
days before the battle)

Casualties

Killed—78
Wounded—195
Missing*—1,055

BRITISH FORCES

COMMAND GROUP
Lieutenant General Charles Lord Cornwallis
Major General Alexander Leslie
Brigadier General Howard (serving as a volunteer)

Regular Army

Brigade of Guards:** Brigadier General Charles O'Hara; 1st Battalion: Lieutenant
    Colonel Norton; 2d Battalion: Lieutenant Colonel Stewart (Muster—481)
7th Regiment of Foot (Muster—167)
Three companies of the 16th Regiment of Foot (Muster—41)
23d Regiment of Foot: Colonel James Webster (Muster—258)
33d Regiment of Foot (Muster—322)
71st Regiment of Foot:† Colonel Fraser; Highland Scots (Muster—530)
Regiment of Bose (German mercenary infantry): Lieutenant Colonel (Major) de Buiy
    (Muster—313); attached jäger riflemen (Muster—97)

Royal Artillery

Three 3-pounders: Lieutenant John MacLeod (Muster—ca. 40–50)

Provincials

British Legion: Lieutenant Colonel Banastre Tarleton; Infantry (Muster—174); Cavalry
    (Muster—ca. 180)

---

*Most of the missing were North Carolina militia who fled the field and made their way to their homes.
**J. W. Fortescue, *A History of the British Army*, Vol. III (London, 1902), pp. 369n, 374n, states that the guards serving at Guilford Court House were not the Royal Guards but selected detachments of the 23d, 33d, and 71st regiments of foot.
†Colonel Fraser is not mentioned among the casualties at Guilford Court House, but seven months later at Yorktown, Lieutenant Colonel Duncan MacPherson commanded the 71st Regiment.

Royal North Carolina Regiment: Lieutenant Colonel John Hamilton (Muster—232)

    The total official muster of Cornwallis's army by regiment was 2,719 on 1 March, two weeks before the engagement. Lieutenant Colonel John Hamilton's North Carolina regiment of 232 infantry supported by 100 regular infantry and 20 dragoons were detached prior to the battle to guard the baggage. Henry Lee in his memoirs estimated the British cavalry at 300, but Tarleton had about 200 dragoons during the march north and 20 were sent with Hamilton, so there could not have been more than 180 present at the battle. This is the number Tarleton led to Virginia from Wilmington, North Carolina. If one reckons 10 or 12 men to each 3-pounder with sergeants and officers the Royal Artillery contingent must have mustered 40 to 50 men. Cornwallis's force at Guilford Court House has been estimated at between 1,981 and 2,253 (the latter number being Cornwallis's return on 14 March, obviously including both cavalry and artilley but excluding officers). Subtract the usual sick, wounded, and stragglers left behind during the skirmishing approach march to the battlefield and there should have been approximately 2,000 British effectives present at Guilford Court House. Nathanael Greene's army still outnumbered Cornwallis's force more than two to one.

Casualties

Killed—93
Wounded—413
Missing—26

The Battle of Hobkirk Hill
25 April 1781

AMERICAN FORCES

COMMANDING OFFICER
Major General Nathanael Greene

Continentals

Maryland Brigade: Colonel Otho Williams, Colonel John Gunby; 1st Maryland
    Regiment: Lieutenant Colonel John Eager Howard; 2d Maryland Regiment:
    Lieutenant Colonel Benjamin Ford

Virginia Brigade: Brigadier General Isaac Huger; 4th Virginia Regiment: Lieutenant
   Colonel Richard Campbell; 5th Virginia Regiment: Lieutenant Colonel Samuel
   Hawes
Delaware Regiment (one company):   Captain Robert Kirkwood

Total Muster of Continental infantry—843

Cavalry

Virginia cavalry (Two regiments, White's and Washington's):   Lieutenant Colonel
   William Washington (Muster—87, only 56 mounted)

Artillery

Three 6-pounders: Colonel Charles Harrison (Muster—ca. 40)

Militia

North Carolina militia: Colonel Reade (Muster—254)

Total Muster of American Troops engaged—ca. 1,200–1,224

Casualties

Killed—19
Wounded—113
Missing—136

BRITISH FORCES

COMMANDING OFFICER
Francis Lord Rawdon

Regular Army

63d Regiment of Foot

Artillery

Two 6-pounders (Muster—ca. 40–50)

Provincials

Volunteers of Ireland: Francis Lord Rawdon
King's American Regiment
New York Volunteers: Colonel George Turnbull
South Carolina Provincial Regiment

Cavalry

One troop, New York Dragoons: Major John Coffin

Total Muster of British Troops engaged:—ca. 900–950

Casualties

Killed—38–39
Wounded—207–218
Missing—12

The Siege of Ninety Six
22 May–19 June 1781

AMERICAN FORCES

COMMANDING OFFICER
Major General Nathanael Greene

Continentals

Maryland Brigade: Colonel Otho Willams; 1st Maryland Regiment: Lieutenant Colonel
     John Eager Howard; 2d Maryland Regiment: Lieutenant Colonel Benjamin Ford
     (Muster—427)
Virginia Brigade: Brigadier General Isaac Huger; 4th Virginia Regiment: Lieutenant
     Colonel Richard Campbell; 5th Virginia Regiment: Lieutenant Colonel Samuel
     Hawes (Muster—421)
Delaware Regiment: Robert Kirkwood's Company: Captain Robert Kirkwood
     (Muster—60)
Lee's Legion: Lieutenant Colonel Henry Lee (Muster of horse and foot—ca. 150)

Artillery

Four 6-pounders (Muster—ca. 80–100)*

Militia

South Carolina militia: Brigadier General Andrew Pickens (Muster—ca. 400)
North Carolina militia: One company (Muster—66)**

Total Muster of American Forces engaged—ca. 1,624

Casualties

Killed—57
Wounded—70
Missing—20

BRITISH FORCES

COMMANDING OFFICER
Lieutenant Colonel John Harris Cruger

Provincials

1st Battalion of de Lancey's New York Brigade: Lieutenant Colonel John Harris Cruger
    (Muster—150)
2d Battalion of New Jersey Volunteers: Major Joseph Greene (?) (Muster—200)

Artillery

Three 3-pounders, no attached artillery men

Militia

South Carolina Loyalist Militia from the Ninety Six District: Colonel King (Muster—200)

Total Muster of British Forces engaged—550

---

*Nathanael Greene began the siege with three 6-pounders, but Henry Lee brought an additional field gun from Augusta. The American commanders may have used captured pieces taken at Augusta since Lee established batteries giving the besiegers a cross fire on the water supply and covered way leading to the outlying hornwork or palisade fort.
**This company also is described as North Carolina Continentals and may have been state troops rather than militia. North Carolina Continentals in regimental strength served later at Eutaw Springs.

Casualties

Killed—27
Wounded—58

Relief Column

Francis Lord Rawdon's Relief Column from Charleston and Monck's Corner
Flank companies (light infantry and grenadiers) from the 3d, 19th, and 30th Regiments of
Foot recently arrived in Charleston from Ireland.†
Lieutenant Colonel John Watson's Corps
Major Archibald McArthur's reinforcing detachment
Colonel John Doyle's holding force at Monck's Corner
Garrison withdrawn from Camden after Hobkirk Hill

Total Muster—ca. 1,850 infantry

South Carolina Regiment of Royalists (one cavalry troop):   Major John Coffin (Muster—
150)

Total Muster of Relief Column (No artillery included)—ca. 2,000

The Battle of Quinby Bridge
17 July 1781

AMERICAN FORCES

COMMANDING OFFICER
Brigadier General Thomas Sumter

Continentals

Lieutenant Colonel Henry Lee's Legion (Muster—ca. 150)

---

†The inference in several accounts is that Rawdon's infantry included only the flank companies and Doyle's holding force. At full strength the flank companies of three regiments could not have exceeded 600, so Rawdon's old command from Camden plus Watson's and McArthur's reinforcements also must have made the march.

Militia

South Carolina militia: Brigadier General Thomas Sumter's five regiments: Colonel
Thomas Polk, Colonel Thomas Taylor, Colonel Edward Lacey, Colonel Wade Hampton,
Colonel Charles Mydleton (Muster—ca. 225); Brigadier General Francis Marion's four
regiments: Colonel Peter Horry, Colonel Hezekiah Maham, Major Alexander Swinton,
Captain John Baxter (Muster—ca. 180)

Casualties

Killed and wounded—ca. 55–60

BRITISH FORCES

COMMANDING OFFICER
Lieutenant Colonel James Coates

Regular Army

19th Regiment of Foot: Lieutenant Colonel James Coates (Muster—ca. 500–600)

Artillery

One field howitzer

Total Muster of British Troops engaged—ca. 500–600*
Casualties

Killed—6
Wounded—38
Captured—100

The Battle of Eutaw Springs
8 September 1781

AMERICAN FORCES

COMMANDING OFFICER
Major General Nathanael Greene

---

*Two flank companies (light infantry and grenadiers) were absent serving with Francis Lord Rawdon and 150 mounted infantry of the South Carolina Rangers (Provincials) were detached prior to the battle.

Continentals

Maryland Continentals: Colonel Otho Williams; Two battalions: Lieutenant Colonel John Eager Howard, Major Henry Hardman (Muster—ca. 250)

North Carolina Continentals: General Jethro Sumner; Three battalions: Colonel Ashe, Major Armstrong, Major Blount (Muster—ca. 350)

Virginia Continentals: Lieutenant Colonel Richard Campbell; Two battalions: Major Sneed, Captain Thomas Edmonds (Muster—ca. 250)

Delaware Continentals (Kirkwood's Company):   Captain Robert Kirkwood (Muster—ca. 60–70)

Lee's Legion: Lieutenant Colonel Henry Lee (Muster—ca. 60 cavalry; 100 infantry)

Virginia Continental Cavalry: Lieutenant Colonel William Washington (Muster—80)

Artillery

Two 3-pounders: Captain William Gaines
Two 6-pounders: Captain Browne or Captain Finn

Total Muster—ca. 80–100

State Troops

South Carolina state troops: Colonel William Henderson, Colonel Wade Hampton (Muster—Cavalry, 72; infantry, 73)

Militia and Volunteers

South Carolina militia
Sumter and Pickens Brigades (combined):   Brigadier General Andrew Pickens (Muster—307)

Marion's Brigade: Brigadier General Francis Marion (Muster—40 cavalry, 200 infantry)

North Carolina militia: Colonel Francis Malmedy (Muster—150)

Total Muster of Nathanael Greene's Forces—2,082–2,100*
Total Muster of American Forces engaged—ca. 1,900

Casualties (according to Colonel Otho Williams's return prepared immediately after the battle)**

Killed—251

---

*The camp guard of about 200 men must be subtracted from the total because these troops did not serve in the battle.

**The official returns of American losses at Eutaw Springs published by Congress are 139 killed, 375 wounded, and 8 missing. David Ramsay says that Marion's losses were not reported by the Congress.

Wounded—367
Missing—74

BRITISH FORCES

COMMANDING OFFICER
Lieutenant Colonel Alexander Stuart

Regular Army

3d Regiment of Foot (Buffs)
63rd Regiment of Foot
64th Regiment of Foot
Six flank companies (light infantry and grenadiers) of the 3d, 19th, and 30th Regiments of
　　Foot recently arrived from Ireland:　Major John Marjoribanks

Artillery

Three 6-pounders
One 4-pounder

Provincials

One battalion of de Lancey's New York Brigade:　Lieutenant Colonel John Harris Cruger
One battalion of New Jersey Volunteers:　Major Joseph Greene(?)
One battalion of New York Volunteers:　Major Sheridan(?)
One troops of cavalry from the South Carolina Regiment of Loyalists:　Major John Coffin

Total Muster of British Forces engaged—2,300–2,400

Casualties (from Alexander Stuart's report to Cornwallis)

Killed—85
Wounded—350
Missing—257
British captured (as reported by Nathanael Greene to Congress) were ca. 430, including 70
wounded left on the field when Stuart fell back on Charleston. In a letter of Stuart to Greene
dated 9 September in Library of Congress Collection of Greene Papers (cited in an analysis of the
Eutaw Springs battle statistics prepared by the South Carolina Department of Archives and History), Stuart stated that he was leaving 54 wounded with a surgeon to attend them. It is probable
that Greene overestimated the number of prisoners taken when he reported to Congress.

Naval Battle of the Capes or Lynnhaven Bay
5 September 1781

BRITISH FLEET

COMMANDING OFFICER
Admiral Thomas Graves
DIVISION COMMANDERS
Admiral Sir Samuel Hood
Admiral Sir Francis Drake
FLAGSHIP
London

Ships of the Line

Two 98-gun ships, twelve 74-gun ships, one 70-gun ship, and four 64-gun ships, supported by four frigates.

Guns

The British fleet mounted 1,400 guns

Ships Companies

ca. 13,000 seamen

Casualties

Killed—90
Wounded—246–256
The 74-gun ship of the line *Terrible* was so badly damaged in the action that Graves ordered it burned and sunk.

FRENCH FLEET

COMMANDING OFFICER
Admiral François Joseph Paul,
Count de Grasse
DIVISION COMMANDERS
Le Sieur de Bougainville
Le Sieur de Monteil

FLAGSHIP
Ville de Paris

Ships of the Line

One ship, *Ville de Paris*, of 104 guns (or possibly 120 guns), three 80-, seventeen 74-, and three 64-gun ships, supported by six frigates.

Guns

The French fleet mounted 1,700 guns

Ships Companies

ca. 19,000 seamen

Casualties

Killed and wounded—ca. 200

The Yorktown Campaign
29 September–19 October 1781

AMERICAN FORCES

COMMANDER IN CHIEF
General George Washington
SECRETARY
Colonel Jonathan Trumbull, Jr.
AIDES-DE-CAMP
Lieutenant Colonel Tench Tilghman, Lieutenant Colonel David Humphreys, Lieutenant Colonel David Cobb, Lieutenant Colonel William S. Smith, Lieutenant Colonel John Laurens
ADJUTANT GENERAL
Brigadier General Edward Hand
QUARTERMASTER GENERAL
Colonel Timothy Pickering
ASSISTANT QUARTERMASTER GENERAL
Lieutenant Colonel Henry Dearborn
COMMISSARY GENERAL
Colonel Ephraim Blaine

CHIEF PHYSICIAN AND SURGEON
Doctor James Craik
CHIEF OF ENGINEERS
Brigadier General Chevalier Louis Du Portail
SUPERINTENDENT OF MATERIALS IN THE TRENCHES
Colonel Samuel Elbert

Continentals

Lafayette's Division, light infantry: Major General Marquis de Lafayette; 1st Brigade:
    Brigadier General Peter Muhlenberg; 1st Battalion: Colonel Joseph Vose (Muster—
    250); 2d Battalion: Major John Palsgrave Wyllys (Muster—250); 3d Battalion:
    Lieutenant Colonel Francis Barber (Muster—200)
2d Brigade: Brevet Brigadier General Moses Hazen; 1st Battalion: Lieutenant Colonel
    Ebenezer Huntingdon (Muster—200); 2d Battalion: Lieutenant Colonel Alexander
    Hamilton (Muster—200); 3d Battalion: Lieutenant Colonel John Laurens (Muster—
    200); 4th Battalion (Hazen's Canadian Regiment):   Lieutenant Colonel Edward
    Antill (Muster—200)
Lincoln's Division: Major General Benjamin Lincoln
Clinton's Brigade: Brigadier General James Clinton; 1st New York Regiment: Colonel
    Goose Van Schaick (Muster—325); 2d New York Regiment: Colonel Philip Van
    Cortlandt (Muster—350)
Dayton's Brigade: Colonel Elias Dayton; 1st and 2d New Jersey Regiments (United):
    Colonel Matthias Ogden (Muster—600); Rhode Island Regiment: Lieutenant
    Colonel Commandant, Jeremiah Olney (Muster—450)
Steuben's Division: Major General Baron Steuben
Wayne's Brigade: Brigadier General Anthony Wayne; 1st Pennsylvania Battalion:
    Colonel Walter Stewart (Muster—275); 2d Pennsylvania Battalion*:   Lieutenant
    Colonel Josiah Harmar (Muster—275); Virginia Battalion: Lieutenant Colonel
    Thomas Gaskins (Muster—350)
Gist's Brigade: Brigadier General Mordecai Gist; 3d Maryland Regiment: Lieutenant
    Colonel Commandant Peter Adams (Muster—550); 4th Maryland Regiment: Major
    Alexander Roxburg (Muster—450)
Sappers and Miners: Captain James Gilliland, Captain David Bushnell (Muster—50)
Delaware Recruits: Captain William McKennan (Muster—60)

*A 3d Pennsylvania battalion under Colonel Craig arrived just as operations were completed.

Cavalry

4th Regiment of Dragoons: Colonel Stephen Moyland; Armand's Legion (Muster—
    100)

Artillery Brigade

2d Regiment of New York and Connecticut: Colonel John Lamb (Muster—225)
1st Regiment (Detachment):   Lieutenant Colonel Edward Carrington (Muster—25)
4th Regiment (Detachment):   Captains Patrick Duffy, William Ferguson, James Smith
    (Muster—60)

State Troops: General Thomas Nelson (governor of Virginia

Virginia State Regiment: Lieutenant Colonel Dabney (Muster—200)

Virginia Militia: General Thomas Nelson (governor of Virginia)

1st Brigade: Brigadier General George Weedon (Muster—1,500)
2d Brigade: Brigadier General Robert Lawson (Muster—750)
3d Brigade: Brigadier General Edward Stevens (Muster—750)

Total Muster of American Forces engaged—8,845

Casualties

Killed—23
Wounded—65

FRENCH ARMY

COMMANDING OFFICER
Lieutenant General Jean Baptiste Donatien
de Vimeur, Count de Rochambeau
AIDES-DE-CAMP
Count de Fersen; Marquis de Vauban; Marquis de Damas;
Chevalier de Lameth; M. Duman; de Lauberdiere; Baron Ludwig
von Closen
MARECHAUX DE CAMP
Major General Baron de Viomenil; Major General Marquis
de St. Simon; Major General Viscount de Viomenil;
Major General Chevalier de Chastellux

BRIGADIER GENERAL
M. de Choisy
INTENDANT
M. de Tarle
QUARTERMASTER-GENERAL
M. de Beville
COMMISSARY-GENERAL
Claude Blanchard
MEDICAL DEPARTMENT
M. de Coste, Physician in chief; M. Robillard, Surgeon
in Chief; M. de Mars, Superintendent of Hospitals
ENGINEERS
Colonel Desandrouins; Lieutenant Colonel de Querenet;
Major de Palys; and nine line officers

Regular Army

Brigade Bourbonnois.　Regiment Bourbonnois:　Colonel Marquis de Laval, Second
　　Colonel Viscount de Rochambeau (Muster—900); Regiment Royal Deuxponts:
　　Colonel Count de Deuxponts, Second Colonel Count Guillaume de Deuxponts
　　(Muster—900)
Brigade Soissonois.　Regiment Soissonois:　Colonel Marquis de St. Maime, Second Colonel
　　Viscount de Noailles (Muster—900); Regiment Saintonge:　Colonel Marquis de
　　Custine, Second Colonel Count de Charlus (Muster—900)
Brigade Agenois.　Regiment Agenois:　Colonel Marquis d'Audechamp (Muster—
　　1,000); Regiment Gatenois:　Colonel Marquis de Rostaing (Muster—1,000);
　　Regiment Touraine (not brigaded):　Colonel Viscount de Pondeus (Muster—1,000)

Cavalry

Lauzun's Legion:　Duke de Lauzun, Arthur Count Dillon (Muster—600)
Artillery:　Colonel Commandant d'Aboville (Muster—600)

Total Muster of French Forces engaged—ca. 7,800

Casualties

Killed—52
Wounded—134

BRITISH ARMY

COMMANDING OFFICER
Lieutenant General Charles Lord Cornwallis
AIDES-DE-CAMP
Lieutenant Colonel Lord Chewton; Major Alexander Ross;
Major Charles Cochrane, acting aide
DEPUTY ADJUTANT GENERAL
Major John Despard
COMMISSARY
—— Perkins
DEPUTY QUARTERMASTER GENERAL
Major Richard England
DEPUTY QUARTERMASTER GENERAL'S ASSISTANTS
Captain Campbell, Captain Vallancy, Lieutenant Oldfield,
Ensign St. John
MAJORS OF BRIGADE
Edward Brabazon, ——Manley, J. Baillie, Francis Richardson
ENGINEERS
Lieutenant Alexander Sutherland, Commanding;
Lieutenants Haldane and Stratton

Regular Army

Brigade of Guards: Brigadier General Charles O'Hara, Lieutenant Colonel Lake (Muster—
467)
Light Infantry: Lieutenant Colonel Robert Abercrombie, Major Thomas Armstrong
(Muster—594)
Lieutenant Colonel Yorke's Brigade. 17th Regiment of Foot: Lieutenant Colonel Henry
Johnson (Muster—205); 23d Regiment of Foot: Captain Apthorpe(?) (Muster—
205); 33d Regiment of Foot: Lieutenant Colonel John Yorke (Muster—225); 71st
Regiment of Foot (Highland Scots): Lieutenant Colonel Duncan MacPherson
Lieutenant Colonel Dundas's Brigade: 43d Regiment of Foot: Major George Hewitt(?)
(Muster—307); 76th Regiment of Foot: Major Francis Needham (Muster—628);
80th Regiment of Foot: Lieutenant Colonel Thomas Dundas, Major James Gordon
(Muster—588)

German Mercenaries

Two Anspach battalions: Colonel de Voit, Colonel de Seybothen (Muster—948)
Hessian Regiment Prince Hereditaire: Lieutenant Colonel Matthew de Fuchs (Muster—425)
Hessian regiment of Bose: Major O'Reilly (Muster—271)
Hessian jägers (riflemen):   Captain Johann Ewald (Muster—68)
Royal Artillery: Captain George Rochfort, Captain Lieutenant Edward Fage (Muster—193)
Pioneers (Muster—33)

Provincials

North Carolina Volunteers: Lieutenant Colonel John Hamilton (Muster—114)
Queen's Rangers (horse and foot):   Lieutenant Colonel J. Graves Simcoe (Muster—248)
British Legion (horse and foot):   Lieutenant Colonel Banastre Tarleton (Muster—192)

Total Muster of British Forces engaged—ca. 5,953

Casualties

Prisoners—5,593–7,157 plus 840 sailors and 80 camp followers
Killed—156
Wounded—326
Missing—70

SOURCE: Henry P. Johnson, *The Yorktown Campaign and the Surrender of Cornwallis, 1781* (New York, 1881), pp. 112–19. This list was compiled from copies of the rolls of the surrender signed by Major Despard, from Gaine's Army Register for 1782, and the official return of the American Commissary of Prisoners. The 7,157 soldiers cited in the text does include officers and must include nearly 2,000 sick and wounded in the hospitals in Yorktown. The number 7,157 is taken from Banastre Tarleton, *A History of the Campaigns of 1780 and 1781 in the Southern Provinces of North America,* (London, 1787), pp. 448–58.

Selected Bibliography

General Sources

Brown, Tarleton. *Memoirs of Tarleton Brown: A Captain in the Revolutionary Army*. Barnwell, S.C., 1894.

Clinton, Sir Henry. *The American Rebellion: Sir Henry Clinton's Narrative of His Campaigns, 1775-1782*. Edited by William B. Willcox. New Haven, 1954.

———. *Observations on Mr. Stedman's History of the American War*. London, 1794.

Closen, Baron Ludwig von. *The Revolutionary Journal of Baron Ludwig von Closen, 1780-1783*. Translated and edited by Evelyn M. Acomb. Chapel Hill, N.C., 1958.

Cornwallis, Charles. *Cornwallis, 1st Marquis, 1738-1805, Answer to Sir Henry Clinton's Narrative of the Campaign in 1781 in North America by Earl Cornwallis*. Philadelphia, 1866.

Cowpens Papers Being Correspondence of General Morgan and Prominent Actors. From the collection of Theodorus Bailey Myers. Charleston, S.C., 1881.

Davie, William Richardson. *The Revolutionary Sketches of William A. Davie*. Edited by Blackwell R. Robinson. North Carolina Department of Archives and History. Bound together with North Carolina Pamphlets Revolutionary War RI, no. 5 of 6.

Draper, Lyman C. *King's Mountain and Its Heroes*. With attached source documents. Reprint. Spartanburg, S.C., 1973.

Encyclopedia Britannica, or a Dictionary of Arts and Sciences compiled upon a New Plan, in three volumes. Vol. 2. Edinburgh, 1771.

Ewald, Captain Johann. *Diary of the American War: A Hessian Journal*. Edited by Joseph P. Tustin. New Haven and London, 1979.

Gadsden, Christopher. *The Writings of Christopher Gadsden, 1746-1805*. Edited by Walter Richard Walsh. Columbia, S.C., 1966.

Gibbes, R. W. *Documentary History of the American Revolution Consisting of Letters and Papers Relating to the Contest for Liberty, Chiefly in South Carolina*. New York, 1857.

Hill, William. *Colonel William Hill's Memoirs of the Revolution*. Edited by A. S. Salley. Columbia, S.C., 1921.

James, William Dobein. *A Sketch of the Life of Brigadier General Francis Marion and a History of His Brigade*. Charleston, S.C., 1821.

Johnson, Joseph. *Traditions and Reminiscences Chiefly of the American Revolution in the South, Including Biographical Sketches, Incidents, Anecdotes . . . Particularly of Residents in the Upper Country*. Reprint. Spartanburg, S.C., 1972.

Lafayette, Marquis de. *Lafayette in Virginia: Unpublished letters to Jefferson, General Wayne, Colonel Davis, and Governor W. Nelson.* Baltimore, 1928.

————. *The Memoirs, Correspondence, and Manuscripts of Marquis de Lafayette.* 3 vols. London, 1837.

Laurens, Henry. *The Papers of Henry Laurens.* Edited by Philip M. Hamer and George C. Rogers. Vols. 1–6. Columbia, S.C., 1968.

Laurens, John. *The Army Correspondence of Colonel John Laurens in the Years 1777–1778.* New York, 1969.

Lee, Henry. *The American Revolution in the South.* Edited with a biography of his father by Robert E. Lee, 1869. Reprint. New York, 1969.

————. *The Campaign of 1781, in the Carolinas: With Remarks Historical and Critical on Johnson's Life of Greene, With Appendix of Original Documents Relating to the History of the Revolution.* Reprint. Spartanburg, S.C., 1975.

Moultrie, William. *Memoirs of the American Revolution, So Far as It Related to the States of North and South Carolina and Georgia.* Reprint. New York, 1968.

Ramsay, David. *The History of the Revolution of South Carolina.* 2 vols. Trenton, N.J., 1785.

The Revolution Remembered: Eyewitness Accounts of the War for Independence. Edited by John C. Dann. Chicago, 1980.

Rochambeau, Jean Baptiste Donatien de Vimeur. *Memoirs of the Marshal Count de Rochambeau.* Translated by M. W. E. Wright. 1838. Reprint. New York, 1971.

Saye, James Hodge. *Memoirs of Major Joseph McJunkin: Revolutionary Patriot.* Greenville, S.C., 1977.

Shelby, Isaac. "Battle of King's Mountain, October 7, 1780." *Magazine of American History,* November 1880, pp. 351–69.

South Carolina Archives, *The Carleton Papers.* List of Warships Microfilm, 9847 (1), Columbia, S.C.

South Carolina Archives, "The Benjamin Lincoln Papers, Return of the Troops Under the Command of Major General Lincoln, 21 September 1779." Microfilm Roll 4, Frame 584. Columbia, S.C.

Stedman, Charles. *The History of the Origin, Progress and Termination of the American War.* 2 vols. London, 1794.

Stevens, Benjamin Franklin, comp. and ed. *The Clinton-Cornwallis Controversy Growing out of the Campaign in Virginia, 1781.* 2 vols. London, 1888.

Tarleton, Lieutenant Colonel Banastre. *A History of the Campaigns of 1780 and 1781 in the Southern Provinces of North America.* 1787. Reprint. New York, 1968.

————. *A History of the Campaigns of 1780 and 1781 in the Southern Provinces of North America.* London, 1787.

Uhlendorf, Bernhard A., trans. and ed. *The Siege of Charleston with an Account of the Province of South Carolina; Diaries and Letters of Hessian Officers.* Ann Arbor, Mich., 1938.

Washington, George. *Correspondence of General Washington and Comte de Grasse, 1781, August*

17–November 4. Edited by the Institut Français de Washington. Washington, D.C., 1931.

———. *Diaries, 1748–1799*. Edited by John C. Fitzpatrick. 4 vols. Boston, 1925.

———. *The Writings of George Washington; Being His Correspondence, Addresses, Messages and Other Papers, Official and Private ... With a Life of the Author*. Edited by Jared Sparks. 12 vols. Boston, 1834–1837.

Williams, Otho. *Calendar of the General Otho Holland Williams Papers in the Maryland Historical Society*. Baltimore, 1940.

Winn, General Richard. "Notes, 1780." Edited by Samuel C. Williams. *The South Carolina Historical and Genealogical Magazine*, 43(1942):201–2; 44(1943):1–10.

General Histories

Alden, John Richard. *A History of the American Revolution*. New York, 1976.

Bailey, J. D. *Commanders at Kings Mountain*. Edited by H. DeCamp. Gaffney, S.C., 1926.

Balch, Thomas. *The French in America during the War of Independence of the United States, 1777–1783*. 1891. Reprint. Boston, 1972.

Bass, Robert D. *Gamecock: The Life and Campaigns of General Thomas Sumter*. New York, 1969.

———. *The Green Dragoon: The Lives of Banastre Tarleton and Mary Robinson*. New York, 1957.

———. *Ninety Six: The Struggle for the South Carolina Back Country*. Lexington, S.C., 1978.

———. *Swamp Fox: The Life and Campaigns of General Francis Marion*. Columbia, S.C., 1959.

Boatner, Mark Mayo. *Encyclopedia of the American Revolution*. New York, 1966.

Boyd, Thomas. *Mad Anthony Wayne*. New York, 1929.

Caldwell, Charles. *Memoirs of the Life and Campaigns of the Honorable Nathanael Greene*. Philadelphia, 1819.

Callahan, North. *Daniel Morgan, Ranger of the Revolution*. New York, 1961.

———. *George Washington, Soldier and Man*. New York, 1972.

Carrington, Henry B. *Battles of the American Revolution: Historical and Military Criticism with Topographical Illustration*. New York, 1876.

Cashin, Edward J., Jr., and Robertson, Heard. *Augusta and the American Revolution: Events in the Georgia Back Country, 1773–1783*. Augusta, Ga., 1975.

Chappell, Buford S. *The Winns of Fairfield County: Colonel John Winn, William Winn, General Richard Winn*. Columbia, S.C., 1975.

Chidsey, Donald Barr. *The War in the South*. New York, 1969.

Coleman, Kenneth. *The American Revolution in Georgia, 1763–1789*. Athens, Ga., 1958.

Curry, J. L. M. *Richard Winn, 1750–1818*. Publications of the Southern History Association, vol. 2, no. 3. July 1898.

Davidson, Chalmers Gaston. *Piedmont Partisan: The Life and Times of Brigadier General William Lee Davidson*. Davidson, N.C., 1968.

Flexner, James Thomas. *George Washington in the American Revolution*. Boston, 1968.

Fortescue, Sir John William. *A History of the British Army*. Vol. 3, London and New York.

Freeman, Douglas Southall. *George Washington: A Biography*. Vols. 4, 5. New York, 1952.

Garden, Alexander. *Anecdotes of the Revolutionary War in America, with Sketches of Character of Persons the Most Distinguished in the Southern States, for Civil and Military Services*. Reprint. Spartanburg, S.C., 1972.

Gerson, Noel B. *Light Horse Harry: A Biography of Washington's Great Cavalryman, General Henry Lee*. Garden City, N.Y., 1966.

Gottschalk, Louis. *Lafayette and the Close of the American Revolution*. Chicago, 1974.

――――. *Lafayette Joins the American Army*. Chicago, 1937.

Graves, Robert. *Sergeant Lamb's America, A Novel*. New York, 1940.

Gregorie, Anne King. *Thomas Sumter*. Columbia, S.C., 1931.

Guide to Virginia Military Organizations in the American Revolution, 1774–1787. Compiled by E. M. Sanchez-Saavedra. Richmond, 1978.

Headley, Joel Tyler. *Washington and His Generals*. New York, 1913.

Hennig, Helen Kohn. *Great South Carolinians*. Chapel Hill, N.C., 1940.

Higginbotham, Don. *Daniel Morgan: Revolutionary Rifleman*. Chapel Hill, N.C., 1961.

――――. *The War of American Independence: Military Attitudes, Policies and Practice*. New York, 1971.

Hilborn, Nat, and Hilborn, Sam. *Battleground of Freedom: South Carolina in the Revolution*. Columbia, S.C., 1970.

Horry, Brig. Gen. P., and Weems, M. L. *The Life of Gen. Francis Marion*. Philadelphia, 1847.

Johnson, William. *Sketches of the Life and Correspondence of Nathanael Greene ... in the War of the Revolution*. 2 vols. Charleston, S.C., 1822.

Johnston, Henry P. *The Yorktown Campaign and the Surrender of Cornwallis, 1781*. New York, 1881.

Jusserand, Jean Adrien Antoine Jules. *The French and American Independence*. New York, 1918.

Kennedy, Robert L., and Kirkland, Thomas J. *Historic Camden, Colonial and Revolutionary*. Columbia, S.C., 1926.

Landers, H. L. *The Virginia Campaign and the Blockade and Siege of Yorktown, 1781, Including a Brief Narrative of the French Participation in the Southern Campaign*. Washington, D.C., 1931.

Landrum, J. B. O. *Colonial and Revolutionary History of Upper South Carolina, 1897*. Reprint. Spartanburg, S.C., 1959.

Lawrence, Alexander A. *Storm over Savannah*. Athens, Ga., 1951.

McCowen, George Smith. *The British Occupation of Charleston, 1780–82*. Columbia, S.C., 1972.

McCrady, Edward. *The History of South Carolina in the Revolution, 1780–82*. 2 vols. Reprint. Columbia, S.C., 1972.

McDowell, Bart. *The Revolutionary War: American's Fight for Freedom*. Washington, D.C., 1967.

Messick, Hank. *Kings Mountain: The Epic of the Blue Ridge "Mountain Men" in the American Revolution.* Boston, 1976.

Mitchell, Joseph Brady. *Decisive Battles of the American Revolution.* New York, 1962.

Montross, Lynn. *Ragtag and Bobtail: The Story of the Continental Army, 1775–1783.* New York, 1952.

Pogue, Forrest Carlyle. *The Revolutionary Transformation of the Art of War.* Washington, D.C., 1974.

Rankin, Hugh F. *Francis Marion: The Swamp Fox.* New York, 1973.

———. *The North Carolina Continentals.* Chapel Hill, N.C., 1971.

———, and Scheer, George F. *Rebels and Redcoats.* New York, 1972.

Roberts, Kenneth. *The Battle of Cowpens: The Great Morale Builder.* Garden City, N.Y., 1958.

Sedgwick, Henry Dwight. *Lafayette.* Indianapolis, 1928.

Simms, W. Gilmore. *The Life of Francis Marion.* 10th ed. New York, 1854.

———. *The Life of Nathanael Greene.* 2d ed. New York, 1856.

Stinchcomb, William C. *The American Revolution and the French Alliance.* Syracuse, N.Y., 1969.

Thayer, Theodore. *Nathanael Greene: Strategist of the American Revolution.* New York, 1960.

Treacy, M. F. *Prelude to Yorktown: The Southern Campaign of Nathanael Greene, 1780–1781.* Chapel Hill, N.C., 1963.

Vining, Elizabeth Gray. *Flora, A Biography.* Philadelphia, 1966.

Wallace, Willard M. *Appeal to Arms: A Military History of the American Revolution.* New York, 1951.

Waring, Alice Noble. *The Fighting Elder, Andrew Pickens (1739–1817).* Columbia, S.C., 1962.

Weigley, Russell F. *The Partisan War: The South Carolina Campaign of 1780–1782.* South Carolina Tricentennial Booklet 3. Columbia, S.C., 1970.

White, Katherine W. *The Kings Mountain Men.* Dayton, Va., 1924.

Wickwire, Franklin B., and Wickwire, Mary. *Cornwallis: The American Adventure.* Boston, 1970.

Wright, Marcus Joseph. *Lafayette's Campaign in Virginia, April, 1781–October 19, 1781.* Southern History Association Publications, vol. 9. Washington, D.C., 1905.

The American Indian in the South during the Revolution

Brown, Douglas Summers. *The Catawba Indians: The People of the River.* Columbia, S.C., 1966.

Brown, John P. *Old Frontiers: The Story of the Cherokee Indians from Earliest Times to the Date of Their Removal to the West, 1838.* Kingsport, Tenn., 1938 .

Gearing, Frederick O. *Priests and Warriors: Social Structure for Cherokee Politics in the 18th Century.* American Anthropological Association, Memoir 93. Menasha, Wis., 1962.

Rockwell, E. F. "Parallel and Combined Expeditions against the Cherokee Indians in North and South Carolina, in 1776." *Historical Magazine*, October 1867.

South Carolina Archives. "Journal of the Expedition v. the Cherokees, 1776," National Archives and Records Service. Record Group 15. Records of the Veterans Administration.

The Loyalists

Allaire, Lieutenant Anthony. "Diary of Lieutenant Anthony Allaire of Ferguson's Corps." In appendix to Lyman C. Draper, *King's Mountain and Its Heroes*. Reprint. Spartanburg, S.C., 1973.

Boucher, Revd. Jonathan. *Reminiscences of an American Loyalist, 1738–1789*. Port Washington, N.Y., 1967.

Calhoun, Robert McCluer. *The Loyalists in Revolutionary America, 1760–1781*. New York, 1973.

Chesney, Alexander. *The Journal of Alexander Chesney, A South Carolina Loyalist in the Revolution and After*. Edited by E. Alfred Jones. Columbus, Ohio, 1921.

Curwen, Samuel. *The Journal of Samuel Curwen, Loyalist*. 2 vols. Cambridge, Mass., 1972.

DeMond, Robert O. *The Loyalists in North Carolina during the Revolution*. Durham, N.C., 1940.

Fanning, Col. David. *The Narrative of Colonel David Fanning, as Written by Himself, from 1775–1783*. Reprinted for Joseph Sabin. New York, 1865.

Harrell, Isaac Samuel. *Loyalism in Virginia: Chapters in the Economic History of the Revolution*. New York, 1965.

Jarvis, Stephen. "An American's Experience in the British Army: Manuscript of Col. Stephen Jarvis ... Revealing the Life of the Loyalists... ." *Journal of American History*, vol. 1, no. 4(1907):727–40.

Sabine, Lorenzo. *Biographical Sketches of Loyalists of the American Revolution*. Vols. 1 and 2. Boston, 1864.

———. *A Historical Essay on the Loyalists of the American Revolution*. 1847. Reprint. Springfield, Mass., 1957.

Smith, Paul Hubert. *Loyalists and Redcoats: A Study in British Revolutionary Policy*. Chapel Hill, N.C., 1964.

Upton, Leslie Francis Stokes, ed. *Revolutionary versus Loyalist: The First American Civil War, 1774–1784*. Waltham, Mass., 1968.

Van Tyne, Claude Halstead. *The Loyalists in the American Revolution*. Reprint. Gloucester, Mass., 1959.

The Negro in the American Revolution

McLeod, Duncan J. *Slavery, Race and the American Revolution*. New York and London, 1974.

Quarles, Benjamin. *The Negro in the American Revolution*. Chapel Hill, N.C., 1961.

Uniforms and Weapons

Bailey, DeWitt. *British Military Long Arms, 1715–1815.* London, 1971.

Berg, Fred Anderson. *Encyclopedia of Continental Army Units.* Harrisburg, Pa., 1972.

Carey, Arthur Merwyn. *American Firearms Makers: When, Where, and What They Made from the Colonial Period to the End of the 19th Century.* New York, 1953.

Guns: An Illustrated History of Artillery. Edited by Joseph Jobé. Greenwich, N.Y., 1971.

Hogg, Ian V. *A History of Artillery.* London, 1974.

Hogg, O. F. G. *Artillery: Its Origin, Heyday, and Decline.* London, 1970.

Hughes, Basil Perronet. *Firepower: Weapons Effectiveness on the Battlefield, 1630–1850.* London, 1974.

Katcher, Philip. *Encyclopedia of British, Provincial, and German Army Units, 1775–1783.* Harrisburg, Pa., 1973.

Klinger, Robert L., and Wilder, Richard. *Sketch Book '76: The American Soldier, 1775–1781.* Arlington, Va., 1967.

Lefferts, Charles MacKubin. *Uniforms of the American, British, French and German Armies in the War of the American Revolution.* Reprint. Old Greenwich, Conn., 1971.

Lossing, Benson J. *Pictorial Field Book of the Revolution.* 2 vols. 1851.

Mollo, John. *Uniforms of the American Revolution in Color.* London, 1975.

Neumann, George C. *The History of Weapons of the American Revolution.* New York, 1967.

———. *Swords and Blades of the American Revolution.* Harrisburg, Pa., 1973.

Papacino d'Antoni, Allesandro. *A Treatise on Gunpowder; A Treatise on Firearms; A Treatise on the Service of Artillery in Time of War.* Translated by Captain Thomson. In *Thomson on Firearms.* London, 1789.

Peterson, Harold L. *The Book of the Continental Soldier... .* Harrisburg, Pa., 1968.

Ricketts, Howard. *Firearms.* London, 1962.

Smith, W. H. B., and Smith, Joseph E. *The Book of Rifles.* Harrisburg, Pa., 1963.

Wilbur, C. Keith. *Picture Book of the Continental Soldier.* Harrisburg, Pa., 1969.

Windrow, Martin C., et al. *Military Dress of North America, 1665–1979.* London, 1973.

Archaeology

"Archaeological Base Map of the Site of the Blockhouse, Defending the North Entrance to the Town of Ninety Six, Greenwood, South Carolina, and the Site of the Fortified Brick Jail." Archaeologist: Stanley South. Institute of Archaeology and Anthropology. Columbia, S.C., 1970.

Cann, Marvin L. "Ninety Six and the South Carolina Back Country, 1700–1783," Institute of Archaeology and Anthropology. Columbia, S.C., 1974.

Carrillo, Richard F. "The Howser House and the Chronicle Grave and Mass Burial, Kings Mountain National Military Park, South Carolina," Research Manuscript Series No. 102. Institute of Archaeology and Anthropology. Columbia, S.C., 1976.

Ferguson, Leland G. "Archaeology at Scotts Lake, Exploratory Research 1972–1973,"
    Research Manuscript Series, No. 68. Institute of Archaeology and Anthropology.
    Columbia, S.C., 1975.

———. "Exploratory Archaeology at the Scotts Lake Site, Santee Indian Mound-Fort
    Watson," Research Manuscript Series, No. 36. Institute of Archaeology and
    Anthropology. Columbia, S.C., 1973.

Holschlag, Stephanie L., and Rodeffer, Michael J. "Ninety Six: Siege Works Opposite Star
    Redoubt: Ninety Six Historic Site," Institute of Archaeology and Anthropology.
    Columbia, S.C., 1976.

———. "Ninety Six: The Stockade Fort on the Right: Ninety Six Historic Site," Institute
    of Archaeology and Anthropology. Columbia, S.C., 1976.

Lewis, Kenneth E. "Camden, a Frontier Town in Eighteenth Century South Carolina,"
    Anthropological Studies No. 2. Institute of Archaeology and Anthropology. Columbia,
    S.C., 1976.

South, Stanley. "Archaeological Excavation at the Site of Williamson's Fort of 1775, Holmes
    Fort of 1780 and the Town of Cambridge of 1783–1850's," Research Manuscript
    Series. Institute of Archaeology and Anthropology. Columbia, S.C., 1972.

———. "Exploratory Archaeology at Ninety Six," Research Manuscript Series. Institute of
    Archaeology and Anthropology. Columbia, S.C., 1970.

———. "Exploratory Archaeology at the Site of the 1776 Fort around the Town of Ninety Six
    and Cruger's Fort of 1780," Research Manuscript Series. Institute of Archaeology and
    Anthropology. Columbia, S.C., 1972.

———. "Fickle Forts on Wind Mill Point: Exploratory Archaeology at Fort Johnson, South
    Carolina," Research Manuscript, No. 81. Institute of Archaeology and Anthropology.
    Columbia, S.C., 1975.

———. "Historical Perspective at Ninety Six with a Summary of Exploratory Excavation at
    Holmes Fort and the Town Blockhouse," Research Manuscript Series. Institute of
    Archaeology and Anthropology. Columbia, S.C., 1971.

———. "Palmetto Parapets: Exploratory Archaeology at Fort Moultrie, South Carolina,"
    Anthropological Studies. Occasional Papers of the Institute of Archaeology and
    Anthropology. Columbia, S.C., 1974.

"Stabilization, Interpretation Map for the Site of Williamson's Fort of 1775 and Holmes Fort
    of 1780 at Ninety Six, South Carolina, Fort Profiles Contemporary with Holmes: 'Fort
    Motte' and 'Fort Granby'," Archaeologist: Stanley South. Institute of Archaeology
    and Anthropology. Columbia, S.C.

Articles

Hale, Richard W., Jr. "New Light on the Naval Side of Yorktown." *Proceedings*,
    Massachusetts Historical Society, vol. 71, 1953–1957.

Lipscomb, Terry W. "South Carolina Revolutionary Battles." *Names in South Carolina.* Part
    I, 20(Winter 1973):18–23; Part II, 21(Winter 1974):23–27; Part III,
    22(Winter 1975):33–39; Part IV, 23(Winter 1976):30–34; Part V, 24(Winter
    1977):13–19; Part VI, 24 (Winter 1978):26–33; Part VII, 26(Winter
    1979):31–39

Index